Anchor manual of
NEEDLEWORK

Anchor manual
of
NEEDLEWORK

 INTERWEAVE PRESS

First published 1958
Reprinted 1960 and 1962
Second edition, 1966
Third edition, 1968
Reprinted 1970
Reprinted 1974
New edition, 1990

ISBN 0-934026-59-9

Library of Congress Cataloging-in-Publication Data

Anchor manual of needlework.
     p.   cm.
  Includes index.
  ISBN 0–934026–59–9 : $26.00
  1. Needlework. 2. Fancy work. I. Interweave Press.
TT750.A5 1990
746 – – dc 20

90–38088
CIP

INTERWEAVE PRESS, INC.
201 East Fourth Street
Loveland, Colorado 80537

7M:890
5M:1191

PRINTED IN HONG KONG

CONTENTS

I *Sewing*

2 *Embroidery in white and colours*

3 *Drawn-thread work*

4 *Embroidery on counted threads*

5 Embroidery upon delicate fabrics

6 Knotted lace

7 *Laces made by needle and bobbin*

8 Crocheted laces

9 *Knitting*

10 *Various types of embroidery*

FOREWORD

In recent decades, fibers have been more likely to come from a vat of chemicals than from a sheep or cotton boll, fabric has been woven by air jets more often than human hands, and clothing and household linens have tended to find their way to the castoff bin after only a season or two. Nonetheless, some of the traditions of fine handwork have continued to hold our attention and compete successfully for our time: cross-stitch, lace making, knitting, crewel work, crochet.

As we reach toward the twenty-first century and discover the limits of the no-iron, drip-dry way of life—as we search for durability, for links between the generations, for stability, for individual expression—we find it's time to deepen our hold on tradition. We need quality and elegance again. We need our growing appreciation for the heritage of "women's work," realizing that the textiles our foremothers produced are diminutive monuments to the human spirit, and that their skills and artistry transcended the mundane responsibilities of their everyday lives. Surrounded by a different set of deadening necessities—traffic jams, taxes, hypermarket shopping blues—we need the tangible and timeless presence of careful activities in *our* lives. Like those who went before, we can stitch meaning into our days, and the days of our children.

We're fortunate that, while we were nearly drawn astray by our fascination with plastic fabrics, the techniques of traditional needlework have been kept well-documented and accessible through *The Anchor Manual of Needlework*.

This important reference work was first compiled in 1958 from instructional pamphlets created by Coats & Clark over a period of many years. This venerable company has its origin with James and Patrick Clark, who began manufacturing cotton sewing threads in Paisley, Scotland, in 1812. J&P Coats was another Paisley thread mill; the two companies developed in parallel, opening manufacturing facilities in the United States after the Civil War, and eventually merging in 1954. Their line of threads for embroidery, crochet, and lacemaking bore the Anchor label; hence the title of this volume.

In reissuing this historic work, we hope to preserve a heritage of accomplishment in everyday endeavors, to provide practical information that can bring a measure of grace to mundane tasks, and to inspire those who take needle in hand today to forge a link between the past and the future.

The Editors
Interweave Press

I Sewing

CHAPTER I

Sewing Equipment and Stitches for Household Linen

Before beginning any kind of needlework it is important to collect together the right tools and threads. To possess these and to know the right way to use them will not only make the work more enjoyable, but give a professional finish to the object being made or repaired. In this chapter the most useful sewing tools and threads are briefly described.

Needles. It seems that the first needles used in ancient times were made from fish bones or vegetable spines, with a hole made in the widest part. In several collections of antique objects there are needles made of brass or iron, which presumably substituted the earliest types with the passage of time. It was only towards the middle of the sixteenth century that the needle, as we know it today, was imported into Europe, and particularly into England, from India. A needle-making industry was thus created which spread so rapidly that it was flourishing by the end of the sixteenth century.

The needle must be made of tempered, best-quality steel; it must be resistant to breaking, but not bendable. A needle which is bent, without a point, or rusty should never be used: these things affect the regularity and neatness of the work. The needle must be suitable for the type of work and the fabric which is used: thus for delicate fabrics, very fine needles are required; for sewing household linen rather short, medium-length needles;

and, for millinery, rather long needles are used.

Many different types of needle are manufactured for different purposes. Crewel needles are of medium length with a long eye and these are used with most embroidery threads. Chenille needles, which are similar in appearance, have a very long wide eye suitable for use with wool. Tapestry needles have a long eye and a rounded point for work upon canvas. Special needles are made for threading beads, for making gloves, for darning and for many other purposes, whilst people with poor sight can obtain a needle with an open eye which closes after threading to allow an easy passage for the thread. These are just a few of the very many kinds of needle obtainable today.

The needle should be slightly thicker than the sewing thread, so that it will open up a sufficiently wide passage for the thread as it passes through the material. Needles should be kept in a needle-book in a dry place to avoid rusting.

Thimble. The thimble is another indispensable tool for the needlewoman. The thimble should sit well on the middle finger of the right hand so that the pad of the finger almost touches the bottom of the thimble. It should be light with fairly deep dents; steel, silver or other metal thimbles are preferable to those made of bone or plastic. Once upon a time the elegant woman possessed artistic

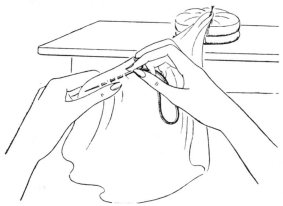

Fig. 1. Position of the hands with work fixed to cushion

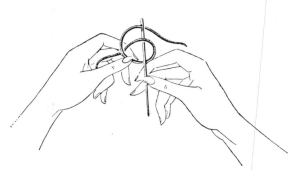

Fig. 2. Position of the hands for sewing

Fig. 3. Method of fixing the thread in the eye of the needle

and valuable thimbles decorated with miniatures and precious stones: such a thimble was generally part of a bride's trousseau and was often a present from her fiancé: but this use has disappeared today and we only look for utility in our modern thimbles.

Scissors. It is a good idea, when working, to have two pairs of scissors: a large pair for cutting fabric (and at this point let us remember that the pointed blade of the scissors should be held below the fabric being cut), and another, smaller pair with sharp points for cutting threads, small pieces of material, scallops, etc. Choose good-quality scissors, made of steel, and always keep them sharp. Nothing is more disastrous than the use of scissors which do not cut well.

There are various types of scissors, such as tailor's shears which are very large, small embroidery scissors, scissors with curved blades for machine embroidery, scissors for cutting buttonholes, and many more.

For cutting hairy materials, fur skins, or mending holes in felt, it is better to use a pen-knife or razor-blade, since scissors, which cut too cleanly, take away the edging of light hairs which should, if possible, be kept intact.

Work-cushion. This is very useful for holding the work and keeping it well stretched, especially when working speedily at Running Stitch, Back Stitch, Hemming, Seaming and Gathering. It is a small felt-covered cushion, round or square, stuffed with bran and weighted with small pieces of lead.

Threads. Many different types of threads are manufactured for sewing, embroidery, knitting, lace making and crochet. These may be made from cotton, linen, silk, wool and the various synthetic fibres available today.

Every needlewoman should have a work-box and, if possible, a drawer where she can keep all the tools and materials necessary for her work. These should include large and small, well-sharpened scissors, packets of needles in various types and sizes, thimbles, a tape measure, shuttles, crochet hooks, knitting needles in their appropriate packets, boxes for cottons, embroidery threads, buttons, pins, hooks and press studs. All these should be neatly placed and kept in good order.

Sewing Position. The position of the worker must be good and it is most important that the proportions between the height of the chair and the table should be right. It is preferable to sit on a rather low chair with the work held high enough for the back to remain upright and the head slightly inclined forward. The work should never be held on the knees as this leads to an uncomfortable and unhealthy position. Use a work-cushion when possible (Fig. 1). If the cushion is not used the work should not be wrapped round the first finger of the left hand, but should be held with the thumb and first finger of the left hand, leaving the work to fall freely over the other fingers. If the work has to be kept stretched, it should be held tightly between the third and little finger (Fig. 2). The stitch should never be so long as to twist the thread and knots should never be used.

For basting or tacking long stitches are used and the thread knotted at the beginning of the stitching. To make this knot, the thread is wrapped round the first finger of the right hand, pressing it against the thumb and rubbing: thus a small knot is formed, helped by the middle finger of the same hand.

When the stitching is finished, the thread must be fastened-off on the back of the work with small hidden stitches, and in the same way the new line of stitching is begun on the wrong side of the work. If the line of stitching is very short and not to be continued further, the thread may be fixed in the eye of the needle by a half-knot as shown in Fig. 3.

For joining on threads in hems and seams, it is sufficient to tuck the two ends of thread, i.e. that of the line of stitching just completed and that of the new line to be begun, under the fabric. In Back Stitch and Stem Stitch, the work is commenced by making small stitches on the back of the work; when joining, the two threads are carried forward for a short distance underneath the joining stitches and then cut off close. For decorative stitches on hems and seams, the same method is used, hiding the ends of the threads under the hem or on the back of the seams.

On beginning work, the needle is taken between the thumb and first finger of the right hand, and with the help of the middle finger, protected by a thimble, it is pushed into the material. Then the thumb and forefinger of the same hand pick up the needle again after the stitch has been made and pull the thread through the fabric.

N.B.—In the illustrations, a dark thread has been used for clarity in illustrating the stitches.

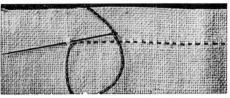

Fig. 4. Running Stitch

Fig. 5. Running Stitch; method of taking up a number of stitches on the needle

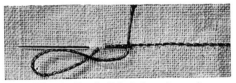

Fig. 6. Back Stitch (continuous)

Fig. 7. Tacking or basting

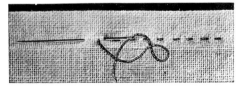

Fig. 8. Back Stitch

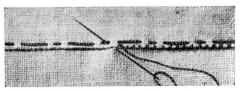

Fig. 9. Hem tacked and hemmed down

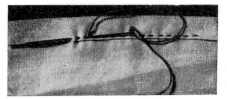

Fig. 10. Hem caught down by Running Stitches

Fig. 11. Hem fixed by Back Stitching, on drawn thread

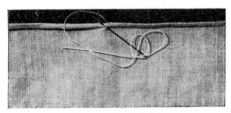

Fig. 12. Rolled hem

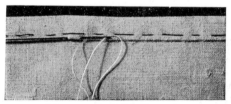

Fig. 13. Invisible hemming

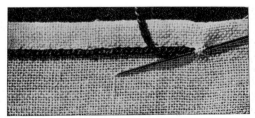

Fig. 14. Stem Stitch over drawn thread

4

Running Stitch. This is the easiest of all stitches. It is used for simple seams, gathering and tacking and is widely used in embroidery, as we shall see later. Two or three threads of the material are taken up on the needle and the same number are passed over. Continue in this way, keeping the spaces as even as possible and working from right to left (Fig. 4).

When the material is fine, it is preferable to take up a number of stitches on the needle at a time, before pulling the thread through (Fig. 5).

Coats Drima (polyester) should be used for this and the following stitches.

Continuous Back Stitch. This consists of a series of Back Stitches with no space between them: three or four threads of fabric are taken up on the needle, which is then replaced at the point where it came out, being drawn through at a point three or four threads ahead of the stitch made. The appearance of perfect Back Stitching can be produced by the sewing machine, but for fine work (lingerie and babies' clothes) Back Stitch is still worked by hand and must be sewn with perfect regularity (Fig. 6).

If the Back Stitch is worked on the straight thread we advise drawing out a thread of the fabric; this drawn thread will be substituted by the continuous Back Stitch. If, instead, the stitch is to be worked diagonally on the material, it is necessary to make a line of tacking stitches to serve as a guide.

Tacking (or Basting). All seams should be properly tacked. Regularity and accuracy are required for tacking as well as for other stitches. As shown in Fig. 7, one long Running Stitch and two short ones are taken up.

Back Stitch. In more ordinary types of sewing, Back Stitch, which is the continuous Back Stitch with spaces, is used. In other words, between one Back Stitch and another, two or three threads of fabric are left (Fig. 8).

The Hem. The hem may be used to finish off the edges of any type of linen. To make a hem the fabric is first of all folded once. This fold should be in proportion to the width of the hem, although, in general, the width of this fold should be sufficient to prevent the fabric from fraying. After the first fold, a second fold is made which should be of the desired width of the hem. It is generally better to tack the hem, as only a very experienced person can make a hem simply by folding. Woollen fabrics, too, should always be tacked, as they do not remain well folded. Once the hem is tacked it is then fixed by hemming.

Hemming. Hemming is worked from right to left, taking up two threads of fabric at the fold of the hem; then the needle is put in obliquely on the edge of the fold (Fig. 9). On the other side, which is actually the right side of the work, a series of regular stitches, forming a perfectly straight line, should be seen.

A Running Stitched Hem. This is worked on sewing of little importance or on old clothing. The hem is folded as explained above and fixed with running stitches one or two threads above the fold (Fig. 10).

Hem sewn with continuous Backstitch. This is used for household linen, such as sheets, towels, pillow-cases, tablecloths, etc. The hem is prepared, then a thread is drawn at a distance of two or three threads above the fold: a regular row of continuous Back Stitch is then sewn in place of the drawn thread (Fig. 11).

Rolled Hem. The rolled hem is used for very fine lingerie and often for handkerchiefs. This type of hem is not tacked. The fabric is rolled between the slightly moistened thumb and index finger of the left hand. The hem is then fixed by hemming, taking up one thread of the fabric (Fig. 12).

Invisible Hemming. This type of hem is used on underwear or clothing when it is desirable to hide the stitching. After preparing a tacked hem, the needle is placed horizontally in the fold taking a rather long stitch; after pulling through the needle, one thread of the fabric to be hemmed is taken up a little more to the left, so that the stitches are not too near to each other, but are well spaced. Then the needle is replaced in the fold of the hem and so on (Fig. 13). An easy-running, resistant, pure cotton thread is required: the best is Coats Drima (polyester).

Decorated Hems. Almost all types of linen, both bed, table and personal, such as sheets, pillow-cases, towels, tablecloths, serviettes, handkerchiefs, slips, underskirts, shirts, etc., are finished off by hemming. The most practical and elegant way of decorating a hem is by Hemstitching. The chapter entitled "Drawn-thread Work" illustrates variations of Hemstitching. In this, the first chapter, there are short descriptions of various stitches for decorating hems on tablecloths, serviettes, towels and other household objects.

To work these stitches, it is best to draw out a thread at the base of the folded hem: this drawn thread will serve as a guide for perfect sewing.

For descriptions and illustrations of the stitches mentioned here, turn to the chapter entitled "Various Embroidery Stitches". Coloured embroidery threads may be used for these decorative hems. Work the stitches in Coats Anchor Stranded Cotton using two, three, four or six strands according to the effect desired, or Coats Anchor Coton à Broder, No. 18.

The first illustration (Fig. 14) shows simple Stem Stitch on the drawn thread at the base of the hem, making a coloured thread outline to the work. Fig. 15 shows three rows of Running Stitch worked in different colours with pleasing effect. Fig. 16 shows "whipping": the needle is put in the material at the beginning on the right, and after throwing the thread over the hem, the needle is drawn out six or seven threads farther to the left; by repeating the movement, the "whipping" stitch is formed, fixing the hem and appearing the same on both sides of the work.

Fig. 17 shows a double working of the same stitch. That is, the same stitch worked back in the opposite direction, from left to right. The needle must go in and out at the same places as the first row of stitches. The two rows of stitches intersect at the fold of the hem.

Fig. 18 shows a hem decorated with two rows of stitching. The first row consists of rather widely spaced Blanket Stitches about a quarter of an inch apart, and a second row of Running Stitches forming a kind of square.

Fig. 19 shows groups of Blanket Stitch, in fours, and a spaced Blanket Stitch with its base on the drawn thread is illustrated in Fig. 20.

Fig. 21 shows a hem decorated with a row of spaced Fly Stitch.

Rather widely spaced Blanket Stitches, ranging from very small to very large and vice versa, are illustrated in Fig. 22. Fig. 23 shows a hem consisting of a double row of Blanket Stitches: one on

Fig. 15. Running Stitches in different colours

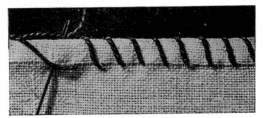

Fig. 16. Whipping

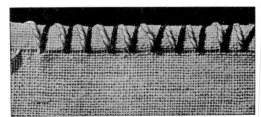

Fig. 17. Double Whip Stitch

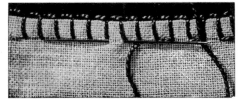

Fig. 18. Spaced Blanket Stitch with Running Stitches

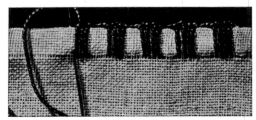

Fig. 19. Groups of four Blanket Stitches

the upper edge of the hem, the other at the base of the hem itself.

The hem shown in Fig. 24 can also be worked in two colours; this consists of two rows of Blanket Stitch with adjoining bases. Finally, Fig. 25 shows another decorative finish which is carried out in the following way: first the long Blanket Stitches covering all the width of the hem are worked at regular, short distances, then different coloured threads are passed in and out three times without taking up any of the material and picking up alternate threads of the stitches.

Fig. 26 shows groups of three Blanket Stitches made in the same hole, and Fig. 27 shows a decoration made with two different lines of stitching. First a row of Chain Stitch is worked along the drawn thread at the base of the fold of the hem. The second line consists of small Blanket Stitches worked on the outer edge of the hem, taking up two or three threads of the hem fabric, then a thread is passed across, from the row of Chain Stitches into the loop of the Blanket Stitch, crossing in the centre, without entering the material.

The coloured illustration shows other stitches for finishing off and decorating hems: these are carried out with Coats Anchor Stranded Cotton, Coats Anchor Coton à Broder or Coats Anchor Pearl Cotton.

Here are the explanations of the stitches in the order of the illustrations (page 8):

1. Simple, spaced Blanket Stitch on hem.

2. The thread is thrown over the edge of the hem, and without taking up any of the fabric beneath the thread, four Blanket Stitches are worked on the thread itself, and then the thread is thrown over the hem again, entering the material at the same point.

3. Alternate groups of four long and two short Blanket Stitches.

4. Five groups of two Blanket Stitches are worked: at the sixth group, the small leaf is worked. The thread is looped and fixed to the edge of the hem, leaving a length of about half an inch. The thread should be double; six rather widely spaced blanket stitches are worked on this protruding thread, repeating the same design on the opposite side, that is, making another six Blanket Stitches, working the stitches between those made previously: a second row of Blanket Stitches is then worked all around. The thread is then slipped from the loop and the leaf is complete.

6

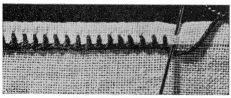

5. This is worked in two rows. First the hem is whipped, working from left to right. On the second row, working instead from right to left, four Blanket Stitches are worked over the whipping stitches, without picking up the material underneath. The thread is passed behind and the needle is placed in the work again at the base of the second stitch, repeating the stitch.

Fig. 20. Blanket Stitch with loop on inside

6. Small circles are marked on the material at equal distances: these are tacked and covered with Buttonhole Stitches radiating from the centre and worked closely and regularly. The spaces between the circles are also covered with Buttonhole Stitch. The circles may be placed at any intervals, or in groups of two or three. This is a very decorative motif. The fabric edge is afterwards trimmed away.

Fig. 21. Fly Stitch

7. Worked in two rows. Firstly, spaced out Blanket Stitch, working alternately one long and one short stitch, and than a Fly Stitch underneath the short stitch.

8. Groups of four or five short Buttonhole Stitches are worked, passing from one group to the other by pushing the needle through inside the hem.

9. Groups of three Bullion Stitches.

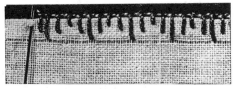

Fig. 22. Graded Blanket Stitch

10. Hem decorated with Stem Stitch band: this is fully explained on page 51, in the chapter on "Various Embroidery Stitches".

False Hems. When a garment is too short or when the full length of the fabric must be used this method of extending a hem may be used.

The right side of the garment is held towards the person, and the piece to be joined on it placed in such a way that the two right sides of the fabric are together; these are then joined, either by hand or machine. Without opening up the seam, the fabric is folded upwards, pressing the seam well with the finger-nail, or, better still, by pressing with a hot iron. Then the work is turned to the wrong side and the hem folded down, making the fold of the hem meet the seam of the two folded edges of fabric; this hem is then caught by hemming it along, after tacking (Fig. 28).

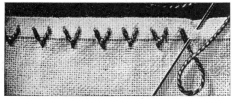

Fig. 23. Double Blanket Stitch

When there is only just enough fabric to allow for a narrow turning, a false hem is made by making a join right at the edge. After joining the two pieces by machining, turn in the hem and press well so that the join lies exactly on the edge of the hem. This is then tacked down carefully and hemmed.

Flat Seam (Run and Fell). This may be used to join two pieces of fabric cut on the straight thread

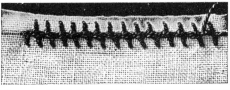

Fig. 24. Variation of Double Blanket Stitch

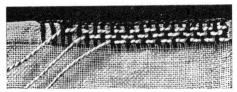

Fig. 25. Blanket Stitch with Running Stitch decoration

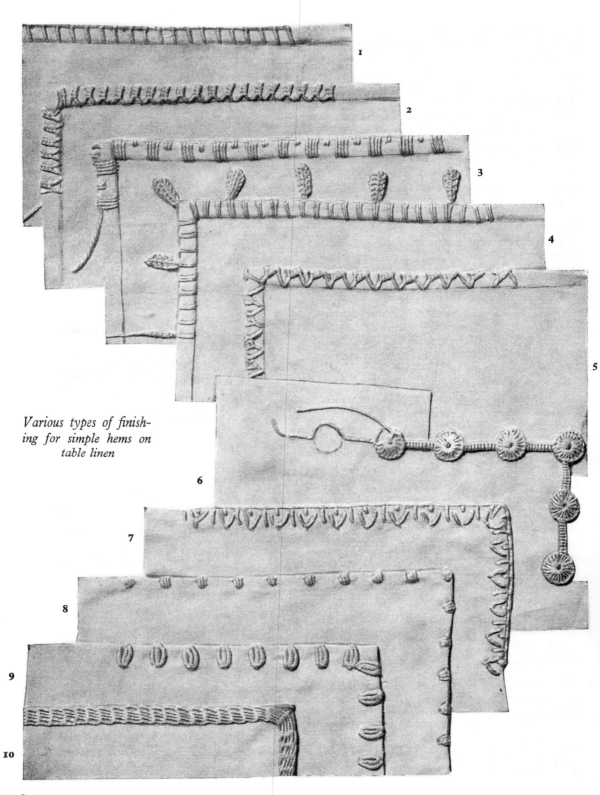

Various types of finishing for simple hems on table linen

8

or on the cross. The two pieces are placed together and tacked carefully. They are then sewn, following the tacking threads, either by a line of Running Stitch, or Back Stitch, or by machining. Then, using a pair of very sharp scissors, the inside part of the turning is cut away to about half its width, the outside piece being folded over like a hem and secured by hemming. Before folding the seam it is a good idea to flatten it by stroking with the scissors or the finger-nail along the line of sewing, so that there are no bulges in the material under the seam, that is, on the right side of the work, but the seam remains flat and well stretched (Fig. 29).

Round Seam (Unpressed Seam). The first row of sewing is prepared as described for the flat seam. Then the inside turning is cut very narrow, that is, very near to the line of sewing. The outside turnover, however, which has not been cut, is rolled over with the thumb and index finger of the left hand, slightly damped, thus enclosing the cutaway piece; this rolled-over hem is then hemmed down without flattening or tacking. On the other side this seam has the appearance of a raised cord (Fig. 30).

French Seam. This type of seam is very useful for garments such as pyjamas, underskirts and housecoats. The two pieces of fabric to be joined are placed together with wrong sides facing, tacked and sewn by machine, or Running Stitch or Backstitch, according to the kind of fabric. After this first seam has been made it is opened out, the part to be folded in is trimmed back with the scissors and the pieces of fabric are turned over and tacked at a distance of about a quarter of an inch from the seam already sewn (Fig. 31). A second row of stitching is made to finish the seam. Care should be taken not to allow the threads of the turning to protrude through the second row of stitching. This seam, which is also called a "double seam", is very practical for joining two pieces of light-weight fabric which may fray easily.

For hand-sewn and machine-stitched seams Coats Drima (polyester), should be used.

Method of joining two Hems. First of all the two edges of the fabric to be joined together are folded in, and then placed one over the other so that the one behind is raised slightly above the other. These are then tacked together. They are sewn, taking care to place the needle first into the higher piece of fabric, and then, holding the

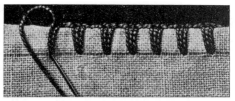

Fig. 26. *Groups of three Blanket Stitches*

Fig. 27. *Blanket and Chain Stitches*

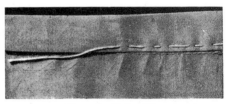

Fig. 28. *False Hem*

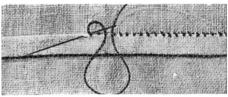

Fig. 29. *Run and Fell Seam (Flat Seam)*

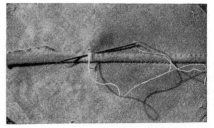

Fig. 30. *Round Seam (Unpressed Seam)*

9

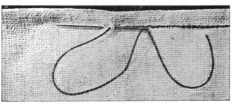

Fig. 31. French Seam

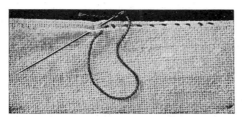

Fig. 32. Oversewing two hems together

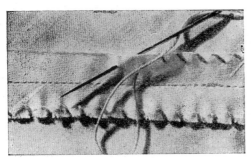

Fig. 33. Overcasting

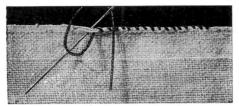

Fig. 34. Joining of selvedges

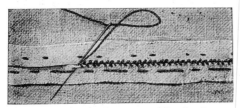

Fig. 35. Joining of turned back edges

needle at an angle, into the front piece (Fig. 32). This seam is used especially for sewing linings into clothing.

Overcasting. This type of sewing serves to prevent the fraying of the fabric and is particularly used in the finishing of articles of clothing. After the fabric has been joined by a row of machine or hand stitching, the seam is opened and pressed flat. The oversewing is made by taking a rather long stitch, placing the needle from the outside to the inside of one side and then returning along the other side of the seam (Fig. 33). When the fabric is very fine the two sides of the seam may be overcast together after having been trimmed.

Overcasting is also used to join two selvedges, for example—repairing sheets, or when the length of material is insufficient and it is desired to join on another piece. To make the joining, it is advisable to tack the two pieces together, or hold them in place with pins placed at intervals, to avoid one piece of the material being shortened more than the other when sewing. The needle is then placed under the first thread of the two selvedges, working either from right to left, or left to right (Fig. 34). When overcasting, the thread should not be pulled too tightly, since the selvedges should appear, on completion of the work, to be joined edge to edge, and not placed one above the other. On completion of the sewing the work should be pressed. When it is desired to join in this way material without a selvedge, the pieces should be folded in along the straight thread, tacking along the fold, then proceed as described above (Fig. 35).

Fishbone Stitch. In order to keep the join flat, Fishbone Stitch may be used, in which, instead of taking up the two selvedges together, the needle is passed under two threads of the selvedge to the right and then under two threads to the left and so on (Fig. 36). The stitch is worked keeping the pieces of fabric open and held close to each other, pinned on the cushion. The stitches may be worked perfectly straight and vertical, or slightly oblique.

Ornamental Hems. When the width of fabric for bed linen or table linen is insufficient and it becomes necessary to make a join, a decorative stitch with coloured threads may be used, thus making the work more attractive. Coats Anchor Stranded Cotton in two, three, four or six strands may be used for this work.

To make the decorative stitches illustrated, the most important thing to remember is to keep the two selvedges or folds exactly parallel. For perfect sewing, we advise the tacking of the fabric on to stiff brown paper before beginning the decoration. To work the stitch shown in Fig. 37, the needle is brought out of the fabric two threads away from the edge of the selvedge or the fold and then passed through the other selvedge, drawing the thread tight with a knot: the needle is then passed back to the other side of the fabric and the movement repeated at intervals of three or four threads along the hem. The decoration shown in Fig. 38 consists of three Blanket Stitches worked alternately first on one and then on the other selvedge, with pleasing effect. Fig. 39 is worked with three different rows of stitches. First a line of spaced-out Blanket Stitches along one of the selvedges, then a row along the other. The two edges are then joined by making a stitch through the loops of the Blanket Stitches on both sides.

Fig. 40 also shows a type of decoration worked with three rows of stitches. First of all a row of Blanket Stitches in groups of two, at intervals of about a quarter of an inch, are worked along both selvedges. Then the two sides are joined by a Cross Stitch. Fig. 41 shows a method of joining together two fabrics of different colour, used in the decoration of underwear or children's clothes. The strips of material to be joined are prepared in the usual way, and then sewn with a crossed Blanket Stitch, making one stitch to the right and one to the left alternately.

Gathering. The most common and necessary form of decoration for children's clothes is gathering.

Gathering consists of very regular Running Stitches worked in a straight line. Three or four threads of the fabric are taken up on the needle, leaving spaces equal to the same number of threads. The thread is pulled through when five or six stitches have been taken up on the needle. When one line of Running Stitch has been worked, the fabric is marked in folds with the needle (Fig. 42). To do this the work is fixed to a cushion; the thread holding the gathering in place is held tight with the left hand and, holding the work between thumb and index finger of the right hand, and using a medium-sized needle, the work is stroked vertically down the length of the fabric from a point after each Running Stitch. As the fold is stroked,

it is firmly pressed into place by the thumb and forefinger under which it is passed. After stroking the first row of gatherings into place, a second row of stitching is made about 15 mm from the first in order to keep the gathers in place.

Gathering is mounted into a cuff or band by first spreading the gathers very regularly over all the material gathered. Then with pins, or a coloured cross-stitch, the half and the quarters of both the gathered fabric and the piece into which it is to be fixed are marked. The marks on both pieces of fabric are then made to correspond and fixed together with rather short tacking stitches. Finally a small hemming stitch is used, taking up one gather to every stitch, in order to produce an even effect and to fix the gathers firmly.

Smocking. One of the best decorations for gathering is, undoubtedly, smocking. This type of decoration is still in use today, especially for children's garments, and has an ancient origin. It is found in many women's national costumes, e.g. Hungarian, Albanian, Roumanian and Russian, especially at the necks and cuffs of blouses. It is best known, however, as the main decoration of the English smock which was worn by countrymen in its most elaborate form during the late eighteenth and early nineteenth centuries.

When preparing for smocking, at least three times the width of the actual measurements required must be calculated; for example, if a 25 cm section is required, 76 cm of material will be needed. A horizontal line is marked along which a Running Stitch is worked with a very strong thread. Coats Drima (polyester) is good for this purpose. The stitches should be about 6 mm long, rather less than more. After the first row of gathering is complete, another line is marked in the same direction, using a needle and marking horizontally, at a distance of about 2.5 cm. Mark other lines in the same way to the required depth of the smocking.

Then, working from top to bottom, beginning from the first line of gathering stitches, stroke vertically down the length of fabric, as explained previously, taking care that these lines do not go beyond the depth of the border required (Fig. 43). After marking, other rows of gathering stitches are worked parallel to the first row, always taking up the same number of threads and using the vertical creases as a guide.

A practical method for working the gatherings

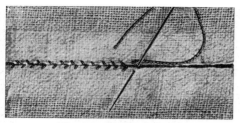

Fig. 36. Fishbone Stitch

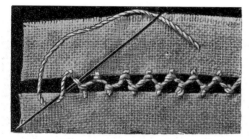

Fig. 37. Ornamental hem

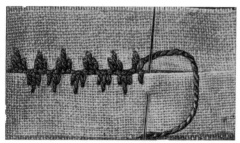

Fig. 38. Joining by groups of three Blanket Stitches

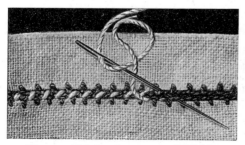

Fig. 39. Joining by means of Blanket Stitch and Whipping

quickly and accurately is by using dots (Fig. 44). A series of dots is marked at perfectly equal intervals on squared paper. Waxed transferring paper is then placed on the material to be embroidered, and then the squared paper is placed on top taking care that the lines of dots follow the straight thread of the material. The dots are transferred on to the material. The distance between the dots must vary according to the type and thickness of the material. On calico, silk, linen and poplin, the distance will be about 6 mm. Transfers with various distances between dots can be bought ready for use.

When this preparation is complete, the gathers are drawn up, pulling the gathering threads so that an even gathering is produced, then stroking into place with a needle in order to produce perfect folds (Fig. 45).

After the gathering is completed and the folds creased, the gathers are let out to the required width and the threads tied securely. Coats Anchor Stranded Cotton or Coats Anchor Coton à Broder are suitable threads to use for the smocking.

There are five basic smocking stitches: Stem Stitch, Cable Stitch, Vandyke Stitch, Chevron Stitch and Honeycomb Stitch.

Stem Stitch. After bringing out the needle on the right side of the material, the thread is passed over two gathers and back under one, pulling the stitch up tightly. Work from left to right. Continue in this way along the desired length so that a straight line of stitching is produced, fixing the gathers in place, one by one. As in ordinary Stem Stitch, the thread, when working, may also be left under the needle, giving the same result (Figs. 46 and 47).

Cable Stitch. Figs. 48 and 49 show Cable Stitch. This stitch is worked from left to right. The thread is passed over two gathers, going back with the

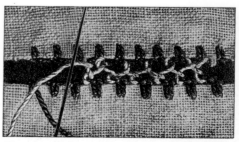

Fig. 40. Other embroidery stitches using crossed threads of different colours

needle under one, holding the thread, alternately above and below the needle.

Vandyke or Wave Stitch. This is worked from left to right. Four projecting stitches are worked, taking the thread each time over two gathers, and bringing the needle out under one, keeping the needle slightly sloping and working upward, in a graduated line; on the upward line the thread is kept below the needle. Proceed to work a corresponding line in the opposite direction, keeping the thread above the needle. The movement is then repeated (Figs. 50 and 51).

Chevron Stitch. This is worked on two levels from left to right.

1st row. The thread is passed over two gathers and the needle is brought back under one: then a second stitch is made taking up the next gather at a higher level keeping the working thread below the needle: then a third stitch is made taking up the next gather on the same level with the thread above the needle: a fourth stitch is made taking up the next gather with the thread still above the needle. The following stitch is taken into the next gather at the lower level with the thread below the needle. Continue in this way, remembering to keep the working thread above the needle for the top stitch and below the needle for the lower stitch.

2nd row. Like the first, but with the direction of the stitches changed so that small diamond shapes are formed.

These two rows repeated form a very effective trellis pattern (Figs. 52 and 53).

Surface Honeycomb Stitch. Here the procedure is slightly different from the other stitches. Working is from right to left. The needle is passed under two gathers, which are fixed with a Back Stitch; then, about quarter of an inch below, two other

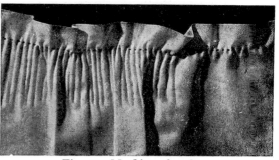

Fig. 42. Marking of gathers

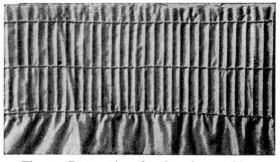

Fig. 43. Preparation of gathers for smocking

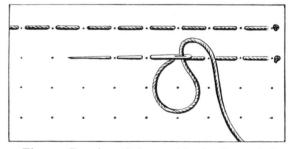

Fig. 44. Running stitches used in the dot method

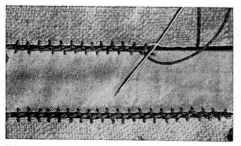

Fig. 41. Two rows of crossed Blanket Stitch

Fig. 45. Gathers after the thread has been drawn up

13

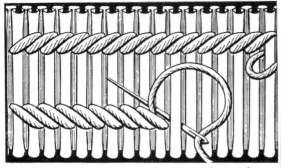

Fig. 46. Stem Stitch on gathers (diagram)

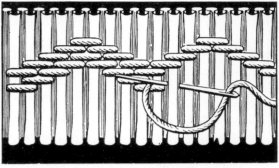

Fig. 50. Vandyke Stitch (diagram)

Fig. 47. Stem Stitch on gathers

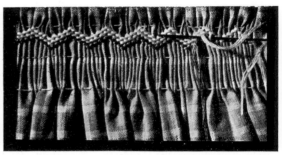

Fig. 51. Vandyke Stitch on gathers

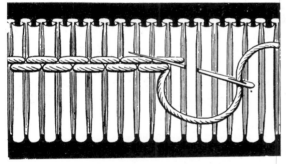

Fig. 48. Cable Stitch on gathers (diagram)

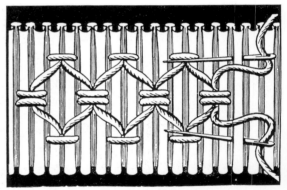

Fig. 52. Chevron Stitch (diagram)

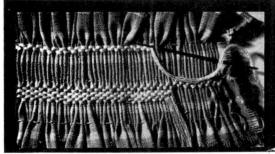

Fig. 49. Cable Stitch on gathers

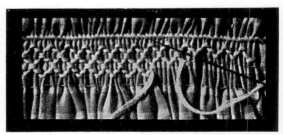

Fig. 53. Chevron Stitch on gathers

14

Carla, Piccolini, Milan

Smocking on children's frocks. The embroidery is worked in Anchor Stranded Cotton and Anchor Coton à Broder
Anchor Coton à Broder

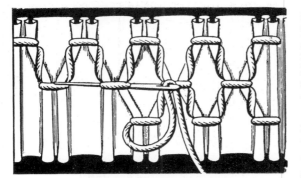

Fig. 54. Surface Honeycomb Stitch (diagram)

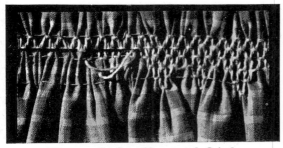

Fig. 55. Surface Honeycomb Stitch

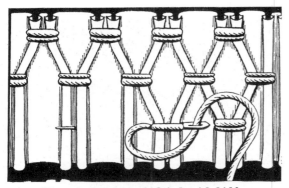

Fig. 56. Honeycomb Stitch with hidden stitch (diagram)

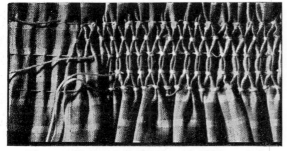

Fig. 57. Honeycomb Stitch with hidden stitch

gathers are taken up (one of them being the last one fixed above by a Back Stitch), and another Back Stitch taken; two other gathers are then fixed by a Back Stitch, by returning to the same level as the first two and so on. In this stitch the thread always remains on the right side of the work.

On the second row, the same procedure is followed, but the Back Stitch is not repeated on the row just worked, but only the gathers below are taken up. These may be taken up in the same grouping as the row just worked or in different groupings, with effective results (Figs. 54 and 55).

The embroidery thread need not always remain on the right side of the work: by passing it below the work, a "honeycomb" effect may be produced; this effect gives its name to the type of decoration shown in Figs. 56 and 57.

Feather Stitch. Another stitch which is very effective on gatherings is Feather Stitch.

Fig. 58 clearly shows how this is carried out. The stitch is worked from right to left: two gathers are taken up on the needle, holding the thread as for Blanket Stitch, then, going down a few threads to the right, two other gathers are taken up, one of them forming part of the preceding stitch, and the other part of the following one: the stitch is continued by taking up groups of two gathers, always moving some threads to the right. When three of these stitches have been completed, the thread is turned and the work continued in the opposite direction, going down to the left, using the same movement.

Herringbone Stitch. This is another stitch which is easily worked over gathers, being worked from left to right. The embroidery thread is thrown over two gathers and both are taken up on the needle; then, going down about quarter of an inch lower, the two following gathers are taken up, keeping the thread above the needle; the next stitch is made by going up again to the level of the first stitch, keeping the thread below the needle, then, by going down again the sequence is continued. The needle must always be kept in a perfectly horizontal position.

Fig. 59 shows the two different stitches.

Fig. 60: a richly embroidered border for a yoke. The pattern is formed by using Cable Stitch.

First of all, two whole lines of stitching are worked; the others are worked in steps, that is five, four, three, and finally one, increasing by one stitch again on the opposite side until once again a complete line of stitching is formed. Four double Back Stitches in a contrasting colour are then worked in the centre of the circles thus formed.

Fig. 61: an example of Cable Stitch worked on squared material. The diamond shapes are worked over eight gathers. No gathers are left free between the groups.

Two horizontal lines of Cable Stitch finish off the border, above and below.

Fig. 62: Love-knot carried out in Vandyke Stitch. The repetition of the same motive makes an attractive decoration.

Fig. 63: double Vandyke Stitch for an effective lozenge design. The stitch holding the two gathers in the centre of the lozenges is worked in a darker shade.

Fig. 64: groups of Cable Stitch, worked over six gathers, make up the border shown in this picture. The groupings of the stitches change on successive lines and are joined together by Vandyke Stitch.

Fig. 65: lines of Stem Stitch enclosing three rows of Chevron Stitch. Below, the same Chevron Stitch worked in triangles to finish off the border.

Fig. 66: five rows of Vandyke Stitch, worked over seven gathers, dividing the gathers into diamond shapes which are then filled in with groups of Cable Stitch worked in steps, that is, first one stitch, then two, three, four, and then again, three, two, one.

Fig. 67: this border consists of Chevron Stitch worked alternately over three and two gathers, forming larger and smaller diamond shapes.

Fig. 68: four lines of Vandyke Stitch in graduated shades for the first section of the border shown in Fig. 68. About a quarter of an inch below, the same line of pattern is worked in the opposite way, working from the lightest to the darkest shades.

Fig. 69: a border embroidered in Cable Stitch in horizontal lines and triangles decreasing by one stitch every row on a background of blue cloth.

Tucks. The tuck is an attractive decoration for underwear. It can be used in various ways, and may be arranged singly or in groups, or in patterns of squares, diamonds, lozenges, etc.

Method of making tucks (Figs. 70, 71). Mark down the fabric with the point of the needle on the straight thread, as many times as the number of

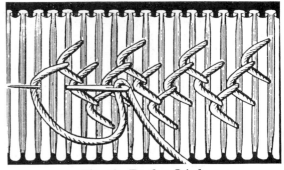

Fig. 58. Feather Stitch

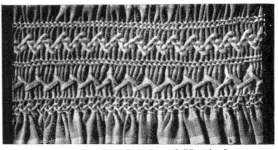

Fig. 59. Feather Stitch and Herringbone Stitch on gathers

Fig. 60. Border in Cable Stitch

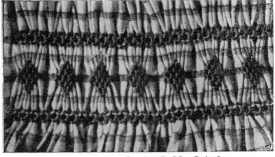

Fig. 61. Border in Cable Stitch

17

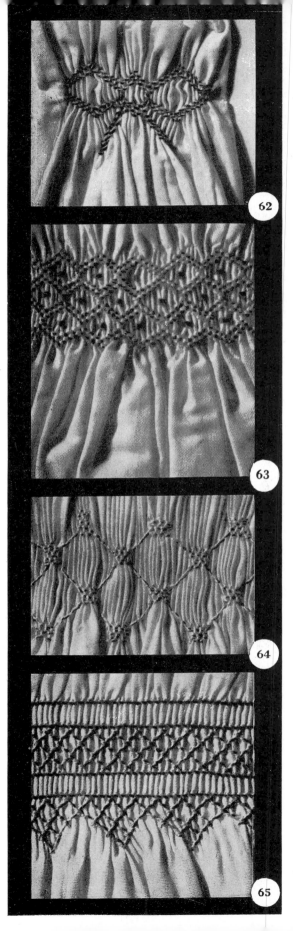

62

63

64

65

tucks required, taking care that the distance between each is equal, measuring them with a piece of card, or with a tape measure. The fabric is then folded on the marked line and then, below the fold and very close to the edge, a small regular Running Stitch is worked, holding the material horizontally.

Experts use a very rapid movement of the hand in making this row of very small, light stitches, running the needle through the fabric until it is filled with very small stitches and only then drawing the thread through, before re-commencing the movement.

In the course of making the tuck, the thread must never be joined or knotted.

As well as a decoration for collars and cuffs, and lingerie, tucks may also serve to control the width of fabric in a garment.

A light soft fabric is required for tucking, such as linen, silk crêpe or chiffon. It is rather difficult to tuck on the cross of the fabric and in this case it is advisable to baste the tuck in position before sewing.

A strong, thin and well-running thread is necessary for sewing tucks: the best is Coats Drima (polyester), or Coats Chain, No. 40.

Finishings for Lingerie. For lightweight or silk materials, the garment can be finished with a decorative stitch instead of the usual hem. Fig. 72 shows how to work an up-and-down Running Stitch on the hem of a garment made of lightweight material: by pulling up this thread slightly small festoons are formed.

Fig. 73 shows a pretty edging stitch. A very narrow hem is fixed down with a coloured thread, using two oversewing stitches pulled rather tight. The needle is then passed through the hem and pulled out at a short distance where a second group of two stitches is made.

Rolled Hem. This is worked as a very narrow hem on handkerchiefs. It is made by rolling the fabric over the needle which, coming out after one turn over, is replaced in the fabric. As shown in the illustration, the needleful of stitches is not drawn through until there are quite a few stitches on the needle (Fig. 74).

False Hems. Another way of finishing off lingerie is by the addition of a false hem. A strip of the same fabric as the garment is cut on the cross. This is obtained by cutting diagonally across a perfect square. The strip is placed on the right side of the work and fixed on by a line of Running Stitch or by machining very near the edge. After this the seam is pressed and the strip is turned over, folded down and hemmed. Take care that the stitches do not show through on the other side of the work (Figs. 75 and 76). If the edge to be finished off is already on the cross, fold it over to the right side and machine stitch very near to the edge of the fold. After pressing the hem is turned back to the other side and fixed down with hemming.

Corded Piping. To make a piping show up better, a cord is used, covered with a half-inch wide strip of fabric cut on the cross. A row of Running Stitches is worked just below the cord. The piping is tacked on the edge to be decorated, and fixed with very close, regular stitches. The work is then turned over, folded in and caught down like an ordinary hem (Fig. 77).

Fixing of Tapes and Ribbons. The end of the tape or ribbon is folded in and attached to the garment by oversewing; however, the joining is more resistant if made by stitching down the folded tape on three sides. The fourth side is held down with Running Stitch or Herringbone Stitch (Fig. 78).

For fixing tapes to the corner of linen to be hung up, such as towels and dish-cloths, the following method is used. A piece of tape about four inches long is folded to form a triangle, as in Fig. 79, the two ends of the tape being folded in and caught down all round the edges on to the corner of the article, using Herringbone Stitch at the joining of the two ends of the tape.

Attachment of Braids. When the garment is to be finished off with a braid edging, this is placed in position on the right side of the work and attached by hand very near to the edge; then it is turned over on to the wrong side of the work and caught down by hemming.

Ric-rac Braid. Is often used as a decoration for collars and cuffs. If placed on the fabric itself, it is sewn down at each point by a small stitch; if, however, it is attached to the edge, then it is sewn down with a well-hidden stitch at the tip of the

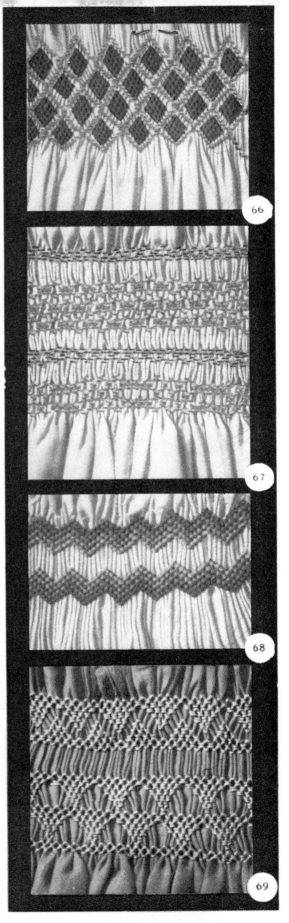

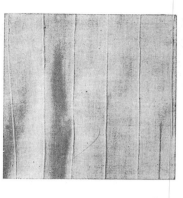

Fig. 70. Simple tucks

Fig. 75. Preparation for binding

Fig. 76. Turning over the cross-piece

Fig. 71. Tucks in diamond pattern worked on the straight thread of the material

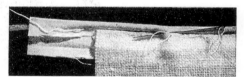

Fig. 77. Piped edging

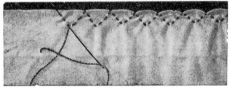

Fig. 72. Finishing of a hem with Running Stitches

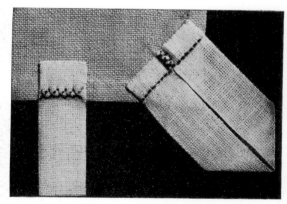

Fig. 78. Attaching ribbons

Fig. 73. Finishing of a hem with groups of two Oversewing Stitches

Fig. 74. Rolled hem

Fig. 79. Attaching tapes

points where they touch the hem of the fabric (Fig. 80).

Attachment of Lace and Insertions. One of the most elegant of decorations for lingerie is undoubtedly lace. There are many types which range from that made on the lace-pillow to the type called "Valenciennes". Lace is always sewn on rather loosely or even gathered. First, it must be tacked on to the fabric, after lightly pulling up a thread at the base of the lace border. The tacking is done by taking up a kind of hemming stitch, in a vertical position, over the edge of the lace. For clarity, the illustrations show both the tacking and hemming stitches in dark thread (Fig. 81).

Attachment of Lace by Oversewing. The fabric is folded over on to the wrong side holding the fold towards the worker. After having tacked the lace with rather close stitches, the lace is then attached by making an oversewing stitch working from right to left, or vice versa, taking up two threads of fabric and two threads of the edge of the lace. After sewing, any excess fabric is cut away (Fig. 82).

To decorate a finished hem with lace. This is simply attached by oversewing, after tacking loosely in position.

Attachment of Lace with Cording. On finely worked lingerie, the lace is often attached by cording. The lace is tacked on as above, and then a rather close row of cording is worked. In order to make this stand out well, a slightly thicker thread than that used for the embroidery is taken across under the stitches (Fig. 83). For this, we advise Coats Anchor Coton à Broder.

Attachment of Lace by Hemstitch. If the lace is to be attached on the straight thread, one or two threads of the fabric are first drawn out: the lace is then tacked on above the drawn threads, and then fixed by Hemstitch, taking up three threads of the space left by the drawn threads and two threads of the fabric, together with the edging of the lace border (Fig. 84). Half Hemstitch may also be used (Fig. 85).

Fig. 86 illustrates another method for attaching lace. After having tacked the lace on to the fabric a double stitch is taken just under the edge of the lace and a second stitch just above the edge. The thread should always be on the right side of the work.

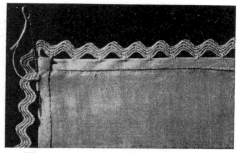

Fig. 80. Attaching Ric-rac binding (wrong side)

Fig. 81. Tacking on lace

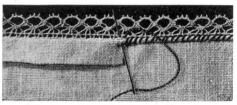

Fig. 82. Attaching lace by seaming

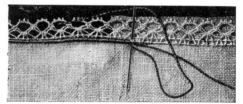

Fig. 83. Attaching lace with cord edging

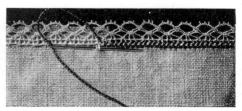

Fig. 84. Attaching lace by hemstitching

21

Fig. 85. Attaching lace by Half Hemstitch

Fig. 86. Attaching lace by Half Turkish Stitch

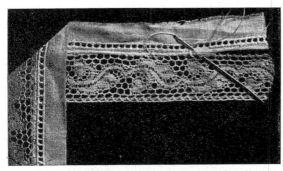

Fig. 87. Attaching an insertion with beading

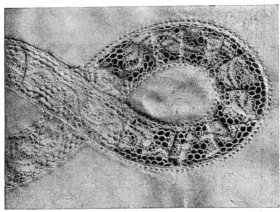

Fig. 88. Attaching curved lace

Another method of attaching lace is by "beadings". These are made by machine and consist of a row of eyelets worked on very fine fabric. The fabric is cut about 6 mm from the line of holes, and then rolled with a damp finger, as for a rolled hem; this is joined to the lace from the back, by a rather close oversewing stitch (Fig. 87).

The attachment of laces must be very firm, therefore a very strong, but at the same time fine and easy-running thread must be used. Coats Drima (polyster) is the best for the purpose.

Attachment of Curved Lace. Joining lace in a curved shape is a little more difficult than the normal method. First it should be tacked along the line of the pattern, after loosening it by pulling the thread along the base, or by overcasting with a thin thread so that the lace is slightly gathered. The gathering should be evened out and then the lace fixed down, using one of the stitches already described. Afterwards, the material is cut away underneath the lace. The same method is used for fixing down the lace at the corners (Fig. 88).

Seams for Fine Lingerie. On silk, or very fine cotton lingerie, the various pieces may be joined by special stitches made with a thick needle and fine thread. Four of the most commonly used of these stitches are illustrated. The most suitable threads for this type of work are Coats Thread, Coats Anchor Stranded Cotton and Coats Anchor Coton à Broder.

Turkish Stitch or Three-sided Stitch. This is worked from right to left. Five or six threads of the fabric are taken up obliquely, the needle being taken back through the fabric at the point where it was first put in, coming out again six threads to the left, horizontally, where another stitch is made, taking up another six threads of fabric. The third stitch is oblique, joining the second to the first in the form of a triangle; then, going back through the place where the needle was drawn out, the needle is brought out below, towards the left, making a stitch which takes up another group of six threads of the fabric in a horizontal direction. This completes the stitch which may then be repeated from the beginning, at regular intervals. The point of the triangles must be directly above or below the centre of the horizontal lines and the oblique lines are double (Fig. 89).

Half-Turkish Stitch. This has already been mentioned as a method of joining lace edgings. Two running stitches are made, taking up four threads of fabric, returning the needle through the same hole, and then a second group of two stitches is repeated four threads below. These alternatively placed groups are joined by an oblique line (Fig. 90).

Paris Stitch. On bringing the needle out of the fabric, it is replaced four threads lower, taking a horizontal stitch to the left. The needle is then replaced in the same hole as it came out of, being withdrawn diagonally four threads higher up to the left. This completes the movement which may then be repeated. To make the stitch stronger, each stitch is gone over twice, pulling the thread tightly (Fig. 91).

Square Turkish Stitch. This is worked from right to left. Four or five threads of material are taken up vertically, going over them twice, then the needle is drawn out four or five threads to the left, making another two stitches. The third stitch of the group is taken by moving in an oblique line below to the left and taking up another two vertical stitches; then point A is joined to point C, closing up the square. The sequence is then begun again (Fig. 93).

Buttonholes. Buttonholes are very important for bed linen as well as for garments.

The buttonhole must have a length proportional to the button to be used. There are special scissors for cutting buttonholes, but with a little practice they can also be cut successfully with ordinary scissors.

As shown in Fig. 94 it is a good idea to enclose the position of the buttonhole by means of Running Stitch. Fig. 95 shows the overcasting of the cut edge which is then covered by Tailor's Buttonhole Stitch.

To make the Buttonhole Stitch, the needle is held with the eye towards the opening of the buttonhole and the thread is passed from right to left under the needle (Fig. 92). The thread is then pulled through in an upward movement, the edge of the stitch being brought as near as possible to the cut edge. After the first stitch, another is made as near as possible to it, so that a regular ridge is formed along the cut edge of the hole. When the first side has been completed, the stitch is continued in a curve around the corner and the work

Legnazzi, Milan

Evening shawls and head-veils, bridal or communi-cants' veils, can be very effectively made by placing lace on a tulle background. First of all the various pieces, flowers, leaves and other patterns are cut out and pinned on to the tulle, keeping a certain symmetry in their arrangement and following a given design. These are then fixed down by very fine over-sewing on the back.

An idea of this kind of work is given in the photo-graph above.

23

Lady's tulle front with lace insertions. The joining is so finely worked as to be invisible

Application of lace on linen

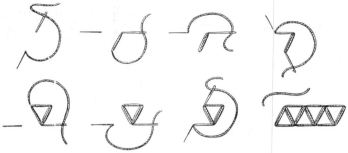

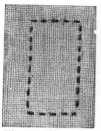

Fig. 94. Marking
out the place for
the buttonhole

Fig. 89. Turkish Stitch or Three-sided Stitch

Fig. 90. Half-Turkish Stitch

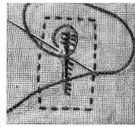

Fig. 95. Oversewing
the cut

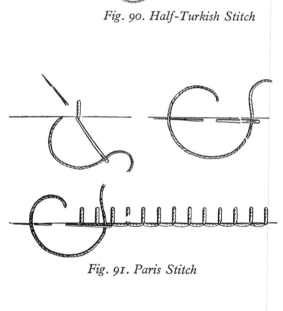

Fig. 91. Paris Stitch

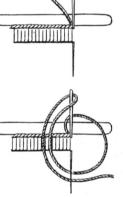

Fig. 92. Tailor's
Buttonhole Stitch

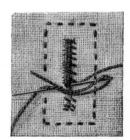

Fig. 96. Method of
working buttonhole

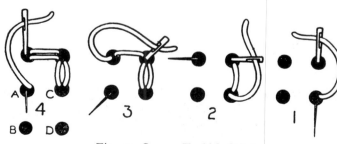

Fig. 93. Square Turkish Stitch

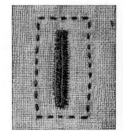

Fig. 97. The finished
buttonhole

continued in a straight line down the other side. When this is also complete, a Back Stitch across three threads is made to join the two sides and these are covered by Buttonhole Stitch so that the knots lie on the inside of the buttonhole (Figs. 96 and 97).

A very strong, resistant and slightly twisted thread is required. Coats Bold Stitch (polyester) or Anchor Button Thread is most suitable.

Buttonhole Loops. Very often buttonhole loops are worked on the edge of an opening. The thread is fastened on at the edge of the fabric, then the needle is replaced at a distance of about half an inch making a loop wide enough for the button to pass through. The thread is passed across three times and then covered with Buttonhole Stitch working from right to left or vice versa, as is most convenient (Fig. 98).

Small loops are also used for fastenings by hooks; these consist of three threads placed horizontally or vertically and covered by Buttonhole Stitch.

Dressmakers sometimes use rings for hooking up dresses, belts, etc. These rings, generally made of metal, are covered by Buttonhole Stitch using a silk thread or cotton in the same colour as the garment.

Attaching Buttons. In order to sew on a button and to fix exactly the place where it must go, the buttonhole, which must always be worked first, is placed in position and the needle to be used for sewing on the button is brought out of the fabric in the exact centre of the worked buttonhole, from below upwards; the button is fixed on with a few stitches (Fig. 99 shows various ways of attaching buttons). Then the thread is brought out between the button and the fabric and the thread wrapped two or three times round under the button, forming a neck or stem; the sewing is fastened off, by taking the thread through to the wrong side of the work, with a few Back Stitches.

When sewing on a button it is well to leave a small space between the fabric and the button itself. Fig. 100 shows how this is done. A pin or needle (or more than one if necessary) is placed above the button and below the thread of attachment. The pins will be taken out before twisting the thread round under the button. When the button must be very strongly sewn on for continual use, in order to avoid the tearing of the fabric (in overcoats, men's clothes, etc.), a smaller

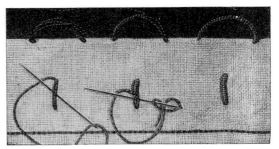

Fig. 98. Buttonhole loops

Fig. 99. Method of attaching buttons

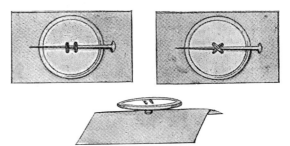

Fig. 100. Method of attaching buttons with stem

Fig. 101. Zip-fastener

Fig. 102. Casing
for elastic

Fig. 103. Casing after
threading elastic

(a) (b) (c)

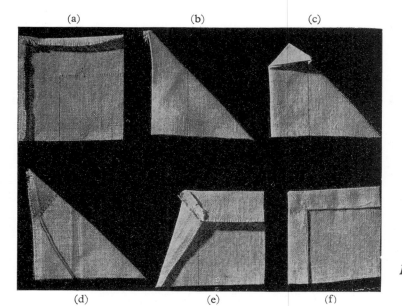

(d) (e) (f)

Fig. 104. Method of mitring
corners

(a) (b) (c)

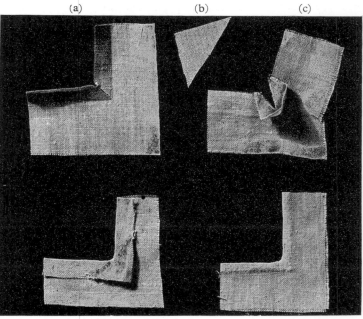

(d)

Fig. 105. Method of finishing
internal corners

28

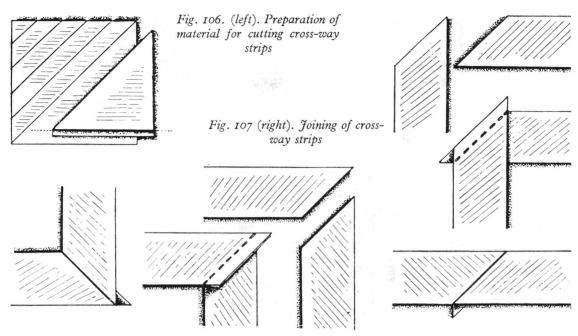

Fig. 106. (left). Preparation of material for cutting cross-way strips

Fig. 107 (right). Joining of cross-way strips

Fig. 108. Corner joining of cross-way strips

button is placed on the reverse side, underneath the larger one, fixing it with the same stitches as the larger one.

Attachment of Hooks and Eyes and Press-Studs. Hooks and press-studs must always be fixed very firmly to the fabric. For press-studs, the stud part is always sewn on first; this is then pressed on to the part of the work where the other side must be fixed, thus marking the place where this is to be sewn.

Zip-fasteners. This is one of the most modern methods of fastening in use today. It can be used for closing dresses, skirts, overalls, jackets, bathing costumes, hand-bags, etc., in a very practical manner. In order to attach a zip-fastener, the fabric which will cover each edge of the tape of the zip is turned back and sewn down by machine or by a row of Back Stitches, taking up the tape of the zip at the same time. A very strong thread must be used. The tape of the zip is then caught down on the wrong side of the fabric (Fig. 101).

Elastic. Figs. 102 and 103 show the methods of making a casing for elastic. Two rows of machine stitching are made on doubled fabric, leaving a space equal to that of the width of the elastic plus a very little extra. A buttonhole is worked across the space and the elastic inserted, using a tape-threader.

Neatening of Corners. When the hem is very narrow, the whole length of the hem is folded in, and then the second side is folded in the same way, leaving a simple fold at the corners and cutting away the inside part of the corner fold. When, instead, the hem is broad, as in tablecloths, serviettes and men's handkerchiefs, the corner must be cut diagonally. One thread is drawn out at the level of the width of the hem to be made, or, if the fabric is very fine, a mark is made by stroking with the needle on the straight thread of the fold and at the base of the hem, both horizontally and vertically (Fig. 104(a)). Then the fabric is folded in a perfect corner, making the two sides (b) meet; then the two upper folds of the corner are folded in a triangle until the points touch the drawn-out thread (c), pressing with the fingers so that a visible mark of the fold is left. The folded work is then unfolded and the diagonal line formed is stitched, either by hand or machine (d). The fabric is then cut very near the line of sewing, removing the corner fold, too; the seam is well flattened with the finger-nail (e) and, lastly, the corner is turned over and the hem is tacked down (f).

Child's dress in white piqué cotton with front of bodice smocked. The details are clearly shown in the enlarged photo. The lozenges are formed by four simple stitches over one gather and two stitches over two gathers. When all the diagonals have been worked four Daisy Stitches or Detached Chain Stitches are worked on the gathers of alternate lozenges

Detail of the embroidery in actual size

Another type of corner is that which is used on the inside of a garment, for example on a square neck. In this case, the cut is made on the perfect diagonal of the corner, for a length which is just sufficient for folding over the hem (Fig. 105 (a)). A right-angled triangle of the same fabric (b) is applied to this cut, separating the cut and applying the triangle with a row of running threads or a line of machining (c); then the applied triangle (d) is turned over to the other side and the narrow hem all round turned in, tacked and hemmed down.

Binding with Crossway Strips. These bindings are very important in the making of lingerie; they are pieces of fabric cut on the cross which serve to bind edges, reinforce hems and cover seams, etc. The cross-way pieces are obtained by folding the fabric so that the two edges meet perfectly on their straight thread, then cutting along the slope of the triangle thus formed.

Fig. 106 shows the procedure and the diagonal lines show where the fabric should be cut. Having thus obtained a number of strips, they are joined by placing them right sides together, Backstitching or machining, as in Fig. 107. Then the two pieces are opened out so that a diagonal join shows on the right side. Fig. 108 shows clearly the same type of join at a corner.

CHAPTER II

Darning and Patching

Materials. The threads used for mending vary according to the work in hand. To make a good darn on cloth, warp or weft, threads of the same fabric should be used: from some articles of underwear a thread may be drawn out of a hem or from an unused piece of the same fabric. For ordinary darning on household, children's and personal linen, it is best to use Chadwick's Mending Cotton. In the chapter entitled "Knitting" the reader will find a clear explanation of how to mend this type of fabric. Here we give instructions for mending in general and for repairing tulle.

Fabric is formed of warp and weft threads, the warp threads being those parallel with the selvedges and the weft the threads going across from one selvedge to another. The formation of the cloth may be studied by taking out a thread from selvedge to selvedge.

Mending may be carried out as follows:
1. Reinforcing of threadbare or worn fabric.
2. Mending a tear.
3. Repairing a hole.
4. Patching.

1. **Reinforcing of Worn Fabrics.** Worn fabric is reinforced on the wrong side, using a thread thinner than that of the fabric for making both warp and weft. The threads should be longer than the worn place in both directions: the work is turned after each row has been worked, leaving a loop at each end of the row, in order to avoid the puckering up of the material if the thread should shrink after washing. The rows of weaving should not all be begun at the same point, but at different levels in order to avoid too much strain. In ordinary fabrics three threads may be taken up and three threads left under the needle, but in very fine fabrics only one thread must be taken to make a perfect repair, the strengthening threads should not be worked between one line of existing threads and another, but exactly over the threads themselves. The illustration (Fig. 1) shows a reinforcement made with a dark thread as seen from the wrong side, a reinforcement made with white thread seen from the wrong side and the two darns seen from the right side.

2. **Mending a Tear.** To mend a tear or a hole use threads drawn from the fabric whenever possible. These should be of three different lengths—short, medium and long. Fix the torn fabric on to a work cushion with fine pins so that the tear or hole may be kept taut. Prepare the three groups of threads and have ready also a needle threaded with fine strong sewing cotton.

The medium thread is woven across beginning six threads to the right of the tear and continuing for six threads to the left, remembering that one stitch consists of one thread over and one thread under. The frayed thread is folded upwards on both sides. With the threaded needle follow the drawn thread at the right but commence working four threads more to the right in order to reinforce the fabric. Continue weaving across to the other side and over four more reinforcing threads on the left.

Short and long threads are inserted in the same way as shown in Fig. 2. The lower illustration shows the mending of a tear as seen from the right side—this is carried out in a dark tone. Fig. 3 illustrates a finished mend carried out with threads of the same fabric. When the mend is finished it should be pressed on the wrong side and the superfluous threads cut away.

3. Repairing a Hole. When a hole has formed in the fabric, a new piece must be created to repair it. The hole should first be trimmed to a square or rectangle, cutting away the broken or worn threads. Then carry on as for the tear, using, however, an equal number of threads for both warp and weft. When making the weft threads, take in the threads which cross the hole (Fig. 4). On the right, the hole; on the left the hole made regular; below, left, introduction of the warp threads and the beginning of the weft. The finished mend seen from the right side, but carried out with coloured thread, is illustrated in Fig. 5.

Application and Insertion of a Patch. When a hole is very large a patch must be placed over it. The hole is made regular and the horizontal and vertical medians must be marked both in the piece to be mended and on the patch itself. Warp and weft threads on both pieces must correspond exactly, so that the insertion is invisible (Figs. 6 and 7). The piece which will form the patch is placed on the wrong side of the fabric making the medians correspond by placing a pin half-way along each side (Fig. 8). It can be seen that the threads coincide with that of the new piece of fabric from which one thread more than the hole is drawn from each side, i.e. two horizontal and two vertical threads. Then the work is turned over on to the wrong side and the piece marked by the drawn-out thread is cut away on the first side on the left, cutting up to the horizontal crossing of the drawn threads (Fig. 9). This detached piece is then fixed down, folding it into a triangle, at the centre of the patch, and then the mending is begun (Fig. 10). The first thread is withdrawn from the piece to be mended: the needle is passed

under and over the threads, taking up one thread at a time, along the line of the withdrawn thread. The frayed edges are worked in with the thread, one by one, until all the new threads have been worked into the torn piece. After completing the first side, the work is turned, the line marked by the drawn thread is cut, the new piece of fabric is folded back in a triangle to the centre of the work and so on, for each side (Fig. 11). When the

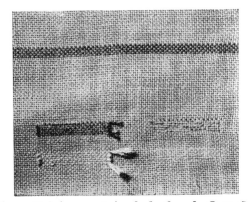

Fig. 1. Reinforcement in dark thread. Seen from both right and wrong sides

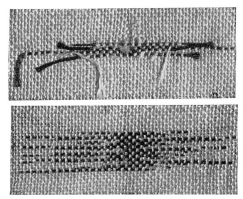

Fig. 2. Mending of a tear. (Upper) Introduction of threads—long, short and medium

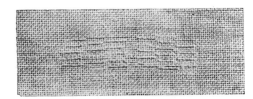

Fig. 3. Mend carried out with threads of the same material

33

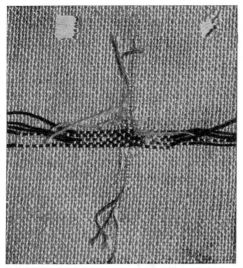

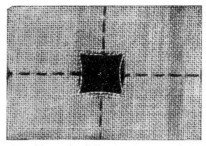

Fig. 4 (Upper). Hole to be mended and hole after being made regular. (Centre) Introduction of warp and weft threads

Fig. 7. Marking of medians on worn piece showing hole after having been made regular

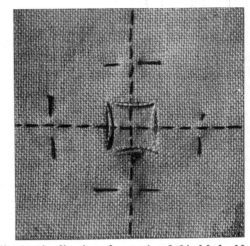

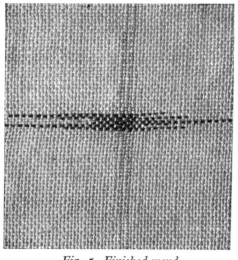

Fig. 5. Finished mend

Fig. 8. Application of new piece behind hole. Notice that the medians remain continuous

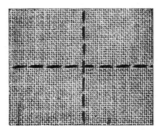

Fig. 6. Marking of the horizontal and vertical medians on piece of material to be placed over hole

Fig. 9. Beginning of insertion: introduction of first new threads on worn piece

insertion of the piece is complete it is pressed on the wrong side and the remaining threads cut away.

Mending a Tablecloth. First of all the type and design of the material must be studied. Let us take as an example a checked tablecloth which is one of the most common types. After studying its weave, other types will be easy to follow.

The tablecloth consists of two types of square, one different from the other, repeated alternately.

In the square consisting of three threads below and one on top, the diagonal from above to below goes down from left to right: in the square consisting of three threads above and one below, the diagonal from above to below goes down from right to left.

To form the two squares, a change of weave takes place every four threads or every multiple of four.

In our pattern the change occurs every twelve threads. Proceed in the following manner:

1st row. 3 threads below 1 above, 3 threads below 1 above, 3 threads below 1 above. 2nd square. 1 thread below 3 above. 1 thread below 3 above. 1 thread below 3 above. 3rd square. As first. 4th square. As second and so on.

2nd row. 2 threads below 1 above, 3 threads below 1 above, 3 threads below 1 above, 1 below. 2nd square. 1 above 1 below, 3 above 1 below, 3 above 1 below, 2 above. Repeat for whole length.

3rd row. 1 below 1 above, 3 below 1 above, 3 below 1 above, 2 below. 2nd square. 2 above 1 below, 3 above 1 below, 3 above 1 below, 1 above.

The following rows repeat the pattern sequence above and so on for 12 rows.

After the 12 rows, that is after having worked one row of squares, the second row is worked by alternating the squares (Fig. 12).

All types of mending which can be worked on smooth cloth may also be worked on tablecloths, following the same rules.

Fig. 13 shows the mending of a tear in a tablecloth, seen from the wrong side.

Fig. 14 shows a mend on a tablecloth seen from the right side.

Fig. 15 shows a darn over a hole in a tablecloth seen from the right side, using coloured threads and still unfinished.

These instructions are intended for the mending and reinforcing of important or valuable items. For very worn or ordinary fabrics, a series of

Fig. 10. Insertion of threads on one side

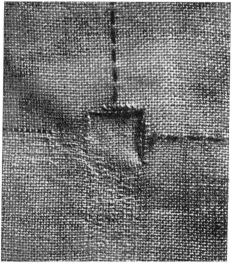

Fig. 11. Mending and insertion completed on two sides

Running Stitches not placed exactly corresponding to the weave may be used, in such a way as to be just sufficient to keep the fabric together and prevent further damage. The needle is held near the eye with the thumb and forefinger of the right hand, working from above down, taking up a few stitches at regular intervals, and then working back from the bottom up, without turning or moving the work.

All mending or reinforcing of fine fabrics should be done by hand, but the sewing machine, prepared

35

Fig. 12. Design on tablecloth—alternate squares

Fig. 13. Mending a tear in a tablecloth (the new threads are dark, to make the process clearer)

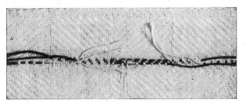

Fig. 14. Finished mend over a tear in a tablecloth

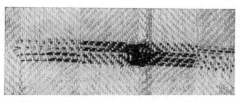

Fig. 15. Mending a hole in a tablecloth

as for machine embroidery, is very useful for darning household linen, thus saving time and trouble and giving a stronger finish. Anchor machine embroidery thread has been produced for this type of work.

4. **Patching.** On patterned fabrics with lines, squares, flowers and other designs, darning is never carried out owing to the difficulty of finding a matching thread. On these fabrics both holes and tears should be repaired by patching with a piece of matching fabric, fixed with invisible stitches.

Joining. The fabric is folded over on to the wrong side along the straight thread, so that the pattern corresponds and the two pieces to be joined are tacked (Figs. 16 and 17). Then with the two folds on the inside, the two pieces are placed together, making the patterns correspond and tacked a second time. Having thus prepared the join, the invisible stitch is begun, working from right to left, with a fine, strong thread—for example Coats Drima (polyester).

Holding the fabric with the turning upmost, two horizontal threads are taken up from the lower piece and then two from the upper, interchanging them. In our pattern on checked fabric, the work is begun at a point where two squares meet, taking up one thread from one square, and one from the other, on the lower piece of fabric, and on the upper two threads from one square only. Work continues by taking up the two following threads from both pieces. If the work is done carefully and the threads of the fabric are strong, the invisible stitch will be easily drawn up. Fig. 18 shows a part of the join seen from the right side and a part seen from the wrong side. The join should be well pressed with a hot iron.

The same system is followed both for the application of a corner or a patch. After working the invisible stitch the work is turned over and trimmed, leaving half an inch of fabric and oversewing both the straight as well as the diagonal parts. Fig. 19 shows a cut corner, tacked ready for sewing. Fig. 20 shows, on one side, a corner seen from the right side, and, on the other, a corner seen from the wrong side. Fig. 21: on the left, the hole to be repaired, and, on the right, the tacked patch ready for sewing. Fig. 22: on the left, a square patch seen from the right side; on the right, the same patch seen from the wrong side. Patches should be well pressed after application.

Darning. However necessary it may be, darning is a rather poor remedy, to be avoided when possible. It is better to change a whole piece, or to replace a piece of fabric to form a decoration, before resorting to darning, in order to hide a hole.

Darning should also be avoided as far as possible on household linen. When a sheet begins to wear in the middle, cut down the centre on the straight thread for the whole length and join together the two selvedges. Make hems on the new sides and reinforce the worn parts, now on the outer edges, by darning them very thoroughly. Pillow-cases, too, generally wear out in the middle: instead of darning, a whole piece may be replaced by joining the new piece to the old by hemstitching, Turkish Stitch or by a lace insertion.

It is more difficult to mend tablecloths, which seem to wear out all over, without any apparent means of mending them successfully. As far as possible small darns should be made, but it is, perhaps, better to cut them up for use as table napkins or kitchen cloths.

When it is impossible to do otherwise, a repair may be made in the following manner:

On white fabric the direction of the threads must be noted, in order to join the warp and weft accurately. For patterned fabrics, the design will serve as a guide. The worn or broken place is first made regular, either as a square or rectangle. A square or rectangle is then cut from new material, slightly larger than the cut-away piece. The new piece is tacked, matching the design and this is stitched round with Running or Back Stitch. The corners may prove to be difficult, as they must not be puckered up. A Back Stitch should pass over the corner in such a way that the last stitch of the line just finished and the first stitch of the new line form a perfect right angle.

When the sides are sewn down, the edges of the worn piece are turned back over those of the new piece and sewn down with small invisible stitches.

Coloured patches are not turned back. The seams are opened out and pressed well down with the finger-nail or iron; they are then trimmed so that they are not too wide and the corners are flattened by cutting diagonally. The edges are then whipped or Blanket Stitched.

Mending Felt-type Cloth. For this particular type of material mending must be carried out differently.

Fig. 16. Folding and tacking of the edge

Fig. 17. Joining of the two pieces with edges folded and tacked so that the pattern corresponds perfectly

Fig. 18. Finished join: the first part is shown from the right side, where no sign of joining can be seen: the second part is seen from the wrong side

Fig. 19. Application of a corner: on right, tacking of new piece

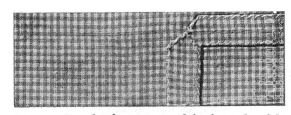

Fig. 20. Completed corner: on left, from the right side; on the right, the wrong side

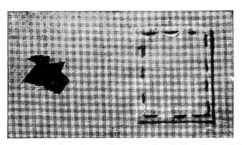

Fig. 21. Application of a patch: left, the original hole; on the right, the patch folded and tacked, ready to be sewn down with an invisible stitch

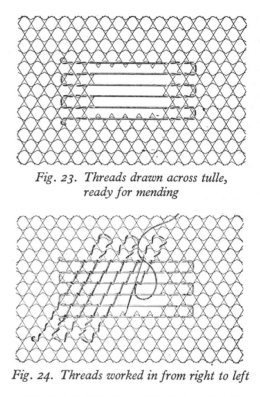

Fig. 23. Threads drawn across tulle, ready for mending

Fig. 24. Threads worked in from right to left

Fig. 25. Threads worked in from left to right

Fig. 22. Application of a patch: on the left, the work seen from the right side, on the right, the inserted piece cut and oversewn, seen from the wrong side

Both for rents and tears the method is the following:

The torn edges are lightly joined by oversewing with long spread-out stitches, using thread of contrasting colour and using a long, thin needle. The edges, which must not be placed over each other, but only just touching, are then properly mended. The needle is threaded with a thin, strong thread (a hair may well be used, as it is very strong in spite of being thin). This thread is worked into the fabric for a distance of about a quarter of an inch beyond the tear. In mending a rent work from the corner, first in one direction and then in the other, so that the corner is mended over twice. The two lots of mending cross each other and give added strength.

It will be easily understood that neither the hair nor the thread should ever come through the surface of the felt and the stitches should be left a little loose. If the felt is very thick, the mending may be repeated, first from the right side and then from the wrong, to make the repair more durable.

When the mend is completed the work should be pressed on the wrong side. Scissors should never

be used for cutting felt for a patch or join, but rather a razor blade, in order to avoid removing the slight hairy surface along the edges, which serves to hide the join.

Mending Tulle. This work is done by skilled workers to preserve precious laces.

The illustrations are clear enough to render any detailed explanation superfluous. To mend tulle successfully, however, the thread chosen should be as similar as possible to the original both in thickness and colour.

38

The torn part is first tacked on to thin card, either coloured or black if the tulle is white, and on to white card if the tulle is black, and then made regular by cutting away the torn edges on the straight thread. Horizontal threads are then placed from one side to the other of the hole following the loops of the tulle (Fig. 23); taking the mending threads a little farther outside the worn place to reinforce the mesh around the hole. The second row of threads is then begun (Fig. 24) by making oblique overcasting stitches over the horizontal lines. On the third row (Fig. 25) another row of oblique stitches is worked in the opposite direction and at the same intervals as the second row.

To reinforce worn places, the same system is followed, going over the loops of the tulle itself.

Patching Tulle. When the hole is too big or too long to darn, it must be patched. A piece of tulle of the same kind is cut, slightly larger all round than the original hole. It is placed over the hole, taking care to make the holes of the tulle coincide. Then with a very fine, strong thread the two pieces are sewn together, following the direction of the loops with an oversewing stitch (one stitch for each side of the small hexagon-shaped hole) for two or three rows, cutting away any spare tulle.

CHAPTER III

The Sewing Machine

The first attempts to build a sewing machine were made in 1755, when a certain Carlo F. Weisenthal invented a little machine containing a double-pointed needle with the eye half-way down its length which, by passing backwards and forwards through the fabric, first in one direction and then in the other, made a stitch. Weisenthal's idea was then adopted by others, but without success.

The most ancient design of sewing machine, still in the possession of the Singer Sewing Machine Company, is that of a patented machine produced by an Englishman, Thomas Steint, in 1790; other attempts were made later by the Englishmen Duncan, Thomas Stone and James Henderson in 1804 and by Giuseppe Madelsperger in 1814; these, however, produced no practical results.

In 1830, the French tailor Bartolomeo Thimmonier of St. Etienne constructed a wooden machine with a needle hooked like a crochet hook, which, passing through the fabric, hooked up the thread which came out of a loading device specially for that purpose and which on the return journey pulled along with it a loop, thus forming a row of chain stitches. Thimmonier's invention was favourably received in Paris where a workroom for military uniforms was set up using eighty of these machines: after some time, artisans, fearing that the machine would be detrimental to their employment, destroyed them. Thimmonier tried again to perfect his invention by making the machine in metal, but

he was unlucky and finished by selling the patent for the machine for a few francs in London.

However, the idea of a sewing machine spread and developed overseas, and the American Walter Hunt of New York is the man to whom we owe the first attempts to sew with two threads and a spool. Hunt, however, did not patent his invention at which he worked from 1832 to 1834 and it was only in 1846 that another American, Elias Howe, took up the principle of Hunt's machine, without, however, obtaining any useful results; finally, in 1851 another American, William B. Wilson, invented a new apparatus with a gadget for producing the same effects of interlaced threads as Howe's machine but substituting the spool with a fixed reel and a rotating disc fitted with a hook for hooking up the thread. In the same year the American, William O. Grover, a Boston tailor, created the double chain stitch with a two-needled machine, and the American, Isaac Merrit Singer took out a patent for a machine fitted with a thin straight needle able to function vertically and alternately.

The Singer machine was the first sewing machine which was at all practical in that it was the first that could function without the need of supervision by skilled mechanics. It became the prototype for the more than one hundred million machines which, from that time on, were produced all over the world. The first machine and the others that

Free style embroidery. This type of work can be done on all Singer Electric Machines. The work is stretched in an embroidery hoop, the feed mechanism covered and the movement of the material is done by the operator.

followed it were not made for family use, but especially for sail-making and industrial purposes. Only after some years was the famous Singer sewing machine with a treadle produced for domestic purposes. Since that time, modifications and developments of all kinds have been added to these first attempts and today modern industry creates technically perfect machines.

Although the machinery and working of the sewing machine is fundamentally the same for all types, each type has its own particular differences and individual instructions for use and care of the machine should always be carefully followed.

The mechanism of sewing machines has been extended to incorporate a zig-zag operation. The needle of this individual type of machine swings from side to side which enables an unlimited scope of practical, decorative and pattern stitches to be formed automatically.

41

The Bobbin. One of the chief parts of the sewing machine consists of the bobbin which is placed under the working surface of the machine. The thread from this bobbin is twisted around the thread from the needle, forming the lock stitch. For filling the bobbin every machine has a device specially for the purpose called a spindle or winder. To free the spindle and make it function independently of the needle mechanism, the knurled knob in the centre of the balance wheel should be turned anti-clockwise with the right hand while the balance wheel is held still with the left hand.

The filling of the bobbin must be regular, that is, the thread must be wound in a uniform manner. The bobbin should be completely filled without the thread projecting beyond the edge.

To fill the bobbin, it should be placed on the spindle which is fitted with a rubber ring and set in motion by slight pressure which puts it into contact with the wheel of the sewing machine.

In many of the latest machines, the bobbin can be automatically filled in the machine. This saves time as it is no longer necessary to unthread the machine to fill the bobbin.

The Needle. The needle of the sewing machine must always be suitable in size for the fabric and thread being used, therefore it is wise to have a varied selection at hand. The needle must be inserted with care, following the instructions. It must be perfectly straight and must move down to a position exactly at the centre of the hole in the sliding plate.

On completing sewing by machine, the work should not be pulled out too hard as this will bend the needle and make it unusable. A needle too short, blunt or too thin in proportion to the thread, or not firmly fixed into the clamp may be the cause of faulty stitches in the row of stitching.

Too large knots in basting, or pins left in the material, cause immediate breakage of the needle.

Sewing Threads. For successful sewing, whether by hand or machine, always choose first quality thread. The following selection will cover all requirements.

Coats Chain Cotton. This unmercerised thread is particularly suitable for stitching all household cottons. It is produced in a range of sizes from No. 10 to No. 50.

Coats Drima (polyester). A superspun multi-purpose thread for home sewing, available in 100 m spools in white, black and a wide colour range. Also produced in 200 m and 500 m spools in a more limited shade range, and black and white.

Being a multi-purpose sewing thread, Coats Drima can be used to sew both natural and synthetic fabrics by hand or by machine. It will give successful results on practically any weight or texture of fabric including the wide range of synthetic dress or furnishing fabrics and the many types of natural fabrics such as wool, linen, cotton and silk. Whatever the fabric, Drima will give neat, inconspicuous seams. Although fine, this thread has great strength, which means that while stitches have a dainty, delicate appearance, seams are strong enough to withstand all the stress and strain which may be imposed on them.

Drima Bold Stitch. This is a new extra strong thread in a 30 m spool which has been produced for decorative top stitching, saddle stitching, sewing on buttons and hand-made button holes. It is available in 38 shades plus black and white. When using it on the machine for bold stitching, use the largest stitch on the sewing machine and a No. 16/100 machine needle; thread the machine with Drima Bold Stitch and fill the bobbin with ordinary Drima in a matching colour.

Coats Anchor Button Thread. This strong thread specially processed for hard wear is particularly suitable for tailored buttonholes and for sewing on buttons.

Gun Basting Cotton. For basting this is an economical thread wound on reels of 1,000 m. lengths.

Anchor Machine Embroidery Thread Nos. 30 and 50. For decorative machine embroidery, free style or swing needle, use Anchor Machine Embroidery thread. No. 50 is the finer thread and it is recommended for use on fine fabrics.

Sewing. Sewing by sewing machine consists of a double stitch formed by the crossing of the thread carried by the needle with that coming from the bobbin. Before beginning any line of sewing on the machine, the thread from the bobbin should be pulled up through the hole in the slide plate.

The speed of the machine can be adjusted to individual requirements in much the same manner as pressing on the accelerator of a car, the harder the pressure the faster the machine will go.

Never stop the machine suddenly but reduce the speed towards the end of the stitching by slowing down, not letting the presser foot run off the end of the material. The reverse feed mechanism which automatically puts the sewing machine into reverse at the flick of the lever can be used to neaten the start and finish of the seam obviating the necessity for tying knots. Once the movement has ceased the balance wheel should be turned towards you until the take-up lever is at its highest point. The foot can then be raised and the work pulled out to the back of the machine and the threads cut, using the special device incorporated in the needle bar for severing the threads.

Tension of Threads. To obtain perfect sewing by machine, the thread must be controlled to the correct tension. There are two tensions: the top tension regulating the tension of the thread passing to the needle from the reel, and the under tension regulating the thread from the bobbin. These tensions should be perfectly equal and may be considered correct when the crossing of the thread

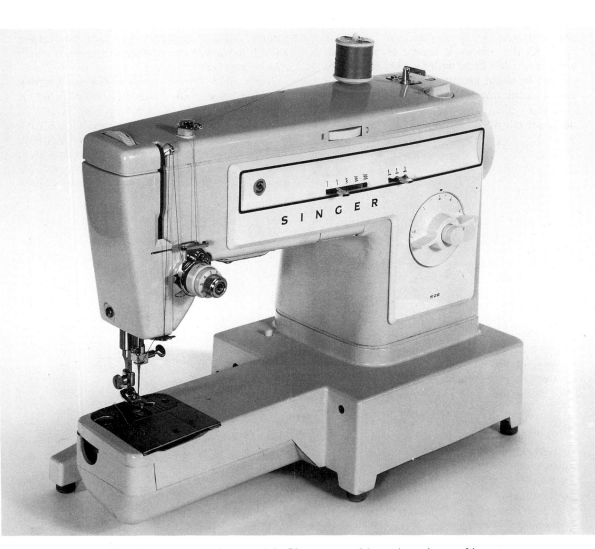

The Singer 522, which is one of the Singer range of domestic sewing machines.

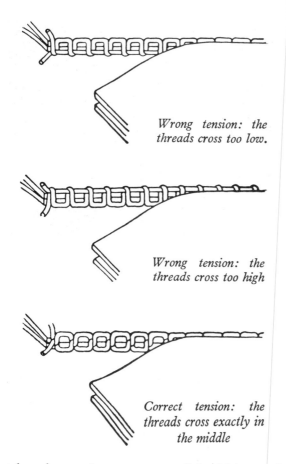

Wrong tension: the threads cross too low.

Wrong tension: the threads cross too high

Correct tension: the threads cross exactly in the middle

takes place at the exact centre of the thickness of the fabric which is being sewn.

A screw, generally to be found in front of the needle-carrying bar, regulates the tension of the top thread: by turning it in a clockwise direction the tension increases and by turning it anti-clockwise the tension is decreased.

The tension of the under thread is regulated by turning a screw which holds the spring on the bobbin race through which the thread from the bobbin passes. The amount of adjustment required is *very* little. To test the tension of the upper and lower threads, the needle should be unthreaded, the presser foot lowered and the tension on the upper and lower threads assessed by pulling them both towards you. The amount of drag or tension on each thread should be about the same.

If the tension is too strong, the sewing will pucker and the thread break easily; if it is too weak, the stitches do not lock properly. The formation of loops above or below the work is also due to ir-

regular tension. If the loops form on top of the work, the tension of the bobbin must be increased. If, instead, they are formed on the underneath, then the top tension should be regulated.

Length of Stitch. The length of stitch should be varied according to the type of material used. Thus for lightweight materials a very small stitch should be chosen, using a longer stitch for heavier fabrics. The length of stitch on the machine may be regulated by moving a small screw to be found generally on the right of the machine. See fabric and thread table, page 48.

Sewing Machine Attachments. Each machine possesses a series of small parts called attachments which serve for various types of specialised work. These gadgets are fixed to the machine in the place of the foot and, with a little practice in their management, they will be found to be really useful.

The uses of the most popular attachments are illustrated here. In addition, most modern sewing machines are provided with a hinged presser foot. The advantages of this device are principally that it will adapt itself to extra thick material and will also enable the user to sew over pins placed at right angles to the lines of stitching.

Chain Stitch. Although the earliest sewing machines invented operated a chain stitch using the top thread only, these machines were superseded by the lock stitch machine which is most commonly in use today. The advantages of a chain stitch are, however, still apparent as it provides a quick method of putting in a temporary stitch for tacking or fitting purposes. The most modern sewing machine today incorporates a chain stitch plate with its Swing Needle machine so that by removing the bobbin, making a small adjustment to the threading order and inserting the special chain stitch plate, a chain stitch is formed. Many of the later models have snap-on feet for easy change over.

Care and Maintenance. The machine must be kept in good working order, dusting it often, oiling it from time to time, freeing it from odd threads and fluff which easily forms under the sliding plate or on the feed mechanism in the slide plate.

The machine should be thoroughly cleaned periodically. When the machine is not in use it should be kept covered from dust, and if possible in an even temperature.

44

The Zipper Foot. This is essential when inserting zip fasteners and it could also be used for piping and cording.

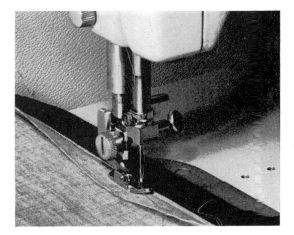

The Zig-Zag Apparatus. This semi-automatic zig-zag machine is capable of seam neatening on all types of fabrics.

Buttonholes and button sewing. This machine will make a perfect machine buttonhole of any size in any material. Buttons can also be stitched on using the Special Button Foot.

The Binder. This will operate successfully on outside and inside curves, seams and all kinds of aprons and children's wear.

The Ruffler. This shows the operation of the six-stitch pleat.

The Edge Stitcher. A useful attachment for joining pieces of material or lace together for special trimming.

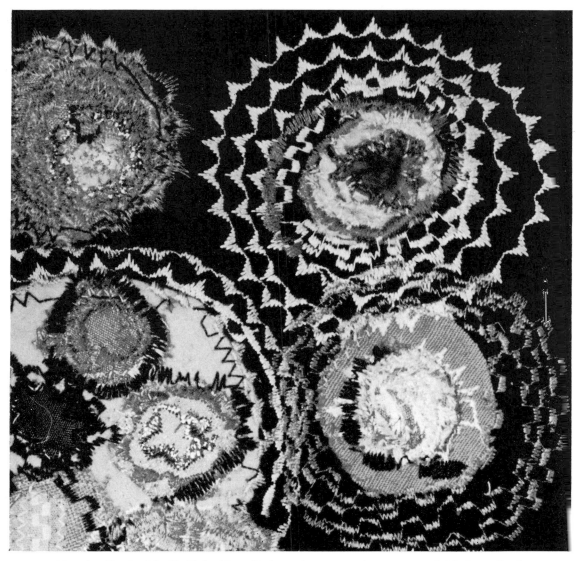

Creative Sewing Needle Embroidery Design using automatic patterns and fabric appliqué

Machine Embroidery. Machine embroidery can be divided into two types.

Free style embroidery is a flowing expression of design, using the needle as a pencil and with the work stretched tightly in an embroidery frame. The possibilities of this type of decoration are unlimited and require only that the operator should be experienced and the sewing machine electrically driven. A few lessons from an expert in machine embroidery are sufficient to learn the technique.

Practice will perfect this. Use Anchor Machine Embroidery Thread, No. 30 or No. 50 in white, black and a wide range of fast colours for all types of embroidery and for mending by machine.

The second more modern type of machine embroidery is that produced by automatic stitches and a Swing Needle Machine. The type of design tends to be much more contemporary, making use of fabric, appliqué, beads, sequins and any other textured materials to create design and colour.

Fabric and thread chart

	Fabric	Thread	Machine needle number B: British C: Continental		Milward hand needle number	Number of stitches to the cm (inch)
			B	**C**		
Fine fabrics	Organdie	Coats *Drima*	9 or 11	70	8 or 9	3–4 (8–10)
	Voile		9 or 11	70	8 or 9	3–4 (8–10)
	Lace		9 or 11	70	8 or 9	3–4 (8–10)
	Silk		9 or 11	70	8 or 9	3–4 (8–10)
	Lawn		9 or 11	70	8 or 9	3–4 (8–10)
	Crepe		9 or 11	70	8 or 9	3–4 (8–10)
	Tulle		9 or 11	70	8 or 9	3–4 (8–10)
	Net		9 or 11	70	8 or 9	3–4 (8–10)
Fine/ mediun fabrics	Cotton	Coats *Drima*	9 or 11	70 or 80	7 or 8	4–5 (10–12)
	Linen		9 or 11	70 or 80	7 or 8	4–5 (10–12)
	Satin		9 or 11	70 or 80	7 or 8	4–5 (10–12)
	Crimplene		9 or 11	70 or 80	7 or 8	4–5 (10–12)
	Glass fibre		9 or 11	70 or 80	7 or 8	4–5 (10–12)
	Plastic		9 or 11	70 or 80	7 or 8	4–5 (10–12)
Medium/ heavy fabrics	Bonded fabric	Coats *Drima*	14	90	7 or 8	3–4 (8–10)
	Vinyl		14	90	7 or 8	3–4 (8–10)
	Jersey		14	90	7 or 8	5–6 (12–14)
	Brocade		14	90	7 or 8	5 (12)
	Wool		14	90	7 or 8	5 (12)
	Corduroy		14	90	7 or 8	5 (12)
	Velvet		14	90	7 or 8	5 (12)
	Terry cloth		14	90	7 or 8	5 (12)
	Flannel		14	90	7 or 8	5 (12)
	Tweed		14 or 16	90 or 100	5 or 6	4–5 (10–12)

2 *Embroidery in White and Colours*

CHAPTER IV

Various Embroidery Stitches

This chapter is an introduction to Embroidery and some of the most useful stitches are described and illustrated. These stitches have remained in the forms illustrated for many centuries, but, as in all forms of art, the way in which they are used has changed with fashion.

There is a wider range of fabrics and threads for embroidery today than has ever been available before and the many beautiful textures and colours obtainable are a challenge to the modern needle-woman. The heavily embroidered bed and table linen of the past has been replaced by machine-embroidered counterparts or by woven or printed patterns. The modern housewife makes instead a colourful supper cloth, luncheon mats to suit her individual needs or a gay sun-suit for her small daughter.

Practise the stitches on a spare piece of the fabric which will be used for the finished embroidery. This will provide an opportunity for trying out different types, colours and thicknesses of thread.

Keep the work fresh by wrapping it in a clean cloth when putting it away. Press from time to time, placing the embroidery face downwards on a well-padded ironing board.

For some kinds of embroidery it is necessary to use a frame. The "Swiss" or tambour frame and the slate frame are described here.

Embroidery Frames. There are various types of frame. The most common and also the easiest to use is the "Swiss" or tambour frame, consisting of two wooden hoops, one fitting inside the other. The outer hoop is fitted with a fastening device which enables it to be fixed to a table by means of a wooden screw; or it may have legs attached to a wooden base, thus allowing it to be held on the knee (Fig. 1).

To fix the fabric in this type of frame, it is stretched across the smaller hoop and then the

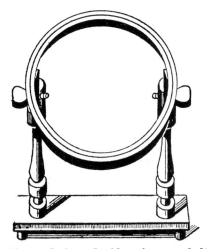

Fig. 1. Swiss embroidery frame to hold on the knee

49

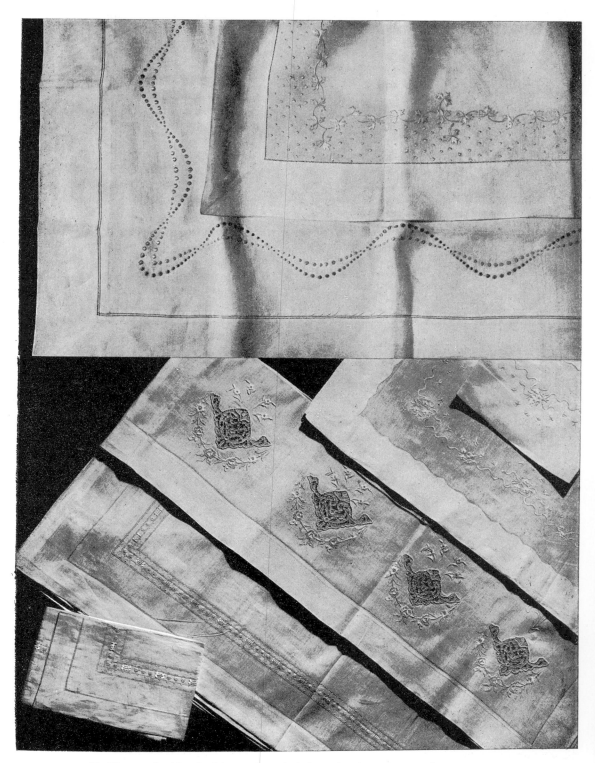

Bed linen embroidered with a variety of stitches using Coats Anchor Coton à Broder

larger one is pressed over it so that the fabric is held tightly between them. This type of frame is advisable for small pieces of work. For large embroideries it is best to use a slate frame resting on two trestles.

The slate frame consists of four pieces: two wooden bars with slots at each end, along the length of which pieces of strong canvas are nailed; the fabric to be embroidered is sewn on to this with close oversewing, and fixed on the other two sides to two perforated strips slotted through the holes in the ends of the bars. After fixing the fabric to the bars of the frame, the part not required for working is rolled over one of the bars. The side strips are fitted into the holes and the fabric is well stretched over them; they are then held in place by means of metal pins fitted through the holes. At the sides of the frame, the fabric is held by string passing round the perforated strips and through the taped or reinforced edges of the fabric (Fig. 2). The fabric must always be attached to the frame on the straight thread.

A slate frame of this type generally measures from 63 cm to 76 cm. For large embroideries, frames which may measure up to 2 m may be necessary. Such frames are often used in training schools and allow several pupils to work at the same time.

For work on all large frames, see that the chair is of the right height in order to ensure comfort in working. The right hand works above the frame, pushing the needle below; this is taken by the left hand under the frame, which pushes the needle back again to the surface with the forefinger. When the material to be worked is very heavy and the passage of the needle must be forced, a thimble is also used on the left hand.

Before beginning any embroidery, wash the hands well in order to keep the work perfectly clean. This should be repeated at intervals, especially if the hands have a tendency to perspire. One of the essentials of embroidery is its freshness and, in white embroidery, its whiteness.

If, in the course of the work, the thread twists and does not run well, turn the needle in the opposite direction to the twist, until the thread is untwisted, or change to a fresh length of thread.

Materials—Threads. The following threads are suitable for many kinds of embroidery:

Coats Anchor Stranded Cotton in one, two, three, four or six strands in 250 fast colours, black and white.
Coats Anchor Coton à Broder.
Coats Anchor Soft Embroidery.
Coats Anchor Pearl Cotton Nos. 5 and 8.
Coats Anchor Tapisserie Wool.
Coats Anchor Machine Embroidery in 10 gram reels in Nos. 30 and 50.

Fabrics. Always use good-quality fabrics. Embroidery requires time and thought, and it is a pity to waste these upon shoddy fabric. Linen, linen crash, even-weave fabric, lawn and good-quality cotton fabrics are worthwhile background fabrics, especially for household objects.

Organdie, which despite its fragile appearance is very resistant if of good quality, is particularly effective because of its transparency. All these fabrics are practical, in that they are easily washed and resist hard wear.

Never tear linens, but always cut straight by drawing a thread from the fabric to give a guiding line. This is a useful hint for the cutting of table-cloths, napkins, sheets, pillowcases, etc.

Always have a good supply of threads when beginning a large piece of work. After some time there may be a slight difference in the colour of new thread, due to a slight change in the dye, a difference which might spoil the effect of the work.

Stem Stitch. This stitch may be used for outlining and for the finer lines of a design. The diagram shows the working of this stitch. Keep the thread below the needle and bring the needle out at exactly the spot at which the previous stitch

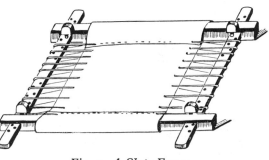

Fig. 2. A Slate Frame

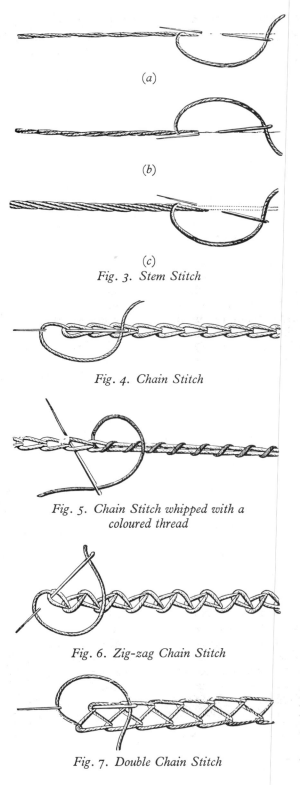

(a)

(b)

(c)

Fig. 3. Stem Stitch

Fig. 4. Chain Stitch

Fig. 5. Chain Stitch whipped with a coloured thread

Fig. 6. Zig-zag Chain Stitch

Fig. 7. Double Chain Stitch

was made (Fig. 3 (a)). Fig. 3 (b) illustrates the same stitch worked with the thread above the needle. Stem Stitch well done should show a row of Back Stitches on the wrong side.

If a rather coarse Stem Stitch is to be made, four or six threads of fabric are taken up, so that the last stitch goes over the preceding one by two threads (Fig. 3 (c)).

For joinings in Stem Stitch, the thread is fastened off on the back and the new thread attached so that the needle comes out two threads behind the last stitch.

Chain Stitch. Chain Stitch is among the oldest embroidery stitches and is often found in Oriental embroidery and in the national costumes of Russian and Roumanian women. It may be worked as a single row, or several adjoining rows may fill a wider space. The needle is brought out of the fabric at a given point and replaced at the same point, leaving the thread in a loop under the needle. The needle point comes out two or three threads below. The needle is then replaced again at the point where it was withdrawn, forming a loop once again. Continue thus, the last stitch being fastened off by a Back Stitch (Fig. 4).

Chain Stitch can also be worked on a frame with a crochet hook, as explained further on in the book. (See chapter on "Embroidery in Beads and Sequins".)

Variations of Chain Stitch. By whipping a coloured thread over the loops of Chain Stitch, without taking up the fabric below, a decorative stitch is obtained (Fig. 5).

Zig-zag Chain Stitch (Fig. 6) is made by placing the needle in the fabric first in one direction and then in the other.

Fig. 7 shows Double Chain Stitch, worked first above and then below.

Fig. 8 shows Cable Chain Stitch in which the thread is wrapped around the needle before drawing it out of the fabric. This is clearly shown in the diagram.

Three Chain Stitches arranged as shown in Fig. 9 may form a simple decorative border, suitable, as are all the others illustrated here, for decorating linen and children's garments. This grouping of the stitch is called Russian Chain Stitch, because of its use by Russian women in their embroidery.

Chequered Chain Stitch. The needle is threaded with two threads of different colour. The stitch is

Fig. 8. Cable Chain Stitch

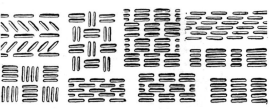

Fig. 14. Running Stitch

Fig. 9. Russian Chain Stitch

Fig. 15. Variations of Running Stitch

Fig. 10. Chequered Chain Stitch

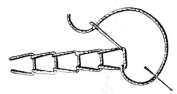

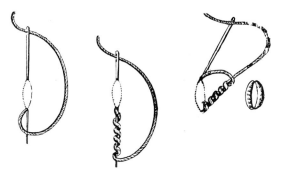

Fig. 11. Twisted Chain Stitch

Fig. 16. Bullion Knot Stitch

Fig. 12. Open Chain Stitch

Fig. 17. Feather Stitch

Fig. 13. Detached Chain Stitch or Daisy Stitch

Fig. 18. Double Feather Stitch

Fig. 19. Feather Stitch and Blanket Stitch

Fig. 20. Feather Stitch Variation

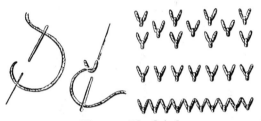

Fig. 21. Fly Stitch

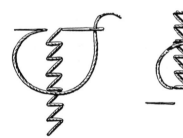

Fig. 22. Triangle Stitch

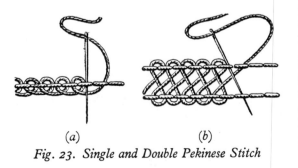

(a)   *(b)*

Fig. 23. Single and Double Pekinese Stitch

made as for ordinary Chain Stitch, using each colour alternately (Fig. 10).

Fig. 11, Twisted Chain Stitch. The thread is placed as for Chain Stitch, but instead of the needle re-entering the fabric at the same point as it came out, it is inserted to the left.

Open Chain Stitch is shown in Fig. 12. The needle, instead of entering through the hole made by the previous stitch as in ordinary Chain Stitch, enters to the rider a space of five or six threads away and is brought out five or six lower down.

Detached Chain Stitch or Daisy Stitch. A single Chain Stitch is made and the needle taken through to the back of the fabric (Fig. 13).

Running Stitch. We have already mentioned Running Stitch, in the chapter on "Sewing Equipment and Stitches for Household Linen", as being the simplest of all stitches. The stitch is worked horizontally, from right to left: two or three threads of material are taken up, passing over five or six (Fig. 14). The length of the stitch may be varied according to the effect required. Running Stitch, worked on the right side of the material, in alternating rows, or by alternating long and short stitches, can, if well done, produce a smooth, uniform effect, similar to Satin Stitch. Fig. 15 shows different ways of varying the rows of Running Stitches.

Bullion Knot. This stitch may be used for working small leaves, flowers or rosettes, which have to stand out from the background. The needle is placed in the fabric and eight or ten threads of fabric are taken up, bringing out the needle only for half its length: it is then held firm with the thumb of the left hand, and with the right hand the thread is wrapped round the needle as many times as the number of threads of fabric originally taken up by the needle. Then holding the spiral so formed, firmly with the thumb of the left hand, the whole length of the needle is drawn through, taking the stitch back to replace the needle in the hole from which it originally emerged. (Fig. 16).

Feather Stitch. The needle is placed in the fabric taking up four or five threads, and, placing the thread under the thumb of the left hand, another stitch is taken a little lower down to the left; then the thread is turned and the movement repeated. The stitch is worked from top to bottom (Fig. 17).

Fig. 18 shows Feather Stitch worked double, that is, with two stitches to the left and two to the right.

Fig. 19 shows a variation of Feather Stitch. Three Blanket Stitches are placed alternately along the points of a simple Feather Stitch. These are worked after the Feather Stitch has been completed.

Feather Stitch Variation. This is suitable for working leaves (Fig. 20). It is composed of two Loop Stitches, one to the right and the other to the left.

Fly Stitch. Fig. 21 shows another decorative and edging stitch. The diagram shows clearly how this is worked.

Triangle Stitch. This is carried out in two stages (Fig. 22). An oblique stitch and a horizontal stitch are made alternately. On the second line of stitching, the movement is repeated in the opposite direction, thus forming small triangles in a pleasant chain effect.

Single and Double Pekinese Stitch. This stitch, like Feather Stitch, is useful for decorating children's clothes, lingerie, collars and cuffs.

Pekinese Stitch is worked in two stages.

Work a line of Back Stitch. Then, with a slightly thicker thread, work the interlacing by passing the thread through the first and third Back Stitches, going back then to the second and so on alternately, without taking up any of the fabric (Fig. 23 (a)).

Double Pekinese Stitch is worked in three stages. First of all work two rows of Back Stitch. Then, a slightly thicker thread is interlaced as shown in the diagram (Fig. 23 (b)).

Threaded Running Stitch. Another decorative stitch is that shown in Fig. 24. This is a line of Running Stitch through which a different coloured thread is passed above and below the line of stitching.

Buttonhole Stitch. Pass the working thread under the thumb of the left hand and take up four or five threads of fabric. Pull up the loop so formed, taking care not to pucker the fabric. The stitches must be even and lie closely side by side without overlapping (Fig. 25).

To make a scallop the same method is followed, with the difference that the stitches must be

Fig. 24. Threaded Running Stitch

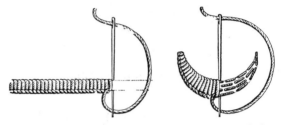

Fig. 25. Buttonhole Stitch. Padded Buttonhole Stitch used for scalloping

Fig. 26. Scalloped Edgings

Wall panel worked in Long and Short Stitch in a rich colour scheme

lengthened or shortened to follow the curve and width of the design. If the scallops are very small, then a simple Running Stitch may be worked round the outline of the pattern before working. If the scalloping must stand out to a certain degree, then the outlines are marked with Running Stitch and the space in between is padded with alternating lines of Running Stitch. The scalloping is worked over these stitches, as explained above (Fig. 25).

Suggestions for scalloped edgings are given in Figs. 26 and 27. These are suitable for babies' dresses, children's blouses and lingerie.

To make a join when working a scallop, fasten off the old thread with a Back Stitch: the new thread is then brought out in the space between two stitches, on the outer edge. For cutting along the outer edge of scalloping, use very sharp scissors and take care that they do not snip the stitching. Fig. 28 shows a Blanket Stitch following the line of the design. This stitch is worked similarly to Buttonhole Stitch, but has spaces between the stitches.

Stem Stitch Band. Work as shown in Fig. 29.

Straight Stitch Filling. Straight Stitch consists of stitches taken horizontally or vertically, never obliquely, over counted threads, following a given shape or design (Fig. 30). In some regions of south Italy and Sardinia, this stitch is worked in bright colours on tablecloths, napkins, table centres and runners. It is advisable to work this stitch in a frame. The material used must have a regular weave and should not be too fine.

Long and Short Filling Stitch is the name of the stitch illustrated in Fig. 31.

Herringbone Stitch. This is worked from left to right. Two or three threads of material are taken up, always to the left of the needle, first above and then below (Fig. 32).

Shadow Stitch is made by working this stitch very closely on the wrong side of transparent or fine fabric. This is fully described in the chapter of the same name.

Variations of Herringbone Stitch. A pretty decoration can be made by using threads of different colours and following the diagram—Fig. 33. Work a row of Herringbone Stitch. With a coloured thread pass the needle through the stitches above and below the point of crossing, without taking up the fabric.

Fig. 27. Scalloped Edgings

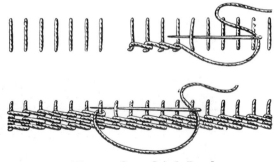

Fig. 28. Blanket Stitch

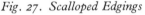
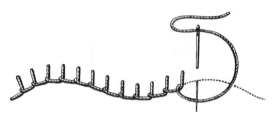

Fig. 29. Stem Stitch Band

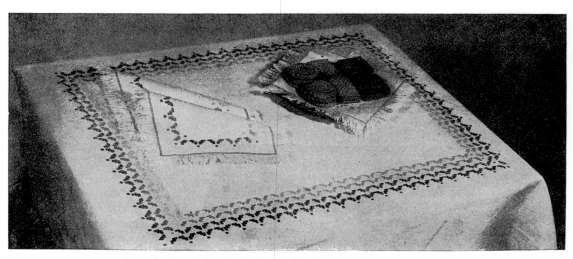

Tea cloth with border in Satin Stitch, worked in tones of pink

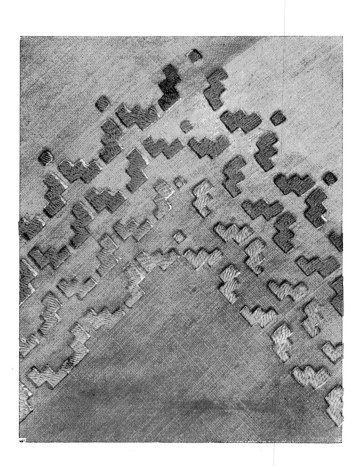

Detail of tea cloth corner

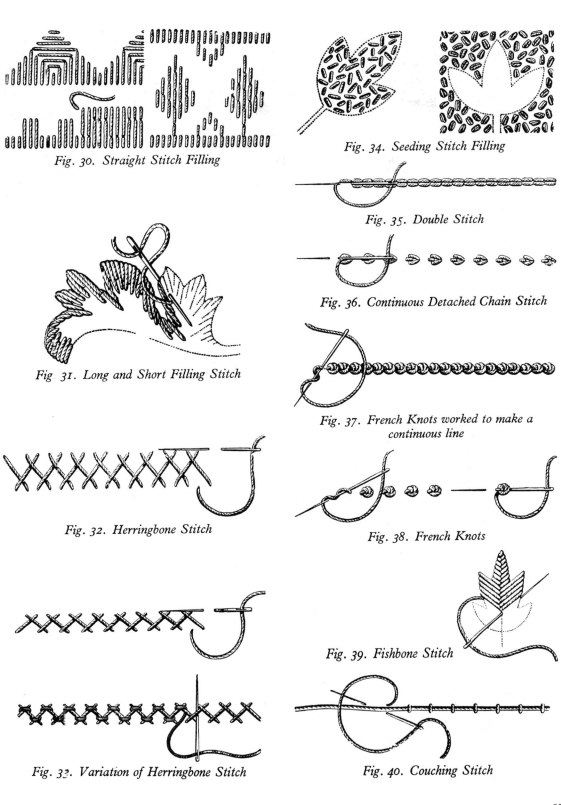

Fig. 30. Straight Stitch Filling

Fig. 34. Seeding Stitch Filling

Fig. 35. Double Stitch

Fig. 36. Continuous Detached Chain Stitch

Fig 31. Long and Short Filling Stitch

Fig. 37. French Knots worked to make a
continuous line

Fig. 32. Herringbone Stitch

Fig. 38. French Knots

Fig. 39. Fishbone Stitch

Fig. 33. Variation of Herringbone Stitch

Fig. 40. Couching Stitch

59

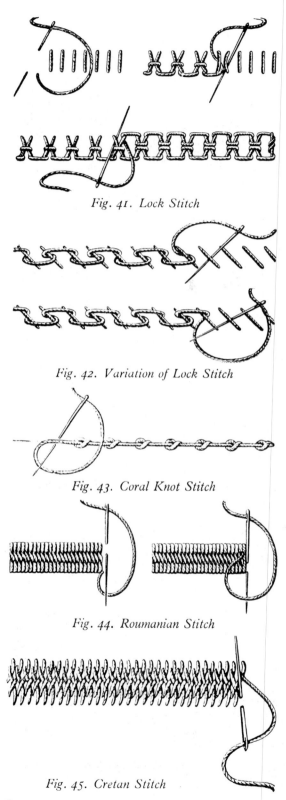

Fig. 41. Lock Stitch

Fig. 42. Variation of Lock Stitch

Fig. 43. Coral Knot Stitch

Fig. 44. Roumanian Stitch

Fig. 45. Cretan Stitch

Seeding Stitch Filling. This is made by small straight stitches taken in all directions to fill in large spaces. To make the stitch stand out better, it can be worked over a second time (Fig. 34).

Double Stitch. This consists of Back Stitch worked so that the needle passes twice through the same hole (Fig. 35).

Continuous Detached Chain Stitch. This is a line of detached Chain Stitches (Fig. 36).

French Knot Stitch. To make a knot, the thread is held between the thumb and first finger of the left hand, wrapped twice around the needle, which is replaced as near as possible to where it came out. The thread must be pulled taut by the left hand until the knot has been completed (Fig. 38). This stitch may be worked as a continuous line as in Fig. 37.

For some types of work and design, the French Knots may be worked so closely that the background fabric is entirely covered.

Fishbone Stitch. The stitches are made, following the outline of the pattern, passing from the outer edge to the centre of the leaf, going two threads beyond the centre line, every time, first to the left and then to the right. The stitches thus overlap in the centre (Fig. 39).

Couching Stitch. This consists of the application of a thick thread or a cord to the fabric by small oversewing stitches worked at equal distances. The stitch should be worked in a frame and the thread or cord should be held firmly in place by the oversewing stitches, and pulled so as to avoid puckering when the work is removed from the frame (Fig. 40).

Lock Stitch. This decorative stitch is found in Siennese work in white or natural thread on coloured Florentine linen.

It is worked in three stages.

First, a series of Straight Stitches all of equal length are worked from right to left at equal distances apart.

The second row of stitches, worked from left to right, passes through the first stitch, without touching the fabric, keeping the thread below the needle, then through the next stitch keeping the thread above the needle; in this way a wavy line is formed.

Motifs worked in Running Stitch in tones of blue suitable for a tea cloth

Tea cloth in heavy linen, with a design in Running Stitch, carried out in dark and light blue. The Running Stitch is worked by taking up two threads of fabric and passing over six. The small triangles are arranged to form a pattern for the sides and corners of the cloth

The third row of stitches is worked as the second, using the same movement on the opposite side of the line (Fig. 41).

The thread used for the wavy line is generally thicker than for the foundation stitches.

Another variation of this type of stitch is used in Parma embroidery; this is shown in Fig. 42.

It is worked in two stages. First a diagonal stitch is worked (like one side of a Cross Stitch) then a thread is interlaced, without taking up the fabric, alternately above and below on the row of stitches.

Coral Knot. This stitch is worked from right to left: the thread is placed along the line to be worked, holding it firmly with the thumb of the left hand, then a slightly oblique stitch is made, taking up two or three threads of fabric. The thread is then pulled through to fix the knot firmly. The knots thus formed may be placed at regular intervals from each other, or very close to each other (Fig. 43).

Roumanian Stitch. This stitch is worked lengthways. It is very easily worked by following the illustration (Fig. 44).

Cretan Stitch. This stitch is similar to Roumanian Stitch and serves for filling in spaces comparatively quickly. The working is shown clearly in the diagram (Fig. 45).

Surface Darning. This stitch perfectly imitates a fabric weave. Threads are first placed vertically, and through these the needle is passed, taking up the threads alternately above and below, from right to left. On the next row, continue from left to right, taking up the thread that was passed over in the preceding row and vice versa. The two rows are repeated alternately, thus forming a compact surface like that of woven fabric (Fig. 46).

Bokhara Couching. This stitch is used for filling in, and worked as shown in Fig. 47. The lines are worked as Couching and may also lie closely together.

Cording. Cording is widely used in all types of sewing and embroidery for outlining designs, attaching lace and different types of decorative motifs and for working initials and monograms. It is also used, unattached to the basic material, in lace-making.

Cording may be worked either from left to right or right to left. Place a thread along the line to be worked and hold it in place by oversewing. Take care that the under thread is rather thick and well-twisted and completely covered by the vertical oversewing stitches, which should be placed close together (Fig. 48).

When a very fine Cording, sometimes named Trailing, is to be worked, pick up only the threads of material comprising the line to be worked, with no thread placed underneath.

To work oblique Cording, the same procedure is followed but the oversewing stitches are placed obliquely.

Broderie Anglaise. This is also called Madeira work because it originated in that island. It is largely composed of small cut-out shapes and Eyelets which are graduated in size. Broderie Anglaise was exceedingly fashionable during the late eighteenth and early nineteenth centuries, when it was extensively used to decorate underwear, collars and cuffs and white cotton dresses. It was used also for baby clothes, particularly christening robes and bonnets, and some of the most beautiful and intricate of these were carried out in Ayrshire, Scotland. Many of these have become family heirlooms and they are in use today. It remained in fashion for only a short period, however, being supplanted by the famous Swiss machine embroidery which imitates perfectly all the designs and stitches once made by hand.

First a running thread is worked round the design, which is then cut out between the two rows of stitching, using very sharp scissors. The fabric is then folded under with the point of the needle and the Cording worked very closely round the edges (Fig. 49). For round holes, instead of cutting, a stiletto is passed through the fabric and the hole so formed is worked in the same way.

Broderie Anglaise is generally worked in white, or in a colour to match the background fabric.

Pisa Stitch. This stitch is worked similarly to Broderie Anglaise. The same Cording Stitch surrounds the cut or pierced spaces, but in Pisa Stitch bars of embroidery are also worked across the spaces. Invented by a Pisan embroideress, the stitch became very fashionable for the ornamentation of household linen, table and bed linen, for curtains, altar cloths and surplices, etc. The rather monotonous designs are based on the classic motifs of

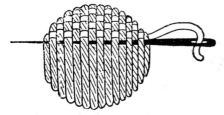

Fig. 46. Surface Darning

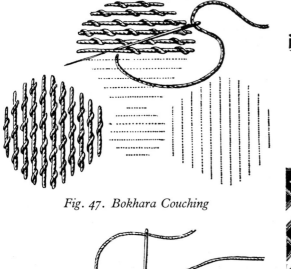

Fig. 47. Bokhara Couching

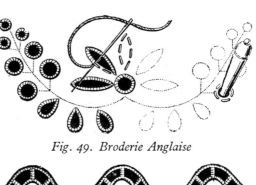

Fig. 49. Broderie Anglaise

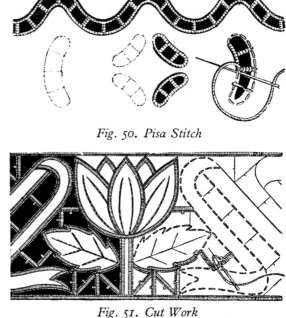

Fig. 50. Pisa Stitch

Fig. 51. Cut Work

Fig. 48. Cording

arcs arranged in many different ways, circles, as in Broderie Anglaise, and long leaves with cross bars. Pisa Stitch is almost always completed by the application of pillow or filet lace, generally in white or natural.

It is necessary to attach the work to stiff paper. The fabric is tacked down along the lines of the design, using the same thread as for the Cording, in a thickness suitable to the fabric being used; the cross bars are prepared by passing the thread three times across the space to be worked, and on the fourth row, working across with a very close Cording Stitch. When the cross bars are complete, the fabric is cut away between the two lines of tacking, using very sharp scissors, and then folded under with the needle, fixing it down with Cording Stitch (Fig. 50).

When Pisa Stitch follows a simple straight or wavy line, as shown above in the illustration, it is called Ladder Stitch.

Cut Work. Cut Work is that type of embroidery in which leaves, flowers and figures are surrounded by Buttonhole Stitch and joined up by bars, the rest of the fabric being cut away. It is more properly called Richelieu embroidery, after the famous cardinal, Minister to King Louis XIII of France. At that time, Venetian laces were held in high esteem, and the lace industry, creation and pride of the Venetian Republic, penetrated into other European countries, undergoing various local changes and taking on different names.

Cardinal Richelieu, in order to further develop industry in France, and after the imposition of

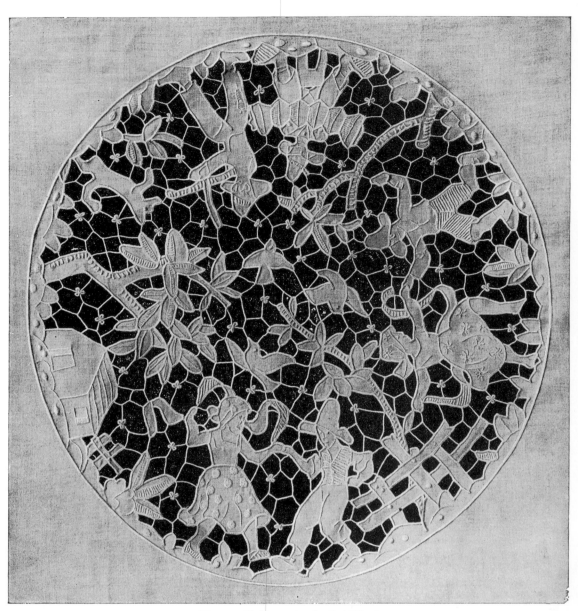

Fig. 52. Table centre in Cut Work

heavy taxes on Venetian laces, which were much in demand by the French aristocracy of the time, called skilled Venetian lace-workers to France, set up schools and workshops, encouraged the application of new techniques and helped to establish the new industry in France. Thus Richelieu gave his name to this new type of Cut-work embroidery. The initiative of the great cardinal was followed by Colbert, minister to King Louis XIV, so that cut

work remained in vogue throughout the seventeenth century, following the extravagant tastes of the times with its designs of large flower sprays and surrounds in high relief.

Cut work was popular right up to the beginning of this century: today, however, it has lost some of its charm and has become neglected. If, perhaps, some artist should design new patterns and an intelligent embroideress were to carry them out in accordance with modern taste, the typical attraction of this embroidery, with its imitation of the light airiness of lace, would return to favour once again.

Cut work is best carried out in white or in natural colour.

Method of Working. After the design has been applied, tack the fabric on to stiff paper so that it is well stretched on the straight thread. Work a line of short tacking stitches around the lines of the pattern; when meeting a bar, fasten the tacking thread off on the wrong side without cutting off the thread. Pass behind the bar and bring the needle out on the far side to continue tacking. After tacking, begin the Buttonhole Stitch. This must be very regular and, to make it stand out, two or three threads of embroidery cotton should first be passed underneath. The Buttonhole Stitch is often decorated with "picots". When the bar is reached, pass a third tacking thread across, over the existing ones, and cover all three with Cording or Buttonhole Stitch, without taking up the fabric underneath. Then continue Buttonhole Stitching (Fig. 51).

To make the bars, care must be taken to see that the tension is regular; that is, neither too slack nor too tight: any irregularity of tension would spoil the work.

To fasten off a thread and recommence work, take small Running Stitches which will be covered by the Buttonhole Stitch. Do not fasten off and rejoin when working a bar. Other stitches may be used to enrich the work. e.g. Stem Stitch, various filling stitches, knots, etc.

The cutting away of the fabric from under the bars is the last operation. Remove the completed embroidery from the paper by cutting all the tacking threads from the back. If necessary, wash in tepid water with soap flakes, squeezing the fabric, but never rubbing it. Press carefully whilst still damp with a rather hot iron. With very sharp and pointed scissors, and taking great care not to touch either the bars or the knots of the Buttonhole Stitches, cut away the fabric along the edges. After cutting, the work should be pressed face downwards on a soft pad.

In the section entitled "Needle- and Bobbin-made Laces", illustrations and explanations of the method of working different types of bar are to be found.

Fig. 52 shows a table centre in Cut Work, with a modern Italian design.

Long and Short Stitch. This is a variation of Satin Stitch. It is a difficult stitch, not because it is difficult to work in itself, but because it requires great care and accuracy in the placing of each stitch.

The variations of Satin Stitch seem to have originated in Asia, where they were used by the Japanese and Chinese. In fact, the national costumes of these people are often richly worked in this type of embroidery.

The Japanese and Chinese always carry out this work on rich materials such as satin, velvet and moiré or upon heavy, shiny or matt silk, with silk threads in rich and varied shades. This wonderful embroidery is worked on kimonos, hangings, screens and fans.

Satin Stitch and its variations must be worked in an embroidery frame. The stitch illustrated consists of long and short stitches, alternating from the top edge of the design and little by little moving down over its whole surface to give a shaded effect.

After a first row in a given colour, a second follows in another tone, either lighter or darker, and then a third and a fourth, until the whole area of the design is covered. If the design grows narrower towards the bottom, as, for example, in the petal of a flower, the stitches should diminish gradually in size and converge in the centre. The stitches should never be too long, or too regular, but should be worked close together, sometimes even taking the needle through half of the preceding stitch. In this way, the whole surface of the work should be quite smooth so that neither the beginning nor the end of any individual stitch can be seen (Fig. 53).

Shading may also be carried out by working lines of Chain Stitch close together. This is very effective, and largely used in Turkish, Russian, Persian and Indian embroideries.

Split Stitch. Like Satin Stitch, this stitch is only worked in a frame, and may be used to form a close smooth background for stylised designs and ornamental motifs. To make the stitch, draw the needle out of the fabric and replace it five or six threads ahead, working from left to right. Go back about half-way along the previous stitch and split it in two with the point of the needle, before passing the thread through to form the next stitch. On the following line, the stitches must be placed so that the point of splitting alternates with the previous

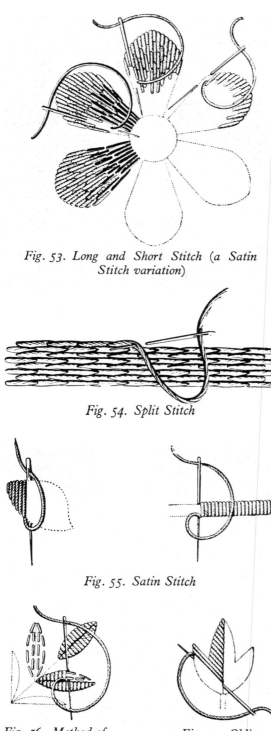

Fig. 53. Long and Short Stitch (a Satin Stitch variation)

Fig. 54. Split Stitch

Fig. 55. Satin Stitch

Fig. 56. Method of working leaves in Satin Stitch

Fig. 57. Oblique Satin Stitch

line. In fact, this stitch is rather like Stem Stitch, except that the needle point, instead of coming out at the side of each stitch, emerges in the middle of the stitch itself (Fig. 54).

Satin Stitch. This stitch is very important for embroidery upon linen. It is very simple, but requires extreme accuracy in working. It consists of vertical or horizontal stitches placed one beside the other, following a given design. The difficulty of working the stitch will be found in making the outline perfectly clean (Fig. 55). The design may be padded with small Running Stitches before working.

When the design is broad it may be worked in two halves. In this case (Fig. 56), after having padded the two parts separately, the left-hand side is worked first, so that the other side is not pressed down by the thimble during sewing, and then the second part is completed. Satin Stitch may be worked obliquely as shown in Fig. 57.

Fig. 58 shows two flower heads worked in Satin Stitch. The design is first filled in with small padding stitches.

Dots. It is said that an embroideress may be judged by her ability to work dots. The same difficulties are met with here as in the previous working of Satin Stitch. If the dot is large, it is padded with small Running Stitches taken round and round and with Cross Stitches in the centre (Fig. 59). When the dot must stand out well, it is first embroidered in one direction and then the other, after the initial padding.

As well as these "classical" dots, there is the more common kind made by taking three or five stitches across the dot without any padding. Of the three stitches, the two outside ones are shorter, in order to form a round shape and the same where five stitches are taken. These dots are used for trimming handkerchiefs, lingerie and table linen.

Initials and Monograms. Satin Stitch is most useful for the working of monograms. The use of initials for marking bed, table and personal linen is very ancient and in the Turin museum, amongst Egyptian work of the fourteenth century B.C., there is a piece of linen worked with signs and initials in brown thread.

The modern initial, used everywhere today, is generally small in size with a simple outline.

Tea cloth worked with Coats Anchor Stranded Cotton on pale-blue linen

Fig. 58. Method of working petals in Satin Stitch

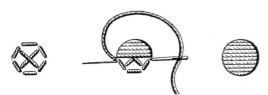

Fig. 59. Dots worked in Satin Stitch

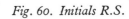

Fig. 60. Initials R.S.

Fig. 61. Initials C.D.

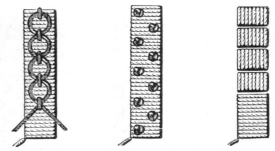

Fig. 64. Decorative stitches for initials and monograms

Fig. 62. The letter B worked in Satin Stitch on a Punch Work background. The surrounding decoration is worked in cording and seeding

Fig. 65. Initials S.T.

Fig. 63. The letter U worked in Cording and Seeding. The added decoration is worked in Cording and Punch Work

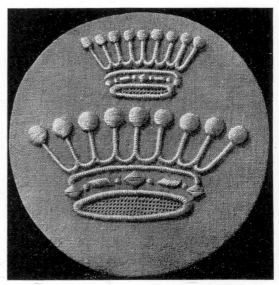

Fig. 66. A Count's coronets (Italian)

Fig. 67. A Viscount's coronets (Italian)

Fig. 68. A Count's coronets (Italian)

Fig. 69. A Marquis' coronets (Italian)

Fig. 70. A Duke's coronets (Italian)

Sheets, pillow slips, tablecloths, lingerie, handkerchiefs, bags, blouses, belts, scarves, etc., often have an initial as their only ornament. The size and type will vary according to the object upon which it is worked.

The working of initials requires precision and discrimination in the placing of the various stitches and in the choice of background and threads. Use Coats Anchor Stranded Cotton, Coats Anchor Coton à Broder or Coats Anchor Pearl Cotton for this work.

It is best to use a frame for this embroidery: the Swiss type mentioned is particularly suitable. The design should be clearly marked on the fabric, so that the outlines are quite definite.

The initials of a monogram may be placed close to each other, first that of the Christian name and then that of the surname, or they may be interwoven. When interwoven, one of them may be worked in a heavier stitch to stand out well, and the other in a lighter stitch.

The illustrations show some different types of interesting monograms for household and personal linen.

Here is an explanatory note on some of the monograms shown:

Fig. 60. The initials R S placed side by side are embroidered in Long and Short Stitch, with the small leaf motifs on the side in Satin Stitch. The coils covering the background are in Cording. The border is worked in the following way:

First work a line of padded Satin Stitch. Then lay two threads on top crossing these at short intervals. The threads are caught down with a small stitch at each intersection (Fig. 64).

The other two small illustrations show different ways of decorating monograms with Satin Stitch, a series of knots in alternate positions, worked on the Satin Stitch, and blocks of Satin Stitch. This last method is clearly visible in the two initials C D in Fig. 61.

The two initials B and U (Figs. 62 and 63) are worked almost entirely in Cording. The Cording defines the designs which are embroidered in Punch Stitch and Seeding.

The letters S T are simply worked in Satin Stitch on the background fabric. The hexagonal frame is worked double, in Satin Stitch and Herringbone Stitch (Fig. 65).

Also shown are coronets which generally surmount the initials of a nobleman. The working of the coronets is carried out in the same way as the monograms.

69

Tea cloth in natural-coloured linen embroidered in Coats Anchor Stranded Cotton in Stem Stitch and Satin Stitch. The sprays of flowers, of which two are shown below in their actual size, are dotted over the whole cloth

*"Sailing Ship." This is worked in
Stem Stitch*

*"Vase." This is worked in Stem Stitch, Satin
Stitch and alternating rows of Running Stitch are
used to fill in the vase shape*

*"Flowers". Leaves and flowers are among some of the many designs which may be worked on tablecloth.
Stitches such as Stem Stitch, Herringbone Stitch, Roumanian Stitch and Satin Stitch are used for
these designs*

An attractive tablecloth for family use. The background is in natural-coloured crash, which shows up the brilliant colours of the motifs dotted about the cloth

3 *Drawn-thread Work*_____

CHAPTER V

Hemstitch

Hemstitching is used in all kinds of Drawn-thread Work. There are many simple and complex variations of the stitch, but all are worked by drawing out threads from the background fabric and grouping and working upon the remaining threads. This technique is seen in Norwegian embroidery, Slav and Hungarian work, and Sicilian Drawn-thread Work.

Hemstitch is generally worked in white or natural, to match the background fabric. Coloured threads may, however, be used and magnificent examples of coloured Hemstitch may be found in Hungarian and Roumanian national costumes, in which the blouses are often decorated with this stitch in bright colours such as turquoise, red, orange and yellow. The stitch is also used for decorating household linen sheets, pillow-cases, towels, tablecloths, table napkins, table centres, cushion covers, lingerie and handkerchiefs.

Hemstitch may be worked on any type of fabric, but the weft and warp threads should be as even as possible. Where there are slight differences which might affect the regularity of the work, these may be overcome by drawing out more threads in one direction than in the other.

The thread used for this type of embroidery must be very strong and smooth. It should be chosen in relation to the thickness of the fabric: for coarse fabrics, like canvas and crash, use Coats Anchor Stranded Cotton (three, four or six strands),

Coats Anchor Coton à Broder, No. 18 or Coats Anchor Pearl Cotton No. 5 or 8. For very fine fabrics, such as organdie and lawn, use Coats Anchor Stranded Cotton in one or two strands.

Method of working Hemstitch. The preparation of a piece of work to be Hemstitched requires great care as the regularity of the finished work depends upon the exact counting of threads.

When two lines of Hemstitching are separated by a wide stretch of unworked fabric, a ruler should be used to measure the distances if it is impossible to count the threads accurately. Measurements should be taken with the fabric stretched on a table and made on the straight thread.

In this type of embroidery, where Drawn-thread Work and other stitches may both be used, the first step is the preparation of the drawn threads, and afterwards the working of the embroidery.

The number of threads to be drawn out for the Hemstitching will naturally vary according to the fabric used and the type of work required. On very fine fabrics, only a few threads are drawn out, whilst more threads must be drawn out for wide and complicated borders suitable for sheets and tablecloths.

Simple Hemstitch. Draw out two or three threads from the fabric, turn the hem to within one thread of the first row of drawn threads, and

73

Handkerchief in white linen with a Hem-stitched border. Small webs decorate the points where the threads cross at the corners

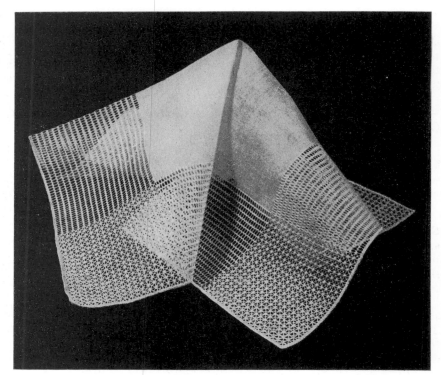

Hemstitched handkerchief

work the stitch on the wrong side from left to right. Begin the thread inside the hem. Take up three or four threads on the needle, placing the needle in from right to left. Pull the needle through drawing up the thread slightly, and then take up two threads of the turned-in hem (Fig. 1).

This simple form of the stitch may also be worked keeping the turned-in hem to the top (Fig. 2).

Ladder Hemstitch. Fig. 3 shows Hemstitch worked on both sides of the space, making a series of vertical groupings.

Saw-tooth or Zig-Zag Hemstitch. Begin this stitch by working a simple Hemstitch, always taking up an even number of threads. From the opposite side half of one group is joined to half of the adjacent group, thus making a zig-zag line (Fig. 4).

The stitches illustrated in Figs. 5, 6, 7, 8, 9 and 10 make interesting finishes for all types of work. These are all worked between two rows of drawn threads, that is, the fabric is prepared with one thread drawn out, then three or four threads are left before another single thread is withdrawn.

Four-sided Stitch. This may be worked in two ways:

1. Work on the right side, from right to left. Take up three fabric threads from the lower line and then take the needle to the back and work the three corresponding threads of the upper row, bringing the needle out below, to the left. Take a vertical stitch from below above, bringing the needle out three threads to the left of the first horizontal stitch (Fig. 5).

2. This is worked on the back of the work and from the other side appears exactly the same as the preceding stitch. It is clearly shown in Fig. 6.

Four-sided Stitch can also be worked in an oblique line without drawing out threads. It makes a useful background filling stitch, having the appearance of a square mesh.

It is worked in two stages, on the right side of the work. Both stages may be seen in Fig. 7. When this stitch is worked diagonally it is pulled tightly and worked with a thick needle and a fine strong thread.

Fig. 8 shows a variation of Four-sided Stitch. Work from left to right on the right side of the

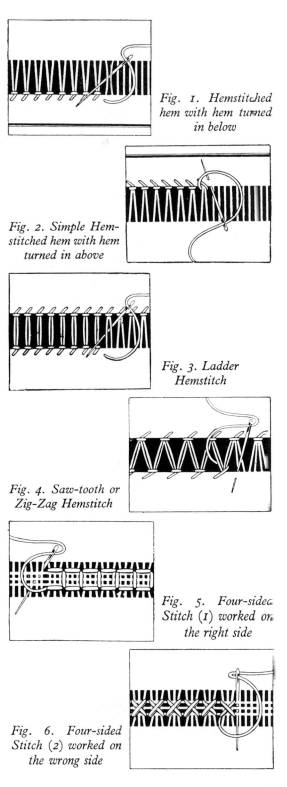

Fig. 1. Hemstitched hem with hem turned in below

Fig. 2. Simple Hemstitched hem with hem turned in above

Fig. 3. Ladder Hemstitch

Fig. 4. Saw-tooth or Zig-Zag Hemstitch

Fig. 5. Four-sided Stitch (1) worked on the right side

Fig. 6. Four-sided Stitch (2) worked on the wrong side

75

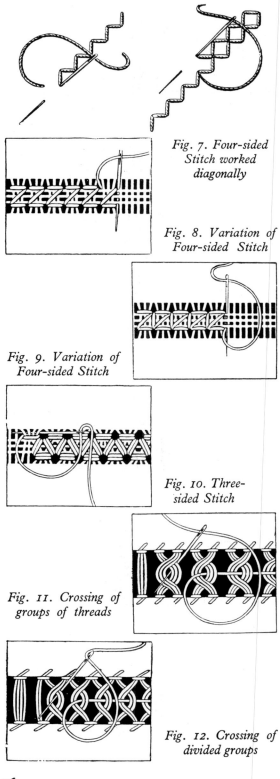

Fig. 7. Four-sided
Stitch worked
diagonally

Fig. 8. Variation of
Four-sided Stitch

Fig. 9. Variation of
Four-sided Stitch

Fig. 10. Three-
sided Stitch

Fig. 11. Crossing of
groups of threads

Fig. 12. Crossing of
divided groups

work. Take up three or four threads with a horizontal stitch from the lower row of drawn threads, and then the corresponding threads of the upper row. Continue with a vertical stitch on the back, from above below thus returning to the lower row of drawn threads.

Fig. 9 shows the same stitch slightly modified.

Three-sided Stitch. This is worked from right to left as shown in Fig. 10.

Crossing of Groups of Threads or Interlaced Hemstitch. The crossing of two or more groups of threads gives rise to many variations.

The groups can be crossed in many ways after working the Hemstitching.

Fig. 11 shows a simple crossing of two groups. The needle is threaded with rather thick thread.

Fig. 12 shows the crossing of threads in groups which are split into two and which must therefore always be formed by an equal number of threads. This border is less open than the previous one.

Fig. 13 shows a combination of two whole groups crossed by four half-groups, and Fig. 14 shows a combination of four whole groups, the first crossed with the third and the second with the fourth.

Whole groups may also be crossed in the way shown in Fig. 15, that is in combinations of four, crossing the first and second over the third and fourth.

Fig. 16 shows a double row of whole groups crossing and alternating on successive lines.

Knotting of Groups of Threads. The knotting of groups of threads also forms an attractive variation of Hemstitch.

The knot which holds the group of threads firmly fixed is obtained by placing the thread as for Chain Stitch and making the needle pass under the group of threads to be knotted. The thread should be taut. The knotting can have two or more knots.

Knotted groups can be made in one or more parallel lines and the thread used for the knotting may be visible and form part of the whole pattern (Fig. 17); it can, on the other hand, be hidden, by wrapping it around the group of threads and bringing it out at the next group of stitches for the following knot (Fig. 18).

The groups may be knotted singly, or in two, three, or more at a time, in simple single lines or alternately.

Fig. 13. Crossing of whole groups and half groups

Fig. 14. A series of crossed groups

Fig. 15. Another type of crossing of groups of threads

Fig. 16. Groups crossed and alternated in two rows

Fig. 17. Groups joined and knotted in groups of three, leaving the thread showing

Fig. 18. Groups joined and knotted in groups of three with the thread hidden

Fig. 19. Groups knotted in twos and alternated

Fig. 20. Groups knotted in fours and alternated

Fig. 21. Method of Cording on two threads

Fig. 22. Cording on eight threads making a zig-zag line

Fig. 23. Joining of four groups by Cording

Fig. 24. Joining of six groups with Buttonhole Stitch

77

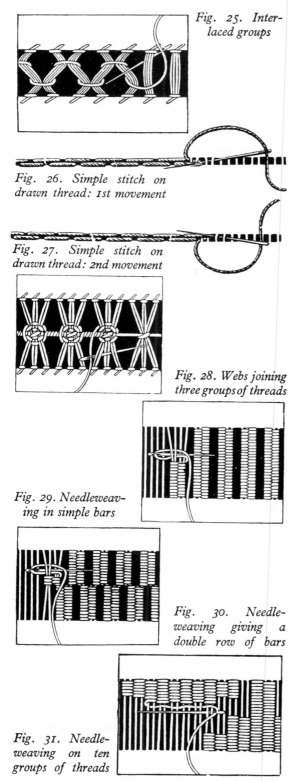

Fig. 25. Inter-laced groups

Fig. 26. Simple stitch on drawn thread: 1st movement

Fig. 27. Simple stitch on drawn thread: 2nd movement

Fig. 28. Webs joining three groups of threads

Fig. 29. Needleweaving in simple bars

Fig. 30. Needleweaving giving a double row of bars

Fig. 31. Needleweaving on ten groups of threads

Fig. 19 shows a series of groups knotted two at a time and alternated on the second row; Fig. 20 shows a double row of groups knotted in fours and alternated.

Generally speaking, the thread used for Hemstitching should be of the same thickness as the threads drawn out; where there is a difference, it should be finer rather than thicker. Cording and Buttonhole Stitch are often used for covering the bars in Hemstitching.

Fig. 21 shows the way in which Cording is worked on groups of threads. Three fabric threads are Corded, beginning from the bottom and covering the whole length.

Fig. 22 shows groups of four threads forming a zig-zag line. At the joinings, a double number of threads meet; these are worked alternately towards the top and the bottom. This same type of work, worked over about a third of the space, first above and then below, is shown in Fig. 23, while Fig. 24 shows the method of combining six groups using Blanket Stitch instead of Cording.

Fig. 25 shows a simple variation in which the thread joining the two groups passes horizontally. The needle is placed first from below above, and then from above below.

When it is necessary to divide a piece of fabric into squares for tablecloths and napkins, the easy stitch shown in Figs. 26 and 27 is most suitable. The fabric is prepared by spreading it out on a table and drawing out two threads, after careful measurements. Work along the line of the drawn thread, passing over four threads and taking up two, first keeping the thread above and then below the needle.

Fig. 28 shows a series of wheels or webs, worked over combinations of three knotted groups and the knotting thread.

Needleweaving. This is another stitch for carrying out attractive decorative work on drawn threads. Spaces worked in this stitch, as well as being rich and very decorative, have the advantage of being solid and hard wearing. When the needleweaving fills the whole space, it is unnecessary to group the threads as for the previous stitches. Needleweaving is usually worked in white on household linen, or in natural, whilst on clothing it is very effective worked in colours.

The simplest use of this stitch is in the form of a series of bars, as shown in Fig. 29. Threads are drawn according to the width of the space required and an equal number of woven threads is worked. Use the needle eye first to avoid catching the fabric threads or, better still, use a tapestry needle which has a blunt point.

Fig. 30 shows a double row of woven bars. There may be three or four of such rows, or even more, so that diagonal lines are formed. To pass from one group of stitches to another, the needle is threaded through behind the group already completed.

Needleweaving can also be worked over three, four or more groups of threads, making the most varied patterns. Fig. 31. Working on ten groups.

Corners. Some difficulty may be found in the working of corners in Hemstitching.

When the two rows of threads have been drawn out, a square, empty space is formed at the corners where the two rows meet. Here the threads should not be cut at the edge of the fabric, but left for about half an inch and folded over to the wrong side of the work by pushing them back with the eye of the needle (Fig. 32). Then, on the right side, a Corded or Buttonhole Stitched edge is worked very closely along the edges of the square (Fig. 33).

If this square is very small, as in very fine work, and the material does not fray easily, it may be left empty, but when the space is rather large, this must be filled with a web to decorate and strengthen the corner. The thread is fastened to one corner and taken across diagonally to the opposite corner, and the same worked in the opposite direction from the other two corners. Where the threads cross, a wheel or web is worked by winding the thread round the centre. When the web is sufficiently large, the thread is taken across to the corner where it is fastened off (Fig. 34).

The number of spokes to the wheel may vary according to the size of the space. When the space is not very big it may be decorated as shown in Figs. 35 and 36. When the space is rather large, there are many and varied ways of decorating and filling in the square.

Figs. 37 and 38 show two decorative methods of finishing off corners.

Sometimes the drawn threads continue right up to the outside edge of the work, instead of finishing some distance from the edge; then it is possible to work Hemstitch on the folded hem, taking up only a few threads on the needle so that the groups of threads do not become too large.

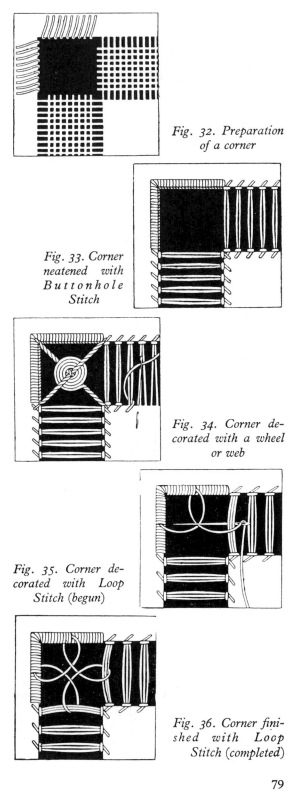

Fig. 32. Preparation of a corner

Fig. 33. Corner neatened with *Buttonhole Stitch*

Fig. 34. Corner decorated with a wheel or web

Fig. 35. Corner decorated with Loop Stitch (begun)

Fig. 36. Corner finished with Loop Stitch (completed)

Fig. 37. Decorative Corner

Fig. 38. Corner for
a broad border

Fig. 39. Corner
of a border em-
broidered in
Satin Stitch,
Bullion Knots
and Drawn-
thread Work

Fig. 39a. Cor-
ner of a Drawn-
thread border
embroidered in
Satin Stitch,
Cording and
Four-sided
Stitch

Figs. 39 and 39(a) show two corners of borders suitable for bed linen, carried out in Hemstitching and other stitches.

Here are some ways of working decorative borders in Hemstitching, suitable for household linen.

Fig. 40. *1st border.* The threads are joined with Needleweaving.

2nd border. Here there is a double row of drawn threads. Eight threads are drawn out, four left in and then again eight threads are drawn out. Herringbone Stitch is worked in the centre, grouping the threads in twos, then the Needleweaving is worked, joining first four groups of threads and then two, alternating the pattern on the line below

Fig. 41. *1st border.* Another decoration in Needleweaving. The threads are first Hemstitched in groups of two. Work eight groups in Needleweaving, working one group less on each side until only two remain. The design is repeated over eight groups, leaving a space of two groups between, on the opposite side. Lastly, join the groups between the triangles.

2nd border. Groups of three threads each are Hemstitched and four groups are worked in Needleweaving and then two on each side: lastly, the four central groups are joined with Needleweaving.

Fig. 42. Four groups of two threads each are joined using Needleweaving as illustrated.

Fig. 43. Six groups of threads worked in Needleweaving alternate with two groups worked in Needleweaving and Cording, between two rows of Four-sided Stitch.

Fig. 44. The threads are Hemstitched in groups of two. These are taken six at a time and decorated with Blanket Stitch.

Fig. 45. Narrow border in Needleweaving and Cording. First prepare groups of two threads and then follow the given pattern.

Fig. 46. Prepare groups of three threads each. Five groups are worked in Cording, joining them in the centre. On the six following groups work Needleweaving, following the pattern.

Fig. 47. A ribbon may be passed through this Drawn-thread border. Use Needleweaving and follow the given design, over ten groups of two threads each. This is alternated with three groups joined with Needleweaving.

Fig. 48. A rich border which looks like lace. Groups of two threads each are joined with small knots and Buttonhole Stitch. The border is made up from ten rows.

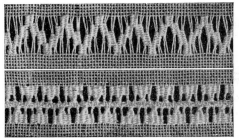

Fig. 40. Borders suitable for sheets, pillow-cases and towels

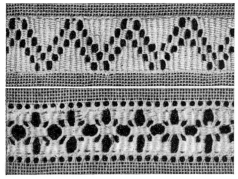

Fig. 41. Borders for household linen

Fig. 42. Border in Needleweaving

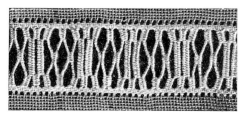

Fig. 43. Another border in Needleweaving

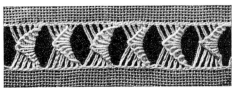

Fig. 44. Border in Blanket Stitch

Fig. 45. Narrow border in Needleweaving
and Cording

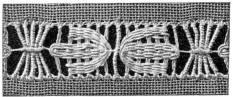

Fig. 46. Border in Needleweaving
and Cording

Fig. 47. Border in Needleweaving for
threading a ribbon

Fig. 48. Border in Buttonhole Stitch
and knotting

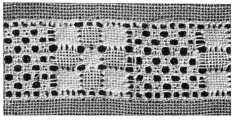

Fig. 49. Pulled Stitch border

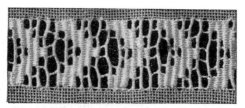

Fig. 50. Narrow border in Needleweaving and Cording

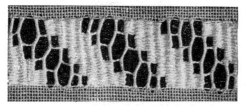

Fig. 51. Another border in Needleweaving and Cording

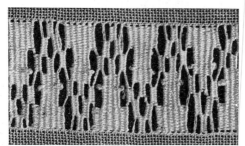

Fig. 52. Richly worked border in Needleweaving decorated with picots

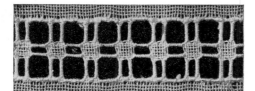

Fig. 53. Open work border in Cording

Fig. 54. Open work border in Needleweaving

Fig. 49. Border worked over pulled threads, that is, the threads have not been drawn out, in alternate squares; one worked in Loop Stitch, the other in Herringbone Stitch on the wrong side.

Figs. 50 and 51 show two pretty borders carried out in Needleweaving and Cording.

Fig. 52. A very decorative border embroidered in Needleweaving and enriched with picots.

Threading. A simple, quick method for decorating borders for napkins, tablecloths and handkerchiefs is "threading". This means substituting the threads of the fabric itself with other coloured threads. Work in the following way:

Take out one thread of fabric, leave the next, and draw out the following one. Thread a needle with Coats Anchor Stranded Cotton twice as long as the length necessary and use double. Join the thread with a simple knot, between the two drawn threads, to the remaining thread of fabric. In this way, by pulling gently on the thread of the fabric, it will draw the coloured thread through to replace it.

These "threadings" are very effective and may be made into wide borders, using a number of different colours.

Open Work. By taking out fabric threads in both directions, an empty space is left which can be decorated very effectively.

This type of work should be executed as far as possible on fabric in which the warp and weft threads are very regular. The number of threads taken out in one direction or the other will depend on the type of open work design and on the thickness of the fabric.

In order to avoid the fraying of the cut edges, these are covered with Buttonhole Stitch or Cording, after the threads have been drawn out, as already explained for corners.

Here are two narrow borders in open work (Figs. 53 and 54). In the first illustration four threads in both directions have been withdrawn, leaving eight threads between. These eight threads are grouped in fours using Cording Stitch.

In the second illustration six threads have been withdrawn lengthways, every eight threads, and four withdrawn in the opposite direction, every eight threads. The eight threads are grouped into fours and worked in Needleweaving.

Backgrounds in Drawn-thread Work. For household linen, backgrounds of Drawn-thread

Work in various geometrical forms—squares, diamonds and circles may be used. To carry out this decorative form of embroidery, the design must first be traced on to the fabric and outlined with Running Stitch which is then covered over with Buttonhole or Cording Stitch, worked very closely. When the outline has been completed, the threads are withdrawn from the fabric. These threads are cut away after fastening off on the back of the work. Then the background is worked.

It is always more difficult to work circular designs regularly. A practical method which generally gives good results is the following. Mark out a circle, using compasses, on a thin piece of card. Cut out round the edge and cover the circle with fabric, fixing it on the wrong side with long stitches starting from the centre, like rays. Then, with a rather hot iron, press over the disc, then cut away the stitching and remove the card. The outline of the circle will be impressed on the fabric and should be immediately outlined with tacking. This system is also effective for the application of circular inlays.

Fig. 55. Take out ten threads and leave ten threads, in both directions. Make a simple Hemstitched edge, taking two threads at a time along the whole length of drawn threads. Then group together the five groups of threads formed in both directions, with a knot. Then pass the two diagonals across forming a web.

The three figures 56, 57 and 58 are worked in Needleweaving.

Fig. 56. Take out six threads from the fabric, leaving an equal number, both horizontally and vertically. Work each group of threads in Needleweaving, dividing each in two. On finishing one line, either vertical or horizontal, proceed to the other and at the same time work the curves in Blanket Stitching and fix these to the corners with Cording.

Fig. 56. Drawn-thread background in Needleweaving, Buttonhole Stitch and Cording

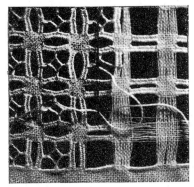

Fig. 57. Drawn-thread background in Needleweaving and Loop Stitch

Fig. 58. Drawn-thread background in Needleweaving Satin Stitch and webs

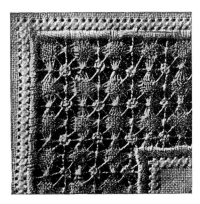

Fig. 55. Drawn-thread background with webs

Fig. 59. Background worked in squares

83

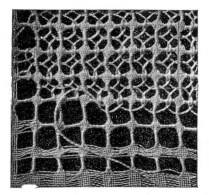

Fig. 60.
Drawn-thread background in Cording and Loop Stitch

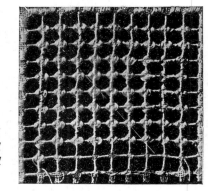

Fig. 61.
Drawn-thread background in Cording and small wheels

Fig. 62.
Drawn-thread background in Button-hole Stitch

Fig. 57. Draw out twelve threads, leaving in the same number, in each direction. Work the groups of threads with Needleweaving, taking up a series of six threads, that is three and three, at a time. On working the last side of the square, work a Loop Stitch as shown in the illustration.

Fig. 58. Draw out nine threads from the fabric and leave in the same number both horizontally and vertically. Work in three series, taking three threads at a time. Then pass the diagonals across the squares to form small webs. The squares of fabric are then decorated with spots worked in Satin Stitch.

Fig. 59 shows squares which have a padded appearance suitable for decorating lingerie. First prepare the drawn threads, dividing the material into as many squares as required for the design to be worked. Divide the larger squares into nine small squares by drawing out one thread and leaving in six, both in a vertical and horizontal direction. Then, on the wrong side of the fabric, work Herringbone Stitch which takes in two threads in one direction and then in the other. These threads, rather tightly drawn on the wrong side, form a slight swelling of the material on the right side which is very effective.

Fig. 60. Take out four threads and leave in the same number in both directions of the work. Cover the remaining threads with Cording Stitch. Pass then from the middle of one square to the middle of the next with a loose Blanket Stitch, and on completing the line, repeat the same movement in the opposite direction to form a series of Loop Stitches.

Fig. 61. Take out four threads and leave in the same number in both directions. Work Cording Stitch on the remaining threads. Where the squares cross, wrap the thread round seven or eight times so that small wheels are formed.

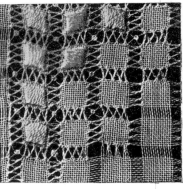

Fig. 63.
Drawn-thread background with Satin Stitch and webs

Fig. 64.
Corner with threads joined by Loop Stitch

Fig. 62. Take out eight threads and leave the same number in both directions. Divide each group of remaining threads in half and work them, on both sides, with Blanket Stitch.

Fig. 63. Draw out six threads and leave fourteen in both directions. Work Serpentine Hemstitch making small webs at the crossing points of the squares. Decorate the squares with Satin Stitch as shown in the illustration.

Fig. 64. Corner of a Drawn-thread border. Draw out eight threads, leaving eight in, and eight again drawn out in both directions This foundation is finally decorated with Loop Stitch enclosed by two lines of Satin Stitch.

Backgrounds in Drawn-thread Work on light-weight fabric give a delightful transparency to the work.

These designs may be worked in Coats Anchor Stranded Cotton or Coats Anchor Coton à Broder depending on the desired effect.

1st design (Fig. 65).

Draw out ten threads in both directions, leaving the same number of threads.

Fix the first group of threads above, with a knot, going down to fix another group of threads below, then returning to a group of threads above and so on alternately.

On the following line, fix the thread on the first knot, then go down to fix the group below; go up again to the knot already formed and so on. Each series of threads is grouped together and fixed by two knots in this way.

2nd design (Fig. 66).

Draw out sixteen threads in both directions, leaving in the same

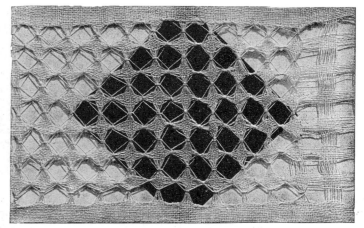

Fig. 65. Drawn-thread background with knotted threads

Fig. 66. Drawn-thread background with Blanket Stitch and Loop Stitch

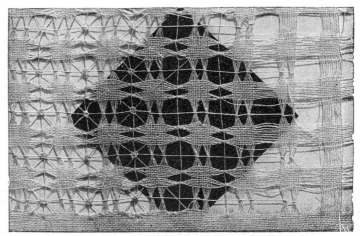

Fig. 67. Drawn-thread background with knotted threads and wheels

85

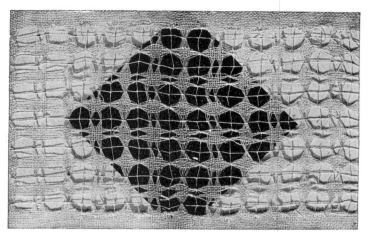

Fig. 68. Drawn-thread background with knotted threads in both directions

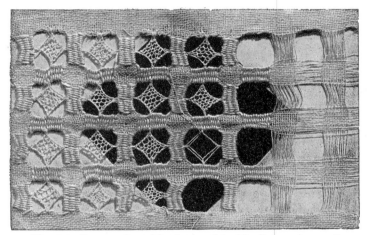

Fig. 69. Drawn-thread background in Needleweaving and Blanket Stitch

Fig. 70 Drawn-thread background with knotted threads and webs

86

number. Fix and join half (that is, eight) of the remaining threads with Buttonhole Stitch, and then the other half. On the last side of every square work a Loop Stitch, passing the needle twice round the thread. Lastly, work a thread in both directions across the empty space, fixing it to the fabric with a Back Stitch.

3rd design (Fig. 67).
Draw out twelve threads in both directions, leaving in the same number: fix the threads by knotting them in sixes in both directions. Lastly, work threads diagonally, fixing them at the crossing points in the empty spaces by a wheel or small web.

4th design (Fig. 68).
Draw out eight threads in both directions, leaving in the same number. Bind the various series of threads with knots which take in alternately eight threads in one group and eight threads in two groups of four threads each, in both directions.

5th design (Fig. 69).
Draw out twelve threads in both directions, leaving in the same number: group the threads using Needleweaving. Then take threads across the squares formed, fixing them twice with Loop Stitch at the centre of each side. In these small diamonds, work five or six widely spaced Blanket Stitches, making six rows in all.

6th design (Fig. 70).
Draw out twenty-four threads in each direction and leave in the same number. Group the threads in three rows. At the crossing points, make a wheel or web.

CHAPTER VI

Sicilian and Sardinian Drawn-thread Work

Sicilian Drawn-thread Work. Drawn-thread Work cannot be mentioned without bringing Sicily to mind. It is the typical embroidery of the island and known all over the world for its technical perfection and characteristic designs.

This Drawn-thread Work has the appearance of a net and is carried out on fine material, taking out and working over threads in both directions of the fabric. The drawn-out sections form a background for patterns which are generally surrounded by Cording. There are many different designs, including flowers, geometrical patterns and allegorical figures. Many of the designs are used for decorating household and personal linen.

There were four types of Sicilian Drawn-thread Work carried out during the fifteenth, sixteenth, eighteenth and nineteenth centuries.

The technique of this Drawn-thread Work is very well known. It consists of drawing out three or four threads in both directions of the fabric and covering the remaining threads with Cording to form an open work background for the designs.

In Drawn-thread Work before the fifteenth century, the design was made by replacing both horizontal and vertical threads with weaving in both directions with the needle so that the design remained solid on a background of open work squares without any kind of outline stitch. Only at Ragusa is it still worked in the traditional manner. In the course of time changes in the technique

were introduced which are characteristic of the sixteenth century—the pattern being made by the background fabric surrounded by Cording. The effect of the design is much the same as that of the fifteenth century, but naturally the latter is more valuable.

Eighteenth-century work shows radical changes. In it, the design is carried out in Drawn-thread Work, leaving the background unchanged. This is more difficult to work than the other types, but is not so effective.

The nineteenth-century work returns to the sixteenth-century style, but shows the influence of the Vittorian workroom (Vittoria being a place in the province of Ragusa), where it originated. It is classical in inspiration, with figures derived from Greek low reliefs and symbolic motifs.

Sardinian Drawn-thread Work. Sardinian Drawn-thread Work, like that of Sicily, is based upon the making of a Drawn-thread Work mesh. Unlike the Sicilian work, however, Sardinian Drawn-thread Work consists of only two types: one, very old type, worked in Campidano, which has not suffered from any changes in fashion. The other, which is similar to Sicilian work, is enriched by motifs decorated in Satin Stitch and Cording.

The background for both types is a Drawn-thread Work mesh and the decorative stitch used is Cording in a horizontal direction, making very

Corner of a richly embroidered cloth in Sicilian Drawn-thread Work, sixteenth-century design, with appliqués in Venetian Stitch and embroidery in Satin Stitch

close stitches. In antique Sardinian Drawn-thread Work, the empty squares are filled in with interlaced threads worked in a similar way to Loop Stitch, as shown in the last chapter.

In Sardinia each village has its own particular type of work, and anyone who really knows the island will have heard of the cloths from Trexena, Sorgonese linen, Isili carpets, Gadoni curtains, and the laces from the hills around Bosa. Sardinian women often make free interpretations of the designs whilst remaining faithful to traditional style.

Technique of Sicilian Drawn-thread Work. Sicilian Drawn-thread Work is carried out on fabric with a very regular weave. It may be worked in the hand, but it is preferable to work in a frame, especially when large pieces such as bedcovers or tablecloths are made. In order to make the work of drawing out the threads easier, leave the fabric slightly loose in the frame. The Cording is also worked in the frame. If the piece of work is small it can be fixed on to card. The number of threads to be drawn out depends on the thickness of the fabric used and on the design chosen.

Use Coats Anchor Stranded Cotton for this type of embroidery. The number of strands may be varied to suit the thickness of the fabric. In working the sixteenth-century type of Drawn-thread Work, the thread must be as near as possible to that drawn out of the background fabric.

Fifteenth-century Drawn-thread Work. Do not draw out all the threads before starting the embroidery, but limit the preparation to small areas which should be completed before going on to the next. After the threads have been drawn out, the design is worked by passing an embroidery thread of the same thickness through the spaces. As the work proceeds, in order not to have to take big jumps from one space to another, a length of thread is left hanging; this may be fastened off later at the back of the work. Then the process is repeated in the opposite direction. The background is afterwards worked in Cording (Fig. 1). The illustrations Figs. 2, 3, 4 and 5 show clearly how to proceed.

Sixteenth-century Drawn-thread Work. This has been very much simplified. Keep the design to hand, drawn on squared paper and count the threads carefully. Work Back Stitch to outline the pattern and allow four threads for each square. At the corners, count two extra for each side. When the work has been thus prepared, outline the

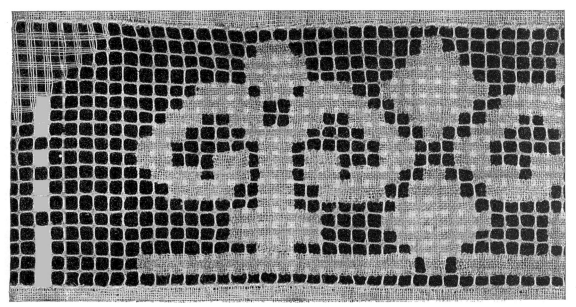

Fig. 1. Sicilian Drawn-thread Work of the fifteenth-century type. The pattern is woven on a drawn background

89

Fig. 2. Drawing out of fabric threads

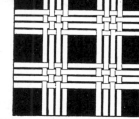

Fig. 3. Cording on background threads

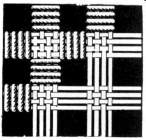

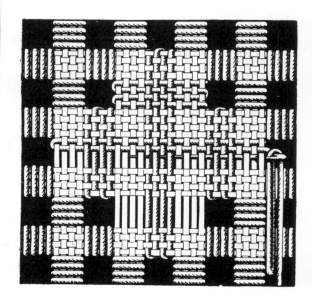

Fig. 4. Weaving of the pattern in fifteenth - century - style Drawn-thread work

whole design in Cording passing over four threads. On completing the Corded outlines, draw out the background threads, taking out four threads in both directions. Finally cover all the remaining background threads with Cording. Fig. 6 shows the method explained here.

In Sicily, too, the women often use Back Stitch to outline the design. They prepare the whole area to be embroidered and work the background before the design. See Fig. 7. A thread, similar to that used for the embroidery, is laid under the Cording as this is worked.

The finishing off of Drawn-thread Work is generally carried out in one of two ways: either by folding in the hem and fixing it down with Hem-stitch or Four-sided Stitch, or by working round the background mesh in Blanket Stitch, following the outline of the design.

Another type of Drawn-thread Work, similar to that described, but which does not form part of the traditional Sicilian and Sardinian work, is that shown in Fig. 8. The illustration shows how, after having drawn out three threads in either direction to form a background, this is then covered with Cording, and embroidered in Needleweaving following a specific design.

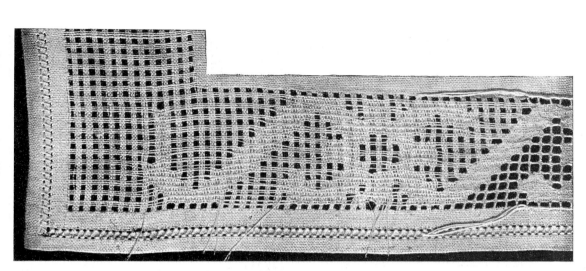

Fig. 5. Sicilian Drawn-thread Work of the fifteenth-century type. From left to right: drawn threads; placing of new threads; a part of the mesh completed

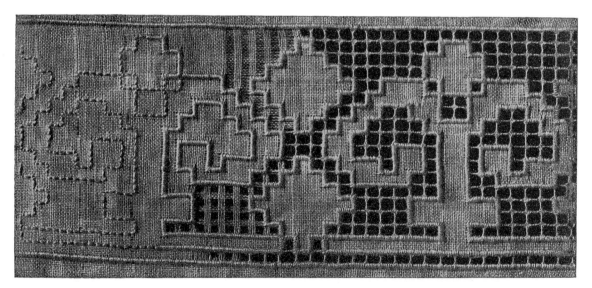

Fig. 6. Sixteenth-century-style Sicilian Drawn-thread Work. The design is formed by the fabric which stands out in relief from a drawn background

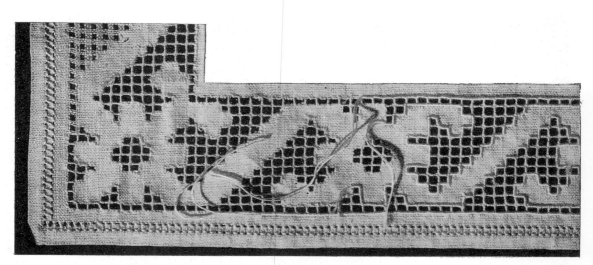

Fig. 7. Sixteenth-century-style Sicilian Drawn-thread Work. From left to right: drawn threads; Corded mesh; a part of the finished work

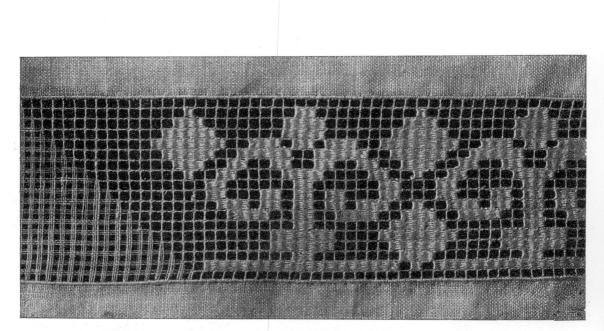

Fig. 8. Needleweaving on drawn threads. The background worked in Cording, over three threads of the fabric

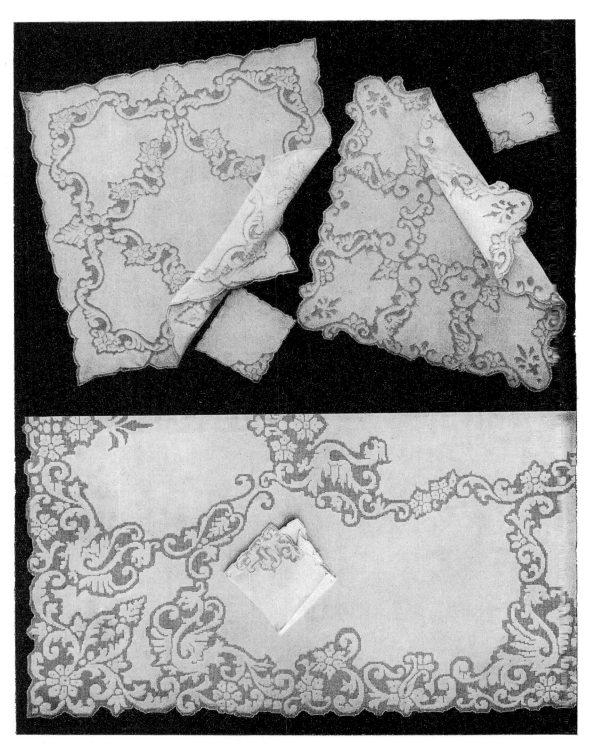

Above: Table centres embroidered in Sicilian Drawn-thread Work. Below: Corner of a tablecloth and napkin in Sicilian Drawn-thread Work

An example of old Sardinian Drawn-thread Work

CHAPTER VII

Hardanger Embroidery

The name of this particular embroidery, which is also called "Norwegian" embroidery, comes from Hardanger, a district situated on the fiord of the same name in Western Norway.

This kind of work, in its original form, is very ancient, and in Persia and Asia a similar type of embroidery was carried out on transparent gauze in coloured silks. Today it is still popular in Northern countries, where the women decorate their personal linen, their dresses and household objects with very elaborate patterns. In Italy, it was fashionable at the beginning of this century, but since then has fallen into disuse.

Fabrics and Threads. Hardanger embroidery is worked on fabric with a very regular weave, in which the warp and weft threads are equal. The most suitable threads for Hardanger embroidery are Coats Anchor Stranded Cotton, using a number of threads suitable for the work in hand, Coats Anchor Coton à Broder and Coats Anchor Pearl Cotton No. 5 and 8. The embroidery is generally worked in white on white or natural fabric, but in some modern designs, colour has been introduced on white fabrics and white on coloured fabrics. For one piece of work, two thicknesses of thread are required: a fine one for Cording Stitch and Needleweaving on the drawn threads, and a thicker one for the Satin Stitch.

Tapestry needles and a pair of very sharp, pointed scissors are the essential tools for Hardanger embroidery.

Method of working Hardanger Embroidery. Although easy and quick to carry out, Hardanger work belongs to the drawn-thread group of embroidery, and it is therefore important that the fabric used should be carefully cut, as any irregularity would spoil the effect of the work. It is always necessary to count both threads and stitches with great accuracy.

In Hardanger embroidery the surrounds for the spaces are embroidered first of all and then the lines of decorative stitching. Finally the work is cut, the threads drawn out and the background mesh completed.

The first part of the embroidery, i.e. working the surrounds and filling in, is best worked in a frame. The working of the spaces and drawing of the threads is done in the hand.

The basic stitches for Hardanger embroidery are: Satin Stitch for the filled-in areas; Needleweaving and Cording Stitch for the bars; Buttonhole Stitch for the edges. Four-sided Stitch is sometimes used for both straight and diagonal lines.

The Satin Stitch is always worked over counted threads in horizontal or vertical directions. When the edges of the various designs have been completed, then the threads are cut and drawn out; the threads are first drawn out in one direction and then in another.

The edge finish is chosen according to the type of pattern and the use to which the embroidery is

Mat worked in Hardanger embroidery using Coats Anchor Pearl Cotton in white on natural coloured cloth. The design of this mat is not very difficult to work and all the different stitches are explained in the following chapter. Begin by working the Satin Stitch and then draw out threads from each single square, working these with Cording and Loop Stitch. The edge is Buttonhole stitched

to be put. Generally a Hemstitched hem is worked in simple form or in Four-sided Stitch. For an embroidery with an irregular edge this may be neatened with Buttonhole Stitch. Fringes are also used to finish off the work where these are appropriate.

Satin Stitch is worked over four threads of fabric, in vertical, horizontal, or diagonal lines (Figs. 1 and 2).

Figs. 3 and 4 show blocks of Satin Stitch, alternated. The small squares in the illustrations 5 and 6 consist of five stitches worked over four threads of material, repeated on four sides. The centre of these squares may be left undecorated or enriched with small eyelets or webs.

Fig. 7 shows two corners: the first is worked in Satin Stitch over six threads of fabric, and the second in Buttonhole Stitch. At the corner, each stitch is decreased by one thread, and then increased again, one thread at a time, until all six threads are again covered. In Fig. 8 the Buttonhole Stitch follows the same design as the Satin Stitch.

Outlining of background spaces. The stitches outlining the drawn-thread backgrounds must be worked over a number of threads corresponding to the number of threads withdrawn, plus one. Thus, if four threads are to be withdrawn, five stitches worked over four threads of material are worked, and after leaving four threads, another five stitches are worked on the four following threads. It may be noted in Figs. 9 and 10 how the direction of the Satin Stitch may be either vertical for the horizontal edges or horizontal for the vertical edges.

Figs. 9 and 10 show a square surrounded with Satin Stitch ready for drawing the threads, and a square with the threads drawn and the Needleweaving commenced.

Cutting of Threads. After preparing the framework of the pattern, the threads are cut very near to the Satin Stitch, and drawn out where the space is required.

The square in Fig. 11 shows the sides worked in Satin Stitch with four threads drawn out at the corners and eight left in the centre, grouped into two bars, with Needleweaving.

In Fig. 12, four small squares are placed in a diamond shape. The fourth side of each square consists of a bar in Needleweaving. In the centre of the four squares a Loop Stitch is worked.

Fig. 13 shows a square outlined on each side by two triangles worked in Satin Stitch over seven threads, each stitch decreasing in height by one thread. At the centre the Needleweaving bars form a cross and are worked with a picot half-way along each bar.

Figs. 14 and 15 show a square with sides in Satin Stitch, consisting of four stitches over four threads, five stitches over eight threads, and four stitches over four threads. At the centre the two bars cross and the illustrations show two different ways in which the centre may be finished.

Fig. 16 shows a square with sides in Satin Stitch, composed of four stitches over four threads, four over eight threads, five over twelve, and another four over eight threads and four over four threads. The space is decorated with double bars of Needleweaving each one worked over two threads and four Loop Stitch motifs.

Figs. 17 and 18 show the outlining of corners with groups of Satin Stitch in straight and diagonal blocks. Fig. 19 illustrates a square. This square, with the threads drawn out and embroidered, is the subject of the following illustrations. After the Satin Stitch is worked and the threads have been withdrawn the background is embroidered.

The threads may be grouped with simple knots, or with Cording or with Needleweaving.

Illustrations Nos. 20 and 21 show backgrounds decorated with Loop Stitch. This stitch is explained elsewhere and the illustrations are so clear that they may be easily followed.

Fig. 22 shows the grouping of threads using Cording, worked diagonally. To enrich this simple square, Loop Stitch and webs, as shown in Figs. 23, 24 and 25, may be used. The first shows a simple Loop Stitch alternating with an empty space. The Loop Stitch is worked half-way along the fourth side of the small square; after it has been worked, go back to the starting point and complete the Cording on the second half of the side. The second illustration shows the same Corded background with Loop Stitches, with the thread twisted round twice. This is worked in the same way as in the first illustration, but here the Loop Stitch is not worked from the sides of the square but from the corners, so that the stitch lies in an oblique direction. The third illustration, Fig. 25, shows a decoration of small webs.

The other four illustrations, Figs. 26, 27, 28 and 29, show backgrounds worked in Needleweaving. After the background has been prepared, Needleweaving is worked diagonally as for the Cording.

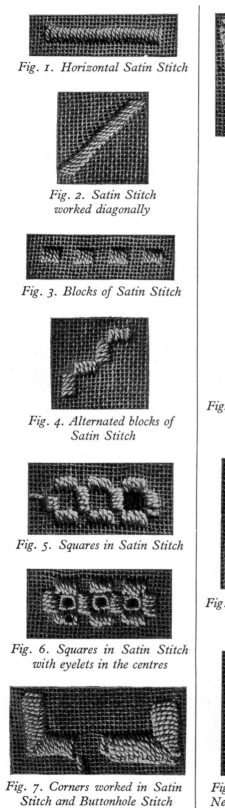

Fig. 1. Horizontal Satin Stitch

Fig. 2. Satin Stitch
worked diagonally

Fig. 3. Blocks of Satin Stitch

Fig. 4. Alternated blocks of
Satin Stitch

Fig. 5. Squares in Satin Stitch

Fig. 6. Squares in Satin Stitch
with eyelets in the centres

Fig. 7. Corners worked in Satin
Stitch and Buttonhole Stitch

Fig. 8. Satin Stitch and
Buttonhole Stitch

Figs. 9 and 10. Two stages in
working an open square

Fig. 11. An open square with bars
in Needleweaving

Fig. 12. A diamond shape with
Needleweaving and Loop Stitch

Fig. 13. Square surrounded with
graduated Satin Stitches

Figs. 14 and 15. Squares with
sides worked in Satin Stitch and
two different fillings

Fig. 16. Large square surrounded by Satin Stitch, with
bars of Needleweaving and Loop
Stitch fillings

98

Fig. 17. Outline in horizontal and vertical Satin Stitch blocks

Fig. 18. Outline in Satin Stitch worked in alternate directions

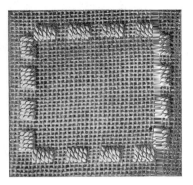

Fig. 19. Outline in Satin Stitch blocks

Fig. 20. Threads grouped with Loop Stitch

Fig. 21. Threads grouped with Loop Stitch

Fig. 22. Threads grouped with Cording

Fig. 23. Decoration of squares using Cording and Loop Stitch

Fig. 24. Decoration of squares with Loop Stitch worked from corner to corner

Fig. 25. Decoration of squares with Cording and webs

99

Fig. 26. Threads grouped with Needleweaving

Fig. 27. Decoration of small squares with Needleweaving and Loop Stitch

Fig. 28. Decoration of small squares with Needleweaving and Loop Stitch variation

Fig. 29. Threads grouped with Needleweaving and picots

The Loop Stitch which decorates the small squares in Fig. 27 alternates with empty spaces. The Needleweaving is interrupted, the Loop Stitch is made, twisting the thread once or twice, then the work is recommenced by going back to the starting point to continue the Needleweaving.

Fig. 28 shows the Loop Stitch twisted twice and worked from the corners.

The working of picots on Needleweaving presents some difficulties. Fig. 29 shows a background where the bars are decorated with picots in the centre of alternate sides. Half-way down the side on which the picot is to be worked, the thread is wrapped twice round the needle, the needle pushed through half the threads, the embroidery thread pulled through and the picot formed in this way. Continue thus and complete the Needleweaving.

Another important feature of Hardanger or Norwegian embroidery is the working of Four-sided Stitch on the diagonal. This has already been explained in the chapter on Hemstitching.

Figs. 30 and 31 show a series of motifs useful for enriching Hardanger embroidery. All are simple and easy to copy and they are always

worked over counted threads. For example, various star shapes, crosses, lozenge patterns, squares, rectangles, diamonds and other geometrical shapes worked in Satin Stitch and other simple Stitches.

Among the decorative stitches met with in Hardanger embroidery, Interlacing Stitch and Couching are particularly interesting.

Fig. 32 shows the method of working Interlacing Stitch. First of all, work a foundation of two rows of Herringbone Stitch with threads evenly crossed. After the foundation has been prepared the interlacing of the threads is carried out in two stages, as shown clearly in the illustration.

Fig. 33 shows a small Interlaced star. Make a foundation as shown in the illustration, passing the threads evenly over and under. Then the Interlacing is completed in one stage only.

Couching is very much more simple. A thread is placed over the exact diagonal of the fabric and fixed with small stitches at perfectly equal distances, that is, by counting the threads. In order to cover an area of fabric with Couching, the movement just explained is repeated and the small stitches are alternated (Fig. 34).

Fig. 35 shows a series of lines worked in three directions. These are useful either to separate patterns or to enrich the different types of decorative motifs.

The Four-sided Stitch worked diagonally is shown in the illustration, being the first on the left.

The second stitch is Four-sided Stitch worked diagonally on the wrong side, forming a series of sloping, parallel stitches on the right side.

The three horizontal lines following are very easy to copy. Two rows of oblique Satin Stitch on two threads of fabric form the first row. The second row is worked in the same way, but with a space of one thread, which is then drawn out. The third line is worked in four stages: first of all the rows on each side are worked with small upright stitches taking in two threads of fabric at a distance apart of two threads which are then cut and removed. Two rows of Stem Stitch are worked in the centre space.

In the same illustration are four vertical stitches which are easy to copy. They consist of a row of Double Stitch over four threads of material, alternating on successive lines. Herringbone Stitch joins three threads above and three threads below, The third is a simple Four-sided Stitch and the last a more open line. Here a thread is drawn out, two are left in and another one withdrawn. Four threads above are pulled together by two Back Stitches, tightly drawn up. Then with another two tightly drawn Back Stitches the two threads of fabric are drawn together. Then four threads below are taken up and pulled tightly, and then another two Back Stitches are worked over the two threads of fabric and the whole process is begun over again.

The design of the cloth, of which we show a section, is simple and very easy to work. All the embroidery stitches have been fully explained in the preceding pages, and therefore it should be

Fig. 30. Stitches and motifs for enriching Hardanger embroidery

Fig. 31. Motifs for Hardanger embroidery

Interlacing on a foundation of Herringbone Stitch

Fig. 32. (Top line): The working of two rows of Herringbone Stitch. (Middle line): The first row of Interlacing is complete and the second row has been started at the left. (Bottom line): The finished row of Interlacing

Table centre in Hardanger embroidery with a cut edge

Fig. 33. Small star worked in Interlacing

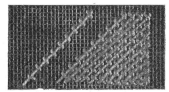

Fig. 34. Threads couched diagonally

Fig. 35. Various stitches for Hardanger embroidery

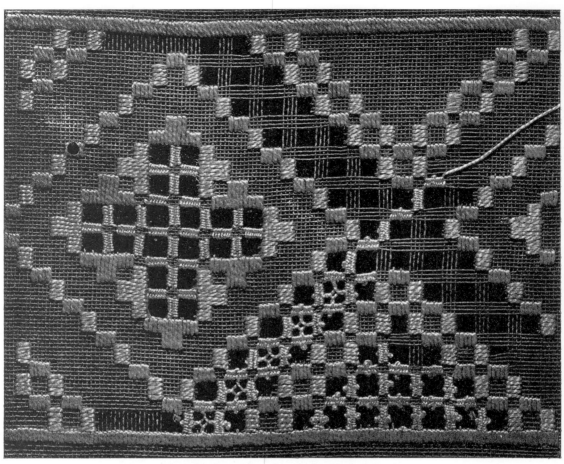

Fig. 36. Actual size detail of tablecloth border

Fig. 37. Corner of tablecloth in Hardanger embroidery

easy for the embroideress to copy them accurately. The background may be any type of thick fabric with an even weave, and the thread used is Coats Anchor Pearl Cotton.

RODI EMBROIDERY

This has nothing to do with Rodi lace, which is described in a later chapter. It is embroidery worked on rather strong fabric, in which the design, outlined with Stem Stitch, stands out on an open work background made by pulling the fabric threads together (Fig. 38).

The designs are based on leaves, flowers, and stylised animal shapes whilst the background is a simple Four-sided Stitch worked diagonally in rows to fill in the entire space. The stitches are very tightly drawn together so that the finished appearance is like a square network. Any kind of fabric with an even weave may be used for this work, although it is best worked on rather coarse fabric, since this type of embroidery is very suitable for cushions, mats, workbags, etc.

The embroidery threads used should be chosen according to the thickness of the fabric. Use Coats Anchor Stranded Cotton in one, two or three strands for the background. For the Stem Stitch outlines four, five or six strands may be used, Coats Anchor Pearl Cotton or Coats Anchor Coton à Broder. It is best to work this embroidery in a frame.

GAYANT EMBROIDERY

This is a type of Drawn-thread Work which takes its name from its place of origin, that is, from a region near Douai in France. As in Rodi embroidery, the background consists of Four-sided Stitch, drawn up very tightly; these lines of stitching, placed close together, create a network of holes, three threads by three.

The various patterns of the embroidery are worked over this background net in Needleweaving, afterwards outlined with Stem Stitch. The contrast between the close work of the pattern and the background holes gives very effective results.

The most suitable thread for working Gayant embroidery is Coats Anchor Stranded Cotton in a thickness suitable to the thickness of the material used. For the embroidered parts use Coats Anchor Coton à Broder, which is soft and has a good shine.

CYPRUS EMBROIDERY

Cyprus embroidery is a rich and elaborate form of Drawn-thread Work. The stitches used include Cording, Satin Stitch over counted threads, Buttonhole Stitch, Richelieu Stitch with bars, with and without picots. These are worked on white or natural linen cloth with a very even weave. In Cyprus embroidery the background fabric is hardly visible, since it is almost entirely covered

Fig. 38. Detail of a cushion cover in Rodi embroidery. Note how part of the embroidery is worked against a background carried out in Four-sided Stitch

Fig. 39. Table mat with border worked in Cyprus embroidery

with embroidery or cut into various types of opening, so that it often resembles lace. The edges are finished with Buttonhole Stitch or Hemstitch. Very often these are placed close together so that the hem may consist of a line of Hemstitching and Four-sided Stitch, followed by a line of Buttonhole Stitching, giving richness and beauty to the work.

Use Coats Anchor Stranded Cotton, Coats Anchor Coton à Broder or Coats Anchor Pearl Cotton for this embroidery (Fig. 39).

4 *Embroidery on Counted Threads*

CHAPTER VIII

Cross Stitch

Cross Stitch is one of the most ancient embroidery stitches, having originated, it seems, in the Coptic period.

It appears in almost all embroidery throughout the world, and especially in the national costumes of Slav and Oriental women, where it is embroidered in brilliant colours. It is a simple, easy, but effective stitch. Whilst many other embroidery stitches look better when combined with other stitches, Cross Stitch can stand alone.

As its name suggests, Cross Stitch is formed by two oblique stitches, crossing in the centre. There are two ways in which it may be worked: by making one complete stitch before going on to the next, or by making a line of oblique stitches in one direction and then completing them by making the stitches in the opposite direction (Fig. 1).

Cross Stitch requires some care in working. It is important to keep the direction of the stitches the same; that is, to make every line with the crossing from right to left, or from left to right, so that the whole surface of the work presents an even, regular appearance.

Sicilian Cross Stitch. In Italy, Cross Stitch is used particularly in Assisi embroidery, of which we shall speak later, and in that of Arezzo, as well as Sicilian embroidery. The last named consists of Cross Stitch worked on rather fine cloth over two threads of fabric. This is typical embroidery of

great delicacy which Sicilian women work with astonishing rapidity. Designs of small figures, animals, Sicilian carts and flowers are worked in bright colours on tea cloths, children's table sets, table centres and babies' bibs. The work is often finished with many coloured fringes.

Materials Required. Cross Stitch must be worked on cloth with a very even weave so that it is easy to count the threads. The most suitable embroidery threads for Cross Stitch are Coats Anchor Stranded Cotton, using from one to six strands according to the thickness of the fabric, and Coats Anchor Coton à Broder or Coats Anchor Pearl Cotton.

Cross Stitch is usually worked in colour, and often in very bright colours. The design is made on squared paper (each square corresponds to a stitch) and then this must be followed by counting carefully square by square.

Cross Stitch on Canvas. If the fabric on which the Cross Stitch is to be worked is too fine to allow for the counting of the threads, the canvas method may be used.

A piece of canvas is placed over the fabric to be embroidered and tacked securely in place, taking great care to see that the warp and weft of canvas and fabric are matching. The embroidery is then worked over the canvas threads and through the fabric lying underneath. When the work is finished

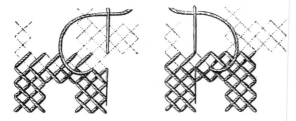

Fig. 1. Simple Cross Stitch in alternating backward and forward lines. The stitches must all lie in the same direction

Fig. 2. Cross Stitch on canvas. On the left, Cross Stitch design embroidered on canvas; on the right, after the canvas threads are removed, the design is shown on the cloth

the canvas threads, both vertical and horizontal, are withdrawn one at a time (Fig. 2).

Of the two methods mentioned for working Cross Stitch, the best is undoubtedly that of working horizontal lines with a backward and forward movement, so that the back of the work is neat and even.

Two-sided Cross Stitch. There is also a method for working Cross Stitch so that it is perfectly equal on both sides of the fabric. Fig. 3 shows the method of working this double sided Cross Stitch. The thread is attached with a small Back Stitch, which will be covered by the first stitch, and a line of stitches is worked across four threads in length and width. An oblique line is thus made both on the right side and on the wrong side of the work, proceeding either from right to left or left to right.

When the first line has been completed, the second is worked in the same way, but in the opposite direction. After working the last stitch of the second row, the third is worked by joining on to the first stitch halfway down, with a half Cross Stitch, and going on with another Cross Stitch to the beginning of the third row, which is worked like the others. The same procedure is followed for the fourth row which finally completes the line, making the embroidery exactly the same on each side of the fabric.

Although simple Cross Stitch is universally used, many countries have their own variations with particular characteristics. Some of these are described and illustrated in this chapter.

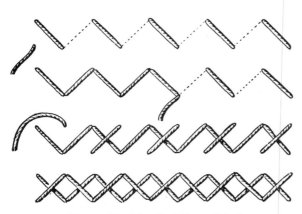

Fig. 3. Double sided Cross Stitch

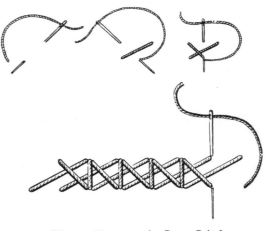

Fig. 4. Montenegrin Cross Stitch

Montenegrin Cross Stitch. This stitch is found in Southern and Eastern Europe and especially in Montenegro (Fig. 4).

The stitch is begun from a point on the material eight threads to the right and four threads higher than the spot where the thread comes out, the needle coming out four threads to the left. The thread then crosses with an oblique stitch over the first four threads. Then a third vertical stitch is made over four threads as shown in the diagram.

Slav Cross Stitch or Long-legged Cross Stitch. This is very similar to Montenegrin Cross Stitch, but is somewhat simpler. Work from left to right. The upright stitch is made six threads to the right of the spot where the thread comes out, and three threads above that level. The threads are made to cross by working a vertical stitch three threads to the left of the first. Then the first stitch is repeated (Fig. 5).

Double-back Cross Stitch or Basket Stitch. The stitch is begun by pulling the needle out on the right side of the fabric and making an upright stitch which begins six threads to the left and four threads above; another stitch is then taken to the right, two threads beyond that already made, and then another is taken by going back over four threads in width, always keeping the stitch four threads high. The working is then repeated, taking another upright stitch two threads beyond the last, going back over four threads with another upright stitch, and so on (Fig. 6).

Algerian Cross Stitch. This is worked from left to right. Three threads of fabric are taken up, and then, going down six threads, another three are taken up. The movement is recommenced, always moving one thread to the right.

Initials in Cross Stitch. Cross Stitch is still used for marking all types of linen with the initials of the owner. Where there are a number of articles of the same kind, a serial number may also be worked in order to avoid losing the articles at the laundry. The alphabets illustrated in Figs. 7 and 8 are suitable for this purpose.

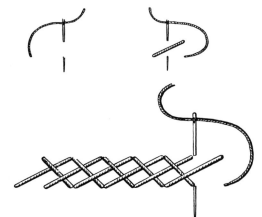

Fig. 5. Slav Cross Stitch or Long-legged Cross Stitch

Fig. 6. Double-Back Cross Stitch or Basket Stitch

Sampler worked in Cross Stitch

Sampler

Materials

Anchor Stranded Cotton: 3 skeins Dusky Pink 0896; 2 skeins each Snuff Brown 0373, Olive Green 0845, Marine Blue 0849, Silver Green 0956; 1 skein each Peat Brown 0358, Beige 0376, 0379, Marine Blue 0779, Olive Green 0843 and Dusky Pink 0894. Use 4 strands throughout.

White evenweave embroidery fabric 50 cm × 40 cm, 21 threads to 2.5 cm.

Picture frame with backing board to fit (purchase on completion of embroidery).

Milward International Range tapestry needle No. 24.

Match the centre of fabric lengthwise and widthwise with a line of basting stitches. The diagram gives a little more than half the design, centre indicated by black arrows which should coincide with the basting stitches. Each background square on the diagram represents two fabric threads. The design is worked throughout in Cross Stitch and Back Stitch worked over 2 threads of fabric. With short side of fabric facing commence the given design centrally and work following the diagram and sign key for the embroidry. To complete the design work the remaining areas in reverse using a mirror to reflect the iamge but remember that the upper half of all Cross Stitches should lie in the same direction throughout. On completion of embroidery, press on wrong side and frame as desired.

Teddy bear pictures

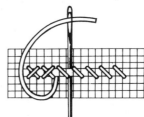

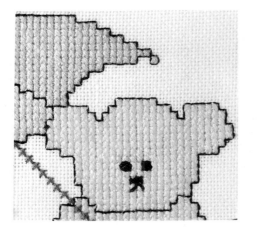

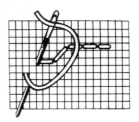

Fig. 7. Alphabet for marking household linen

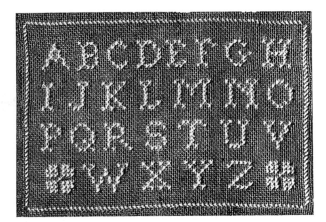

*Fig. 8. Alphabet in small letters
for marking household linen*

*Fig. 8. Alphabet in small letters
for marking household linen*

*Fig. 9. Cross stitch alphabet
worked with 3 strands of Anchor
Stranded Cotton over 2 threads of
evenweave fabric, 21 threads to
2.5 cm*

Cross Stitch and Cutwork picture

Cross Stitch and Cutwork picture

This picture combines two traditional forms of embroidery. The Cross Stitch insert may be mounted and framed as a picture on its own right. The cutwork mount may also be used as a mat where the centre is not cut away.

The Cross Stitch is worked on a 40 × 40 cm square evenweave fabric in Anchor Stranded Cotton (1 strand). The Cutwork embroidery, worked in Buttonhole Stitch using Pearl Cotton on a similar size piece of fabric.

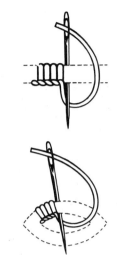

Cross Stitch Cushion

**Soft Embroidery
Stranded Cotton**

◥ - 0168

☒ - 0387

Tapisserie Wool

◥ - 0168

☒ - 0899

116

CHAPTER IX

Assisi Embroidery

Assisi, the beautiful Italian town which was the birthplace of Saint Francis, is renowned for the embroidery which bears this name. In past centuries this work was used to enrich ecclesiastical linen as well as the household articles and clothing of the peasants. Towards the beginning of this century a band of enthusiastic workers, under the guidance of Maria Bartocci Rossi assisted by her daughter Chiara, were responsible for a renewal of interest in this typical work of Assisi. Taking their inspiration from early examples preserved in the churches of the town they revived the ancient designs of stylised animals and birds and the geometrical patterns suggested by fragments of mosaic, wrought-iron work and marble inlays. Assisi embroidery is well known throughout the world.

Materials. In Assisi embroidery the background is generally worked solidly in Cross Stitch in blue or rust colour leaving the design in the background fabric. The design is often outlined with Holbein Stitch sometimes called Double Running Stitch in black or another dark colour. Since Assisi embroidery is worked by the counted threads, the cloth used must have a very even weave. It is generally of a natural colour and sometimes called "Assisi cloth". The thread used may be Coats Anchor Stranded Cotton, Coats Anchor Coton à Broder or Coats Anchor Pearl Cotton.

Method of Working Assisi Embroidery. Assisi embroidery is worked in three stages:

1. The Outlines.
2. The Background.
3. The Finishing Off of hems and edges.

1. **The Outlines.** Draw the design on squared paper. Begin the outline by working Running Stitch, taking up three threads of fabric above and three below. Work back in the opposite direction to fill in the spaces. At the same time as the outline is worked, the lines of the pattern inside the shapes should also be worked, thus completing all the linear part of the design.

2. **The Background.** When the outlines, generally worked in black, are complete, proceed with the filling-in of the background with Cross Stitch in horizontal lines. When working these lines of Cross Stitch take each one to the farthest limits of the design. Any empty spaces not included in the rows of stitching should be filled in separately.

The wrong side of Assisi Stitch should be perfectly even. Do not, therefore, carry a thread over or change the direction of the stitch.

Fig. 1 shows how to work Assisi embroidery in the necessary stages.

When the outlines follow a diagonal direction and it is impossible to make an entire Cross Stitch,

C.A.R.A., Assisi

Tea cloth worked in Assisi embroidery. The border reproduced in actual size is worked in Cross Stitch for the background, whilst the outer part of the design is worked in Double Running Stitch. The napkin is decorated with Double Running Stitch. The edging of cloth and napkin is in Four-sided Stitch with corners in tatting

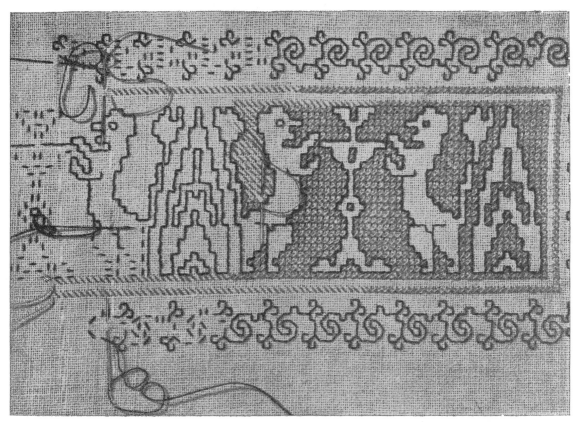

Fig. 1. The working of Assisi Embroidery Outlines in black in Holbein Stitch and background in Cross Stitch

Fig. 2. Mark indicating original Assisi work

Fig. 3. Assisi-work border

Fig. 4. Border in Assisi work

Fig. 5. Table mats in Assisi embroidery

Fig. 6. Another Assisi-work border in Cross Stitch and Holbein Stitch

Fig. 7. Cushion covers in Cross Stitch and Holbein Stitch. The first shows a hunting scene and the second is worked with a design composed of traditional animal shapes

the spaces are filled in by sloping half stitches, but it is better to plan the design so that this is not necessary.

3. The Finishing Off of Hems and Edges.

Embroidery in Assisi work is generally finished off with a hem in Four-sided Stitch. In the chapter on Hemstitching there is a full explanation, with illustrations, of this stitch. In Assisi work the hem, folded over and worked in Four-sided Stitch, should be very small and look like a corded edge, since it is not really folded but rolled tightly between the first finger and thumb of the left hand, as the work proceeds. This hem is then caught down and often decorated with whipping in the same colour as the embroidery. The corners of cloths are sometimes decorated with three small tassels, each of which is made by passing the thread eight or ten times through a hole in the Four-sided Stitch and round the first finger of the left hand, held always at the same distance from the work. The tassel is then fastened off with two or three stitches into the fabric.

All, or most, Assisi embroidery, worked in its place of origin, bears a small Franciscan cross in one corner, or the heraldic emblem of the town of Assisi, a lion rampant and a cross (Fig. 2). The illustrations on pages 117 to 121 show examples of Assisi embroidery.

CHAPTER X

Holbein Stitch or Double Running Stitch

This stitch is worked on the counted thread of the fabric. In Tuscany it is also called "Volterrano" Stitch because in the region of Volterra it is used to embroider tablecloths, napkins, blouses, and children's clothes. At Assisi it is called "St. Chiara" stitch and it is, as we mentioned earlier, the complementary decorative stitch in Assisi embroidery. It consists of Running Stitch worked

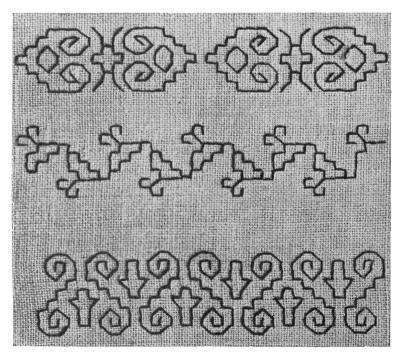

Fig. 1. Borders in Holbein Stitch

Tea cloth worked on natural-coloured linen in Holbein or Double Running Stitch

in both directions. Three or four threads of fabric are taken up and an equal number left and the spaces are filled in on the second row, by

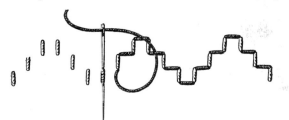

Fig. 2. Working of Holbein or Double Running Stitch

passing under the stitches already worked and over the empty spaces (Fig. 2). The Running Stitch may be worked horizontally, vertically, or diagonally, according to the design, and if the embroidery is well done, the wrong side of the work will be just like the right side.

As for all work on counted threads, Holbein or Double Running Stitch requires a very evenly woven fabric which is not too fine. The most suitable threads for the embroidery are Coats Anchor Stranded Cotton, Coats Anchor Coton à Broder or Coats Anchor Pearl Cotton. It is usual to use black or some dark colour for this embroidery.

Cartotto Maria, Milan

Runner for table or chest. The same design is repeated on the opposite end of the runner. The embroidery is worked in brown on natural-coloured fabric

*Fig. 3. Borders with corners
suitable for table linen*

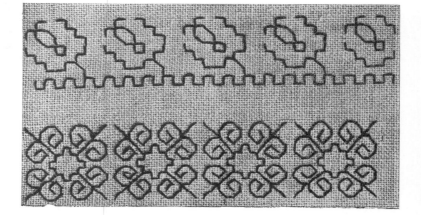

*Figs. 4 and 5. Borders worked in
Holbein Stitch*

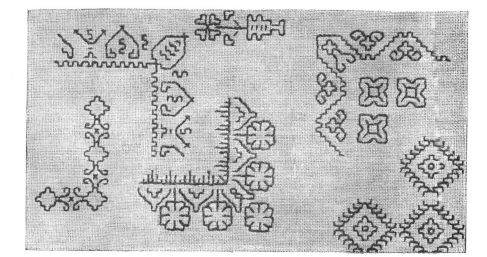

Figs. 6 and 7. Corners and narrow borders for various uses

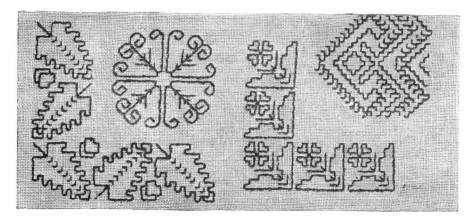

More suggestions for using Holbein Stitch

Figs. 8 and 9. Borders and corners in Holbein Stitch

Border for tea cloth embroidered in Holbein Stitch and Cross Stitch on natural-coloured linen

C.A.R.A., Assisi

CHAPTER XI

Filling Stitches

Although some embroideries can be carried out successfully in one stitch others require a great number of stitches in order to give variety of line and texture in the interpretation of a design. The many embroidered fillings given in this chapter will suggest ways in which background spaces and large areas in a design may be treated.

The modern Italian embroideries illustrated are all carried out in white on fine white organdie with great technical skill. In these, the embroidered fillings of many different kinds are used to enrich parts of the designs. Sometimes extra layers of organdie are applied to give more opaque areas and Satin Stitch is skilfully worked so that the play of light and shade gives variety to the work.

For such embroideries as these use Coats Anchor Stranded Cotton and Coats Anchor Cotton à Broder or Coats Anchor Pearl Cotton.

The embroidered fillings given in this chapter include Drawn or Pulled Fabric Stitches as well as more solid fillings worked in Satin Stitch over counted threads. The Pulled Fabric Stitches differ from Drawn Thread Work in that the background threads are pulled tightly together in forming the stitches and not withdrawn from the fabric as in Drawn-thread Work.

Fig. 1. This is sometimes called Rodi Stitch. Proceed as for diagonal Four-sided Stitch. Take four threads of fabric with a vertical stitch. Go back into the same stitch for a second time and draw out the needle four stitches more to the left. Make a horizontal stitch and go back into the same stitch for a second time, coming out four threads below. All the lines are worked in the same way.

Fig. 2. This is worked in four stages. Take four threads of fabric with a horizontal stitch, going down with the needle to four threads below the first stitch and making a vertical stitch in that position. Then go down four threads to the left and four threads below making a diagonal stitch and so on. The second row of stitching, which is like the first, closes the square and covers the diagonal stitch a second time. On the third row, start from one corner of the square with a diagonal stitch, then make a vertical stitch and another diagonal stitch, one horizontal and another diagonal, which joins the corner of the second square with a double stitch. The fourth row is like the second, therefore, in effect, the third and fourth rows only are repeated.

Fig. 3. Filling worked in small squares of five Satin Stitches over six threads in height. Work diagonally, moving the square down by three threads.

Fig. 4. Filling in Satin Stitch over an area of 12 threads both in height and width. Inside the diamonds the threads are pulled together and joined in twos with Cross Stitch. Use a thicker thread for the Satin Stitches and a finer one for the Cross Stitches.

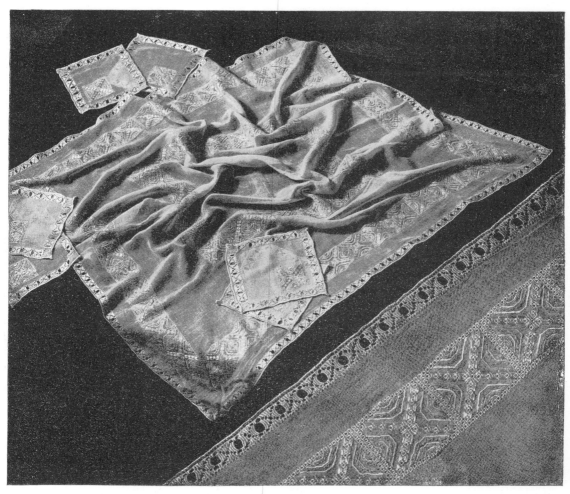

Afternoon cloth in natural-coloured linen, worked in Coats Anchor Stranded Cotton in natural

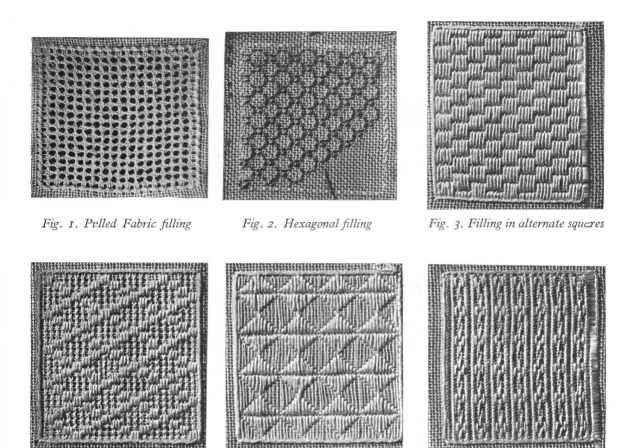

Fig. 1. Pulled Fabric filling   *Fig. 2. Hexagonal filling*   *Fig. 3. Filling in alternate squares*

Fig. 4. Filling in Satin Stitch and   *Fig. 5. Filling in Satin Stitch*   *Fig. 6. Filling in vertical lines of*
Cross Stitch   *using threads of different thickness*   *Cording and Satin Stitch*

Fig. 5. Filling worked in Satin Stitch placed vertically over twelve threads in height and fourteen in width. The variation in texture is made by working the stitch in threads of different thickness.

Fig. 6. Background consisting of double vertical lines in Cording over two threads of fabric. Between the double lines, single Satin Stitches over four threads are worked to form a pattern.

Fig. 7. Vertical lines of Satin Stitch over four threads of fabric every twelve threads. Four rows of slanting stitches make a zig-zag filling in between the vertical lines.

Fig. 8. Groups of two Satin Stitches.

Fig. 9. Single Satin Stitches worked to form a trellis or Diamond.

Fig. 10. Each triangle consists of five stitches taken over an area of eight threads by five threads.

An original design by L. Righetti showing women's costume throughout the ages. Each figure is separated from its neighbour by a wide Satin Stitch. The enlarged details which are also reproduced give a clear idea of the rich effect which can be achieved with filling stitches and Satin Stitch. Under each figure there is a small panel decorated in the same style as the costume and bearing the date (pages 133-4).

This embroidery is intended for the decoration of a long, narrow table so that the design is planned to look right from each side of the table. The runner would be placed under plate glass.

Fig. 11. Satin Stitches over four threads of fabric in steps of one thread both increasing and decreasing.

131

Fig. 12. A closely filled in background worked in Satin Stitch.

Fig. 13. Filling consisting of Satin Stitch over an area of seven threads in width and eight in height. Between the geometrical shapes, work pulled stitches, each joining three threads.

Fig. 14. Filling consisting of Satin Stitch over four threads in width and six in height. When these are complete, join them with stitches which thread under the rectangles without entering the fabric. These are worked alternately one above and one below each line.

Fig. 15. Satin Stitch filling over an area of five threads in width and eight in height.

Fig. 16. Filling with threads withdrawn. Two drawn threads, two left in. Work Cross Stitches backwards and forwards diagonally, first in one direction and then in the other.

Fig. 17. Filling consisting of diagonal lines, using Holbein Stitch in vertical or horizontal lines over an area of six stitches both in width and height.

Fig. 18. Filling with pulled threads consisting of double Cross Stitches worked over an area of four threads in width and height.

Fig. 19. Background consisting of Satin Stitch worked diagonally, over an area of six threads in width and height.

Fig. 20. Pulled Fabric Filling consisting of horizontal lines of stitches joining two threads above and two below a line of four threads.

Fig. 21. Filling consisting of lines of Cording over two threads of fabric worked vertically and horizontally. In each square work five stitches all starting from the same point.

Fig. 22. Satin Stitch filling over an area of six threads in width and eight in height.

Fig. 23. Pulled Fabric filling over an area of eight threads in width and height.

Fig. 24. Pulled Fabric filling over an area of five threads in both directions worked both horizontally and vertically. Complete the stitching in one direction and then work the opposite way.

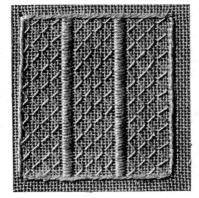

Fig. 7 (left). Filling with lines of Satin Stitch

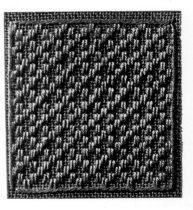

Fig. 8 (right). Filling with groups of Satin Stitch

Fig. 9 (left). A trellis pattern

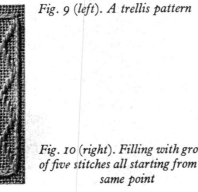

Fig. 10 (right). Filling with groups of five stitches all starting from the same point

Fig. 25. Pulled Fabric filling in squares of Shadow Stitch over an area of eight threads in width and nine in height, alternated with lines of Cording worked over three threads in height and eight in width.

Fig. 26. Pulled Fabric filling consisting of three rows of Cording over three threads of fabric worked vertically and then horizontally. Work over an area of nine threads in width and height.

Fig. 27. Filling with threads withdrawn. Two drawn out and four left in in width and height. Overcasting worked in each small square, passing the thread through the centre.

Fig. 28. Filling consisting of double vertical lines of Cording worked on two threads every six. Between the rows, Back Stitches pulled tight in order to form small holes.

Fig. 29. Filling with threads withdrawn. Two drawn out and four left in place, both in width and height. Overcast the four horizontal and vertical threads in pairs. Pass diagonal threads through each square.

Fig. 30. Filling with threads withdrawn. Two drawn out and two left in. Overcast two threads horizontally and vertically. Pass across a diagonal thread, making a wheel or web at the intersection of the threads.

Fig. 31. A herringbone pattern worked in Cording over two threads over an area of seven threads in width and height.

Fig. 32. Pulled Fabric Filling in Cording over five threads of fabric in vertical and horizontal

Enlarged detail of some of the figures decorating the table runner illustrated

Fig. 11. Filling in zig-zag lines

Fig. 12. A closely filled background

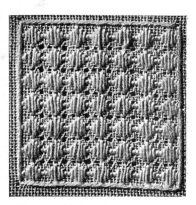

Fig. 13. Diamond shapes alternating with pulled threads

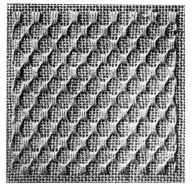

Fig. 14. Filling in threaded Satin Stitch

Fig. 15. Satin Stitch filling

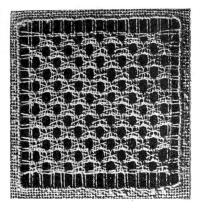

Fig. 16. Drawn-thread Work filling

directions over an area of ten threads in width and height. Work diagonally.

Fig. 33. Filling consisting of six Satin Stitches and three rows of Cording.

Fig. 34. Filling with threads withdrawn. Four drawn out and four left in. At the intersection of the threads work seven sloping stitches forming a small square. Take the thread across the empty space. This thread will then be crossed with the thread of the next row.

Fig. 35. A filling imitating rush-work, carried out in Satin Stitch worked vertically and horizontally over an area of seven threads in both width

and height. First work the horizontal lines, and then those in the opposite direction.

Fig. 36. Pulled Fabric filling consisting of five vertical Cording Stitches alternating on succeeding lines.

Fig. 37. Filling worked over an area of ten threads by ten. Work the corners, formed by five Satin Stitches over 1, 2, 3, 4 and 5 threads respectively on each side. At the centre of each square work eight pulled stitches forming a small eyelet.

On pages 139 to 141 is shown a very original table runner. The design is inspired by the Opera. The embroidery is worked in white on white organdie with great technical skill.

135

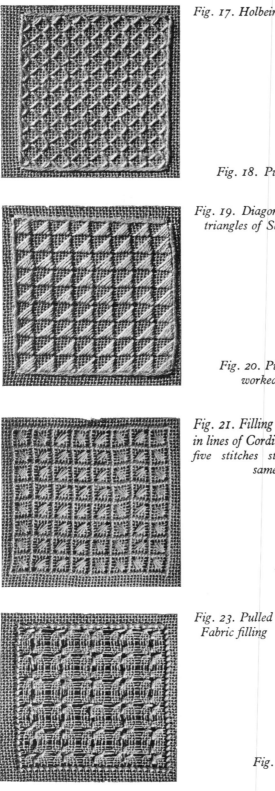

Fig. 17. Holbein Stitch filling

Fig. 18. Pulled Fabric filling

Fig. 19. Diagonally worked
triangles of Satin Stitch

Fig. 20. Pulled Fabric filling
worked horizontally

Fig. 21. Filling in squares worked
in lines of Cording. In each square
five stitches starting from the
same point

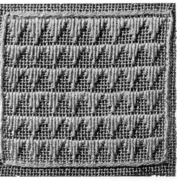

Fig. 22. Filling in
Satin Stitches

Fig. 23. Pulled
Fabric filling

Fig. 24. Pulled Fabric
filling

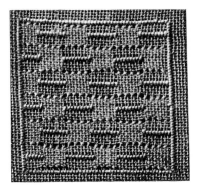

Fig. 25. Filling in squares of Shadow Stitch and Cording

Fig. 26. Pulled Fabric filling worked in Cording

Fig. 27. Filling with threads withdrawn

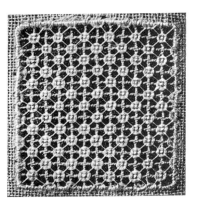

Fig. 28. Filling in vertical lines of Cording and Back Stitch

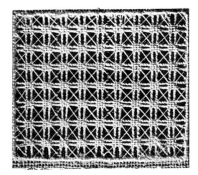

Fig. 29. Drawn-thread filling

Fig. 30. Drawn-thread filling

Fig. 31. Herringbone pattern worked in Cording

Fig. 32. Filling in Cording with the threads pulled tightly

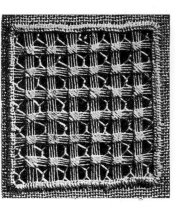

Fig. 33. Background in squares
of Satin Stitch and Cording

Fig. 34. Drawn-thread filling

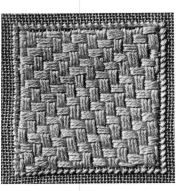

Fig. 35. A filling imitating
rush work

Fig. 36. Pulled Fabric filling

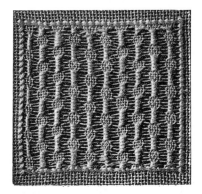

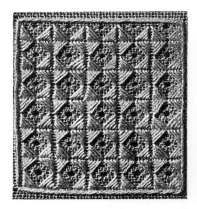

Fig. 37. Diagonally worked
Satin Stitch and Eyelets

Table runner with original design based on scenes and characters from operas

Ist. Dell'Addolorata, Milan

Details of the table runner

Actual size reproductions of details from the table runner

Detail of table centre. Many stitches are used including Satin Stitch and a great variety of filling stitches. Extra layers of organdie are applied by means of Cording

Table centre in organdie embroidered in Coats Anchor Stranded Cotton and Coats Anchor Coton à Broder

CHAPTER XII

Canvas Stitches

The stitches illustrated in this chapter are all suitable for working upon canvas and the finished embroidery is excellent for enriching any object which will have to withstand hard wear. Chair seats, stool tops and kneelers may all be worked in canvas embroidery and even rugs and carpets are successful when carried out in thick wool upon a coarse canvas.

In Elizabethan times huge table carpets were worked for the purpose of covering tables and some interesting examples can be seen in our museums. During the seventeenth and eighteenth centuries the upholstered chairs of the period were covered with canvas work—sometimes sets of chair coverings were worked each showing some variation in the design.

Canvas stitches may be worked upon single or double mesh canvas—the chief characteristic of this embroidery being that the canvas background is completely covered by the stitches. The work is usually carried out in wool of a thickness suitable for the canvas which is used. Cotton threads are also successful for some types of canvas embroidery. Coats Anchor Stranded Cotton may be used in any desired thickness from two to six strands at a time. Coats Anchor Soft Embroidery cotton resembles wool in appearance and Coats Anchor Tapisserie Wool is pleasant to work on a canvas with an appropriate mesh.

It is advisable to frame up the canvas before starting to work as this helps considerably to prevent stretching. The design may be made on squared paper, letting one square represent one stitch. Use tapestry needles for working upon canvas as these have rounded points and therefore do not split either the mesh of the canvas or the working thread.

Upright Gobelin Stitch. The design must first of all be "trammed", that is, horizontal threads in the appropriate colours are passed over the design as shown in the illustration (Fig. 1). When this is

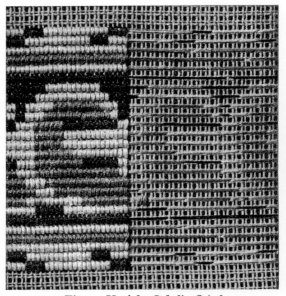

Fig. 1. Upright Gobelin Stitch

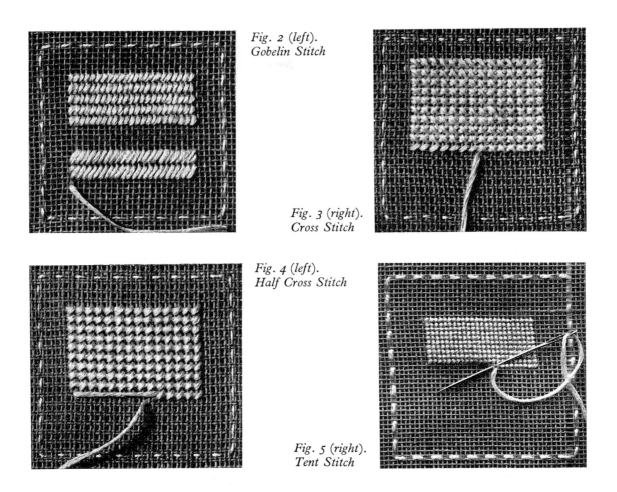

done, cover the threads with straight up and down stitches working from left to right or right to left.

Gobelin Stitch. For the oblique stitch the same procedure is followed, but, instead of covering the "trammed" threads with straight stitches, these are covered with oblique stitches (Fig. 2). The upper row of stitches takes in two threads of canvas, the lower row, three, but both are only one thread wide.

Cross Stitch. This stitch has already been described in detail. Work in two stages, backwards and forwards, taking care that the crossing of the stitches always takes the same direction (Fig. 3).

Half Cross Stitch. When the thread is too thick for a complete Cross Stitch, a half stitch is made (Fig. 4).

Tent Stitch. Very fine work can be carried out with this stitch and it is very beautiful in its effect, especially when using a variety of colours. Figure 5 shows this stitch very clearly.

Alternating Cross Stitch. This consists of a lengthened Cross Stitch worked over six threads of canvas in height and two in width, and a small Cross Stitch over two threads in height and width, at the centre of the preceding stitches and alternating with these (Fig. 6).

Double Cross Stitch or Smyrna Cross Stitch. This consists of a simple Cross Stitch worked on four threads both in height and width. A second Crossing Stitch is worked over this (Fig. 7).

Encroaching Gobelin Stitch. This may be worked from left to right or right to left. Take four threads of canvas in a vertical direction. On the following line, work in the same way, entering into the previous row (Fig. 8).

Herringbone Filling or Stem Stitch. Take the thread diagonally over four threads in height and width, working from above below and vice versa. When one line is complete, repeat the process in the opposite direction. At the intersections of the diagonal stitches, Back Stitch may be worked in a contrasting colour (Fig. 9).

Fig. 10 shows how a stitch fixing down the diagonals with the same thread may be worked. This is worked immediately after the diagonal stitch.

Hungarian Stitch. This consists of vertical stitches of different lengths. It is worked in horizontal rows as shown clearly in Fig. 11.

Fig. 12 shows a variation of Hungarian Stitch.

Diagonal Stitch. This is worked diagonally with five stitches, of which the first takes up one thread of canvas and the longest, the third, three threads (Fig. 13).

Variation of Diagonal Stitch. This is very easy to copy from the illustration shown in Fig. 14.

Parisian Stitch. This is worked in horizontal rows; it consists of alternating long and short stitch (Fig. 15).

Web Stitch. This gives the impression of a smooth woven fabric. It is worked by taking a thread in a perfectly diagonal direction and fixing it down with small stitches. On the following line the stitches are alternated (Fig. 16).

Fig. 6 (left). Alternating Cross Stitch

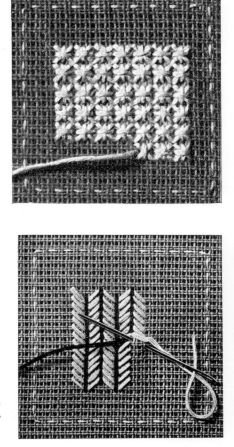

Fig. 7 (right). Double Cross Stitch or Smyrna Cross Stitch

Fig. 8 (left). Encroaching Gobelin

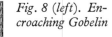

Fig. 9 (right). Herringbone Filling or Stem Stitch

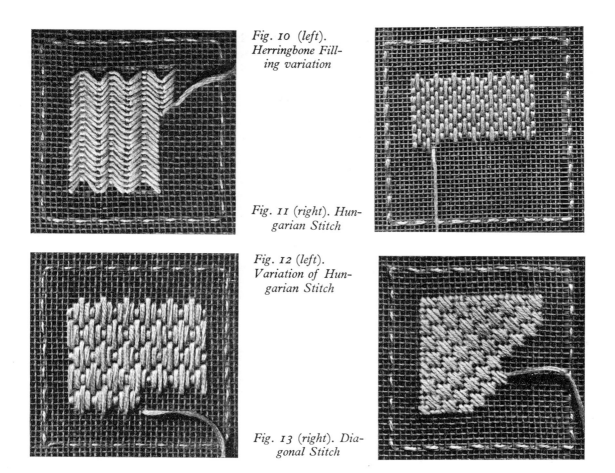

Fig. 10 (left). Herringbone Filling variation

Fig. 11 (right). Hungarian Stitch

Fig. 12 (left). Variation of Hungarian Stitch

Fig. 13 (right). Diagonal Stitch

Mosaic Stitch. This is worked diagonally. It consists of rows of long stitches worked over four threads in length and width alternating with rows of short stitches worked over two threads in both directions (Fig. 17).

Florence Stitch. This is similar to Mosaic Stitch and is also worked diagonally. Each row consists of short and long stitches worked alternately (Fig. 18).

Alternating Stitch. This is worked horizontally as shown in Fig. 19. This stitch is very suitable for filling in spaces with graduated shading.

Long Stitch or Straight Stitch Filling. Work as shown in Fig. 20.

Variations of Long Stitch or Straight Stitch. These are shown clearly in the illustrations (Figs. 21 and 22).

Crossing Stitch. Work from top to bottom and vice versa diagonally over four threads of canvas, both in height and width. Repeat the same movement on the following line crossing the first two threads of this over the last two threads of the preceding row (Fig. 23).

Crossing Stitch Variation. This stitch is also worked from top to bottom as shown in the illustration (Fig. 24).

Crossing Stitch Variation. Take six threads of canvas in height and two in width, then place the needle in again two threads below, making a crossing stitch (Fig. 25).

Crossing Stitch Variation. Take four threads of canvas in width and two in height. On the following line the diagonal threads are placed in the opposite direction and take up four threads,

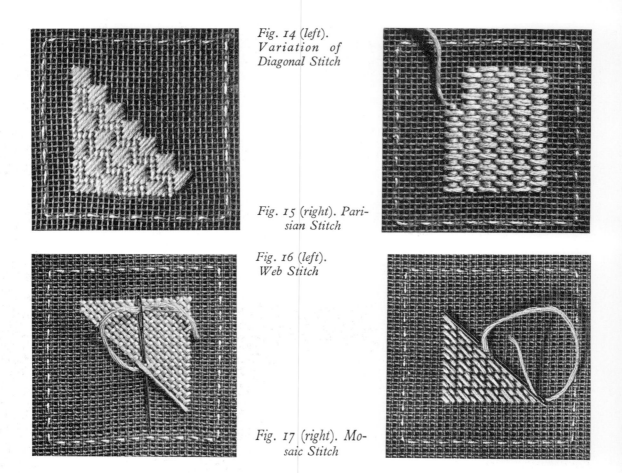

Fig. 14 (left).
*Variation of
Diagonal Stitch*

Fig. 15 (right). Pari-
sian Stitch

Fig. 16 (left).
Web Stitch

Fig. 17 (right). Mo-
saic Stitch

two of which belong to the previous line
(Fig. 26).

Back Stitch Filling. This is worked in two
stages. First a row of Back Stitch over two threads
of canvas in a horizontal direction, then a line of
vertical Back Stitches (Fig. 27).

Ray Filling. Groups of five stitches are worked
over four threads of canvas always starting from
the same point. Note that the direction of the
stitches is alternated for every group (Fig. 28).

Knitting Stitch. Illustrations 29 and 30 show
Knitting Stitch, so-called because of the similarity
of appearance to Stocking Stitch.

Fig. 29 shows the stitch worked on four threads
in height and two in width. It is worked from
bottom to top and back again and the needle
passes horizontally under two threads of canvas to

take up the same two threads again, four threads
higher. In the example illustrated Running Stitch
is also used in a contrasting colour.

Fig. 30 shows Knitting Stitch closely worked in
horizontal lines over four threads in width and
two in height. This stitch has given rise to a very
attractive type of embroidery in which cushion
covers, rugs and carpets are worked in very bright
colours and with distinctive geometrical designs. It
is also called Kelim Stitch.

Fig. 31. A background of squares worked in
horizontal and vertical lines of small slanting
stitches. In the centre of the squares are small stars
worked with eight stitches.

Jacquard Stitch. This stitch, formed by two
alternating rows, is very suitable for large areas.
One row in diagonal stitches over four threads
both in width and height, the other in smaller
stitches worked over two threads (Fig. 32).

Fig. 18 (left).
Florence Stitch

Fig. 19 (right).
Alternating Stitch

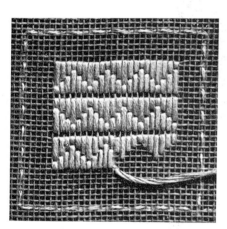

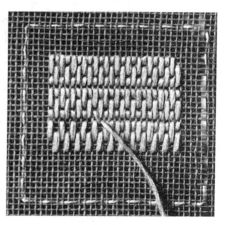

Fig. 20 (left). Long
Stitch or Straight
Stitch filling

Fig. 21 (right). Vari-
ation of Long Stitch
or Straight Stitch

Fig. 22 (left).
Another variation
of Long Stitch
or Straight Stitch

Fig. 23 (right). Cros-
sing Stitch

Fig. 24 (left). Variation of Crossing Stitch

Fig. 25 (right). Variation of Crossing Stitch

Fig. 26 (left). Variation of Crossing Stitch

Fig. 27 (right). Back Stitch filling

Fig. 28 (left). Ray filling

Fig. 29 (right). Knitting Stitch

Fig. 33 shows the same stitch worked on single mesh canvas.

The following stitches make interesting backgrounds for cushion covers, covers for benches and chair seats.

More and varied examples are shown in the coloured illustration. All these stitches are described and illustrated in this chapter.

Florentine Stitch. The most famous examples using this stitch are the coverings of the chairs in the Palazzo Vecchio in Florence.

Generally Florentine Stitch is worked in gradations of tone, from dark to light or vice versa, in colours such as bright red, blue, old gold, or green, with a striking decorative effect. The stitch is worked vertically and varies in height to form wavy lines of pattern. On successive lines the needle is replaced in the same holes, following the wavy line with the next gradation of tone. Figs. 34 and 35 show two different types of Florentine Stitch.

Fig. 36. Filling with lines of small straight stitches over two threads in height, forming a diamond pattern. At the centre there are small cubes in various colours.

Fig. 37. Background in small straight stitches over three threads of canvas, forming small lozenge shapes.

Fig. 31. Stars worked on a squared background

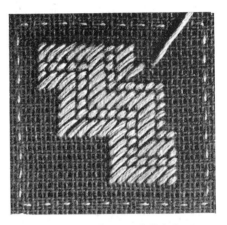

Fig. 32. Jacquard Stitch

Fig. 30. Kelim Stitch. (Variation of Knitting Stitch)

Fig. 33. Variation of Jacquard Stitch

Fig. 38. Filling consisting of three vertical stitches over four threads of canvas worked in one colour, and three more stitches worked in the opposite direction in a contrasting colour.

Fig. 39. Filling worked in vertical stitches over three threads in height, alternated on successive lines. The design can easily be copied from the illustration.

Fig. 40. A honeycomb filling composed of two vertical stitches over six threads and two diagonal stitches of two threads each forming hexagons. The centres may be worked in a contrasting colour.

Canvas embroidery, even when worked on a frame, tends to pull diagonally. The fault may be rectified in the following way. Place the embroidery right side down on a clean board and pin out to the original rectangular shape with drawing pins. Keep the pins well away from the embroidered area as they may leave rust marks. Damp the back of the embroidery and leave it to dry thoroughly before removing from the board.

When beginning an important piece of work see that enough threads have been purchased. After a period of time there may be a slight difference in the colour of the threads.

Fig. 34. Florentine Stitch

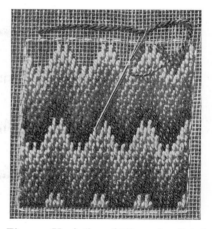

Fig. 35. Variation of Florentine Stitch

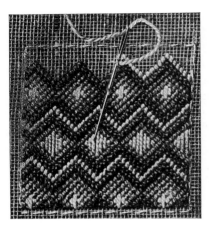

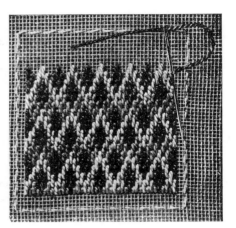

Fig. 36 (left). Dia-
mond pattern filling

Fig. 37 (right).
Lozenge filling

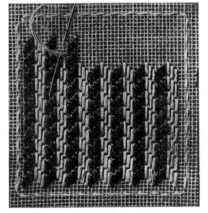

Fig. 38. Filling in vertical lines

Fig. 39 (left). Lozenge
pattern worked in
vertical stitches

Fig. 40 (right). Honey-
comb background

153

*Church kneeler design
for Wells Cathedral*

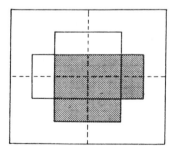

Anchor Tapisserie Wool: 22 skeins 0860; 14 skeins 0402; 1 hank or 6 skeins 0862; 4 skeins 0309; 1 skein each 0264, 0279 and 0848.

69 cm double thread tapestry canvas, 10 holes to 2.5 cm, 60 cm wide.

1 Milward International Range tapestry needle No. 18.

Piece of furnishing velvet to match, or tailor's linen 36 cm × 43 cm.

Filling—Foam chips, Kapok or pad to fit.

The finished size of the kneeler is approximately 30 × 38 × 9 cm deep.

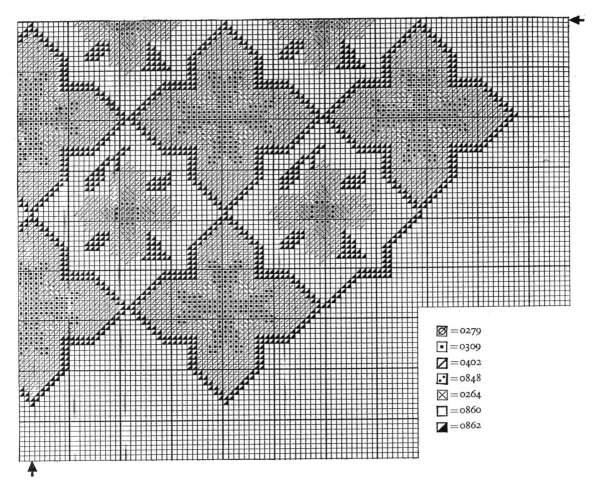

⊘	= 0279
⊡	= 0309
◪	= 0402
⊡	= 0848
⊠	= 0264
☐	= 0860
◪	= 0862

The centre of the canvas should already be marked. Each background square represents the double thread of the canvas. The above diagram also gives the right-hand quarter of the design, centre indicated by black arrows, which should coincide with the basting stitches. Commence centrally and work the given quarter. Repeat on other three quarters to correspond.

Norweave Embroidery

This style of embroidery originated in Norway where it is known as Åkle embroidery and is extremely popular in the Norwegian homes of today.

The designs are built up from 'blocks' of satin stitches, which can vary in number, and the length depends upon whether a double thread or single thread canvas is used.

The blocks consist of four Satin Stitches over four threads of single thread canvas (A) or three double Satin Stitches over three double threads of double thread canvas (B). The blocks are worked side by side to form horizontal lines of stitchery across the entire canvas (C). This formation must be kept to maintain the characteristics of this style of embroidery.

Satin Stitch may be worked from right to left or left to right. When worked on canvas, if the canvas is correctly stretched on the frame, it is impossible to make the stitch in one movement, although for the purpose of the diagrams the stitch is shown in this way. With a little experience, speed and regularity of stitch can be obtained by using both hands. The method is as follows: with right hand on top, insert the needle downwards through the canvas and pull the needle through with the left hand. With the left hand, push the needle upwards through the canvas and pull the needle up and out with the right hand (vice versa if you are left handed). Diagram D shows Satin Stitch worked over four threads of single thread canvas and diagram E shows Satin Stitch worked twice into each hole over three double threads of double thread canvas to form double Satin Stitch.

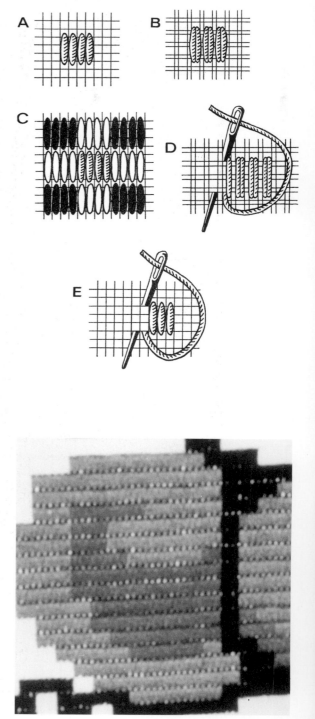

156

Norweave design for pouffe
Worked in Anchor Tapisserie Wool on 70 cm
square double thread tapestry canvas, 10 holes to
2.5 cm.

5 *Embroidery upon Delicate Fabrics*

CHAPTER XIII

Embroidery upon Organdie

Organdie is one of the most delightful fabrics upon which to embroider and has become increasingly popular in recent years. This work is very attractive when carried out in white threads upon white organdie or in any self-colour scheme. Interesting effects can be achieved by applying extra layers of organdie in order to increase the density of the background fabric and net and tulle may be used in the same way to give greater delicacy to the design.

The illustration (Fig. 3) shows a tray cloth worked by the Countess Pia di Valmarana from a design by Vittorio Zecchin and another interesting piece of work, also carried out on organdie, is reproduced in Fig. 5. This design, inspired by the four seasons, is worked mainly in Satin Stitch using Coats Anchor Stranded Cotton. The coloured embroidery on white organdie is worked in tones of pink for Spring, golden yellow for Summer, rust red for Autumn, and grey for Winter. The embroidery illustrated in Fig. 1 was worked in Coats Anchor Stranded Cotton in white using Satin Stitch and Stem Stitch.

The christening robe (Fig. 4) is a superb example of design and craftsmanship. This beautiful old embroidery is worked on fine linen lawn.

Embroidery on organdie may be worked in the hand, but it is generally advisable to use a frame. Coats Anchor Stranded Cotton is a very suitable thread for this work as the number of strands may be selected according to the effect required.

Method of Applying Organdie to the Background. Trace the design on to the organdie background and frame up in the usual way. On another piece of organdie trace the parts of the design to be applied. Cut out these sections, leaving a margin of about half an inch all round, and lay them in position on the back of the fabric. Two, three or even more layers may be used if necessary. Take great care to match the straight threads of background fabric and applied shapes. Fix securely by means of tacking and then outline the design with small Running Stitches passing through all the layers of organdie. Cover the Running Stitches with Cording.

With a pair of very sharp scissors, cut away the projecting edges and complete the design by working any other embroidery stitches. Fig. 2 shows an embroidery of this type. The figures are applied in organdie attached by means of Cording.

Work on Double Organdie. (Illustrated in Fig. 8.) Trace the whole design on to a piece of organdie and place this over another piece of the same size, taking great care to see that the straight threads of both pieces match exactly. Tack the two pieces together. Work round all the lines of the design with small Running Stitches passing through both layers of organdie. Cover the Running Stitches with Cording or Buttonhole Stitch, taking care not to pucker the fabric by pulling the stitches too

Fig. 1. *White organdie cloth embroidered in Coats Anchor Stranded Cotton.*
(Technical School of Matelica (Macerata).)

Fig. 2. *Table runner in*
white organdie

159

tightly. When this outlining is complete, cut away the fabric on the back with very sharp, pointed scissors, leaving the upper layer intact. Other stitches may be worked on the single organdie after the under layer has been cut away.

Piave Embroidery. Some interesting modern embroideries have been carried out at the Marta Balbi Valier School at Piave di Soligo. In these embroideries organdie is combined with tulle and both fabrics are often richly decorated. Sometimes the organdie is cut away leaving the tulle uncovered and sometimes it is left so that the tulle shows through the organdie. A great variety of filling stitches is used and the outlining is carried out in Cording.

The two illustrations, Figs. 6 and 7, show details of a tablecloth from the Marta Balbi Valier workroom. This was exhibited at the 7th Triennale Exhibition in Milan. The more opaque parts consist of layers of organdie applied to the background by means of Cording. The dresses of the two figures are in tulle worked with stars and dots and lines of Cording which suggest drapery.

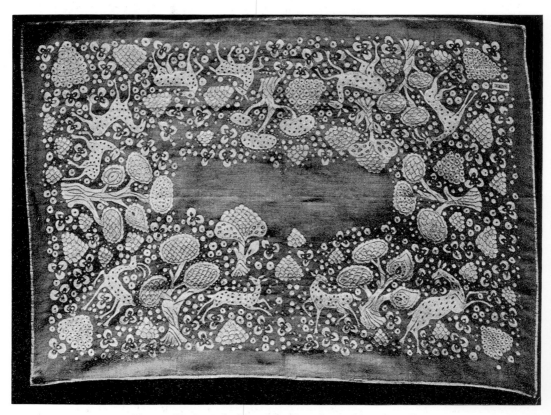

Fig. 3. Cloth worked in white thread on white organdie

Fig. 4. Christening robe in fine white linen lawn embroidered in Satin Stitch, French Knots, Stem Stitch, Cording and many filling stitches

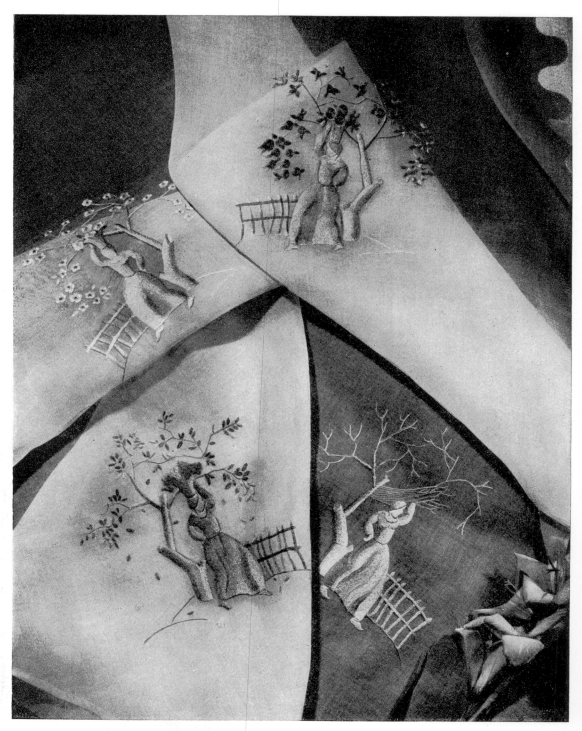

Fig. 5. Cloth, "The Four Seasons", embroidered in shades of camellia pink for Spring, golden yellow for Summer, autumn leaf rust for Autumn and grey for Winter. (Technical School of St. Caterina da Siena, Milan.)

Fig. 6 Example of Piave embroidery

Fig. 7. Example of Piave embroidery

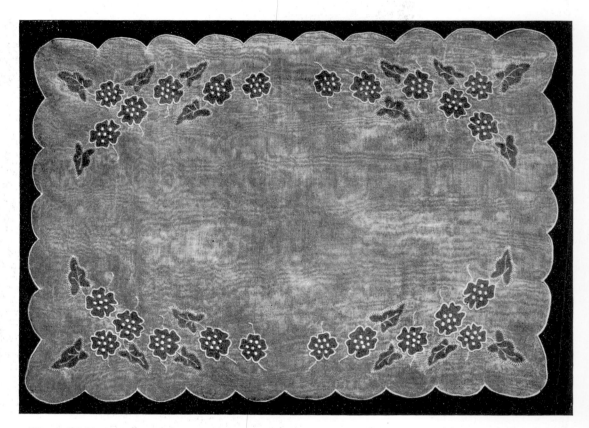

Fig. 8. Embroidery on double organdie. The design is outlined with Cording and Buttonhole Stitch, and then cut away on the underside

Richly worked cloth for a round table. The floral motif shown here is repeated at regular intervals. The background fabric is a very fine linen lawn and the embroidery, in white, is carried out in various filling stitches, Satin Stitch, Shadow Stitch and Pulled Fabric Stitches. This cloth is worked in Coats Anchor Stranded Cotton

CHAPTER XIV

Shadow Stitch

Shadow work is carried out on transparent or very fine fabrics in Double Back Stitch, which is a variation of Herringbone Stitch. The crossing threads of the stitch lie on the back of the fabric, so giving to the worked areas a more opaque quality. Organdie, fine linen lawn and muslin, crêpe de chine and nylon are all suitable fabrics for this embroidery which may be used for babies' and children's dresses, blouses and lingerie, table and dressing table mats, lamp shades and curtains.

The most suitable thread for the embroidery is Coats Anchor Stranded Cotton using one or two strands according to the type of background fabric. Although white thread is most often used upon a white background fabric, colours are very successful and give variety to the work.

Method for carrying out Shadow Work. The designs used for this embroidery have their own particular characteristics, as the decoration is often worked between two parallel lines.

Embroider on the right side of the fabric with the work in a frame. Double Back Stitch is worked, very evenly, passing alternately from one side of the design to the other so that the threads cross on the back of the fabric (Figs. 1 and 2). On curves, the stitches must be smaller and closer on the inside of the curve and slightly wider apart and larger on the outside. In any case, care should be

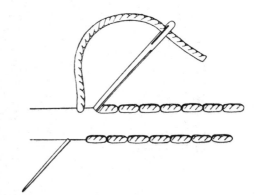

Fig. 1. Double Back Stitch; worked on right side of fabric. 1st stage

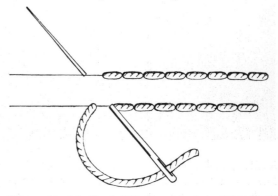

Fig. 2. Double Back Stitch; worked on right side of fabric. 2nd stage

taken not to slope the stitches too much, but make them always perpendicular to their base.

For less important embroideries, work in the hand on the wrong side of the fabric. Trace the design on to the wrong side of the fabric and work with a very close and even Herringbone Stitch (Fig. 3), so that, on the right side, a double row of Back Stitch appears.

Many other surface and filling stitches may be used with the Shadow Work.

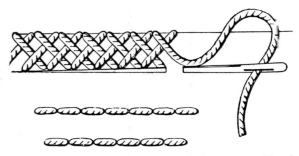

Fig. 3. Herringbone Stitch, worked on wrong side of fabric and showing also the right side of the stitch, which is Double Back Stitch

Shadow Work Tablecloth. Instructions for making see overleaf

Illustrations 4, 5 and 6 show the method of carrying out Shadow Work. In Fig. 5, which represents the back of the work, it can be seen that the stitches filling in the leaves are divided by veins worked on the right side in Back Stitch.

Anchor Stranded Cotton

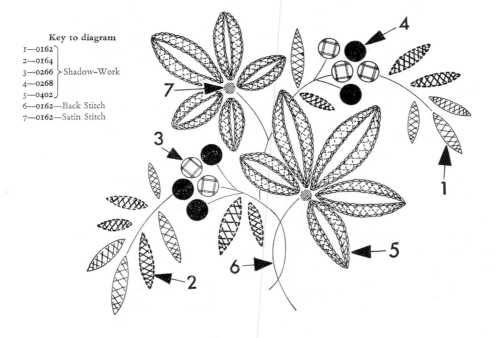

Key to diagram
1—0162 ⎤
2—0164 ⎟
3—0266 ⎬ Shadow-Work
4—0268 ⎟
5—0402 ⎦
6—0162—Back Stitch
7—0162—Satin Stitch

Shadow Work Tablecloth

The finished size of the cloth is 109 cm square.
Fold the fabric across the centre both ways creasing lightly, these folds act as a guide when placing the design. Follow the diagram and number key for the embroidery. All parts similar to numbered parts are worked in the same colour and stitch. Press the embroidery on the wrong side. Make up, taking 12 mm hems.

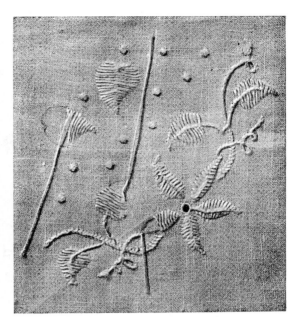

Fig. 4. Shadow work. Right side of work in a frame   *Fig. 5. Shadow work. Wrong side of work in a frame*

Fig. 6. Motif in Shadow Work, with Back Stitch and Satin Stitch dots

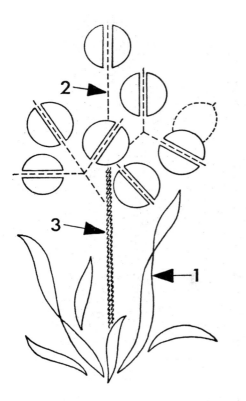

The Finishing of Edges. The edges of objects embroidered in Shadow Work may be finished in a variety of ways and Figs. 7, 8 and 9 show three examples.

Fig. 7. Prepare the hem and work Double Back Stitch on the turned-in fabric so that the stitches go through both thicknesses. On completing the embroidery cut away any spare material on the underside using very sharp, small scissors.

The second illustration, Fig. 8, shows another type of edge finish. Work small, close Buttonhole Stitching along the edge of the work, following the shape of the outline. This is decorated with picots placed at regular intervals. On completing the edging, cut away any spare material around the edges.

A third method is shown in Fig. 9. Buttonhole Stitch closely around the design and then work Back Stitch about a quarter of an inch inside the edging, imitating Shadow Work.

Very fine Hemstitching is also a good finish for Shadow Work. Fig. 10 shows a motif in Shadow Work and Cording on a Pulled Fabric background.

Anchor Stranded Cotton (2 strands)

1—Shadow-Work
2—Back Stitch
3—Stem Stitch

Shadow Work Lampshade
Worked on organdie or similar transparent fabric. Lined with fine silk.

Fig. 7. Finishing of a folded hem. The stitches are worked through both layers of fabric

Fig. 8. Finishing of edge with Buttonhole Stitch decorated with picots. The Buttonhole Stitches follow the outline of the Double Back Stitch

Fig. 9. Finishing of edge with Buttonhole Stitching and Back Stitch

Fig. 10. Motif for lingerie in Shadow Work and a Pulled Fabric filling

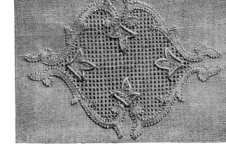

171

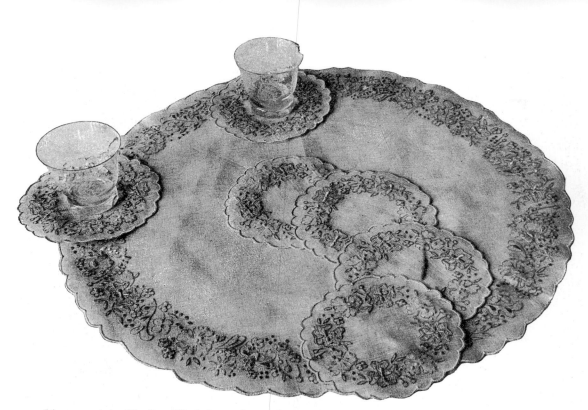

Liqueur set in Shadow Work in various colours. The background fabric is a fine linen lawn

Cushion cover worked entirely in white on fine linen

Octagonal table centre in organdie, in Shadow Work, in white. Embroidered spots and Pulled Fabric fillings enrich this example

Richly embroidered tablecloth in fine white linen embroidered in blue

Detail of the embroidery on the tablecloth. The design is placed round the edge of the cloth and repeated in the centre and on the napkins. The embroidery is in Shadow Work, Stem Stitch, Cording, Satin Stitch and various filling stitches

Detail of the tablecloth. The design, which is worked in the centre and along the outside edges of the cloth, is in Shadow Work, Stem Stitch and Satin Stitch in tones of blue. Part of the tablecloth design is repeated on the napkins. The cloth is finished off with a Hemstitched hem

Richly embroidered luncheon cloth worked in Coats Anchor Stranded Cotton in three tones of blue

177

G. Calegari, Milan

Lunch cloth in fine natural-coloured linen

Motif from the cloth shown in the illustration. The motifs are scattered over the whole cloth and the stitches used may easily be seen in the illustration

Tea cloth (above) in white organdie in Shadow Work and Satin Stitch. Liqueur set (below), enlarged details of which are also shown in this chapter

Liqueur set in white organdie in Shadow Stitch and Hexagonal Filling Stitch in white. The illustration shows a glass mat and part of the centrepiece in actual size

Table runner in a fine natural-coloured linen. In the centre a plain with fleeing deer is worked in Cording and Satin Stitch. The design is applied to a net background whilst the borders surrounding the scene are worked in Shadow Stitch and Satin Stitch

Details of a table centre. Coiling leaves surround the arms of the town of Siena

Detail of a table centre. The design is in Shadow Work, Satin Stitch and Pulled Fabric Fillings

CHAPTER XV

Embroidery on Tulle and Net

Although transparent, light and airy as a veil, a good quality tulle is a hard wearing fabric. The name is derived from Tulle, a town in France, where it was first manufactured. Today it is made in many places all over the world. The mesh, consisting of small hexagons, provides a framework for patterns which may be embroidered by taking threads in and out of the holes in various directions. This type of embroidery is excellent for enriching bridal and communion veils, and for trimming lingerie. It may also be used for household furnishings such as small window curtains, table runners and luncheon mats.

Materials for Tulle Embroidery. For embroidery on tulle, a very soft thread must be used. For fine tulle Coats Anchor Stranded Cotton using one, two or three strands at a time is the most suitable. Coats Anchor Machine Embroidery Cotton may also be used. Clark's Anchor Coton à Broder or Coats Anchor Pearl Cotton are useful when a coarser thread is required.

Method of Working Embroidery on Tulle. Paint the design in white outline on black paper, and tack the tulle in position so that it is smooth but not stretched too tightly. This preliminary work is very important and must be done carefully, since, if it is badly carried out, the finished work will be ruined.

Outline the design with a running thread and then fill in the patterns by working over the counted threads of the mesh. Use rather long threads to avoid too many joins. On finishing a thread, do not fasten off but join by making a small knot in the thread. (See the Chapter on "Tatting", page 210.) The outlines of the design may be worked in Running Stitch (Fig. 1) or in Stem Stitch (Fig. 2) or in Cording (Fig. 3). Cording should be worked over a foundation of Running Stitch.

The illustrations given in this chapter are so clear that the fillings can easily be copied. Brief explanations are given in the text.

Fig. 4. Running Stitches worked over one thread of tulle alternately, changing on successive lines.

Fig. 5. Running Stitches worked by taking up alternate threads and alternating on successive lines to form a diagonal pattern.

Fig. 6. Running Stitch worked diagonally, leaving a space between each line of stitching.

Fig. 7. Rows of diagonal Running Stitches worked in double thread.

Fig. 8. Diagonally worked Running Stitches, as in Fig. 7, but with a single thread. Work in both directions.

Fig. 9. Work diagonally, taking up one thread of tulle above and one below.

Fig. 10. Rows of stitches as in Fig. 9, but worked

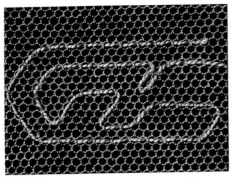

Fig. 1. Running Stitch on tulle

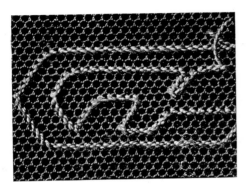

Fig. 2. Stem Stitch on tulle

Fig. 3. Cording on tulle

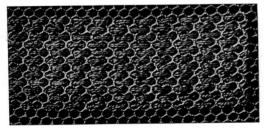

Fig. 4. Alternating Running Stitch

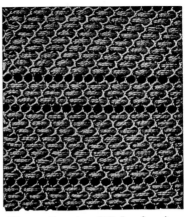

Fig. 5. Running Stitches forming
a diagonal pattern

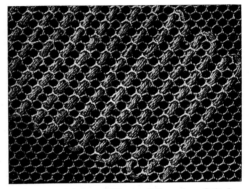

Fig. 6. Diagonal lines of Running Stitch

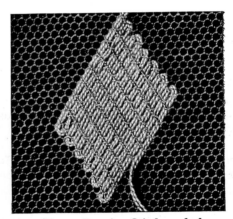

Fig. 7. Running Stitch worked
with a double thread

185

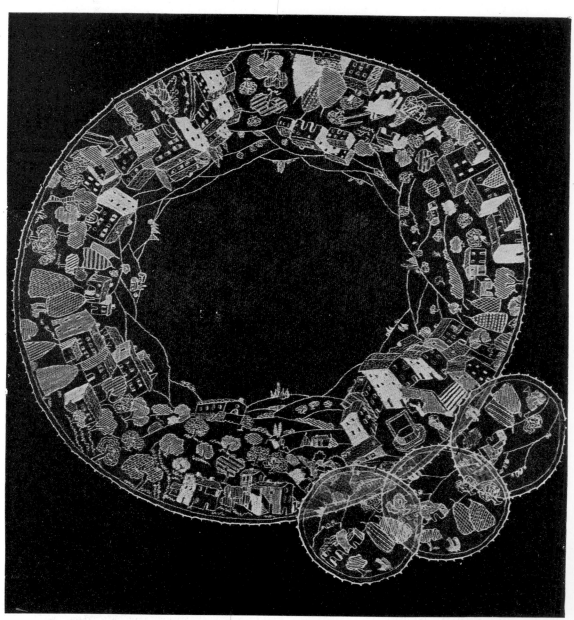

Circular cloth worked on white tulle, with an original design all around the edge. It is worked in Coats Anchor Stranded Cotton. Note the richness and variety of the stitches used for the little houses and trees. The cloth and napkins are finished at the edges with Buttonhole Stitch and picots

horizontally first from right to left and then from left to right, to make a series of waves.

Fig. 11. Work in two stages. First, a row of vertical stitches over one mesh, one hole apart and changing on every line, then pass a thread through these stitches without taking up the tulle.

Fig. 12. Cross Stitch worked in two stages from left to right and then from right to left.

Fig. 13. Three rows of stitching form this pattern. First, work a series of slightly oblique stitches taking up alternately one hole towards the right and another to the left. On the second row work horizontally a Wave Stitch as in Fig. 10. Repeat the second row.

Fig. 14. A two-row filling. The first row is composed of two Back Stitches worked over one hole of tulle, leaving a space of one hole. The second row is the same as in Fig. 10, that is, a wavy line of stitches in two directions.

Fig. 15. Two rows of wavy lines.

Fig. 16. Back Stitch worked over two rows of mesh and a double wavy line.

Fig. 17. This threaded pattern may be worked easily from the photograph. Use two different thicknesses of thread.

Fig. 18. This filling consists of a running thread, passing at intervals round a hole in the mesh.

Fig. 19. Two rows of Running Stitches. The second row intersects the first and is worked from left to right.

Fig. 20. This is a more closely worked version of the filling shown in Fig. 19.

Fig. 21. Filling worked in close rows of diagonal Running Stitch together with the stitch shown in Fig. 18.

Fig. 22. This illustration and Figs. 23, 24, 32 and 33 are so clear that they can be easily copied. They are useful for borders and insertions.

Fig. 25. Filling consisting of groups of three rows of stitching which alternate diagonally. A very much finer thread is passed through the line of holes left free in between the groups.

Fig. 26. Filling consisting of alternating lines of Running Stitch worked diagonally. Wavy lines are worked in between the diagonal rows.

Fig. 27. Filling consisting of lines of stitches forming a herringbone pattern. Work first in one direction and then in the other.

Fig. 28. Rows of overcasting worked alternately over a hole and a thread of the tulle. The stitches are alternated on successive rows.

Fig. 8. Crossing lines of Running Stitch

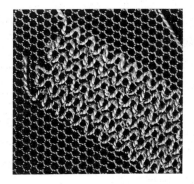

Fig. 9. Wavy lines worked diagonally

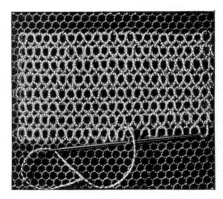

Fig. 10. Crossing wavy lines worked horizontally

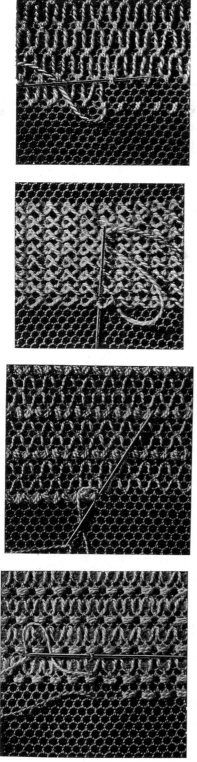

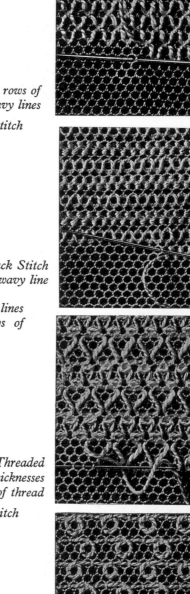

Fig. 11 (left). *Vertical Stitches and threaded wavy lines*

Fig. 15 (right). *Two rows of wavy lines*

Fig. 12 (left). *Cross Stitch on tulle*

Fig. 16 (right). *Back Stitch and a double wavy line*

Fig. 13 (left). *Wavy lines alternating with rows of oblique stitches*

Fig. 17 (right). *Threaded lines worked in two thicknesses of thread*

Fig. 14 (left). *Back Stitch and wavy lines*

Fig. 18 (right). *Running Stitches forming circles*

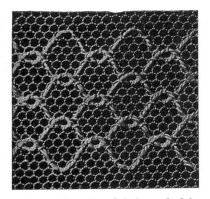

Fig. 19. Running Stitch worked in
wavy lines with wide curves

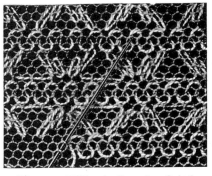

Fig. 22. Filling in Running Stitch

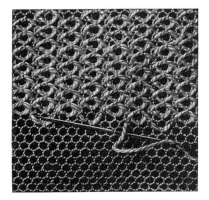

Fig. 20. A closer version of the pattern
shown in Fig. 19

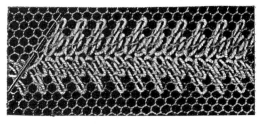

Fig. 23. Border in graduated Running Stitches

Fig. 24. Another border in Running Stitch

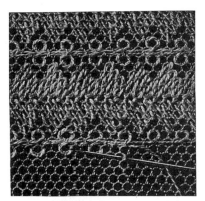

Fig. 21. Filling in Running Stitch

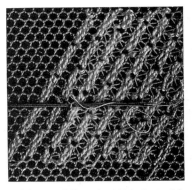

Fig. 25. Diagonal Running Stitches with thread
of different thickness

189

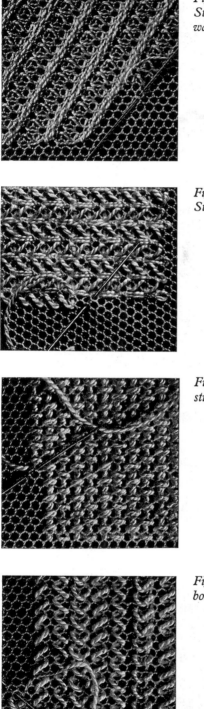

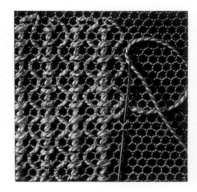

Fig. 26. Diagonal Running Stitches alternated with wavy lines

Fig. 30. A wavy line and rows of overcasting worked alternately

Fig. 27. Horizontal Running Stitches and overcasting

Fig. 31. Another Herring-bone pattern

Fig. 28. Filling worked in stitches of two sizes

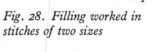

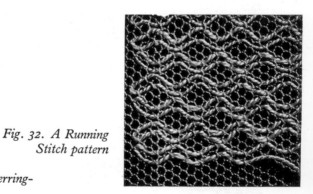

Fig. 32. A Running Stitch pattern

Fig. 29. A herring-bone pattern

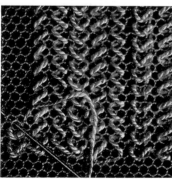

Fig. 33. A border in Running Stitch

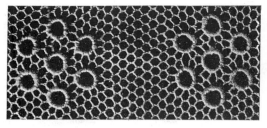

Fig. 34. Eyelet holes on tulle

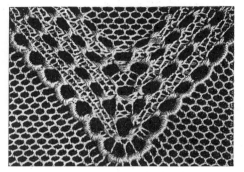

Fig. 37. Corner of a border

Fig. 35. A star worked in Running Stitch

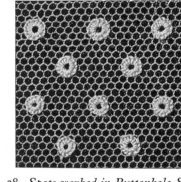

Fig. 38. Spots worked in Buttonhole Stitch

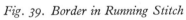

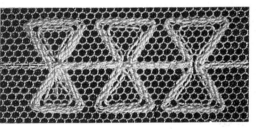

Fig. 39. Border in Running Stitch

Fig. 36. Star in Cording and overcasting

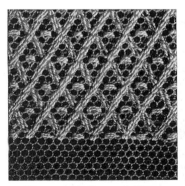

Fig. 40. A diamond filling

Fig. 41. Filling in Running Stitch

Fig. 42. Another filling in Running Stitch

Fig. 43. A chevron filling

Fig. 44. A star filling

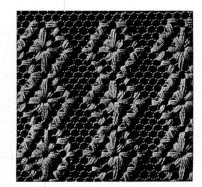

Fig. 45. A diamond and star filling

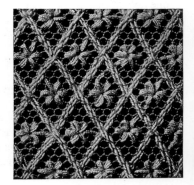

Fig. 46. Another diamond and star filling

Fig. 47. A solid filling

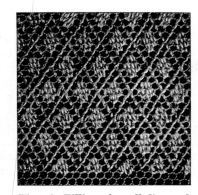

Fig. 48. Filling of small diamonds in a trellis worked in Cording

Fig. 49. Another diamond filling

Fig. 29. Rows of diagonal stitches, worked first in one direction and then in the other.

Fig. 30. Filling consisting of a wavy line and a row of stitching as in Fig. 28. They are worked alternately.

Fig. 31. Another herringbone pattern.

Fig. 34. Groups of eyelet holes forming stars. Work in Cording, pulling up each stitch, over a foundation of Running Stitches.

Fig. 35. Begin in the centre to work this star with Running Stitch.

Fig. 36. A decorative star formed by overcasting stitches over one thread of tulle. First work the outline of the diamonds and afterwards the centre stitches as shown in the illustration.

Fig. 37. This corner is worked by drawing up the threads tightly. The tulle is not cut away.

Fig. 38. Spots worked in Blanket Stitch around one hole of tulle at equal distances from each other.

Fig. 39. Border in Running Stitch.

Fig. 40. Diagonal lines and horizontal stitches forming diamonds.

Fig. 41. Blocks of Running Stitch arranged as shown in the illustration.

Fig. 42. A different arrangement of the stitch shown in Fig. 41.

Fig. 43. A chevron pattern worked in Running Stitch, Herringbone Stitch and overcasting.

Fig. 44. Star filling. The six rays of the star are formed by threads passed twice over each hole of tulle.

Fig. 45. Diamond shapes formed by threads passing twice through each hole of tulle in a zig-zag movement. Work a star with eight rays at the centre of each diamond.

Fig. 46. Diamonds worked in Running Stitch. The stars at the centre are like those shown in Fig. 44.

Fig. 47. A heavy filling worked in six strands of Clark's Anchor Stranded Cotton.

Fig. 48. Filling consisting of small diamonds within a framework of Cording.

Fig. 49. This filling is similar to those shown in Figs. 45 and 47.

Fig. 50. Border formed by a double row of triangles worked in Running Stitch. A thread is passed through the centre as in Fig. 18.

Fig. 51. Narrow border in Running Stitch and Cording.

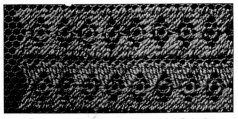

Fig. 50. Border in Running Stitch

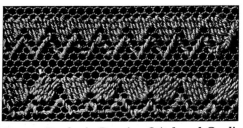

Fig. 51. Border in Running Stitch and Cording

Fig. 52. Border in Buttonhole Stitch and Running Stitch

Fig. 52. Narrow border worked in Buttonhole Stitch and Running Stitch. The tulle may be cut away around the scalloped edge.

Tulle Background. Sometimes in cut work embroidery the background, usually worked with bars, is substituted with tulle. When this method is used, tack the fabric and tulle together very carefully and work round the design with Running Stitch. Work Buttonhole Stitch or Cording over the Running Stitch foundation, taking care to pass the needle through both fabric and tulle. When complete, press and cut away the fabric with very sharp scissors without snipping the tulle.

193

Cushion cover for a bedroom embroidered in white on white tulle

Decorative panel with a religious theme, carried out on fine tulle

Curtain in grey tulle with a floral design in various fillings

Detail of a tulle runner embroidered in many filling stitches by the pupils of the Bon Brenzon School of Verona

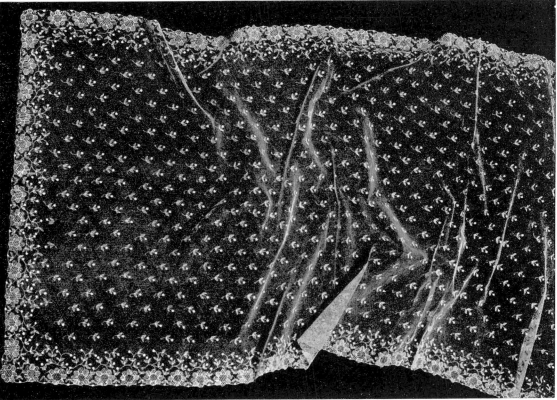

White tulle stole with a delicate floral border. A larger detail of this stole is also illustrated

CHAPTER XVI

Lingerie

Changes in fashion are reflected in the changing style of lingerie and the last seventy years have seen heavy underclothing give place to thin and pretty garments. With the change in style have come changes in colour and in the type of fabric used. Today a wide range of fabrics is available from pure silk crêpes and satins to the man-made fibre fabrics such as nylon and Terylene. Much of the lingerie manufactured today is decorated with machine embroidery, but fine handwork is still the best medium for enriching the more precious fabrics.

Very good technique is necessary for fine work upon lingerie fabrics and a good embroidery thread such as Coats Anchor Stranded Cotton must be used. The stitches most often used are Satin Stitch, Cording, Broderie Anglaise, Shadow Work and many kinds of Pulled Fabric and Drawn-thread Work.

Nightdress in heavy white silk, with smocking at neck and cuffs

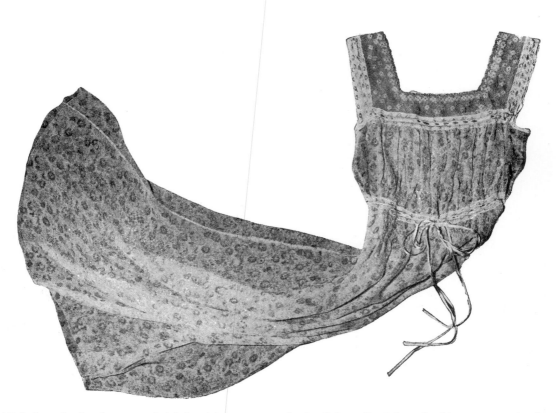

Nightdress in floral patterned fabric with a square yoke in plain voile. The embroidery repeats the floral motif in Shadow Work. The enlarged illustration shows this clearly

Nightdress in pink satin with a deep neckline. Two embroidered bands form a background for the decoration which is carried out in Shadow Work and Pulled Fabric Stitches in self colour as shown in the larger illustration

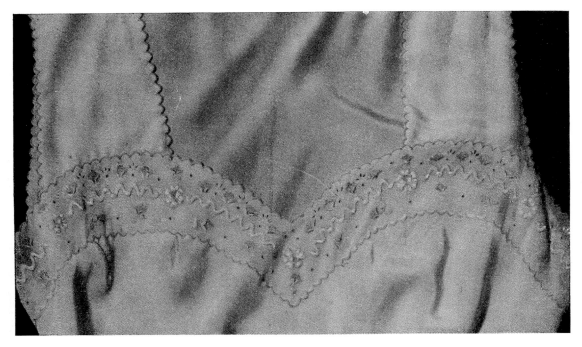

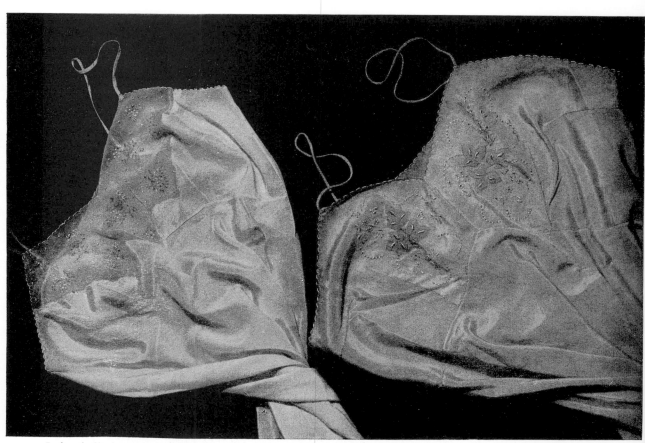

Left: A slip in rose pink silk with a panel of embroidered net at the front of the bodice. Right: Pale blue satin slip with a richly embroidered bodice. The design is also shown in the actual size and it is carried out in Satin Stitch, Cording and embroidered fillings

Details of the two embroidered slips are shown here

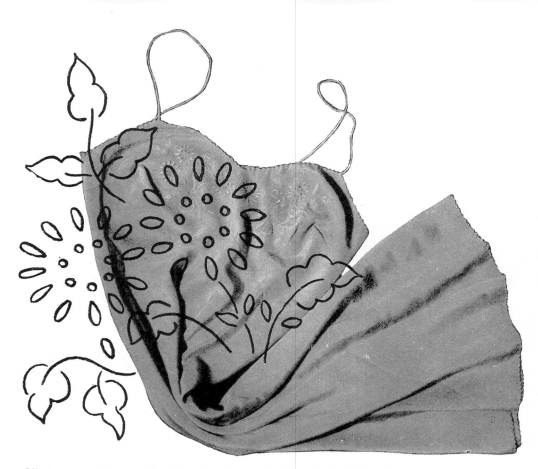

Slip in rose pink silk with rich embroidery on the front of the bodice. Satin Stitch is used to work the daisies and the leaves are in Shadow Work. The two "truelovers' knots" are enriched with Pulled Fabric fillings and Shadow Work

Above: Nightdress in pale blue satin, embroidered in filling stitches and Satin Stitch. Below: Nightdress in pale blue crêpe with self-coloured embroidery. Satin Stitch and filling stitches are worked for the small flowers and spots and Shadow Work for the decorative lines. Fine pleating gathers in the fullness below the yoke and at the waistline

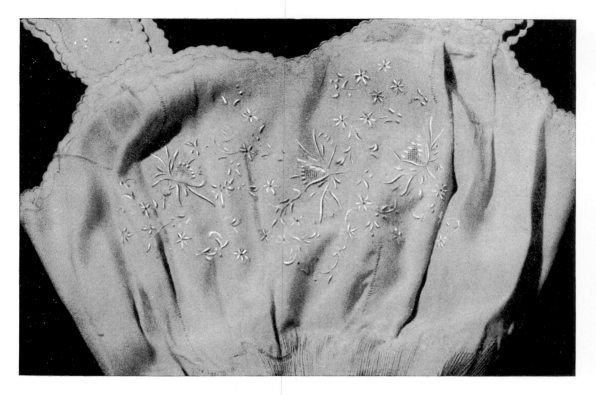

Details of the embroidery on the two nightdresses are shown in this illustration

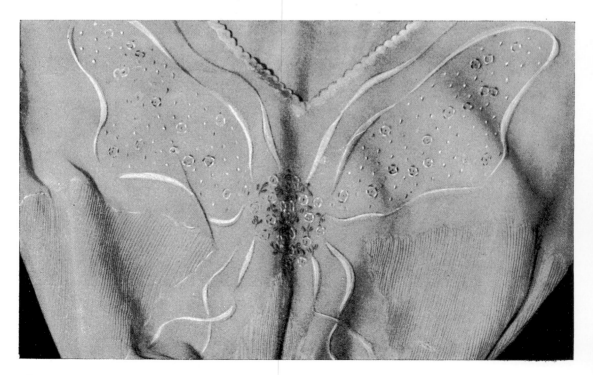

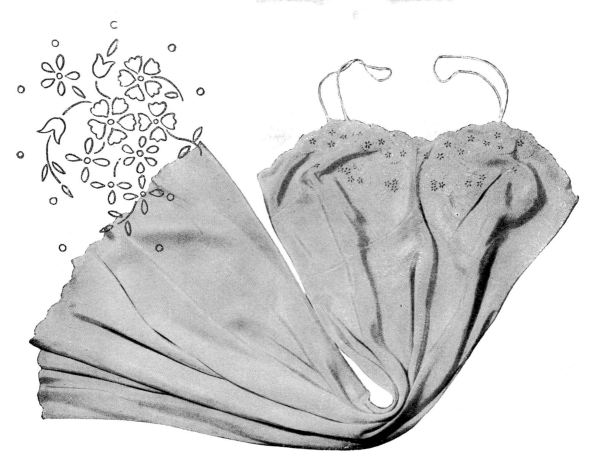

Slip in pale blue silk worked in Broderie Anglaise and Satin Stitch. The scalloped edging and the embroidery are worked in a tone darker than the background fabric. This design would also be suitable for a nightdress

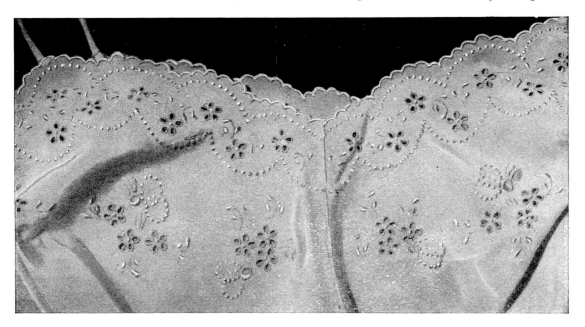

Nightdress with short sleeves and high collar, in white silk, embroidered at the front with Shadow Work, Satin Stitch and Pulled Fabric Stitches. Small butterflies have been worked separately and applied as if alighting on the fabric. This design could be worked on the front of a blouse

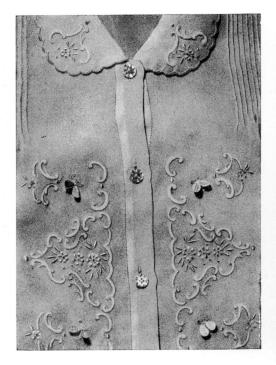

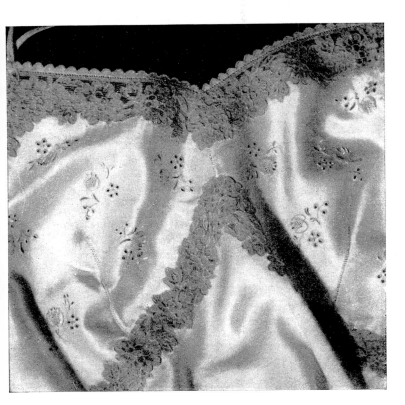

A slip in ivory-coloured satin. Ecru lace trims the neckline, waist and hem. Between the two strips of lace there is a small sprig pattern in Broderie Anglaise, Satin Stitch and Pulled Fabric fillings

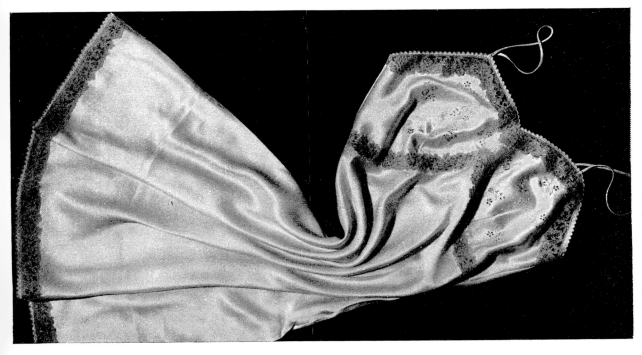

6 *Knotted Lace*_____

CHAPTER XVII

Tatting

Tatting is simple work which does not require any special preparation, while it is also not bulky and therefore easy to carry round and work in company, in the open air, in the garden, in the train, etc., using two small shuttles and a little thread.

The French call this work "frivolité"—frivolity—Eastern people call it "makouk", a name which means shuttle, and in Italian it is called "chiacchierino", a word whose origin is uncertain but possibly derives from the word "chiacchierare", to gossip, the work being easily carried on whilst the daily gossip is being held.

At the end of the last century, tatting was used on a vast scale to decorate feminine clothing: it was worked in silk, for preference, in various colours and in various decorative forms.

Today tatting still takes its place along with crochet work. It is more solid and elegant than crochet work but both kinds of lace are often used in combination for decorative edgings for underwear and children's clothing. It is generally worked nowadays in rather fine cotton in white or natural.

Tatting is also used in the house for various types of decoration, such as runners, edgings for table centres, serviettes, and cushion covers.

Necessary Materials. The Shuttle. To work tatting, the small tool called a shuttle is necessary. Once upon a time the shuttle was much larger than that in use today. An ordinary shuttle measures

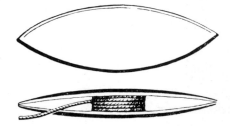

Fig. 1. Shuttle

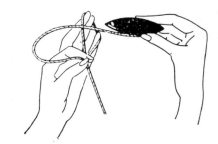

Fig. 2. First movement: winding the thread on the left hand to begin work

*Liqueur set in white organdie with tatting edge, worked in Coats Mercer-Crochet, No. 60.
(See p. 226 for explanation as to how it is worked.)*

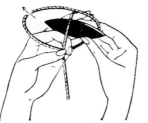

Fig. 3. *The shuttle passing through the loop from right to left*

Fig. 4. *Position of the thread for the first half of the knot*

Fig. 5. *A series of half knots left loose on the thread*

Fig. 6. *Second movement: the shuttle passes from left to right through the loop*

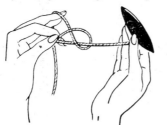

Fig. 7. *Position of thread in the second stage of the knot*

about 7.6 cm in length and 2.5 cm in width; it used to be made in wood or bone; today celluloid or plastic are the most common materials.

Inside the shuttle there is a small reel with a hole through it. The thread is fixed through the hole and wound round the reel (Fig. 1), without, however, protruding beyond the edges of the shuttle, so that the thread does not get dirty. When buying the shuttle, care should be taken that the two ends of the two halves of the shuttle fit perfectly, so that the thread is held tightly and firmly and cannot slip through, as this is very inconvenient, especially when working with two shuttles.

The most suitable thread for this type of work is Coats Mercer-Crochet in the various thicknesses. We recommend Nos. 40 and 60 for fine work and Nos. 10 and 20 if a bolder effect is desired.

Method of Working Tatting. Tatting consists of a simple knot formed in two stages, making the basis of the lacework.

After preparing the shuttle as described above, leave a length of thread free for about 50 cm, then, taking the end of the thread between finger and thumb of the left hand, wrap it around the other three fingers in a large circle (Fig. 2); then, holding the shuttle in the right hand, pass it through the circle of thread, from right to left as shown in Fig. 3. Now, before moving the left hand, pull through the thread with the shuttle, then raising the third and fourth fingers of the left hand, slip the loop along the stretched thread (Fig. 4). Thus the first movement, making half the complete knot, has been worked. Fig. 5 shows a series of half knots left loose on the stretched thread. The beginner must learn this first movement very well and practise it often before attempting the second stage.

The second half knot is worked in the opposite direction: after having wound the thread round the fingers of the left hand, as explained in the first stage, pass the shuttle, held in the right hand, from left to right through the circle (Fig. 6). The right hand, as already in the first stage, holds the thread and remains still (Fig. 7) while the left hand closes up this second half knot, thus completing the whole knot (Fig. 8). On completion of the two stages, the whole process is begun again.

Figs. 9 and 10 show the looping of the thread to make the knots.

The thread must always run freely through the knots which are formed. If the knots stick, it means that a stitch has been wrongly made and the work must be begun again. Although tatting is easy, the work must be followed carefully and the knots counted with attention, keeping in mind that the work cannot easily be unpicked and that the whole effect of the work is spoiled if the thread has to be cut and knotted again.

After working a given number of knots, necessary to form a circle, the basic circle is left free from the fingers of the left hand, and the thread from the shuttle is slightly pulled in order to close up the circle.

Picots. One of the characteristic decorations in tatting is picots, that is, part of the thread left free between one knot and another. Figs. 11 and 12 clearly show the method: after completing a second half-knot, leave a length of thread free, pushing it up against the preceding knot, before proceeding to the formation of the first half of the next knot. This loop is a picot.

Keep in mind that in the following descriptions the picot is separate from the knot, therefore in calculating, the knot near the picot must always be counted.

Josephine Knot. By making a series of first-stage half knots and then drawing up the thread, the so-called Josephine knot is obtained. This is very decorative and may be alternated with simple picots (Fig. 13).

Working with Two Shuttles. Work with one shuttle gives a circle, while if semicircles or arcs are desired, two shuttles must be used.

When working with two shuttles, proceed as follows: knot the ends of the two threads, and to avoid confusing the shuttles use two differently coloured threads. The thread from one shuttle passes over the middle and third fingers of the left hand, then it is wrapped twice round the little finger and left to fall free together with the shuttle (Fig. 14). Take the other shuttle in the right hand and work the same movements as if working with only one shuttle.

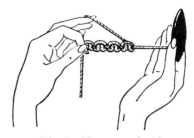

Fig. 8. *Knot completed*

Fig. 9. *The two positions of the thread to make the knot*

Fig. 10. *Complete knot left loose. Complete knot drawn up tight*

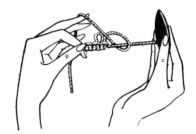

Fig. 11. *Method of working picot*

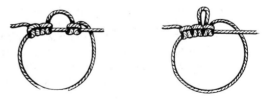

Fig. 12. *Open picot. Closed picot*

*Fig. 13. Josephine knot: 5 half knots.
Closed knot*

Fig. 14. Working with two shuttles

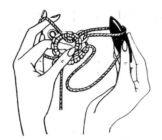

Fig. 15. Method of attaching picots

Fig. 16. Position of threads when joining picots

*Fig. 17. Second method of working tatting:
first movement*

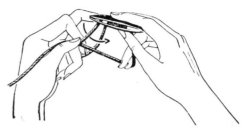

*Fig. 18. Second method of working tatting: second
movement*

Attachment of Circles and Arcs to Picots. In tatting both circles and semicircles are joined together at the point where there is a picot. To do this, pass the running thread from the left hand and through the picot, using a crochet hook or needle, and then push the shuttle through the loop which leaves the picot, and draw up the thread before beginning the following knot (Fig. 15).

Fig. 16 illustrates the attachment of picots.

Joining of Threads in Tatting. To join on thread in the course of the work, make a weaver's knot, taking at least one of the threads through the following knot: the thread can never be joined when making a circle or arc, but only at the beginning or end of them.

Second Method of Working Tatting. The two illustrations Figs. 17 and 18 show another method of working tatting, a method which allows, especially for the expert, greater speed in working. The shuttle first passes under and then over the loop of thread around the left hand, whilst the thread is held tightly stretched by the little finger of the right hand. In this way, the length of thread from the shuttle to the work itself must be very much shorter than in the other method.

Abbreviations used in the course of the text:

sh.	shuttle
k.	knot
p.	picot
tn.	turn work
prec.	preceding
p.r.	preceding row
sep.	separate
rep.	repeat
a.a.	as above

(*) When, in the course of the work, an asterisk is shown, continue the work until the directions indicate that the work should be repeated from the asterisk sign.

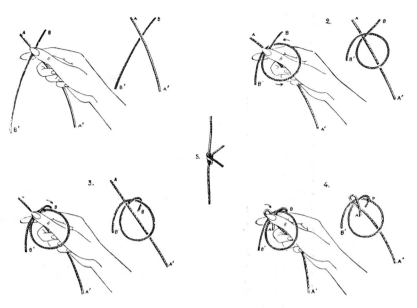

Sketch showing the making of a weaver's knot, used for joining on threads when working almost all types of lace and nets

Weaver's Knot. 1. Hold the two ends of the threads AA' and BB' firm and crossed between the thumb and the first finger of the right hand, placing AA' over BB'.

2. With the left hand, take the end B' and pass it around the right thumb between the shorter ends B and A.

3. Fold the end B over the first finger of the right hand and hold it firm with the middle finger of the same hand.

4. Fold the end A over and hold firm under the thumb of the right hand: then, without leaving hold of the threads, pull up the end B tightly. The knot is thus completed.

Fig. 19. Work with one shuttle only. Make a circle of 6k. 1p. very small, 6k. 1p. like the other, 6k. Close the circle leaving it open for about 6 mm (*) make another circle of 6k. joining 6k. 1p., 6k. to the second picot of the prec. circle. Close a.a. and rep. from (*).

Fig. 20. With one sh. work a circle of 4k. 1p. rather long, 2k. 3p. sep. by 2k. 2k. 1p. long, 4k. Close. Turn. With 2 sh. work 6k. With the left sh. work a Josephine knot (10 half knots) 6k. Turn. Rep. from beginning joining first picot in the new circle to last picot along the prec. circle.

Fig. 21. Work with one sh. only. Work a circle of 5k. 3p. sep. by 5k. 5k., close. (*). Turn. Leave a short length of thread and work a Josephine knot (10 half knots). Turn. Leave a very short length of thread equal to the other, work a circle of 5k. attach 5k. 1p. 5k. to last picot of prec. circle. Close. Rep. from (*).

Fig. 22. With one sh. work a circle of 5k. 3p. sep. by 5k. 5k. Close. Work another circle of 5k. attach 5k. 1p. 5k. 1p. 5k. to last picot of prec. circle. Close. Still using one sh. work a third circle of 5k. attach 5k. 1p. 5k. 1p., 5k. to last picot of prec. circle. Close. Turn. With two sh. work 8k. 1p. 8k. Turn Rep. from beginning attaching second picot of new circle to second picot of prec. circle.

Fig. 23. (With one sh. work a circle of 3k. 5p. sep. by 3k. 3k. close) twice. Turn. (*). With two sh. work 3k. 3p. sep. by 3k. 3k. Turn. With one sh. work a circle of 4k. join to centre p. on prec. circle. 4k. 2p. sep. by 4k. 4k. Close. Turn. With two sh. work 7k. Turn. With one sh. work a circle of 8k. join to last p. on prec. circle. 4k. 2p. sep. by 4k. 8k. Close. Turn. With left hand sh. work a circle of 2k. 5p. sep. by 2k. 2k. Close. With two sh. work 7k. Turn. With one sh. work a circle of 4k. join to last p. on prec. circle. 4k. 2p. sep. by 4k. 4k. Close. Turn. With two sh. work 3k. 3p. sep. by 3k. 3k. Turn. With one sh. work a circle of 3k. 2p. sep. by 3k. 3k. join to last p. on prec. circle. 3k. 2p. sep. by 3k. 3k. Close. Circle of 3k. 5p. sep. by 3k. 3k. Close. Turn and rep. from (*).

Fig. 19

Fig. 20

Fig. 21

Fig. 22

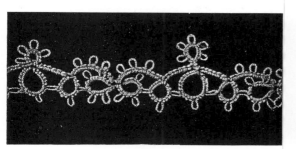

Fig. 23

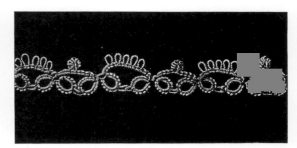

Fig. 24

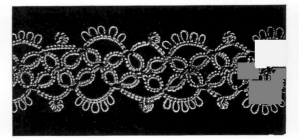

Fig. 25

Fig. 26

Fig. 27

Fig. 24. With one sh. work a circle of 7k. 1p. 7k. Close. With two sh. work 5k. With the left sh. work a Josephine knot (8 half knots) then with two sh. 5k. Turn. With one sh. work a circle of 7k. joining 7k. to the prec. picot. Close. Work another circle of 7k. 1p. 7k. Close. Turn. With two sh. work 3k. 5p. sep. by 2k. 3k. Turn. With one sh. work a circle of 7k. joining 7k. to picot of prec. circle. Close. Repeat from beginning.

Fig. 25. Inset consisting of fine lace work, as above, worked from two sides. First work the lace, as above, for the required length. Then work from the other side in the same way joining p. on second strip to joining of p. on first strip.

Fig. 26. Work in two stages.
1st stage. With one sh. work a circle of 10k. 1p. 10k. Close. Work another equal circle. Turn. (*). With two sh. work 3k. 5p. sep. by 3k. 3k. Turn. With one sh. work a circle of 10k. attached to picot of prec. circle. 10k. Close. Work another circle of 10k. 1p. 10k. Close. Rep. from (*) for desired length.
2nd stage. (**). With one sh. work a circle of 10k. attach to joining of the two circles of first row, 10k. Close. Turn. With two sh. work 3k. 5p. sep. by 3k. 3k. Turn. With one sh. work a circle of 10k. attach as above 10k. Close. Rep. from (**).

Fig. 27. With two sh. work 2k. 1p. 2k. Turn. Change sh. and work 12k. 1p. 2k. Turn. Change sh., and work 2k., attach to first picot worked, 12k. 1p. 2k. Turn. Change sh. and work 2k. attach to picot of nearby arc, 12k. 1p. 2k. Rep. always in the same way.

Fig. 28. With two sh. work 9k. 1p. 9k. Turn. With one sh. work a circle of 7k. 1p. 7k. Close. Circle of 5k. 2p. sep. by 7k. 5k. Close. Turn. (*). With two sh. work 9k. Turn. (With one sh. work a circle of 5k. join to last p. on prec. circle. 7k. 1p. 5k. close) 3 times. Turn. With two sh. work 9k. Turn. With one sh. work a circle of 5k. join to last p. on prec. circle. 7k. 1p 5k. Close. Circle of 7k. 1p. 7k. Close. Turn. With both sh. work 9k. join to p. on corresponding semicircle. 9k. join to p. on prec. circle. With two sh. work 9k. 1p. 9k. Turn. With one sh. work a circle of 7k. join to same p. on prec. circle. 7k. Close. Circle of 5k. join to last p. on 3rd last circle. 7k. 1p. 5k. Close. Turn and rep from (*).

Fig. 28

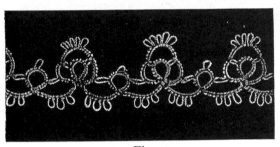

Fig. 29

Fig. 30

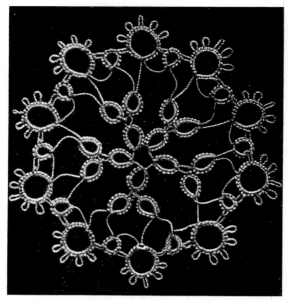

Fig. 31

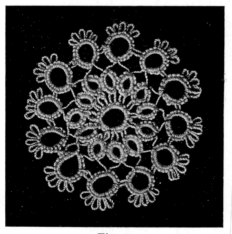

Fig. 32

Fig. 30. With one sh. work a circle of 2k. 5p. sep. by 2k. 2k. Close. (*). Turn. With two sh. work 3k. 3p. sep. by 3k. 3k. Turn. With one sh. work a circle of 2k. 1p. 2k. attached to fourth picot of prec. circle 2k. 3p. sep. by 2k. 2k. Close. Rep. from (*) until 7 circles and 7 semicircles have been worked. Cut threads and knot.

This completes the central star. Now work one row thus: (*). With one sh. work a circle of 2k. 2p. sep. by 2k. 2k. attach to central picot of first semi-circle of star, 2k. 2p. sep. by 2k. 2k. Close. With two sh. work 8k. 5p. sep. by 2k. 8k. Turn and rep. from (*). Join the last semicircle to the base of the first circle. Cut threads and knot.

Fig. 31. This star is worked with a single sh.
1st row. Work a circle of (*) 8k. 1p. 8k. Close. Rep. from (*) another 4 times then cut threads and knot.
2nd row. Work a large circle of 5k. 7p. sep. by 3k. 5k. Close. Turn. Leave a short length of thread of about quarter of an inch and work a circle of 8k. Attach to picot of first circle of first row, then, 8k. and close (**). Turn. Leave 6 mm thread, work a small circle of 4k. attach to last picot of largest circle, 4k. 1p. 4k. Close. Leave 6 mm thread, work another large circle of 5k., attach to picot of small circle, 3k. 6p. sep. by 3k. 5k. Close. Turn. Leave 6 mm thread. Work a circle of 8k. and attach to same point on the circle of the first row, 8k. Close. Turn. Leave 6 mm thread. Work a small circle of 4k. attach to last picot of large circle, 4k. 1p. 4k. Close. Leave 6 mm thread. Work a large circle of 5k. attach to picot of prec. circle, 3k. 6p. sep. by 3k. 5k. Close. Turn. Leave 6 mm thread. Work a circle of 8k. attach to picot of second circle of first row, 8k. Close. Rep. from (**) all round. At the end of the star attach the second picot of last small circle to first picot of first large circle.

Fig. 32. This star is worked with a single sh. Work a circle of 1k. 12p. sep. by 2k. 1k. Close. Cut threads and knot. *1st row*. Work a circle of 6k. attach to one picot of central circle, 6k. Close. Turn. Leave a short length of thread. Work a circle of 4k. 1p. 4k. 5p. sep. by 1k. 4k. 1p. 4k. Close. Turn. (*). Leave a.a. and work a circle of 6k. attach to picot following central circle, 6k. Close. Turn. Leave as above. Work a circle of 4k., attach to last picot of nearby circle, 4k. 5p. sep. by 1k. 4k. 1p. 4k. Close. Turn. Rep. from (*).

Attach last picot of last circle to first picot of first circle nearby.

Fig. 29. With one sh. work a circle of 5k. 3p. sep. from 5k. 5k. Close. (*). Turn. With two sh. work 4k. 3p. sep. from 2k. 4k. Turn. With one sh. work a circle of 6k. 1 small picot, 6k. 1 small picot, 6k. Close. With two sh. work 5k. attach to picot of circle nearby, 6k. attach to first small picot of last circle worked, 5k. 5p. sep. by 1k. 5k. attach to the other picot of the same circle, 6k. 1p. 5k. attach to base of small circle. Turn. With two sh. work 4k. 3p. sep. by 2k. 4k. Turn. With one sh. work a circle of 5k. attach to picot of nearby semi-circle, 5k. 1p. 5k. 1p. 5k. Close. Rep. from (*).

218

Fig. 33. With one sh. work a circle of 10k. 3p. sep. by 5k. 10k. Close. (*) Work a second circle of 10k. attach to third picot of prec. circle 5k. 1p. 5k. 1p. 10k. Close. Rep. from (*) until 8 circles have been worked. Attach last to first. Cut threads and knot. With two sh., attach threads to central picot of a small circle, then with two sh. work 6k. Turn. (**). With one sh. work a circle of 10k. 1 small picot 10k. Close. With two sh. work 3k. 3p. sep. by 3k. 3k. attach to small picot of prec. circle, work a Josephine knot (10 half knots) with left sh., 3k. 3p. sep. by 3k. 3k. attach to base of prec. circle so that two concentric circles are formed. Turn. With two sh. work 6k. attach to picot of circle following central rosette, 6k. Turn. Rep. from (**). At the end, join the last 6k. to the first worked at the beginning of the row.

Fig. 33

Fig. 34. With one sh. work a circle of 6k. 3p. sep. by 6k. 6k. Close. Work another three the same. Cut the threads and knot.

1st row. With one sh. work a circle of 4k. attach to first picot of first circle of the four-leaved clover then work 2k. attached to third picot of nearby circle, 4k. Close. Turn. With two sh. work 5k. 1p. 5k. attach to central picot of first circle of four-leaved clover, then work again 5k. 1p. 5k. Turn. Rep. until 8 semicircles have been formed. Cut the thread and knot.

2nd row. (*). With one sh. work a circle of 4k., attach to picot of first semicircle, 4k. Close. Turn. With two sh. work 5k. 1p. 2k. With left sh. work a circle of 3k. 3p. sep. by 3k. 3k. Close. Work another two circles the same, attaching the first picot to the third prec. circle. With two sh. work 2k. 1p. 5k. turn and rep. from (*) until 8 three-leaved clovers and 8 semicircles have been formed. Cut threads and knot.

All these star and clover shapes may be used for household linen. If worked in fine cotton such as Coats Mercer-Crochet, Nos. 60 and 80, they may be appliquéd on to underwear or used as trimming for dresses and blouses. To appliqué these motifs to material proceed thus: mark a perfect circle of the same diameter as the star shape to be inserted, on the material. Fix the star to the centre of this by basting, taking care that the straight threads of both materials and insertion are in a straight line. Tack the outside edges of the star, fixing down all the picots on the edge of the circle. This tacking will be covered by buttonhole stitching or cording worked very closely and evenly. With small, sharp scissors,

Fig. 34

cut away the material along the edges of the cording. Combined with a central star, these stars can form wonderful lace patterns with original designs.

Figs. 35 and 36. The place-setting shown on the following page is worked in natural-coloured crash: it consists of a mat for the plate and a serviette. The large strip for the centre of the table can be decorated with the same tatting and the whole will stand out nicely on dark, polished wood.

Fig. 35. American table settings in natural-coloured crash with border in tatting

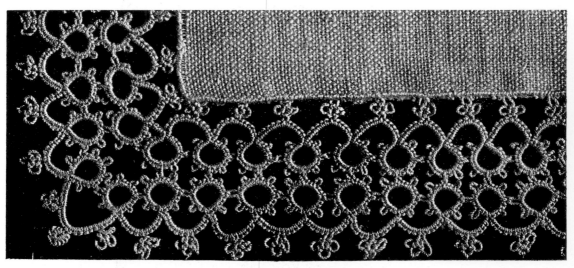

Fig. 36. Detail of border worked in Coats Mercer-Crochet, No. 20, in écru

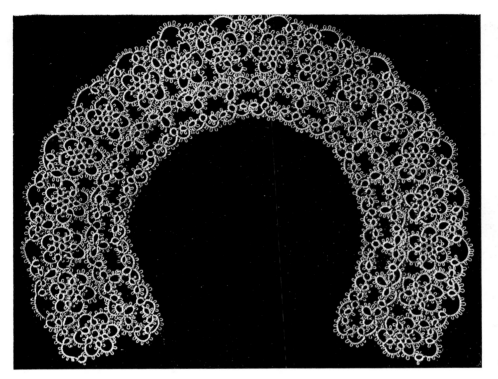

Fig. 37
Ladies' Collar

Necessary Materials. The length of cloth required will vary according to the number of place mats and serviettes and the size of the central runner. For the tatting Coats Mercer-Crochet, No. 20, in 20-gm. balls will be required and one ball for two mats and serviettes should be calculated.

The place mats measure 30 × 45 cm completed.
The serviettes measure 22 × 22 cm completed.

Place-setting. Worked in two stages.

1st row. With one sh. work a circle of 3k. 7p. sep. by 3k. 3k. Close. (*). Turn. With two sh. work 6k. With the left sh. work a small circle of 1k. 3p. sep. by 1k. 1k. Close. With two sh. work 6k. Turn. With one sh. work a circle of 3k. 1p. 3k. attach to sixth picot of prec. circle, 3k. 5p. sep. by 3k. 3k. Close. Rep. from (*).

Corner. After making the last circle turn, with two sh. work 6k. With left sh. work a small circle of 1k. 3p. sep. by 1k. 1k. Close. With two sh. 6k. with left sh., 1 Josephine knot. With two sh. 6k. with left sh. work a circle of 1k. 3p. sep. by 1k. 1k. Close. With two sh. 6k. Turn. With one sh. work a circle of 3k. 1p. 3k. attach to next to last picot of nearby circle, 3k. 5p. sep. by 3k. 3k. Close.

2nd row. The second row is the same as the first worked from the opposite side. The central picot of the circles on the first row is attached to the central picot of the circles on the second row.

At the corner work two circles sep. by 3k. as shown in the illustration.

Serviette. The first row is like that of the large circle; the second consists of arcs as in the first row, worked with two sh. and attached to the central picot of the circles on the first row.

Fig. 37. Collar.

Necessary Materials. Coats Mercer-Crochet: 1 20-gm. ball in No. 60. Two shuttles.

1st row. With one sh. work a circle of 3k. 5p. sep. by 3k. 3k. Close. (*). Work another circle the same. Turn. With two sh. 3k. 5p. sep. by 3k. 3k. Turn. With one sh. work a circle of 5k. attach to third picot of last circle, work 5k, 1p. 5k. 1p. 5k. Close. Turn. With two sh. 3k. 4p. sep. by 3k. 3k. Turn. With one sh. work a circle of 3k. 1p. 3k. 1p. 3k. attach to last picot of last circle worked 3k. 1p. 3k. 1p. 3k. Close. Rep. from (*) for required length.

Now proceed to turn the collar in this way: after the last couple of equal circles work with two sh. 3k. 5p. sep. by 3k. 3k., turn. With one sh. work a circle of 3k. 1p. 3k., attach the third picot of last circle 3k. 3p. sep. by 3k. 3k. Close. Turn. With two sh. work 3k. 5p. sep. by 3k. 3k. Turn and with two sh. work a circle of 3k. 1p. 3k. attach to fourth picot of last circle, 3k. 3p. sep. by 3k. 3k. Close.

2nd row. With two sh. work 3k. 5p. sep. by 3k. 3k. Turn. (*) With one sh. work a circle of 3k. 3p. sep. by 3k. 3k. attach to last picot of last circle worked, 3k. 3p. sep. by 3k. 3k. Close. With one sh. work a second circle very near to the other of 3k. attaching to last picot of circle prec. 3k. 3p. sep. by 3k. 3k. attaching to circle of 20k. and 3p. of first row, 3k. 4p. sep. by 3k. 3k. Close. With one sh. work a third circle very near to the second of 3k. attaching to last picot of prec. circle 3k. 6p. sep. by 3k. 3k. Close. Turn. With two sh. work 3k. 5p. sep. by 3k. 3k. Turn. With one sh. work a circle of 4k. attaching to fourth picot of nearby circle, 3k. 4p. sep. by 3k. 4k. Close. Turn. With two sh. work 3k. 5p. sep. by 3k. 3k. Rep. from (*), always attaching the single trefoils to the circle of 20k. on the prec. row; at the end of the row, proceed as for the beginning and attach last circle to the first on prec. row. Cut threads and knot.

3rd row. This is formed by a number of stars which are attached one by one to the first two rows worked. Begin at the centre of the first star, working with one sh. to make a circle of 1k. 6p. sep. by 3k. 2k. Close. Cut threads and knot. Then work a circle of 3k. 1p. 3k. 1p. 3k. attaching to a picot on the central circle, then 3k. 1p. 3k. 1p. 3k. Close. Turn. With two sh. work 3k. 5p. sep. by 3k. 3k. Turn. With one sh. work 3k. 1p. 3k. attaching to fourth picot of last circle worked, 3k. attaching to second picot of central circle 3k. 1p. 3k. 1p. 3k. Close. Turn. With two sh. work 3k. 2p. sep. by 3k. 3k. attaching to third picot of first arc of prec. row 3k. 2p. sep. by 3k. 3k. Turn. Continue to work in this way until 6 circles and 6 arcs have been worked, attached to each other as shown in the illustration. When the first star is complete, cut the threads and knot. Repeat the stars, attaching them together and to the prec. row. The number of stars will be the same as the number of trefoils on the prec. row, i.e. a total of 18.

4th and last row. With one sh. work a circle of 5k. 1p. 5k. attaching to central picot of first arc of first star, 5k. 1p. 5k. Close. Turn. With two sh. work 3k. 5p. sep. by 3k. 3k. Turn. (*). With one sh. work a circle of 5k. 1p. 5k. attaching to third picot of second arc of same star, 5k. 1p. 5k. Close. Turn. With two sh. work 3k. 3p. sep. by 3k. 3k.

Fig. 37(a). Detail, worked in actual size, of collar illustrated on preceding page

Turn. With one sh. work a circle of 3k. 1p. 3k. attaching to third picot of prec. circle 3k. 2p. sep. by 3k. 3k. Close. With one sh. work, very closely to prec. circle, a circle of 3k. attaching to last picot of prec. circle 3k. 2p. sep. by 3k. 3k. attaching to first picot of third arc of same star 3k. 1p. 3k. attaching to last picot of nearby arc of following star, 3k. 3p. sep. by 3k. 3k. Close. With one sh. work a third circle very near to prec. one of 3k. attaching to last picot of circle just worked. 3k. 3p. sep. by 3k. 3k. Close. Turn. With two sh. work 3k. 3p. sep. by 3k. 3k. Turn. With one sh. work 5k. attaching to central picot of first free arc of following star, 5k. 1p. 5k. Close. With two sh. work 3k. 6p. sep. by 3k. 3k. Turn. Recommence from (*) and continue until the end of row. The last arc will be of 3k. 5p. sep. by 3k. 3k. as the first.

Fig. 38. Table centre on right.
Necessary Materials. Coats Mercer-Crochet, No. 60, in white, écru or colours. 20-gm. ball.
Circle of 1k. 15p. sep. by 1k. Close. Cut threads and knot.

1st row. Circle of 6k. attaching to first picot of circle just completed, 6k. Close. Turn. Leave a very short length of thread, and work a circle of 5k. 1p. 5k. 3p. sep. by 3k. 5k. 1p. 5k. Close. (*) Turn. Leave as above and work a circle of 6k. attaching to following picot of central star, 6k. Close. Turn. Leave as above. Circle of 5k. attaching to last picot of circle nearby, 5k. 3p. sep. by 3k. 5k. 1p. 5k. Close. Continue thus repeating from (*) until 15 small circles and 15 larger circles have been worked.

2nd row. Attaching two threads to central picot of a first circle and using two sh. work 5k. 3p. sep. by 3k. 5k. attaching to central picot of following circle. Rep. all round until 15 arcs have been worked. This completes the first star at the centre of the table centre. Now, proceeding in the same way, work a smaller star, that is of 12 picots at the centre, of 12 small circles and 12 larger circles. Attach central picot of last two circles to central picot of the 2 arcs. Work thus for another 4 small stars and attach all of them to the central star leaving out one arc. Thus a table centre with one central star and five surrounding stars is formed. Between one star and another a free arc is formed.

Work separately a circle of 5k. 3p. sep. by 3k. attaching then to central picot of free arc 3k. 3p. sep. by 3k. 5k. Close. Leave a short length of thread as above and work a circle of 10k., attach to first picot of second free circle of star, 5k. 1p. 5k. 1p. 8k. Close. Work, very near to this, another circle the same, attaching it to the corresponding picot of the following star. Pass a thread through these two circles, place in the sh. and draw up tightly. Leave a short length of thread as above, and work a circle of 7k. attaching to last picot of nearby circle, 5k. 1p. 5k. 1p. 7k. Close. Very near to this work another circle in the same way. Pass the thread through these two new circles as above. Leave a length of thread and work a circle of 5k. attaching to last picot of nearby circle, 5k. 1p. 5k. 1p. 6k. Close. Very near to this work another circle in the same way. Pass the thread through these two new circles as explained above. Leave a length of thread and work a circle of 4k. attaching to last picot of nearby circle, 6k. 3p. sep. by 1k. 6k. attaching to last picot of corresponding circle nearby, 4k. Close.

Rep. the work between each star of the table centre.

Fig. 38. Table centre on left.
Necessary Materials. Coats Mercer-Crochet, No. 60: 20-gm. ball.
Circle of 10k. 1p. 2k. 1p. 8k. Close. With two sh. work 7k. 1p. 3k. Turn. Circle of 7k. 1p. 2k. 1p. (rather long) 2k. 1p. 7k. Close. Turn. With two sh. 3k. 4p. sep. by 3k. 3k. (*). Turn. Circle of 7k. attaching to picot on circle just worked, 2k. attaching to long picot of same circle, 2k. 1p. 7k. Close. Turn. With two sh. 3k. 4p. sep. by 3k. 3k. Turn. Circle of 7k. attaching to picot of prec. circle 2k. attaching to long picot of first circle, 2k. 1p. 7k. Close. Turn. Circle of 7k. attaching to picot of prec. circle 2k. attaching to long picot of first circle 2k. attaching to free picot of first circle, 7k. Close. Turn. With two sh. 3k. 4p. sep. by 3k. 3k. attaching to base of four-leaved clover formed. Turn. With two sh. 3k. attaching to picot of nearby semicircle, 7k. Circle of 8k. attaching to first picot of circle nearby, 2k. 1p. 10k. Close. With two sh. 7k. Turn. Circle of 7k. attaching to second picot of arc of four-leaved clover, 7k. Close. With two sh. 3k. with left sh. work a circle of 3k. 5p. sep. by 3k. 3k. Close. With two sh. work 3k. Turn. Circle of 7k. 1p. 7k. Close. With two sh. 7k. Circle of 10k. 1p. 2k. 1p. 8k. Close. With two sh. 7k. 1p. 3k. Turn. Circle of 7k. 1p. 2k. 1p. (rather long) 2k. 1p. 7k. Close. Turn. With two sh. 3k. 1p. 3k. attaching to picot of circle of 7k. 1p. 7k. then 3k. 1p. 3k. 1p. 3k. Rep. from (*).

After working 11 four-leaved clovers, finish off the table centre by joining the last semicircle of 7k.

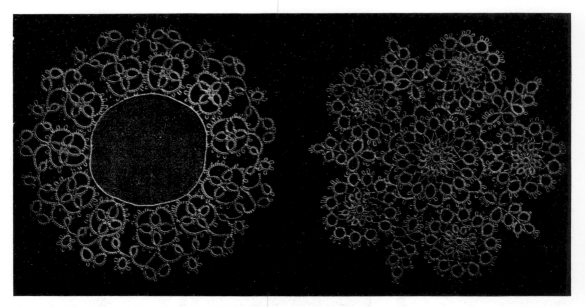

Fig. 38. Table centres in tatting worked in Coats Mercer-Crochet, No. 60, in white or natural

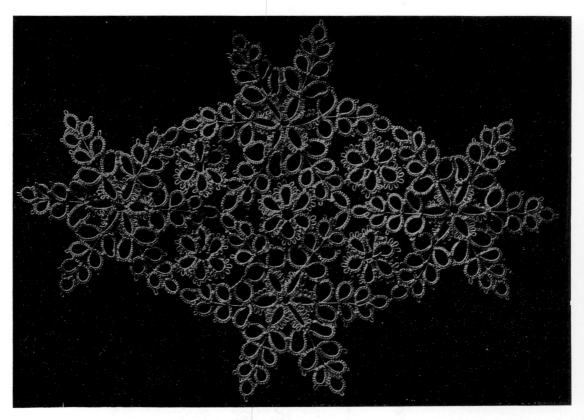

Fig. 39. Table centre in tatting worked in Coats Mercer-Crochet, No. 40, with a single shuttle

Table centre with richly-worked border in tatting, carried out in Coats Mercer-Crochet, No. 40, in white. From the detail given below, in actual size, it will be easy for anyone familiar with the work to follow the simple, easy motif. Each ray begins from the centre and goes towards the outside, being joined, in its turn, to the other rays

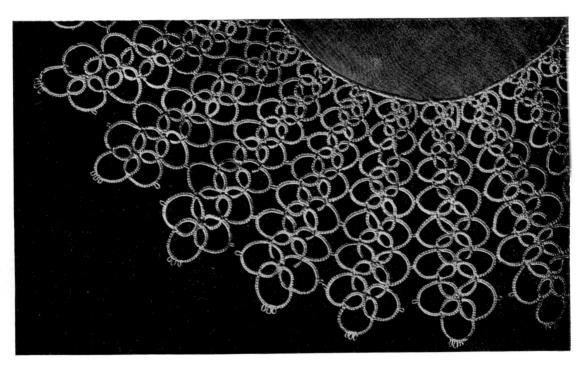

to the first circle worked at the beginning. Attach the lace to the material with Cording.

Fig. 39. Table centre.
Necessary Materials. Coats Mercer-Crochet, No. 40, in white: 1 20-gm. ball. Work with one shuttle.

Circle of 2k. 5p. sep. by 2k. 4k. 1 long p. (about 6 mm 4k. 5p. separated by 2k. 2k. Close. Circle of 10k. 3p. sep. by 5k. 10k. Close. (*). Turn. Very near to the prec. one work another circle of 10k. 3p. sep. by 5k. 10k. Close. Pass the thread, with a knot, through the centre of the two circles just worked. Leave about ¼ inch of thread and work a circle of 4k. attaching to last picot of nearby circle, 8k. 1p. 4k. 1p. 8k. Close. Turn. Very near to prec. one work another circle of 4k. attaching to picot of circle nearby 8k. 1p. 4k. 1p. 8k. Close. Pass the thread with a knot through the centre of the two circles just worked, leaving a length of thread of about ¼ inch and work a circle of 3k. attaching to picot of nearby circle, 7k. 1p. 3k. 1p. 7k. Close. Turn. Very near to this, work another circle of 3k. attaching to picot of nearby circle, 7k. 1p. 3k. 1p. 7k. Close. Pass the thread with a knot through the centre of the two circles just worked, leaving a short length of thread and work a circle of 3k. attaching to picot of nearby circle, 7k. 1p. 7k., attaching to corresponding picot of last circle worked 3k. Close. This completes the first ray of the star. Cut the thread and knot. Now proceed to work

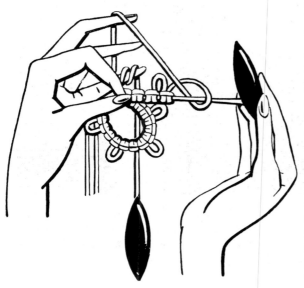

the second ray with a circle of 2k. 4p. sep. by 2k. 2k. attaching to corresponding picot of central circle of first ray, 4k., attaching to long picot of circle, 4k. 5p. sep. by 2k. 2k. Close. Turn. Circle of 10k. attaching to corresponding picot of first ray of star, 5k. attaching to following picot of same circle, 5k. 1p. 10k. Close. Rep. from (*) all round 6 times in all, not forgetting to attach last ray to the first.

When the first star has been completed work another three in the same way, arranging them as shown in the illustration and filling in the empty spaces with a star consisting of 6 circles all alike (4k. 9p. sep. by 2k. 4k. close), attaching them together to the first nine picots and to the large star, at the points which are clearly shown in the illustration.

Liqueur Set consisting of a large bottle mat and four, six or eight glass mats, illustrated on p. 211.
Necessary Materials. Coats Mercer-Crochet, No. 60 in white: 1 20-gm. ball.

Bottle Mat

1st row. Circle of 4k. 3p. sep. by 4k. 4k. Close. With two sh. work 5k. With left sh. work a circle of 5k. 3p. sep. by 5k. 5k. Close. Change sh. and work 5k. Turn. (*). With left sh. work a circle of 4k. attaching to picot of nearby circle 4k. 2p. sep. by 4k. 4k. Close. Change sh. and with two sh. work 5k. Turn. With left sh. work a circle of 5k. attaching to picot of nearby circle, 5k. 2p. sep. by 5k. 5k. Close. Change sh. and with two sh. work 5k. Turn. Rep. from (*) all round until 48 small circles and 48 larger circles have been formed. Join the last two circles to the first two.

2nd row. Circle of 5k. 1p. 5k. attaching to central picot of first outer circle of first row, 5k. 1p. 5k. Close. With two sh. 5k. Turn. With left sh. work a circle of 5k. 3p. sep. by 5k. 5k. Close. Change sh. and with two sh. work 5k. (*). Turn. With left sh. work a circle of 5k. attaching to picot of nearby circle 5k. attaching to central picot of following outer circle on first row, 5k. 1p. 5k. Close. Change sh. and with two sh. work 5k. Turn. With left sh. work a small circle of 5k. attaching to picot of nearby circle, 3k. 1p. 5k. Close. Work a second circle very near to the prec. one with 5k. attaching to picot of last circle, 5k. 1p. 3k. 3p. sep. by 1k. 3k. 1p. 5k. 1p. 5k. Close. Work a third circle with 5k. attaching to last picot of prec. circle 3k. 1p. 5k. Close. Change sh, with two sh. work 5k. Turn. With left sh. work a circle of 5k. attaching to picot of nearby circle, 5k. attaching to picot at centre of following circle outside, on first row, 5k. 1p. 5k. Close. Change sh. and with two sh. work 5k. Turn. With left sh. work a circle of 5k. attaching to last picot of nearby circle 5k. 2p. sep. by 5k. 5k. Close. Turn. Change sh. and with two sh. work 5k. Turn and rep. from (*) all round. At the end there should be 24 trefoils around a large centre.

Trace a circle on the material and attach the lace with buttonhole stitching. For the small mats proceed in the same way but omit the first row. Each mat will have 14 trefoils and 24 small circles.

Table centre in tatting worked in Coats Mercer-Crochet, No. 40, in white. This same thread, No. 40, allows the work to be carried out in colours too; we advise pale pink 624, pale green 573, pale blue 680, golden yellow 442, all very delicate shades which are easily made to fit in with the chinaware or colour scheme of the room

CHAPTER XVIII

Macramé Work

During last century, this unique type of work was very much in vogue; it is worked with knots and its origin is very ancient.

"Macramé" is an Arab word which in its original form means "fringe", so we must therefore assume that the work was imported from the East where it was very much in use. In Italy, in ancient terminology, it was called "Knotted stitch"—"punto a groppi" or "punto gropposo".

Like almost all Oriental embroidery it is very decorative work and its designs, twists or braids in geometrical forms are characteristic and unmistakable.

Today, macramé work has re-appeared in the vast production of handbags, very much admired by women, which are made in Sardinia, in Liguria and at Forli, and which maintain all the characteristics of the ancient type of work.

In macramé work, above all, fringes are worked, as the name indicates; these fringes are of all types, but very resistant materials may be formed from them, allowing the production of bags, handbags, chair coverings and decorative edgings of all kinds.

The work is different from the other types of lace-making which are produced with the aid of a needle, hook or shuttle, in that in macramé work only the worker's hands, with their agile movements in arranging, knotting, and braiding the threads, are necessary.

Necessary Materials. Since the basis of macramé work is the knot, it will be easily understood that the quality of the thread used is of the greatest importance. For macramé work the thread must be very easy running, well twisted and very strong. All these qualities are to be found in Coats threads, amongst which Coats Mercer-Crochet Nos. 3 and 10 may be chosen according to the fineness of the work to be done. This thread offers a wide range of fast colours for edgings and decorative household objects.

Technique of Macramé Work. Macramé is worked by fixing the threads to a rather heavy pillow: for smaller pieces of work, the usual lace-pillow will serve. Another method is that of using two supports to be screwed to the table at distances which can be regulated, and stretching the knot-carrying thread between the two upper edges; this gadget is, however, not on sale nowadays.

Knot-carrying and Knotting Threads. As we have already mentioned, macramé consists of a series of threads twisted or braided together in various ways to form the most varied designs. First of all it is necessary to arrange a horizontal thread, which we shall call the "knot-carrying" thread, on the pillow or between the two supports. On this thread, the other threads will be knotted little by little; we shall call these the "knotting"

Ciottoli, Faenza

Bags in macramé work. The first, on the left, as well as the bag on the right, is worked in two parts which are then mounted on strips of leather as shown in the picture. The stitches used are explained and illustrated in the course of the chapter dealing with this type of work

Fig. 1a. Loose knot
Fig. 1b. Drawn-up knot

Fig. 2. Series of knots attached to material

Fig. 3a. Simple knot with loop on left
Fig. 3b. Simple knot with loop on right

threads. These two threads may, in the course of the work, change their function: the knot-carrying thread may become the knotting thread and vice versa. Here we call the reader's attention to some important details; the knot-carrying thread must always remain fixed and stretched, both horizontally, or at any point during the work where it must be held in the hand whilst the other hand manoeuvres the knotting threads. In order to make rapid progress in this work, it is necessary to understand clearly that the knot-carrying thread must never move, and that it is the other, the knotting thread, which forms the knot on the fixed thread.

The base of every fringe or macramé work is given by the attachment of the knotting threads to the knot-carrying thread. First of all prepare a large number of threads of equal length: this length will vary according to the design to be worked. It is as well to calculate a length of four times that of the finished length. If the work has a large design, the threads must be wound on bobbins, off which the thread can be wound little by little as work proceeds.

To join threads in the course of the work, knot the old thread to the new with a single weaver's knot, trying to hide it on the back of the work, so that it cannot be seen on the right side.

Setting-on. There are various methods of setting-on the threads on the knot-carrying thread. Let us begin with the simplest. Fig. 1 is very clear: pass a double knotting thread from above below, behind the knot-carrying thread; fold over the ends, passing them through the loop and drawing up the knot tightly.

If, instead of attaching the thread to a knot-carrying thread, it has to be joined to material directly, proceed in the same way, using a crochet hook (Fig. 2).

Simple Knot. The first and simplest movement of macramé work is that of making a simple knot. Take one of the two threads of the first pair—the right-hand one—and hold it still and pulled tight with the right hand, whilst the left hand wraps the first thread around the pulled thread. Repeat this movement several times and a vertical chain will be formed of simple knots like that of Blanket Stitching, with the ridge on the left (Fig. 3 (a)).

Fig. 4 (a). Chain with two simple knots alternated
Fig. 4 (b). Chain with double thread

Fig. 6 (a) and 6 (b). Setting-on in simple loop
and chains

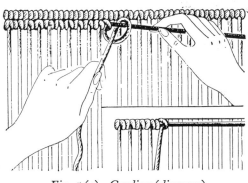

Fig. 5 (a). Cording (diagram)

Fig. 5 (b). Cording

Then practise in the reverse direction, i.e. with the ridge on the right (Fig. 3 (b)). In this case the first thread is held firm with the left hand, whilst the right hand holds the moving thread.

By alternating these two knots, worked as explained above, that is, one to the left and one to the right, a "chain" is formed as shown in Fig. 4 (a). Fig. 4 (b) shows a vertical, double chain worked, that is, with a double instead of a single thread.

Cording. Cording is one of the basic movements of macramé work. After setting on and in the course of the work itself, cords are often worked horizontally. After lining up the various threads on a knot-carrying thread, a second thread is immediately placed in position below, horizontally. On this, the knotting threads are wrapped around one by one. Each thread passes twice, moved by the left hand, whilst the right hand holds the horizontal knot-carrying thread well stretched. Then, beginning with the first knotting thread pass it from above below once, then the second time pass it again from below, above, so that the thread remains fixed and firm between the two twists (Figs. 5 (a) and 5 (b)).

Setting-on of Simple Loops. Fig. 6 shows the setting on of simple loops which is one of the easiest movements. Fix the double threads to the pillow with pins, then work a cord as explained above on a horizontal knot-carrying thread.

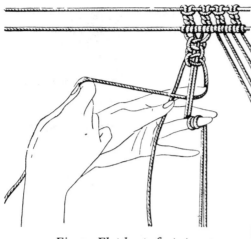

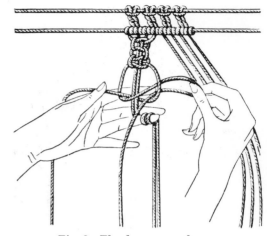

Fig. 7. Flat knot: first stage   *Fig. 8. Flat knot: second stage*

Setting-on in Chains. (Fig. 6 (b)). Fix the doubled threads over a horizontal knot-carrying thread, and then taking two threads at a time work four knots alternately (that is, one to the right and one to the left). Then fix the threads on the horizontal knot-carrying thread with cording. Before going on to other details, let us stop for a moment to consider a flat knot.

The Flat Knot. Figs. 7, 8, 9, 10, 11 and 12 show the method of working the "flat knot", which recurs so often in macramé work. The position of the hands and the twisting of the threads is very clearly shown in our illustrations. We would say, however, that in the flat knot, too, the central threads must remain stretched and unmoving, while the actual knot itself is worked by using the side threads. The flat knot is generally worked on four threads, but sometimes it can be worked on a twist of six or eight threads.

It is worked in two stages: set four threads on to the knot-carrier: hold the two central threads firmly, wrapping them round the third finger of the left hand, or simply by squeezing them between the third and little fingers (Fig. 7). Now take the fourth or first thread on the right, forming a loop on the right under the two stretched threads and above the first thread on the left: this first thread on the left is taken through the loop formed by the fourth thread (Fig. 8) and both ends are pulled, making a twist which is pulled up to the top over the two stretched threads (Fig. 9).

This is the first half of the flat knot. For the second part, proceed in the same way from the opposite side, i.e. taking the first thread forming a loop to the left (Fig. 10) below the two stretched threads in the right hand, and above the first thread on the right, which is taken through the loop formed by the first thread (Fig. 11), pulling the two ends and pulling the knot up to the top below the first half of the flat knot, thus forming the complete knot (Fig. 12).

Fig. 13 (a) shows a line of flat knots and Fig. 13 (b) shows a twisted row obtained by working the twist of the first half of the knot only.

Alternated Flat Knots. Fig. 14 shows a series of alternated flat knots: these are worked by making an entire flat knot taking four threads set-on, and then working other flat knots of four threads each. On the following row the threads for the flat knots are taken two from the first knot made and two from the second, alternately. This produces a kind of material which is very strong and practical for work-bags, etc.

Treble Flat Knot. Proceed as for the whole flat knot but follow this by the first half of the knot worked again (Fig. 15).

Flat Knot on Six Threads. Group together three doubled, that is, six, threads. First work the whole flat knot with the four central threads, then with the two lateral threads make a second whole flat knot which comprises also the first knot,

232

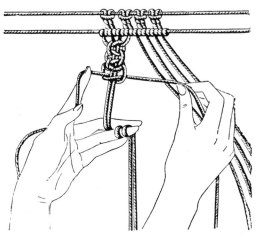

Fig. 9. Half flat knot

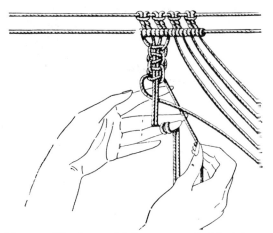

Fig. 10. Flat knot: third stage, as first but in opposite direction

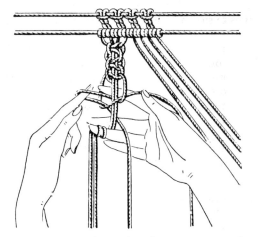

Fig. 11. Flat knot: fourth stage, as second but opposite

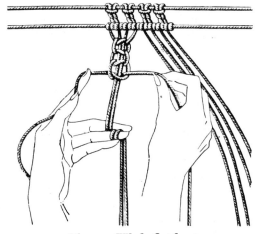

Fig. 12. Whole flat knot

making it bigger. Continue with a second knot, working in the same manner (Fig. 16).

Flat Knot with Picots. After making a whole flat knot. work a second one leaving a length of thread free (about half an inch). Then work a second flat knot, making it run up over the two central threads, thus forming a picot at either side (Fig. 17).

Nowadays, lace worked in macramé is very fashionable, worked in fine thread, substituting that made in crochet or tatting. We advise Coats Mercer-Crochet, No. 20.

Flat Knot with Second Knot. After working a whole flat knot, knot the two side threads, as shown in the illustration, drawing them up so that they form two knots, thus a second flat knot is formed (Fig. 18).

Balls. Another very nice decoration in macramé are the little balls standing out from the rest of the work. Set on four threads with two double threads each, on the knot-carrying thread, and work four or five whole flat knots over the four threads. Thread the two central threads between the two knots at the exact spot where they were set on.

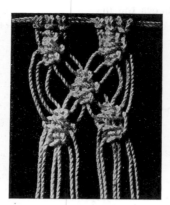

Fig. 13 (a). Series of whole flat knots
Fig. 13 (b). Series of half flat knots

*Fig. 16. Flat knots with
six threads*

Fig. 19. Small balls on flat knots

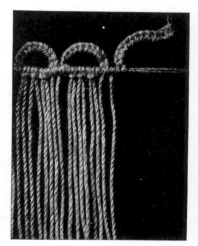

*Fig. 14. Flat knots interchanged
and alternated*

Fig. 17. Flat knots with picots

Fig. 20. Setting-on in chain loops

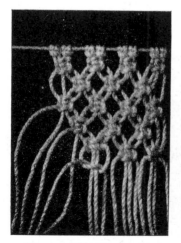

*Fig. 15. Flat knots with
three knottings*

*Fig. 18. Flat knots with small
side knots*

*Fig. 21. Setting-on with three loops
and two cords*

and pull up until the last knot touches the first. The ball is fixed here by working a whole flat knot immediately after it (Fig. 19).

Setting-on in Chains. Another interesting way of setting-on the work is by chains (Fig. 20). Above the right-hand thread, knot the left-hand thread eight or ten times, so that the loop formed is on the outside, that is, on the left. The two threads of the loop, when complete, are fixed by cording on the knot-carrying thread. Under the curve of the loop work two or three simple knots. After ten knots, turn the thread upwards and fix it by wrapping round the horizontal knot-carrying thread. The threads to be used for the loops should be longer than the others.

Setting-on with Three Loops. Work as for simple loops. Fix the doubled knotting threads to the pillow with pins, then work a flat knot with six threads, using four in the centre. Lastly, fix the threads by cording on the horizontal knot-carrying thread (Fig. 21).

Setting-on with Chain Drops. Take two doubled threads and fix them with pins to the pillow, work four simple knots, alternated, and then fix the threads to two horizontal knot-carrying threads with cording (Fig. 22).

Setting-on Flat Knots. Take two doubled threads and fix with pins to the pillow, one near to the other; then, with four threads work a whole flat knot and fix the threads to the horizontal knot-carrying thread with cording. If the setting-on band is to be broader, work two consecutive whole flat knots, before fixing the threads to the knot-carrier (Fig. 23).

Here is given a list of the most common ways of setting-on the work. In addition, after this setting-on and before working the actual fringes, an edging border is generally worked. This border may be worked in different ways; some of them are given here.

Border of Flat Knots. After having set on the threads doubled, two by two, work five or six whole flat knots, with four threads. Then close with another knot-carrying thread on which the cording will be worked (Fig. 24).

Border of Twisted Columns. These columns are obtained by working a series of five or six half

Fig. 22. Setting on in chains in double threads and cording

Fig. 23. Setting-on in loops, flat knots and cording

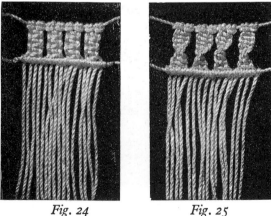

Fig. 24   *Fig. 25*

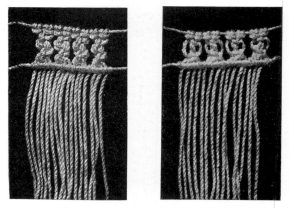

Fig. 26   Fig. 27

Fig. 28. Border with small columns in flat knots
and cording

Fig. 29. Border with simple and double
chains and cording

flat knots. That is, always repeating the first movement of the whole flat knot. As for the other border, close with another knot-carrier on which the cording will be worked (Fig. 25).

Border of Columns of Double Chains. After setting on the threads doubled two at a time, work in twos making six chain stitches alternately and double (i.e. one knot to the right and one to the left). Close with a border made by the usual knot-carrying thread covered with cording (Fig. 26).

Border of Flat and Simple Knots. After setting on the threads, doubled, two by two, take four and work the first half of a flat knot: then knot the two central threads with two simple knots, pulling up the threads tightly, and then immediately below this knot, make a whole flat knot. This border is also closed by a second knot-carrying thread, covered with cording (Fig. 27).

Border with Flat Knots and Cording. (Fig. 28). Set on six pairs of threads on the horizontal knot-carrier (★). On the first four threads work five whole flat knots. Then work on the following eight threads. The fourth thread will be a knot-carrying thread: wrap the first three threads round making a bar to the left. Then take the fifth thread as a knot-carrier and wrap the last three round it, making an oblique bar to the right.

Join the four central threads with a whole flat knot. The thread on the left will now be the knot-carrier and wrap round it the three following threads making an oblique bar to the right; the last thread on the right will be the knot-carrier for the oblique bar to the left.

Repeat from (★) for the desired length.

Then wrap the threads around a horizontal thread.

Border in Double and Simple Chains (Fig. 29). After setting-on in chains worked with four threads, work a cord, horizontally, then a series of simple chains on two threads with six twists, and lastly a horizontal cord.

Border with Twists of Cording (Fig. 30). Set-on six pairs of threads on the horizontal knot-carrier. Wrap the threads over a second horizontal knot-carrier using the usual cording. Then take the first threads as knot-carrier, holding it in the right hand and wrapping round it the following five threads, making an oblique bar to the right;

then take the twelfth thread as knot-carrier, holding it in the left hand and wrapping the five nearby threads round it, making an oblique bar to the left. Then cross and knot the two central, inside threads, that is, pass the sixth thread to the place of the seventh and vice versa. Take the seventh thread in the left hand and wrap the five left-hand threads around it, then take the sixth thread in the right hand and wrap the five threads on the right around it. Lastly, wrap all the threads around a new knot-carrier, with cording.

Oblique Cording to Left and Right. Fig. 31 shows an oblique cording worked on five doubled knots, i.e. on ten threads. In this case, the knot-carrier is always the same. It is the first thread on the left, and is held stretched in the right hand while the knots are made with the left, i.e. on the knot-carrier all nine threads are knotted, one after the other, passing them twice as for horizontal cording. After completing the wrapping of the threads, proceed to make the oblique cording to the left, keeping the same thread as knot-carrier, but holding this firm with the left hand, whilst the following nine threads are knotted with the right hand.

Fig. 32 shows a pretty twist of oblique bars, giving the various stages of the work. Here is the method:

After setting-on the doubled threads on a knot-carrier, place another knot-carrier and work the usual cording. Then work the first six threads (three pairs) in the following way:

Fig. 30. Border in horizontal and oblique cording

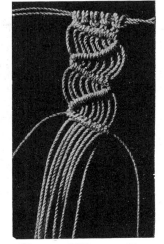

Fig. 31. Oblique cording

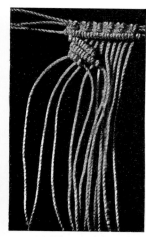   

Fig. 32 (a) *Fig. 32 (b)* *Fig. 32 (c)* *Fig. 32 (d)*

237

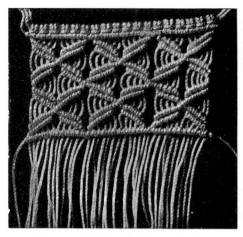

Fig. 33. Fringe in oblique cording

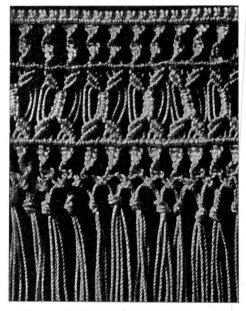

Fig. 34. Fringe in flat knots and cording

The first thread acts as knot-carrier, and the other five threads are wrapped round it successively, passing them twice, as for cording. Then take the first thread on the left as knot-carrier, and knot the five threads on to it. For the third time, take the first thread on the left as knot-carrier and knot the five threads on to it. Thus a small diamond shape is formed of three bars of oblique cording (Fig. 32 (a)).

Now leave the first six threads idle and work on the six following ones. Take the last thread on the

right in the left hand; this thread will be the knot-carrier for the other five. After completing the first bar, take, once again, the last thread on the right in the left hand; this will, in its turn, form the knot-carrier for the wrapping of the five threads. For the third time, take the last thread on the right to wrap the five threads as previously (Fig. 32 (b)).

On completing this second diamond, which will be the same as the first, but placed in the opposite direction, join the two central threads by knotting. The thread of the diamond on the right will now act as knot-carrier, being held in the left hand, whilst the five threads are wound round the knot-carrier. The first thread on the inside will now act as knot-carrier for the second bar, and then again, the first thread on the inside will be the knot-carrier for the third bar (Fig. 32 (c)).

Finally, for the fourth diamond, take the first thread in the centre, and, holding it with the right hand, use it as knot-carrier for the five threads to be wound round it. In the same way, as already explained, the first central thread will be the knot-carrier for the second and for the third bar (Fig. 32 (d)).

Here are some illustrations of macramé fringes for the working of which we advise the use of Coats Mercer-Crochet, Nos. 3 and 10, in white or écru.

Fig. 33. *1st row.* On horizontal knot-carrier, knot a number of pairs of threads, in multiples of six.

2nd row. Cording.

3rd row. Two oblique bars to the right with six threads: the first thread acts as knot-carrier and is held in the right hand.

4th row. Two oblique bars to the left with six threads: the sixth thread acts as knot-carrier and is held in the left hand. On completing the four crossed bars, twist them, the last thread on the left with the first on the right. These two threads have thus changed positions, becoming at the same time knot-carriers. Work two other bars to the left and two to the right. This completes the first motif which is then repeated for the desired length.

Last row. Cording.

Fig. 34. *1st row.* On the horizontal knot-carrier knot a number of pairs of threads in multiples of four.

2nd row. Cording.

3rd row. Columns of flat knots on four twisted threads (i.e. composed of the first half of flat knots). Work ten knots in all.

4th row. Cording.

5th row. Two oblique bars to the right worked on four threads: the fourth thread, held in the left hand, acts as knot-carrier. Two oblique bars to the left: the first thread acts as knot-carrier and is held in the right hand.

6th row. Four whole flat knots worked on the four central threads between the two oblique diamonds.

7th row As 5th, but follow the illustration so as not to mistake the direction of the bar.

8th row. Cording.

9th row. Columns of flat knots on four twisted threads (i.e. composed of the first half of a flat knot). Work eight knots in all.

10th row. Two chain stitches alternating with four threads. Knot the fringe four threads at a time.

Fig. 35. *1st row*. Horizontal flat knot with threads knotted in twos, up to a total which is a multiple of twenty.

2nd row. Columns of six whole flat knots on four threads.

3rd row. Cording.

4th row. Three columns of four whole flat knots worked on four threads. Leave eight threads idle and repeat the columns. Work two columns of four flat knots, each under the three already worked, and then a column of four under the two already made. Return now to work the eight threads left aside. The second thread will be the knot-carrier and is held in the left hand. Wind the first thread round it and then the other four of the column, four times each. They thus form an oblique bar to the left.

Repeat, taking the fourth thread as knot-carrier and making a second oblique bar to the left. Repeat the same work on the four successive threads, working two bars to the right. Lastly, work a whole flat knot at the centre with eight threads; four at the centre and two at each side.

5th row. Cording.

Repeat from beginning, changing the motif as indicated in the illustration.

Fig. 36. *1st row*. Horizontal knot-carrier with knots in a multiple of sixteen.

2nd row. Cording.

3rd row. On four threads work two oblique bars to the left (wind the first three threads on to the fourth as knot-carrier).

4th and 5th rows. Two cords.

6th row. With the first twelve threads work three columns of whole flat knots (two knots over four threads each) then, interchanging the threads, work another two below, and lastly a third, below the previous two. Leave aside the four following threads and repeat the same process as already described on the twelve following threads and so on.

Then take up again the four threads left aside. The second thread acts as knot-carrier. Wind the first and then, one by one, the other six threads, coming from the columns of flat knots on the right, round this. Thus we have two groups of eight threads each, i.e. sixteen threads. Now work three oblique bars to the left and, interchanging the threads, which, from being knotting threads become knot-carriers and vice versa, work three oblique bars to the right, alternating with three worked to the left and three to the right. Now the first and last of the sixteen threads with which the twists were made become knot-carriers and seven threads on either side are wound round them. When the squares have been worked, repeat the groups of six columns from bottom to top, i.e. first one on four threads, then two on eight threads and lastly, three on twelve threads.

7th and 8th rows. Two cords.

9th row. As 3rd.

10th and 11th rows. Two cords.

12th row. Knot with chain of ten simple knots, alternating all the threads four at a time and lastly knotting the chains in twos.

Fig. 37. *Corded edging*. Set-on to the horizontal knot-carrier, eight double threads or sixteen single threads. Work the first eight threads (the eighth being the knot-carrier held in the left hand), and work an oblique bar to the left, then a second and a third. Repeat the process on the following eight threads, but in the opposite direction (the first thread of the second group of eight threads, held in the right hand, acts as knot-carrier).

Now join the eight central threads with a flat knot (four central threads and two lateral). Take up again the threads to the left of the oblique bar to the right and with the right-hand threads, the oblique bars to the left (the fourth thread counting from the outside will be the knot-carrier). On completing the bars on both sides, join the four

Fig. 35. Fringe in flat knots and cording worked in Coats Mercer-Crochet, No. 3

Fig. 36. Rich fringe in horizontal cording, oblique cording and flat knots

Fig. 37. Edging in cording, chains, flat knots and balls

Fig. 38. Fringe worked in Coats Mercer-Crochet, No. 10, in two colours

Fig. 39. Fringe similar to preceding figure with a different arrangement of colours

central threads and work six whole flat knots, and with them work a ball (see explanation and illustration 19), fixing it with a whole flat knot: then work the six threads to the left in the following manner: work two chains of simple knots with the first two threads, work another two chains of simple knots with the second pair of threads. Now work an oblique bar to the right, winding the five threads round the first, which is the knot-carrier. Repeat the chains of knots and bars another three times. Repeat the same work on the six threads to the right, while the four central threads remain fixed.

Begin again from the beginning making bars from the centre to the left and from the centre to the right and continue as explained above.

Figs. 38 and 39 show two fringes worked with threads of different colours. In working them the reader's attention is drawn to the explanation and to Fig. 32; as to the thread used, the two fringes were worked in Coats Mercer-Crochet, No. 10.

For the fringe in Fig. 38 set on to the horizontal knot-carrier three pairs of threads in 503, and three pairs in 621. For the work in Fig. 39 set on, above the usual horizontal knot-carrier, a pair of threads in 623 and a pair in 442, then two pairs in 523 and one in 442 and one in 623. Repeat the same arrangement for the following pairs.

Macramé work in colours is very decorative. For fringes it is wise to keep in mind the colour of the article to which the fringe is to be applied. For handbags, choose a colour which matches the wardrobe, not forgetting that bags all in white are very elegant.

Fig. 40. *1st row.* Set on to the horizontal knot-carrier, a number of pairs of threads in multiples of ten.

2nd row. Cording.

3rd row. Two oblique bars to the right: the first thread acts as knot-carrier and the other five are wound round it.

4th row. Cording.

5th row. Five knots in chain on two threads, four knots in chain on two threads, five knots in chain on two threads, two knots in chain on four threads, five knots in chain on two threads, four knots in chain on two threads, five knots in chain on two threads.

6th row. Eight Buttonhole Stitches with ridge on left with six threads of first three chains: the thread on the left takes up the other five.

Two knots in chain with eight threads joining the two following chains, and two knots in chain on four threads each. Eight Buttonhole Stitches with ridge on right, taking up the threads of the last three chains. The last thread makes the Buttonhole Stitch, taking up the five threads.

241

7th row. Five knots in chain on two threads. Two knots in chain on six threads, five knots in chain on two threads, five knots in chain on the following two threads, two knots in chain on six threads, five knots in chain on two threads.

8th row. Two whole flat knots with eight threads to the left and two knots in chain with eight knots to the right. The two external side threads take in the four inside threads.

9th row. Two whole flat knots binding all twenty threads (the two side threads on the outside bind sixteen threads).

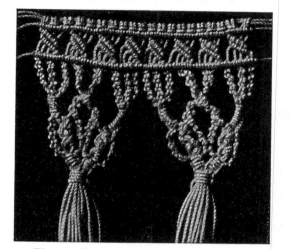

Fig. 40. Fringe in bars, cording and chains

Fig. 41. Fringe in flat knots and chains, introducing beads

Fig. 42. Fringe worked with bars on the wrong side

Fig. 43. Model of a bag in macramé work

242

Fig. 41. Beads, or glass or wooden balls can also be applied to macramé work. Here we give a pattern of an easy fringe decorated with two balls to each pattern.

1st row. Set on a number of pairs of threads in multiples of sixteen.

2nd row. Cording.

3rd row. Join the threads in fours with whole flat knots.

4th row. Alternate the whole flat knots with those of the previous row.

5th row. With the first four threads on the left, work a chain of five knots, alternated, then two whole flat knots on four threads each, and then, on the last four threads work a chain of five knots alternated.

6th row. Thread the balls below the two whole flat knots.

7th row. Two whole flat knots below the balls.

8th row. Three whole flat knots alternated with those of the preceding row.

9th row. On the first four threads to the left work a chain of five knots, then two whole knots and lastly, on the last four threads, a chain of five knots alternated.

10th row. Thread a bead below the two whole flat knots.

11th row. Two whole flat knots joining all sixteen threads. The two side threads on the outside take up the other twelve threads.

Fig. 42. Set on to a horizontal knot-carrying thread a number of double threads in multiples of six and work the usual cording over a new knot-carrier.

Turn the work and on the wrong side work as in Fig. 32. The bars are formed here by four oblique cords on six threads each. Join the two diamonds with two threads on each side, making a whole flat knot, and then repeat the working of the diamonds with the cording in the opposite direction. Each group of diamonds on six threads is joined to the following by means of a whole flat knot on four threads.

On completing the groups of four bars to the required length, turn the work and on what is now the right side, work a whole flat knot every two threads, with four threads. Then knot the threads over a new horizontal knot-carrier.

Fig. 43. *Bag.* The bag is formed by two equal pieces of work, sewn together at their base. The pieces measure about 10 inches in height and 2 inches in width.

Set on forty pairs of threads: each thread will be about about 3 m long.

Immediately after this simple setting-on, which will be folded to the inside and not seen, work four rows of cording, each row very close to the next, then eight rows of whole flat knots alternated, and immediately after, another two rows of cording

Towels with rich fringes in macramé work

The central part of the work follows, worked in groups of oblique bars joined four at a time as in Fig. 32.

Seven rows of flat knots, alternated, are worked immediately after the central panel. Then work another two rows of cording and two rows of three oblique bars, once to the right and once to the left. Lastly, finish off the piece with three rows of cording.

When the two pieces are completed, they should be perfectly equal, and then they are joined at the base.

Work, separately, two circles of single crochet with a diameter of about 15 cm. Sew the two sides of the pieces of work to the circumference of these circles, gathering the upper strip a little, to give the curved line of the bag, as is clearly shown in the illustration. The handle is made of a cord worked in whole flat knots over about a dozen threads.

Details, in natural size, of the fringes for towels illustrated on page 243. The fringes were worked in Coats Mercer-Crochet, No. 10, in white

◄ *Macramé coasters worked in two different shades of cord*

245

CHAPTER XIX

Cavandoli Work

The Head of the "Casa del Sole" in Turin, Mrs. Valentina Cavandoli, created this stitch which takes its name from her, in order to amuse and occupy the children in her care, during their long hours out of doors. It is, actually, another version of macramé, explained in the previous chapter. Cavandoli is a compact material, closely worked, in threads of two colours—one for the background and the other making the design. We advise Coats Mercer-Crochet.

It is amusing work, and not at all tiring, with a characteristic appearance and which may have many and varied uses. In fact, Cavandoli work is very suitable for book-covers, book-marks, bags and handbags, belts, covers for boxes and seats, children's slippers, fringes for towels, etc.

A design in cross-stitch, when very simple, can be worked in Cavandoli Stitch.

The children of the open-air school "Casa del Sole", even the very young ones (five or six years old), and both boys and girls, are able, under the guidance of the older children and the teachers, to become quickly expert in this work, and from their small hands come, as if by magic, the thousands of practical articles, which are generally offered or sold to the benefactors of the Institution.

Necessary Materials. As for macramé work, Cavandoli is work based on knots, and therefore only thread is necessary for its successful accomplishment. This thread must, however, be of the best quality, and must offer the greatest guarantee of strength, easy running and fast colours. Coat's Mercer-Crochet, Nos. 3 and 10, is the best thread, giving the most perfect results.

Attempts to work Cavandoli stitch in more than two colours have not given good results and have been abandoned.

Technique of Cavandoli Work. As we have already mentioned, the design for this work is based on cross-stitch designs, that is, geometrical shapes, flowers, leaves and even stylised animals and figures. It should not be forgotten, however, that in all Cavandoli work the figures are slightly deformed, as the stitch elongates them, and for this reason a certain practice in choosing suitable designs is necessary. The motifs of the pattern are worked to stand out, vertically, on a background which is worked horizontally. In fact, on looking closely at our illustrations, the two different directions of the stitches are clearly visible. Each square of the design is worked with two horizontal stitches for the background and two vertical stitches for the pattern itself.

There are three movements in the work, and the diagrams show the procedure: the winding of the knotting-thread round the knot-carrier for the horizontal stitches (see Cording in chapter on Macramé), and then a vertical stitch to the right and one to the left.

Now let us explain in detail the method for following the pattern given in Fig. 1. Once the procedure has been well learned, the sewer will be able to follow any other Cavandoli design.

The pattern, traced on the squared paper, is placed on the left of the worker.

On a pillow fixed to a table, fix a knot-carrying thread on which seven double threads in the background colour are set on; in this case, natural (see explanation in chapter on Macramé). There will therefore be fourteen threads in all, just as there are fourteen squares in the design. If there is an odd number of squares, leave out one thread at the end of the first row, later fixing it to be back of the work, since the threads are always double.

Separately prepare a ball of Coats Mercer-Crochet, No. 10, in this case red is used. This thread is always carried through the work, whether it be visible or invisible, and is only cut away when the work has been completed.

High up to the left, fix the end of the ball of thread to the knot-carrying thread (later, this will be taken through to the wrong side), and begin to knot the first thread in natural colour with the red thread. The illustrations Nos. 2 and 3 show clearly how the braid is worked: make the first natural thread pass over the red one and then braid according to the pattern. When the braid is complete, pull the natural thread, the knot-carrier, with the left hand, sliding the red thread on it to form a vertical stitch immediately under the setting-on (Fig. 4). Repeat the same movement with the same threads and form a second vertical stitch under the first. Then pass on to the second natural thread, working the same braid and forming two further vertical red stitches. Now the red thread forms the knot-carrier, and the ten following natural threads are wound round it in cording (i.e. winding twice for each thread (Fig. 5)). At this point, repeat the braiding worked at the beginning, i.e. twist the natural thread with the red, forming two vertical red stitches on the

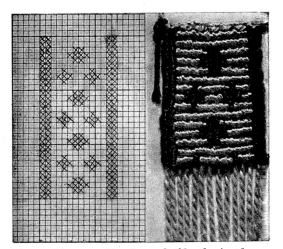

Fig. 1. Diagram of border and of border just begun

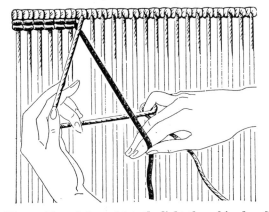

Fig. 2. From left to right: the light thread is placed over the dark one

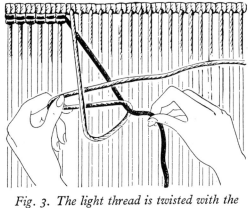

Fig. 3. The light thread is twisted with the dark one

247

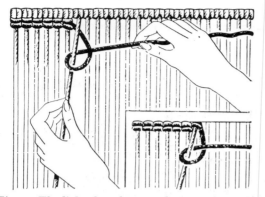

Fig. 4. The light thread acts as knot-carrier and the dark thread as the knotting thread

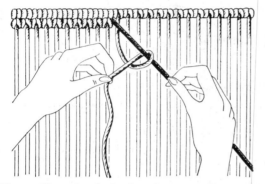

Fig. 5. Here the dark thread acts as knot-carrier and the light as the knotting thread

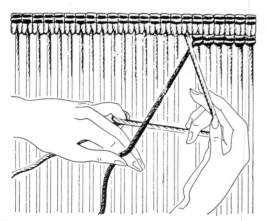

Fig. 6. From right to left: the light thread is placed over the dark one but in the opposite direction to Fig. 2

next-to-the-last thread and another two vertical red stitches on the last.

When the row is finished, proceed from right to left in the same way. The braiding of the natural thread with the red (shown in Figs. 6, 7 and 8) is actually the same as the first, but worked in the opposite direction. Now the natural-coloured carrier-thread is held in the right hand and the red thread slides up this, pushed by the left hand. As in the preceding row, work two red stitches, ten natural and two red. The third line, from the left towards the right, is formed by two red stitches, four natural, two red. The fourth line consists of two red stitches, three natural, two red. The fifth line is like the third and the sixth like the first and second. The seventh is formed of two red stitches, two natural, one red, four natural, one red, two natural, two red. The eighth line is formed of two red stitches, one natural, three red, two natural, three red, one natural, two red. The ninth line is like the seventh, and at this point in the work begin again from the second line.

The outside threads which always form the coloured borders are never shortened, or only very little; for the other threads, however, a length of at least seven times the length required, in proportion to the design to be worked, should be used. In Cavandoli work, the hands must hold the work high, that is, very near to the rows which are being worked, so that the stitches are well drawn-up, forming a compact and even piece of material.

It is as well to calculate always the length of the threads before starting to work, so that it is not necessary to make joins. If necessary try to hide the join, or the ends of the threads, between the rows on the back of the work. Cavandoli work is, however, double-sided, that is to say, the wrong side should also be free from imperfections.

The illustrations on pages 250 and 251 show some articles worked in Cavandoli Stitch.

Fig. 9 shows a needle case finished at the bottom with a fringe in macramé, the instructions for which will be found in the appropriate chapter.

The needle case is double, that is, worked in the form of a book, and the threads of both sides are set-on in the centre. First work one half and then the other. The background is worked in Coats Mercer-Crochet, No. 10, in écru 609; the design is in Coats Mercer-Crochet, No. 10, in blue 621.

Fig. 10 shows a small rectangle for covering a box. The background here is dark and worked in

Rich fringe in Cavandoli work; it may be used for curtains, chair-back covers, car-seat covers, etc. The work is carried out in Coats Mercer-Crochet, No. 10, in blue 621 for the background and the pattern in écru 609. The actual fringe is macramé, work which is very similar to Cavandoli. In the previous chapter we have clearly explained the different stitches in macramé work. Each small fringe shown here is formed by alternate chains, oblique cords and flat knots

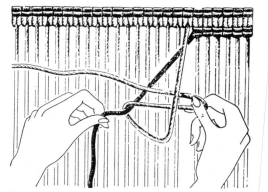

Fig. 7. *The light thread is twisted with the dark one in the opposite direction to Fig. 3*

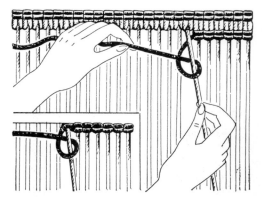

Fig. 8. *The light thread acts as knot-carrier and the dark thread as the knotting thread*

Fig. 9. *Needle case worked in Coats Mercer-Crochet, No. 10, in écru 609 for the background and fringe, and in blue 621 for the design: it consists of two equal parts*

Fig. 10. *Design for a box-cover worked in Coats Mercer-Crochet, No. 10, in green 623 for the background and écru 609 for the design*

Coats Mercer-Crochet, No. 10, in green, whilst the design is worked in Coats Mercer-Crochet, No. 10, in écru.

Lastly, Fig. 12 shows a design for a bookmark in blue 621 in Coats Mercer-Crochet, No. 10, and in écru 609 of the same thread.

The illustration at the top of page 251 shows the beginning of a piece of material for covering a bench. The work, as in all types of Cavandoli work, is carried out in two colours: pink 503 and écru 609 in Coats Mercer-Crochet, No. 10, and follows a simple geometrical design which is very effective. To reproduce the design it is only

necessary to count the stitches and substitute them with crosses on squared paper.

The material produced on working Cavandoli Stitch is very strong and closely woven like tapestry work and can be used for furniture coverings, bags, folders, book-covers and finger pads, etc.

Cavandoli work is little known in Italy and even less so abroad. It is limited to the small group of the Instituto del Sole in Turin, where, however, teachers continue to create and improve new work with all their zeal and good taste. It is mentioned here as being an interesting type of work which will probably be widely developed.

Fig. 11. Work in Cavandoli stitch just begun. There are forty pairs of threads in Coats Mercer-Crochet, No. 10

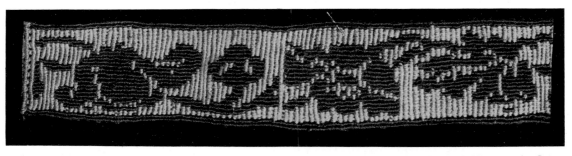

Fig. 12. Small bookmark worked by children of the Casa del Sole, Turin. The design is blue 621 in Coats Mercer-Crochet, No. 10, on a background worked in écru 609

CHAPTER XX

Teneriffe Lace

Teneriffe lace takes its name from the biggest of the Canary Islands, where it is made and sold very profitably to tourists travelling to Europe or America, on their way through the Islands. The term "Brazilian" or "Bolivian" lace, however, makes us think that its origin was probably Latin-American. In any case, Teneriffe lace is one of the famous "Sun" laces which were very fashionable in Spain in the sixteenth century, with the difference that, whilst these were worked on a background of material, Teneriffe lace is worked separately and possesses all the characteristics of real lace, with the delicate braids of threads, which, grouped together in the centre, open into rays towards the outer edge.

Teneriffe lace is, in fact, formed by many circular star shapes. Squares, ellipses, diamonds, insertions and borders may also be worked, but the characteristic form is the star. Each star or each square is worked separately and then appliquéd to the material, or they are joined to each other with subsidiary stitches. It is, therefore, a type of lace which is especially suitable for trimmings and which can be successfully used to substitute Venetian lace or Aemilia-Ars, which are more difficult to work. At the beginning of this century it was also used to decorate feminine wearing apparel.

Necessary Materials. A long needle with a blunt end and very strong thread is necessary for this work. The best type of thread is Coats Mercer-Crochet in varying thicknesses, or Coats Anchor Coton à Broder, or Coats Anchor Pearl Cotton is also suitable for heavier types of work. Like all laces, Teneriffe is generally worked in white or écru.

Technique of Working Teneriffe Lace. This work is much easier and quicker than it may at first seem. There are various ways of working

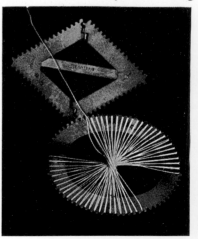

Fig. 1. Steel frames with saw-toothed edges for Teneriffe work

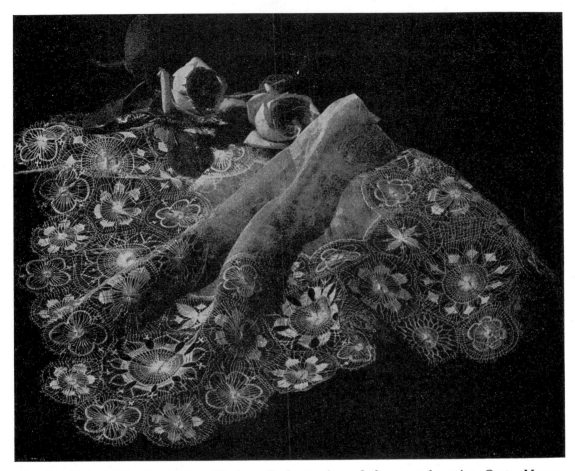

Handkerchief with border in Teneriffe lace. Each star is worked separately, using Coats Mercer-Crochet, No. 80. On page 257 we show a detail of one corner of the handkerchief, in actual size. As can be easily seen from the enlargement, each star is formed of crossed threads, drawn together at the centre by a wheel or web and then decorated with all stitches found in hemstitching and which have already been clearly and carefully explained in the chapter headed "Hemstitch"

Teneriffe lace. At one time it was worked on small, round or square pillows, covered with cloth on which the star design was traced. Steel pins were placed all around the outside edge of the star at a distance of about 3 mm one from the other, and with the points facing the centre.

Starting from the centre the thread was taken from one pin to that exactly opposite on the diameter, and from here to the pin on the left of the starting point, going back to the opposite one until

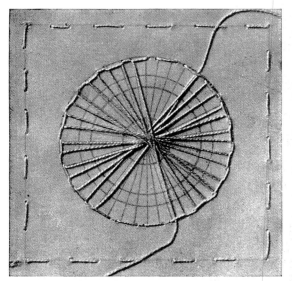

Fig. 2. Stretching the threads

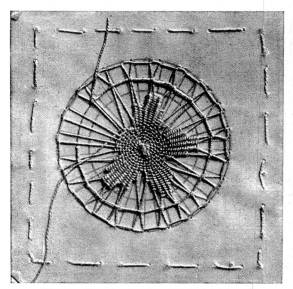

Fig. 3. Star in darning stitch, just begun

the rays of the star had been filled in. After placing these threads, the internal part of the star was worked.

Later, special metal frames were produced, with saw-toothed edges (Fig. 1) in all shapes and sizes, on which the threads could be fixed and which were fitted with a special gadget for opening to allow the work to be removed on completion. This gadget is difficult to find nowadays, as Teneriffe has gone out of fashion, so there is no longer that wide variety of choice of shapes which the embroideress once had, and therefore a third procedure is described which is considered to be easy and not at all expensive.

Trace the outline of a circle about 6 or 7 cm in diameter on to rather strong card, with a number of rays crossing it (one every 3 mm) and with other concentric circles inside which will serve as a guide during work. Place tracing paper over this, as this allows the pattern to be seen below, and fix it down with long tacking stitches. Then, using very strong thread (Coats Drima (polyester)), work the stitches which we shall call "supporting" stitches, and which touch all the rays at the circumference of the circle. With the thread chosen for working the star, and which in the example is Coats Mercer-Crochet, No. 40, begin work from the centre to a supporting stitch. Then take the thread over to the opposite side, take it through the opposite supporting stitch and then take it back through the following supporting stitch and so on until all the stitches have been worked and the circle of card appears to be covered with threads like a wheel with a large number of spokes (Fig. 2). To avoid joining thread during work use a Milwards Gold Seal tapestry needle No. 21, which allows of a greater amount of thread in use. The threads of the rays should never cross each other, except at the centre. On completing the fixing in place of the spokes, using the same thread work a wheel or web at the centre (Fig. 3).

The wheels at the centre of the stars worked in Teneriffe are worked in darning stitch. A variety of stitches may now be worked on the stretched threads of the stars or squares; these stitches may follow a particular pattern or may be left to the good taste and choice of the embroideress. Before beginning the filling-in work, it is wise to arrange the division of the threads in order to be sure there are neither too many nor too few for the design desired. All the stitches in Teneriffe work

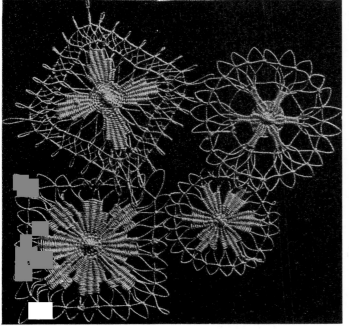

Fig. 4. Stars in Teneriffe lace worked in Coats Mercer-Crochet, No. 40

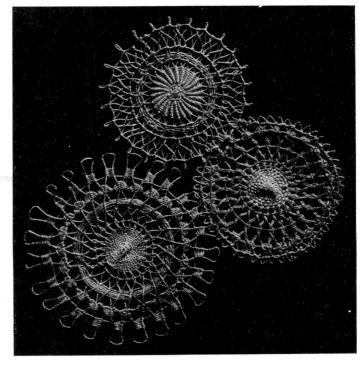

Fig. 5. More stars worked in Coats Mercer-Crochet, No. 40

Fig. 6. Other
stars in Tene-
riffe lace
worked in
Coats Mer-
cer-Crochet,
No. 40

are those used in Hemstitching which we have
already clearly and fully explained in the
chapter under that heading. Therefore, anyone
who has experience of Hemstitching should easily
be able to overcome any slight difficulty which
Teneriffe work presents. Darning Stitch columns
joined or alternated, Cording, webs, half wheels,
knots, etc., are all used in this type of work.

Working always from the centre towards the
outer edge (Fig. 3), it should be easy to copy any
design. Our illustrations are quite clear and show
some easily copied designs (Figs. 4, 5 and 6).

Each star or square has, almost always, on the
outer edge some type of loop which serves for its
attachment to the material and this is obtained by
working a series of knots on alternate threads. To
join threads when working, use a weaver's knot.

Since Teneriffe lace must, like all laces, show
perfectly even work on both sides, the knot should
be as small and flat as possible; it can then be
easily hidden in the work. When threads are
passed from one place to another, they should also
be invisible; the needle will pass easily through the
darning stitch, so to pass from one position to
another a series of overcasting stitches should be
made, avoiding as far as possible, long stretches of
thread.

Fig. 7. Border for a dress worked in Teneriffe lace
on a drawn-thread background

When the star is complete, cut the supporting threads on the back of the card, pulling them out; the star will then come away by itself.

In its time, a special border made by machine, consisting of a perforated border to which long loops of thread were attached, substituted the work of fixing the rays, when the loops were joined at the centre. It is not necessary to point out, however, how much more valuable is the work done entirely by hand.

Details in actual size of the handkerchief illustrated at the beginning of the chapter. Note the variety of design, each star different from the other, but all worked in the same manner

CHAPTER XXI

"Puncetto" Work

The so-called " puncetto" work is a lace from Valsesia, worked by the women of the valley for years. It originated in the sixteenth century but never became sufficiently diffused to give rise to commercial activity.

It is a needle-made lace with a classical design which is very small and worked with very fine thread. It is very suitable for many varied types of work, just because of its subtlety, whilst the manner in which it is worked and the quality of the thread used, guarantee that it is very durable.

It is one of the many fine traditions of the Italian mountain passes which help to give a foundation in fact to the poetry of art and of hard work instilled in the humble yet strong Alpine people, so dear to the Italian heart, and so much admired beyond her borders.

The name "puncetto" comes from a Piedmont word which, in dialect, means "stitch". It is also called "Valsesian" stitch and is often used to decorate the women's national costumes in Piedmont and the Alps.

A white shirt or blouse embroidered on the front with this lace and with a collar in the same type of work is worn with a very tight bodice made of felt or velvet in brown or black, matching the skirt, which differs slightly from region to region. The wide sleeves, joined to the blouse at the shoulders with an inset of puncetto work two or three inches wide, are gathered at the bottom

into a cuff of lace closed with small buttons. The blouses worn by the youngest women are also embroidered in red and blue cross-stitch, worked very precisely over counted threads. An apron in blue cloth completes the costume: this is worked in the brightest and most varied colours such as red, green, yellow, orange, pink, purple, with borders of puncetto and insets down the centre. Altogether the costume is very picturesque and is worn by the women for folk-gatherings, national holidays, processions, etc. Each village has its own dominating colour which distinguishes it from the others.

The uses of "puncetto" lace are many and varied: tablecloths, serviettes, sheets, pillowcases, in fact all household linen and personal linen may be decorated in this way, as the puncetto is a lace which is very pretty as well as being hardwearing. The women of the Valsesian valley learn a number of designs by heart and they work them with astonishing rapidity. But for anybody who has learned to work the stitch well, it should not be difficult to copy the photographs of laces in the chosen design.

Necessary Materials. A very well-twisted thread is necessary for working puncetto lace; it should be strong and of even thickness. All these qualities are to be found in Coats Mercer-Crochet in its various thicknesses. The numbers most

Table centre in linen with rich border in puncetto work, consisting of twelve medallions all worked in the same way, using Coats Mercer-Crochet, No. 60, in white

Enzio Guala Ida, Alagna Valsesia

Enzio Guala Ida, Alagna Valsesia

Original table centre worked entirely in puncetto with a simple motif repeated

259

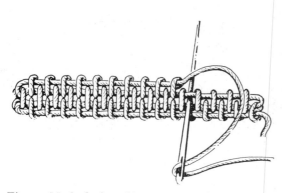

Fig. 1. *Method of working puncetto: first movement of forward row*

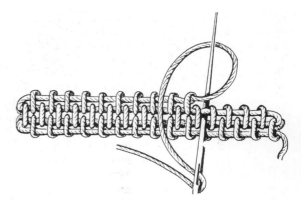

Fig. 2. *Method of working puncetto: second movement of forward row*

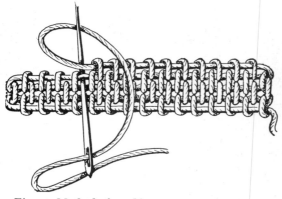

Fig. 3. *Method of working puncetto: return row*

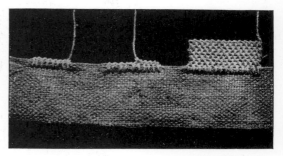

Fig. 4. *The stitch worked on material*

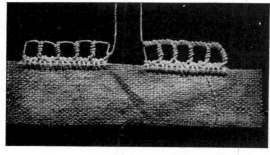

Fig. 5. *Method of working columns*

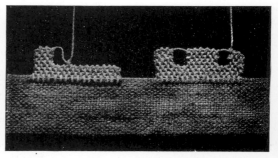

Fig. 6. *Method of working filled-in and empty spaces*

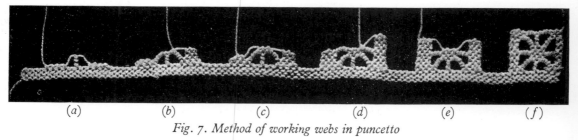

(a)   (b)   (c)   (d)   (e)   (f)

Fig. 7. *Method of working webs in puncetto*

generally used are 40 and 60; the former offers a wide choice of fast colours, such as red 469 and 700, blue 621 and 459, pink 693 and 402, yellow 582, orange 513 and purple 612. Naturally, the work can be carried out in other thicknesses of thread, according to the thickness of lace required.

Technique for making Puncetto Lace. As has already been said, puncetto is a lace formed solely of knots made by the needle, in rows going backwards and forwards. It is always worked on the right side and must never be turned over. In order to understand how it is made, we advise the beginner to learn to work it on material and then it will be easy to understand how it can be worked separately.

Take a piece of material in the left hand and fix on it the needleful of thread. Starting from the left, place the needle vertically from below above (that is, with the point towards the upper part of the work), taking up two threads, and holding the needle under the thread held firm by the first and second fingers of the left hand (Fig. 1). With the thumb and first finger of the right hand, now take two threads of the needleful, near to the eye of the needle and twist them round the needle from left to right (Fig. 2). Pull the needle through towards the upper part of the work, pulling the knot which has been formed up tight. After this first knot, continue to work a series of other knots in the same way, placed very near to each other. On completing the first row, work a second row back, i.e. from right to left, without turning the work. Always place the needle in the work from below (Fig. 3), i.e. with the point towards the top of the work, placing it in the space between two knots of the previous row, taking care that the needleful of thread, held firm by the first and middle fingers of the left hand, is always above the needle. Pull out the needle towards the top of the work in the same way as for the first row, and thus a new knot is formed. Continue as before, to make a row of similar knots. The third row is like the first; the knot is worked in the spaces of the knots on the row above. The fourth row is like the second.

By thus repeating the two rows of knots, as explained above, a solid, compact material is formed (Fig. 4), which is the basis of puncetto work. Spaces now have to be worked into this basic material and the method of working columns is now explained.

Method of working Columns. Working to the left, omit two spaces, i.e. three knots, and replace the needle, always from below, in the third space, and then work the usual knot (as for first row), but before drawing it up, arrange with the needle a length of thread which has to form the three sides of a small square (following this, for two only, as the first will have already been given by the preceding column). Draw up the knot, and place the needle through the hole which has been formed and work three or four knots around the thread, holding the needle firm with the thumb and first finger of the left hand and working the knot as for the second row. Then again, miss out two spaces, or three knots, and repeat as second square. At the end of the row there will be a series of columns separated by a line of unworked thread. This thread will be covered by a row of knots worked from right to left (second row). There are three knots to each hole (Fig. 5).

Method of alternating Empty and Filled-in Spaces. Working from left to right (the work may also be done from right to left if the design allows) miss out three knots and make a square of thread as already explained. If, after working the knot which fixes down the thread of the square, six knots, for example, are worked, continuing on the same row (as for a first row), the work is continued, without turning it over; on the six knots just worked (as for the second row), and on coming to the square, the needle is placed through the hole; another knot can be made so that the thread is hidden in the knot itself, and then the work can be continued working another six knots on the six knots of the preceding row (as for a first row); turn back a second time (as for a second row) and work a knot in the hole again. Then continue with another row forward and another row back, so that a space is formed between the two pieces worked in close knots (Fig. 6), the uncovered thread appearing only above; this will then be covered by a row of knots.

All the stitches, knots and spaces in puncetto work must be carefully counted, and here lies the secret of successful results.

Method of working Webs. One of the motifs which very often occurs in puncetto work is the web. Fig. 7 shows the various stages in working a web.

Above a strip of knots worked lengthways or

Fig. 8. Square in puncetto using Coats Mercer-Crochet, No. 60

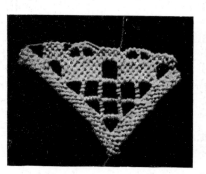

Fig. 9. Detail of centre of square shown in Fig. 8

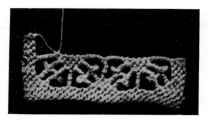

Fig. 10. Detail of outside border

widthways, work four knots (forward row), miss two spaces, and then work a knot, leaving a length of thread which will be covered for half its length by four knots on the row coming back. Miss two spaces and work another four knots, leaving a length of thread, as shown in Fig. 7 (a). Work back, then, again working four knots on the four already worked, covering the first length of thread with four knots (Fig. 7 (b)); then cover the second thread with four knots and work four more knots on those of the preceding line. Now go back over these same knots with a forward row and then again with a return row, then a third time with a forward row, and then, leaving a short length of thread, work three knots at the centre of the web. Fig. 7(c) shows how, at this point, another length of thread is left, going down to work on the right side of the web, taking up, amongst the knots, a part of the thread which will form the fifth ray of the web. Fig. 7(c) also shows how the fourth and fifth rays of the web are covered with knots using a return row. Now continue on the left side of the web, working three rows of knots. On the fourth row, leave the lengths of thread for the sixth and seventh rays (Fig. 7 (e)) and, lastly, Fig. 7 (f) shows the completed web with the eighth ray.

The best type of thread for puncetto work is Coats Mercer-Crochet, a thread which runs easily and is very strong, therefore being very suitable for this type of work.

When these different procedures for puncetto work have been understood, an intelligent worker can copy practically any design. Shown here are some medallions worked in puncetto lace. Fig. 8 shows a square medallion worked in two stages. Begin at the centre at a corner. The enlargement in Fig. 9 should be sufficiently clear. Begin the work at a corner over a thread held firm by a tacking stitch, which will later be removed. On this thread work four knots, and then work eight rows in all, backwards and forwards. On the ninth row (a forward row) go down, leaving a length of thread, as explained above, working four knots to begin the corner. After four rows (two forward and two back), begin the fifth, making four knots, then four knots on the thread to form the first space, then four knots on the opposite side. Continue in this way, following the pattern and alternating empty spaces with filled-in spaces, always counting the knots, the columns and spaces. On finishing the central square, the outer edge is worked from the inside to the outside, composed of rows of knots and small filled-in squares, working always around the design.

Fig. 10 shows an enlarged picture of how to work the outside border.

The medallions in Figs. 11 and 12 are also worked in two stages. First of all work the centre, beginning from a corner, as before, and then the outer border which consists of a series of diamond shapes inside squares, a motif which is often found in puncetto work. Fig. 12 shows the procedure.

On a thread fixed down by a tacking stitch which will be removed when the work is completed make 13 knots (return row). Then turn back, place the needle in and after four knots, work a knot (Fig. 13 (a)). In the hole so formed, work four knots (return row). After four knots work another knot and then work four knots in the new hole formed; then repeat, making a third square in the same way. We thus have three small squares, with the upper thread uncovered. With a return row cover the thread working four knots to each square (Fig. 13 (c)). The first square on the left will have one side formed by a single thread. Now turn back again (without turning the work over) and work back in the same manner, thus forming another six squares (Fig. 13 (d)), making a total of nine. Cover the upper thread with a return row making four knots to each square. In the third square of the last row turn, without turning the work over, and work another four knots, and then, again four knots in the two following squares. Thus nine small squares are formed (as shown in Fig. 13 (e)) all complete. These square-framed diamonds joined together form a very fine finishing for puncetto lace. To join thread in this type of work, try to join at the beginning or end of a row of knots. The thread which is finished and the new thread are taken under the new knot so that the ends are entirely covered.

Sometimes, for example, in the working of collars and cuffs, the puncetto lace is attached to

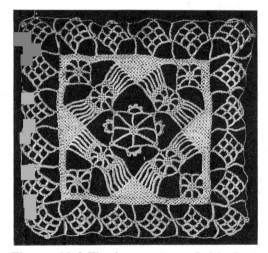

Fig. 11. Medallion in puncetto worked in Coats Mercer-Crochet, No. 50

Fig. 12. Another medallion in puncetto worked in Coats Mercer-Crochet, No. 50

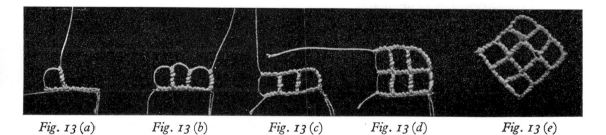

Fig. 13 (a)   Fig. 13 (b)   Fig. 13 (c)   Fig. 13 (d)   Fig. 13 (e)

263

Braid in puncetto

a braid which the women of the place make very quickly. This braid is formed of five threads and here is an explanation of the manner in which it is worked, which we hope is clear enough to be understood.

Braid for Puncetto Work. Take five threads, doubled, and fix them together; or wrap a thread round five times to a length of 63 or 76 cm, so that five threads are formed.

Place two in the right hand (the third finger holding one, the first and second fingers holding the other). Place three in the left hand (the third finger holding one, the middle finger another, and the first finger the third). Now, with the first finger of the right hand, helped by the thumb, take the last thread in the left hand, i.e. that on the third finger, and pass it on through the first double thread on the right hand, so that it is placed on the first finger of the same hand; in this way there will now be three threads on the right hand and two on the left. Take care to move the fingers at every twist of the threads, so that they are always arranged in the same way as described above. In the second stage, take the last three threads from the right hand, with the first finger of the left hand, and pass them into the first thread of the left hand, holding them with the first finger. These two movements are repeated alternately, thus forming braid. At each movement, spread out the hands and pull the threads, so that in the upper part the braid is even and firm.

264

Detail of border of a tablecloth in actual size, worked in puncetto

Table centre with rich border in puncetto worked in Coats Mercer-Crochet, No. 60, in écru

CHAPTER XXII

Rodi or Smyrna Stitch

Let us complete the section on laces made by knotting with a few words on a lace made entirely of small knots, without the help of a design, and that is Rodi lace.

Rodi or Smyrna or Nazareth stitch, as it is called and from whose name we assume that it originated in the East, especially since it is to be found in the dresses of Moslem women, is an interesting type of work, particularly if worked with fine thread, for decorating personal linen and children's clothes, and for finishing-off other kinds of work.

Italian Franciscan nuns, in Palestine, work this lace on a large scale, and by means of local, permanent exhibitions sell it by the metre as table centres, or as a decoration.

Materials. The thread most suitable for this type of work is Coats Mercer-Crochet, a well-running thread which is very strong and whose twist gives a certain strength to laces made with it, in spite of their fragile appearance.

Technique of Rodi or Smyrna Stitch. There are various ways of placing the needle and twisting the thread, but the result is the same in each case.

Rodi lace may be worked directly on to material (e.g. on hem, already prepared for handkerchiefs or linen), or attached to woven braid edgings decorated with loops. Fig. 1 shows knots worked

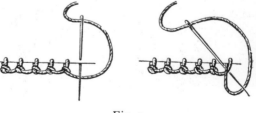

Fig. 1

Fig. 2

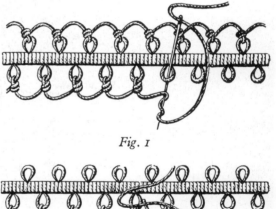

Fig. 3

Table centre worked in Smyrna or Rodi in natural. Begin from centre and work round with small knots made with the needle, as explained in the following chapter

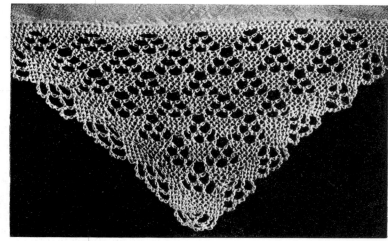

Fig. 4 (above). Method of beginning a star in Rodi stitch

Fig. 5 (right). Corner of a handkerchief worked in Rodi lace

on woven braid. The needle is placed in from above, at the base of a loop, the thread wrapped twice round it with a movement from left to right and then the needle is pulled through and the knot is thus formed.

Fig. 2 shows a double loop. After having worked the first knot in the loop of the woven braid, leave the thread rather long and fix it with a simple knot. This simple knot is clearly visible in Fig. 3.

Rodi work can also be made in another way:

Hold the work towards the top, bring out the needle from the turned-in hem and rest the thread on the first finger of the left hand. Then pass the needle below the thread, bringing it out two or three times below the edge of the hem, and then pass the thread on the front, as if making a button-hole stitch, pulling the needle towards the top of the work. In other words, the knot is the same as that made in Puncetto work, on the forward row.

In Rodi or Smyrna Stitch, however, the work must always be done from left to right. When one row is finished, turn the work and begin again, once more from left to right.

As well as lace by the yard, table centres, medallions and insets for underwear can also be made in Rodi lace. To begin a medallion in Rodi work, wrap the thread over the first finger of the left hand and make several knots as shown in Fig. 4. Then pull the thread and the knots will join together at the centre; then from the centre proceed to the outer edge.

Fig. 5 shows a corner of a handkerchief, worked in close triangles, separated by arcs. The triangles consist of nine knots, decreasing on every row, one

knot on each side, and the arcs consist of three knots worked on the thread.

Fig. 6 shows a series of borders worked in Rodi stitch for decorating handkerchiefs or underwear. The nun who made them said that it was a real relaxation for her to work and create these small laces, one prettier than the other, without any pattern to follow, and they are, in fact, very easy and effective to work. With a thicker thread these borders become effective and elegant decorations.

Very similar to each other, all these stitches illustrated on the right of page 269 can be used to finish off babies' shirts, bibs, handkerchiefs, etc., without a traced pattern and without any technical difficulties. They all begin from the edge of the material to which they are to be attached, making the first row of the knots, as explained above, very near to one another. On completing this first row turn the work and make a second row, and so on, always working from left to right. These outer edges, in scallops, which at first glance appear to be worked in Buttonhole Stitch, are instead formed by a series of small knots, very close to each other, and picots, which are formed by leaving a very short length of thread between the knots themselves.

A very fine thread was used for the examples shown here. But even worked in thicker thread such as Coats Mercer-Crochet, No. 20, the same stitches can be used to decorate articles in heavier, stronger material.

It should be pointed out that the fourteenth lace from the top is the simplest and therefore the easiest to copy. Begin by making the knots very close to each other, leaving a short length of thread between them, then go through the single arcs of thread again on the following row, making other knots. Repeat the same procedure for ten rows, and on the eleventh work a line of scallops, missing out two knots each time and covering the thread with six knots to each scallop.

When this procedure has been fully understood, this lace is very easy to reproduce in all its various designs.

Fig. 6. Stitches for various decorative borders, worked in Rodi lace

7 *Laces made by Needle and Bobbin*

Laces

This special branch of feminine handwork can be called "the aristocrat of embroidery" since it really is the best part, as well as being the most beautiful and most difficult and precious of women's work in this field.

Needle-made laces have a common technique and in all of them the basic stitch is Blanket Stitch, carried out so as to obtain varied designs and which, in less valuable laces, is attached to machine-made cords and edgings.

There is a vast range of very different types of laces: the most precious are Venetian and Burano laces, together with all those laces which are very well known abroad, such as the famous Alençon and d'Argentan, Brussels and Bruges laces, Cluny and English laces, etc.

It is not intended here and, in fact, it would be impossible to give detailed instructions for the making of these wonderful laces, whose best exponents are their countries of origin and which, like Venetian lace, from which the others are derived, reach such heights of perfection as to constitute a real source of wealth for their countries.

Made entirely by hand, it is not difficult, even today, to find local women who carry on the glorious tradition, working entirely by hand those precious and wonderful laces. But the art and industry of lacemaking, which at the courts of the most famous kings of France were protected and valued at their true worth, suffered great changes with the coming of the Revolution, which abolished privileges, put down the aristocracy and suppressed the incredible luxury of the upper classes. The machine did the rest: cords, rosettes, flowers, which had arisen from the able fingers of the lacemakers like magic, began to be made by machine, and then to be mass-produced, destroying all the originality and classic quality to be found in the work of a specialised artisan.

We have divided this chapter into five parts, each dealing with laces:

1. Netting and Aemilia-Ars
2. Renaissance Lace
3. Venetian and Burano Laces
4. Modano Lace
5. Bobbin Laces

and in each chapter we give details about the origins of the different laces and methods of working them, so that the embroideress may have a clear idea and a sure guide in working the basic stitches, which will allow her to understand the type of work done and, if desired, to continue to study it more deeply.

Portrait of Maria Capponi Pecori, by an unknown artist (1500), in the Uffizi Gallery, Florence. Note the richness and incomparable elegance of the collar framing the beautiful face

271

CHAPTER XXI

Netting and Aemilia-Ars

"Netting" belongs to a group of laces made with a needle. The use of lace was in vogue in Venice and elsewhere long before "Venetian" stitch had been heard of. Portraits of noblewomen and noblemen of the fifteenth and sixteenth centuries show perfectly how lace was used in that period in both masculine and feminine wardrobes.

In the fifteenth century, in fact, linen was embroidered with medallions, and sometimes cut away in order to obtain greater light and shade effects. This was called "Cut-out" Stitch. It is the least complicated of needle-worked stitches, very similar to netting and, together with this last, one of the most ancient. The illustration, Fig. 1, of an example of lace-making forming part of the collection of embroidery and laces at the Palermo Museum, will certainly be of great interest to the intelligent reader. In this example (Fig. 1) the partly finished work can be seen. In the unfinished part of the work, it seems as if the hand of the embroideress were suspended only to show more clearly how her wonderful work was produced. In Venice, many figures in the pictures of Gentile Bellini seem to have their garments decorated with netting and some of Carpaccio's pictures, too, show figures whose clothes are decorated with Cut-out Stitch.

From this Cut-out Stitch we pass to so-called "Netting", taking out from the material threads in both directions, so as to trace out a geometrical background on which the needle will work a flower, a star, a heart, etc. Often this work alternates with Royal Stitch and Whirl Stitch.

During the whole of the fifteenth century, netting in its various forms dominated the field of embroidery. Ladies worked Netting to decorate sheets, tablecloths and dress decorations, the nuns worked religious garments, altar cloths and covers, and also contributed to spreading this new art throughout Italy, sending designs and articles from one convent to another and teaching the secrets of the stitches.

Aemilia-Ars. The Bolognese lace called "Aemilia-Ars" originated from Netting. This type of work also has its own history and has produced artistically rich and valuable examples.

Aemilia-Ars laces are very similar to Venetian laces as regards technique, but they differ substantially in design, the decorative motifs not being placed on a tulle background, but very often on a kind of coarse net in squares or geometrical designs which appear here and there through the designs of leaves, vases, heraldic beasts and armorial bearings of ancient Bolognese families. Again it differs from Venetian lace, which is purely lace work, in that it is sometimes worked into the material itself, so that as well as the Aemilia-Ars lace stitch it is often necessary to work on drawn threads and place the lace into the material, using

Royal, Whirl and Vapour Stitches, etc., to enrich the surrounding material with varied and characteristic designs.

Aemilia-Ars lace, too, was abandoned for a time, and it was at Bologna, at the end of last century, that a corporation of artists and art-lovers was formed, on the instigation of the painter, Alfonso Rubbiani, to give new life and to aid the spread and development to all forms of art and to promote artisan activity. This lasted for several years, being called "Aemilia-Ars" or Emilian Art.

Valuable beaten metal work, wood insets, leather work, wrought-iron, furniture and, above all, embroidery and lace-making, were some of the activities which the Aemilia-Ars corporation attempted to encourage and diffuse. But out of such a profusion of art initiative the lace, still famous for its elegance, beauty and richness of design, is the only branch which continues to be active.

The illustrations show some examples of this wonderful lace stitch.

Naturally, detailed explanations cannot be given here. We would, however, like to teach those who amuse themselves with embroidery the method of working those Aemilia-Ars used for decorating bed and table linen.

Necessary Materials. The most suitable thread for this work is Coats Anchor Coton à Broder or Coats Mercer-Crochet.

Technique for Aemilia-Ars Insets. The working of Amelia-Ars lace is neither easy nor quick. It requires good eyesight, an agile hand and a great deal of patience.

Figs. 6 and 7 show the procedure for working an inset. By the method we shall now explain and which we consider to be the best and clearest, any design can be worked.

After preparing the design, which must be particularly clear and exact, in all its details, draw it on a card and cover it with tracing paper, shiny side uppermost, so that the design underneath can be clearly seen.

Begin, first of all, by putting in all the stitches (called "supporting stitches"), which, crossing the card, touch all the lines coming to the edge of the design and which will be cut away when the work is finished. Work supporting stitches inside the design itself, at all points where the lines intersect. The illustration shows a star prepared for working with the supporting threads in dark thread so that they are clearly visible on the light background. Cording, Buttonhole Stitch and picots are the stitches used for insets of Aemilia-Ars.

Taking Fig. 7 as a model, begin first of all to work the diagonal lines, i.e. those that cross the circle. The thread passes three times from one part to the other, through the supporting stitches and is then covered with cording. After working the first part we come to two arcs formed by two parallel lines. Here work is stopped to begin the pattern. Pass the thread through the supporting stitches on the first from left to right and then from

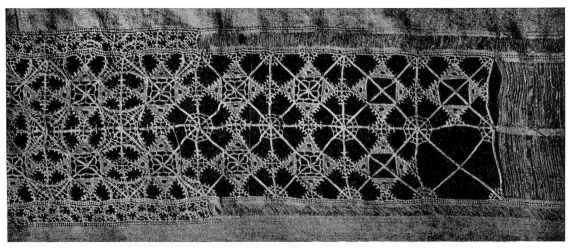

Fig. 1. Antique embroidery, still incomplete, showing the procedure for working netting. Note the richness of the pips which decorate the finished part of the work

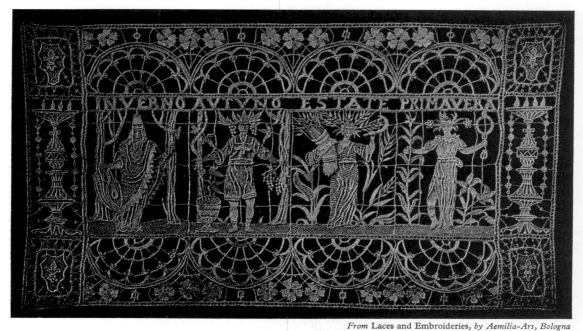

"The Four Seasons." The half-way border is worked in loop stitch

Lace formed by all the elements of the bearings of the Bentivoglio Aemily, ancient lords of Bologna. The design is an imitation of the family terracotta, with some details taken from the armorial bearings of the castle

Fig. 2. Example of antique lace: detail of a cushion worked in alternate squares in netting and whirl stitch

right to left, that is, working in the opposite direction and thus coming back to the cording. Fill in this small space as far as the second parallel line and then proceed as for the first, not forgetting the picots. Having thus come back to the cording, work up to the point diametrically opposite and work the second pair of arcs. On completing the first diagonal, proceed to work the second which, however, will not be completed. In fact, immediately after the centre, proceed to work the first circle, first passing three threads and covering them with Buttonhole Stitch with a picot in the centre. On completing the first circle work the short length of cording on the second diagonal, up to the second circle.

Pass the usual three tacking threads and begin the filled-in parts; in this case the first of the four small triangles of the star. On the tacking begin to work twelve Buttonhole Stitches, then work back and forth, taking off one stitch on every row, until arriving at the point which should then be fixed to the supporting stitch. Now go back with hidden stitches along the right side of the triangle as far as the second central circle; then work the second triangle in the same manner. And so on for the third and fourth. After the fourth, take the cording of the second diagonal up again, and work the last two arcs. On completion of the star pass

one or two reinforcing threads around the circumference of the circle, and then cut the supporting stitches on the back of the work, leaving the star to come away by itself.

These Aemilia-Ars medallions are generally inserted into the material as decorations for table and bed linen, and much more rarely they are left separate and joined together to make richer decorative insertions. Fig. 4 shows a very pretty modern tablecloth consisting of insertions of Aemilia-Ars stars between two rows of square stitch and decorated with Whirl Stitch. The background is ivory-coloured bissum, and the stars are worked in Coats Anchor Coton à Broder, No. 18, in white.

To insert the medallions into the material, proceed as follows: place the medallion on the outlined space previously marked on the material and fix it there with tacking stitches at the centre, taking care that the straight thread falls along the sides of a square insertion along the diagonal of a circular one; then tack around the edges with small, close stitches. Then work a Buttonhole Stitch or cording all around the edges, being careful to take up with the needle all the parts of the insertion which come up to the edge of the outline and which must be firmly fixed to the cloth. On completion of the cording or Buttonhole Stitch cut away the material within the marked outline.

275

Fig. 4 (below). Modern tea cloth in natural-coloured bissum: the insertions are worked in Aemilia-Ars, and the smaller decoration on the material itself in Whirl Stitch

J. Benegiamo, Maglie (Lecce)

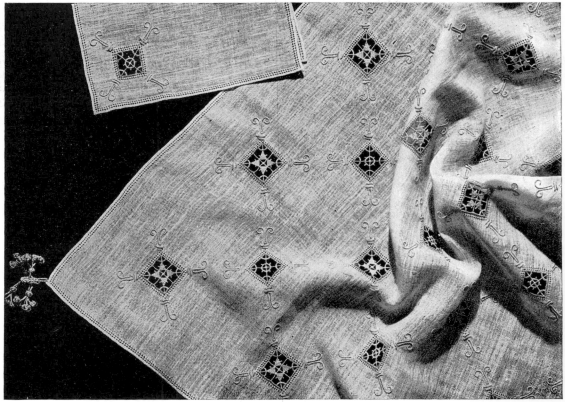

Fig. 5. Table centre with a magnificent border consisting of alternate squares of Aemilia-Ars

Fig. 6. Method of working medallions in Aemilia-Ars: card prepared for work

Fig. 7. Work on the star begun in cording, Buttonhole Stitch and picots

Fig. 8. Stars in Aemilia-Ars worked with Coats Anchor Coton à Broder, No. 18, for insertions for bed linen, table and personal linen

Fig. 9. Tea cloth in white linen with corners worked in Aemilia-Ars and Whirl Stitch

J. Benegiamo, Maglie (Lecce)

Example of insertion on towels, worked in Aemilia-Ars with Coats Anchor Coton à Broder, No. 18

Fig. 10. Table centre with rich border in Aemilia-Ars in a classical style, worked by the Aemilia-Ars School, Bologna

Fig. 11. Table centre made by the same school in Bologna, with a modernised design

Detail, in actual size, of a piece of Aemilia-Ars work for table cloth or table centres. The central border is antique in style, whilst the decorations on the edges were worked to a design by Passerotti

CHAPTER XXIV

Renaissance Lace

"Renaissance" Lace consists of a braid with bars attached at the curves and where the patterns join, and filled in by netting; it was very fashionable in France and Italy in the sixteenth and seventeenth centuries: it went out of use in the eighteenth century, to flourish again in the nineteenth, a period in which this type of work was used everywhere. It was, in fact, used to such an extent as to become monotonous and boring, although in itself, it is very beautiful, with very decorative designs, in wide curves and with flowers consisting of rich and varied netting. About twenty years ago, an attempt was made to modernise this kind of lace, altering its characteristic design a little and substituting more elaborate braids and bindings for the usual, more simple ones. Good workers obtained good results from this and produced valuable work, but Renaissance lace has never returned to its ancient splendour.

Necessary Materials. As well as the braids already mentioned, good thread is necessary for Renaissance lace. The most suitable is Coats Mercer-Crochet thread, in its various thicknesses, which allows very fine, light work to be executed.

The thread must always be chosen according to the thickness of the braid used, whilst a finer thread is used for the netting and a thicker thread for the bars. When working with a rather heavy

braid, Coats Mercer-Crochet, No. 20, gives good results.

Technique of working Renaissance Lace. The designs for this lace are always marked in double lines, i.e. they are traced with two parallel lines between which the braid is tacked. The design is first copied on to tracing paper, on the opaque side, with Indian ink. The tracing paper is then placed on a piece of strong cotton material, to reinforce it, and fixed down with Tacking Stitches.

Attaching the Braid. At first the braids for Renaissance laces were worked by hand, using bobbins, but were later substituted by these made by machine, with a great saving of time and labour. The shapes and sizes of these braids, which can be obtained in Italy, are very varied: broad, narrow, perforated, with picots, smooth with self design, or with various geometrical shapes, etc., in cotton or silk; in white, natural and black. Fig. 1 shows types of braids amongst those in common use. When the design has been prepared, proceed to tacking the braid between the two parallel lines of the design, fixing it to the tracing paper with short, close stitches, and following the lines of the pattern very closely and carefully. At the corners the braid is folded (Fig. 2), whilst at the curves it is sewn close to the outer edge so that the inside curve

An example of Renaissance lace worked with braid and a wide variety of nets

Fig. 1 (left). Various braids

Fig. 4 (right). Netting in Buttonhole Stitching, worked alternately
with wide and narrow spacing

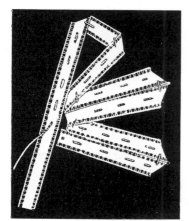

Fig. 2 (left). Application of braid:
folding for corners

Fig. 5 (right). Net in rows of
Buttonhole Stitch, alternated

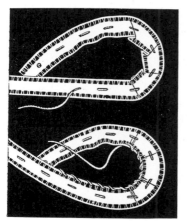

Fig. 3 (left). Application of braid:
procedure for curves

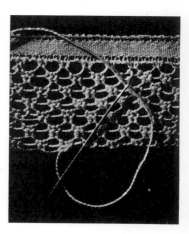

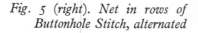

Fig. 6 (right). Netting in groups
of three Buttonhole Stitches

is slightly gathered. When tacking is completed, outline the braid on both sides with overcasting, using a very thin but strong thread (Coats Mercer-Crochet), going into each perforation or the selvedge of the braid. By pulling lightly on this thread, especially on the inside of curves, all the braid will lie flat and smooth (Fig. 3). After fixing the braid in lace, proceed to work the netting, filling in the spaces designed for them.

Nets. Here are given some examples of nets, from which it can easily be seen that the basic stitch is Buttonhole Stitch, worked backwards and forwards. The illustrations should be sufficiently clear to allow the patterns to be followed easily. But the embroideress can also easily create new designs, because there is an infinite variety of ways in which the threads may be twisted. These same nets are met with in Venetian and Burano laces.

Fig. 4. Take the thread from left to right and working back from right to left with a fairly close Buttonhole Stitch, taking up the pulled thread. On the fifth row work a Buttonhole Stitch every two stitches and repeat the motif with wider spaces on the following three rows. Then begin from the beginning.

Fig. 5. Work two rows of Buttonhole Stitching back and forth, leaving the stitches rather widely spaced and loose: on the following row work four Buttonhole Stitches in each space of the preceding row.

Fig. 6. Work three Buttonhole Stitches, leaving a short length of thread between one group and another. Then go back, from right to left with three Buttonhole Stitches in each space of the preceding row. The third row is like the second but worked from left to right. On the following row alternate the filled-in spaces with those left free and vice versa.

Fig. 7. Working from right to left, work two Buttonhole Stitches leaving a free length of thread. Go back from left to right working eight Buttonhole Stitches in each space of the preceding row. On the third row, work as for the first, making two Buttonhole Stitches at the centre of the eight stitches worked on the preceding row.

Fig. 8. Take the thread from left to right, and go back working groups of three Buttonhole Stitches separated by short lengths of thread. On the following row move the work along by one stitch so as to form diagonal lines.

Fig. 9. As for all the others, this net is worked in rows going backwards and forwards. Begin from left to right, making two Buttonhole Stitches close together and leaving a length of thread free. On the following row work three Buttonhole Stitches in the space and two into the two stitches of the preceding row.

All the nets are worked in fine thread: the best is Coats Mercer-Crochet in 20-gm. balls.

Fig. 10. Here the small lozenge shapes are formed by diagonal threads, worked over counted threads. Take the thread from left to right and work from the right towards the left, always leaving out an equal number of threads, in this case two at first, then six, then four and again four, then again six and lastly, two.

Figs. 11, 12, 13. These three nets are similar to each other and very easy to work. The threads must be counted, following the illustration Fig. 11, which consists of filled-in triangles of seven stitches each, decreasing one per row. The second (Fig. 12) consists of small lozenge shapes formed by one stitch, then two, three, four and again three, two and one. The third (Fig. 13) is like the first with triangles of four stitches decreasing on each row and alternated.

Figs. 15, 16 and 17 show the method of working the so-called "tulle" stitch, imitating this well-known material. This is the background most used in laces. In Burano and Milan laces it forms the background entirely, substituting the usual bars.

In Fig. 15, the first illustration of the group, the forward row of the stitch can be seen; the needle should be placed so that the thread is crossed. In Fig. 16 the return row can be seen from right to left together with the position of the needle and thread which is the same as that in the preceding figure but in the opposite direction. Fig. 17 shows, instead, Tulle Stitch worked on the forward row from left to right, while on the return row, from right to left, an overcasting stitch is worked into each hole. Fig. 14 shows Tulle Stitch worked with overcasting.

In leaf patterns the inside can be filled in with simple bars, as well as with netting, as shown in Fig. 18. Take the thread across the space, fix it on the opposite side and work back with overcasting, then taking the thread through the holes in the selvedge, repeat the bar a little farther along.

This is the simplest form of bar used in lace-making, but it is also the most fragile and consequently little used in very delicate, accurate work.

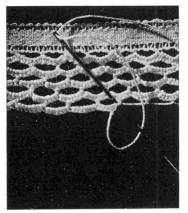

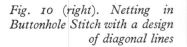
Fig. 7 (left). Netting with arcs in Buttonhole Stitch

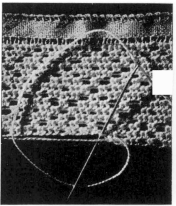

Fig. 10 (right). Netting in Buttonhole Stitch with a design of diagonal lines

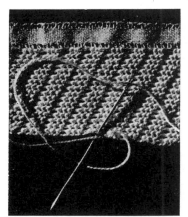

Fig. 8 (left). Netting in diagonal lines, formed by three Buttonhole Stitches

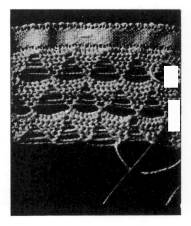

Fig. 11 (right). Netting in groups of Buttonhole Stitches in lozenges

Fig. 9 (left). Netting in loose Buttonhole Stitching

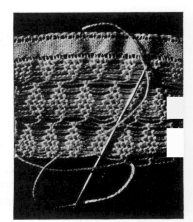

Fig. 12 (right). Netting with groups of Buttonhole Stitches in alternate triangles

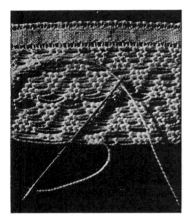

Fig. 13 (left). Netting with groups of triangles in Buttonhole Stitch

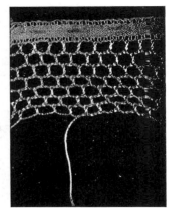

Fig. 14 (right). Tulle Stitch with overcasting on return row

The other leaf, shown in Fig. 19, shows a Crossed Stitch filling in the whole space between the lines of the design.

Fig. 20 shows a widely spaced Blanket Stitch worked alternately to the left and right, taking in the underneath threads and giving a pleasant effect of crossed stitches.

Bars. Bars are worked after the netting and filling-in have been completed. Here are some different types of bars which can be used in Renaissance laces as well as in Venetian, Richelieu laces, etc.

Bar in Cording. This is one of the simplest types. Over three tacking threads, work back with very close cording so that the threads below are hidden (Fig. 21).

Bar in Buttonhole Stitch. Cover three tacking threads with Buttonhole Stitch worked evenly, either from left to right or right to left (Fig. 22). Bar with picots in Chain Stitch. Work Buttonhole Stitching half-way along the bar, replace the needle in the last stitch and work three or four Chain Stitches on the thread, and then go back to the start and continue with the Buttonhole Stitches (Fig. 23).

Bars with Simple Picots. Work Buttonhole Stitching half-way along the bar. Place the needle through the last stitch, bringing it out to three-quarters its length. Wrap the thread three times round the needle with a right to left movement, and push the needle through, drawing it out through the wrapped threads. This forms the picot, and the

other half of the bar is then covered with Buttonhole Stitching (Fig. 24).

Bar with Picots in Vapour Stitch. Work Buttonhole Stitching half-way along the bar, placing the needle through the last stitch and bringing it out to three-quarters its length. Wrap the thread round the needle ten or twelve times from left to right, push the needle through the threads and pull out so that a kind of circle is formed; then continue with the other half of the bar (Fig. 25).

Bar with Looped Picots. Work Buttonhole Stitching half-way along the bar; pass the thread over the stretched tacking threads without making the knot, and fix the loop with a pin; then place the needle in from left to right under the three threads and pull the thread strongly. Then continue with the Buttonhole Stitching (Fig. 26).

Bar with Venetian Picots. This type of picot is very much used in Venetian Stitch, from which it gets its name. Proceed as for the preceding bar; after placing the pin, take the thread back behind the pin making as many Buttonhole Stitches as to work Buttonhole Stitching on the other half of the bar (Fig. 27).

Bars in Double Buttonhole Stitch. On the usual three tacking threads work the first row of widely spread Buttonhole Stitches then, turning the work, work a second row on the other side of the bar, fitting the stitches in between those of the first row (Fig. 28).

287

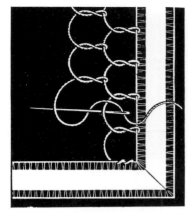

Fig. 15. Tulle Stitch: first forward row

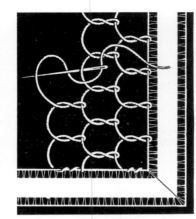

Fig. 16. Tulle Stitch: second return movement

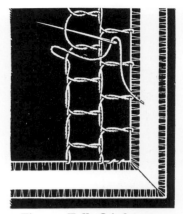

Fig. 17. Tulle Stitch: over-casting on stitches

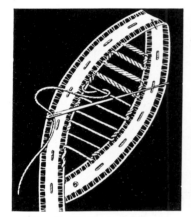

Fig. 18. Method of filling in leaves: bars in overcasting

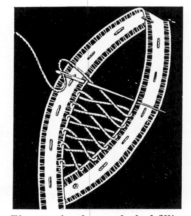

Fig. 19. Another method of filling in leaves: crossed stitches

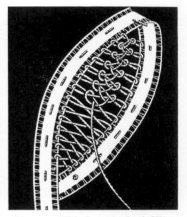

Fig. 20. Third method of filling in leaves: crossed stitches and Buttonhole Stitch

Bar in Darning Stitch. This, like the preceding bar, is very strong and rather thick. It requires four tacking threads. Pass the needle (preferably with the eye first) through the middle of the four stitches, dividing them into twos, and work alternately on the two groups of threads so that the bar turns out to be a kind of double cording (Fig. 29).

Bar with Buttonhole-Stitched Loop. Work Blanket Stitching three-quarters of the way along the bar, taking the thread back and fixing it six or seven stitches behind, then going back to the starting point and then again, going backwards. Cover the three threads of the loop with Buttonhole Stitching and then continue with the bar (Fig. 30).

When the spaces are too large to be joined by simple bars, a group of branching or webs is worked.

Branching Bars. Stretch three tacking threads between points A and B (Fig. 31), going back to work Buttonhole Stitch up to point C; from here stretch other threads up to point E and go back, working Buttonhole Stitches up to D; from here stretch other threads up to point F, work back with Buttonhole Stitches, covering the length between F and D, then that between D and C and lastly, that between C and A.

When there is a greater number of branches, work small supporting stitches at the corners where they join; these will be cut away when the work is finished.

288

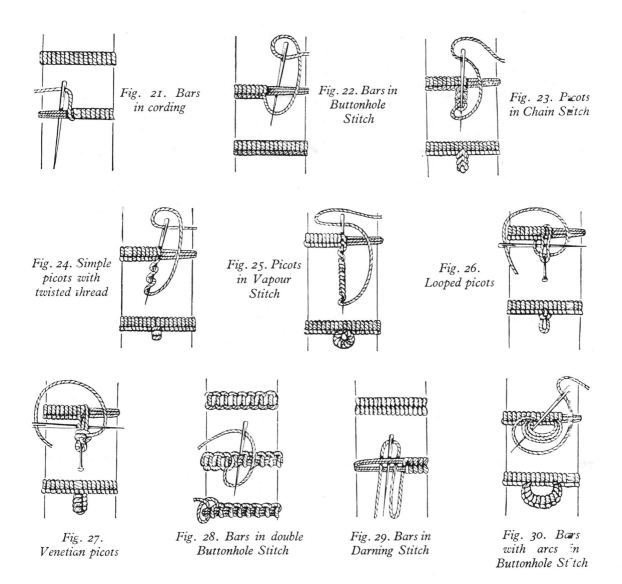

Fig. 21. Bars in cording

Fig. 22. Bars in Buttonhole Stitch

Fig. 23. Picots in Chain Stitch

Fig. 24. Simple picots with twisted thread

Fig. 25. Picots in Vapour Stitch

Fig. 26. Looped picots

Fig. 27. Venetian picots

Fig. 28. Bars in double Buttonhole Stitch

Fig. 29. Bars in Darning Stitch

Fig. 30. Bars with arcs in Buttonhole Stitch

Webs. To work a simple web, fix the needleful of thread at one point, stretch it out in a diagonal direction and fix it to the opposite corner, working back with cording half-way along the stretched thread; then, holding the ray just worked firm with the thumb of the left hand, stretch another thread from the centre, and so on, for all the rays. When these have all been stretched into position, the thread is found at the centre of the web: here wrap the thread over the thread, going above and below the rays themselves (Fig. 32), covering the last ray, too, with cording. This last ray is half of the thread used for the first. The number of rays can vary at will. When there is an equal number, two rays must be taken together at the end of each row, so that on the following rows, the stitches of the central wheel are well twisted (Fig. 33).

A very effective wheel is that worked in Rib Stitch, as shown in Fig. 34, which clearly shows how the thread is wrapped on each ray with a Back Stitch and taken below two rays every time. When necessary, heavier webs can be worked, all in Buttonhole Stitch, as shown in Fig. 35. Fig. 36 clearly shows how the threads should be placed for tacking, in order to form the various rays which collect at the centre in a circle. First of all

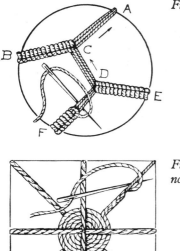

Fig. 31 (left). Branching bars

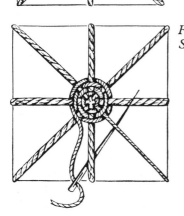

Fig. 34 (right). Web in Rib Stitch

Fig. 32 (left). Web in Darning Stitch, not alternated

Fig. 35 (right). Web with rays

Fig. 33 (left). Web in Darning Stitch, alternated

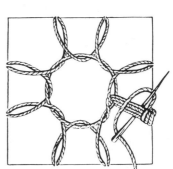

Fig. 36 (right). Tacking of a web with rays

cover the rays always with Buttonhole Stitches, starting to work from the outer edge and, lastly, working the inner circle.

Sometimes the wheels of the web are replaced by Buttonhole-Stitched loops, attached to the tracing paper with two or three Tacking Stitches and from which the rays start. To work Buttonhole-Stitched loops, wrap the thread ten or twelve times round a sliver of wood or bone, slipping the loop along with the thumb and first finger of the left hand and covering the threads with Buttonhole Stitching (Fig. 37).

Medici Stitch. This is the name of the net which takes the form of small regular hexagons, which very often form a background, instead of bars.

The Medici background may be worked in cording or Buttonhole Stitch. The three illustrations showing this stitch are very clear; a few words of explanation will be added.

First of all work several supporting stitches in each corner of the hexagon. These stitches serve only as a basis for the placing of the threads of the net and will be pulled out on completion of the work. Then put in the real tacking threads. Take the thread into the first supporting stitch above on the right, going down then to the second and then into the two stitches marking the vertical side of the hexagon. Now go up to the upper stitch and from here take the needle into the supporting stitch at the corner of the second hexagon and so on along the whole row (Fig. 38). On the following

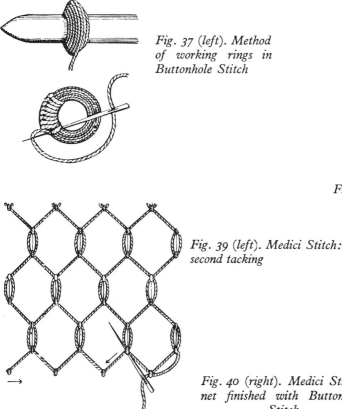

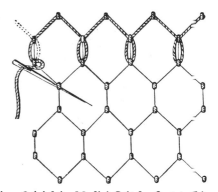

Fig. 37 (left). Method of working rings in Buttonhole Stitch

Fig. 38 (right). Medici Stitch: first tacking

Fig. 39 (left). Medici Stitch: second tacking

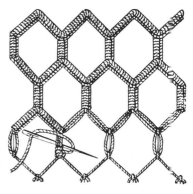

Fig. 40 (right). Medici Stitch: net finished with Buttonhole Stitch

row, work a second line in the same way, from left to right. Fig. 39 shows how the second thread is passed into the broken horizontal line, first from left to right and then going back from right to left so as to form a net on three tacking threads.

Fig. 40 shows the Medici background finished off with Buttonhole Stitches. After having covered the two upper sides of the hexagon, go down with the third tacking thread on the vertical side, cover this with Buttonhole Stitches and carry on working on the two upper sides of the hexagon and so on.

On completing the bars, the work is then ready to be taken off the supporting stitches. First iron with a cool iron, on the wrong side, and then cut away the tacking threads fixing the braid and pull them out.

MILAN LACE

The real Milan lace is that classical lace made with bobbins. However, good results can also be obtained using machine-made braids and expensive

work can be produced in this way. The motifs of the pattern are spread over a tulle background, which gives the lace a light delicate appearance.

For needle-worked Milan lace, the procedure is similar to that already explained for Renaissance lace; the braids are tacked over the design traced on tracing paper. First fill in the network, which in Milan lace is not very varied, and then proceed to the background which, instead of being worked in bars, is worked entirely in Tulle Stitch like Burano lace, but very much closer. Tulle Stitch has been clearly explained in the preceding pages.

ARDENZA LACE

Ardenza lace must be mentioned amongst the Renaissance laces. It is very tasteful and beautiful and takes its name from a district near Leghorn where it is made. This lace in its classical form has a braid worked with bobbins: later, this was substituted by a fine linen edging. There are few

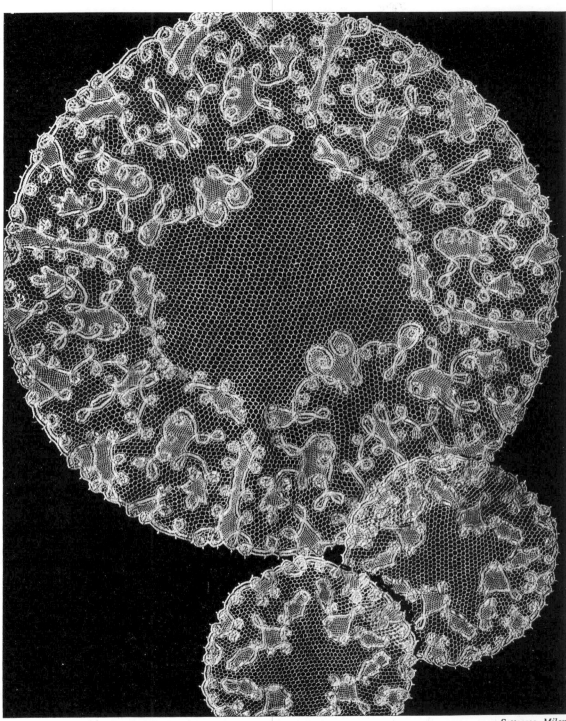

Sottocasa, Milan

Liqueur set in Milan lace: the effect of light and shade is given by the different thicknesses of the tulle stitch which forms a background for the braid design

*Table centre in
Ardenza lace*

nets in the work; the bars, however, must be worked very carefully as they must appear like material without showing the point of attachment to the braid. This type of lace, attached to linen, very often has the same motifs repeated on the material itself. These are worked in Whirl Stitch, Royal Stitch or Cording.

A group of ladies in Leghorn revived this beautiful work some time ago, with modernised designs, so that it is a private enterprise which encourages its production, keeping the secrets of its designs and procedures.

Much Ardenza lace goes abroad, where it is much sought after as an expensive creation.

VENETIAN-TYPE RENAISSANCE LACE

Before the machine-made braid was invented, a linen tape was used for Renaissance laces. This was very heavy and rather stiff, so that it had to be applied with strong, well-pulled stitches. Even today, this lace is amongst the most valued for its appearance. All the joining bars are worked in Blanket Stitch as well as the two sides of the tape, and thus it acquires an appearance very much less fragile than Renaissance lace, and more similar to Venetian lace. To accentuate this similarity the bars are decorated with several picots and cords covered with Buttonhole Stitches.

293

Table runner in Milan lace-type stitch, with thick braid and wide nets

CHAPTER XXV

Venetian and Burano Laces

Venetian laces have their own history; but this is not sufficient to describe them. They are so fragile and airy that a poetic legend has grown up around them, which says:

A young Venetian fisherman, leaving for the Eastern wars, left his loved one a rare and beautiful seaweed. During her long, faithful wait, the girl, fearing that the seaweed would die, began to copy it with her needle among the holes of the fishermen's nets which she worked for her father and brothers by the sea at Burano. This was the first Burano lace.

The importance of a legend should never be overlooked, whatever it may refer to. Here, besides its idealistic meaning, there is also a hint at the principle that it was Venice herself, more than any other place, which gave birth to lace-making.

Many writers are of this view. Venice was the inventor of needle-worked lace, and probably began lace-making based on the study of laces from the East, with which she was intimately connected.

Tradition has it that a woman Doge, Giovanna Malipiero, famous for her support of printing and her encouragement of all the arts, gave an impulse to the lace-making industry of Venice. Later on another woman, the wife of the Doge Marino Grimani, dedicated her interest and care to lace-making, setting up, at her own expense, a workshop for laces in the district of St. Fosca. Historians affirm that 130 people worked there under the surveillance of the teacher, Cattina Gardon, and they worked exclusively for the Doge's wife, who made presents of some of the laces produced in her workshop to the gentlewomen of the European Courts.

Venetian laces were named according to the procedure used in their making. So we have "Knot" Stitch, "Square Loop" Stitch, "Drawn Up" Stitch, "Space" Stitch, one of the most valuable, and Venetian and Burano Stitch. The richest of all is the "stitch cut in branches of flowers", and which, appearing towards the second half of the seventeenth century, was used to decorate the richest dresses of Venetian ladies, and gentlemen, too, as well as for church decorations.

In order to spread the knowledge of how to work these stitches, a strange assortment of books and pamphlets was printed, in which the art of lace-making was explained and illustrated, together with helpful advice.

Niccolo d'Aristotele, called "Toppino", published an *Example of Work for young Maidens and other Noblewomen* (1520). Juan Andrea Vavassore (1532) published another book in which he proclaimed that the work designed by him could be worked by "a virtuous woman". Both noble and

Luxurious tablecloth in Venetian and Burano lace. The tulle stitch, characteristic of Burano lace, can be seen at the corners and at the centre, and also forms a background for the figures shown in the various motifs

common people were very enthusiastic about lace-making. Viena Vendramin Nani, to whom Cesare Vecellio, grandson of Titian, dedicated his "Crown for Noble and Virtuous Women", was an expert in lace-making, and taught it to the young noble-women of the town in her own house.

This beautiful and magnificent work fell into disuse after two centuries of popularity, for many and varied reasons which need not be explained here. However, it soon regained its lost popularity. About 1866, when the old Venetian stitches had almost been forgotten and the lace-making industry had died, the population of the lagoon was reduced to making a living from fishing and had become poor, when a group of kindly ladies, presided over by the M. P. Paolo Fambri, tried to revive the lace-making industry.

Countess Andriana Marcello, lady-in-waiting to Queen Margherita, a person of elevated feelings, cultivated and active, undertook the task of reviving these stitches, especially the Burano lace which no one had worked for more than thirty years. She traced an old woman, the seventy-year-old Cencia Scarpariola, the only remaining soul who knew how to work the ancient Venetian laces, and, in spite of her ripe old age, she was able to teach Bellorio d'Este, a teacher in a Burano school. Thus, the first group of eight students learned the secrets of this glorious lace. And this was sufficient to revive the ancient art and renew the splendour of Venetian lace-making.

The Burano School. In 1873, under the patronage of Queen Margherita of Savoy, then Princess

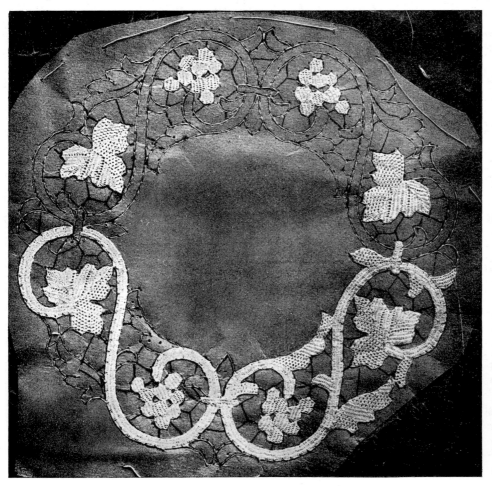

Fig. 1.
Procedure for working Venetian lace. tacking of the design and beginning of "Guipure" Stitch

of Piedmont, a small capital was collected and a school set up on the first floor of an old palace in Burano; it was called the Burano School and at first the number of students was very limited. But little by little the number increased, and since there was no lack of orders, because the Queen, her ladies-in-waiting and all the aristocracy passed orders continually, in a few years the school became a rich workshop of valuable laces.

The First World War put a stop to the work for a time, but it started up again after the peace, so that in 1925 the school had about 800 workers, and continued to develop until the outbreak of the Second World War.

Today the Burano School is still feeling the crisis it suffered during the war. The great increase in wages has made the price of lace rise to incredible heights; young people, now used to the freer life in factories, have left the needle and bobbin, whilst the older women alone try to keep the flame burning, and work faithfully on in the old traditions so that it can still be said that none of the lace manufactured in other places is so finely and carefully worked as that which is still produced by the Burano School (Fig. 3).

Method of working Venetian and Burano Laces at the Burano School. The workers at the Burano School are divided into sections; each of these sections carries out a particular stitch, always the same one, and this allows them to specialise in certain stitches which they can then work with great rapidity and skill. All the pupils pass through the various sections, and little by

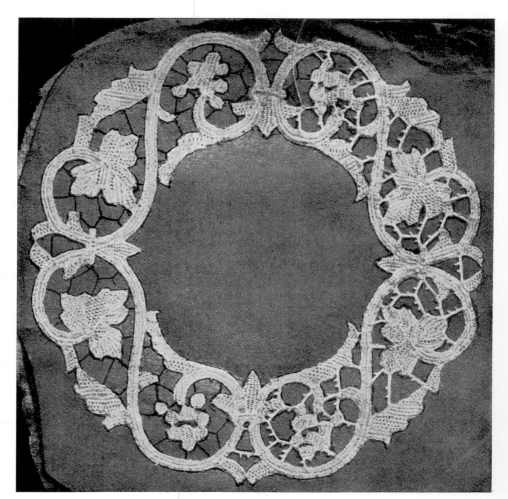

Fig. 2. The finished "Guipure" Stitch and showing commencement of bars in Buttonhole Stitch with picots

Fig. 3. The Burano School: women intent on their lace-making, all dressed alike in white overalls

little the best go on to the more difficult branches, reaching finally a very high level of ability.

Necessary Materials. The design, almost always inspired by the old traditions (attempts at modernisation have been unsuccessful), is in ink on a special paper made at Fabriano; this is rather strong and green or blue in colour. Each design serves once only.

For Venetian laces, a very fine thread is required. With Coats Mercer-Crochet, Nos. 60–80, excellent results can be obtained.

Technique for Venetian and Burano Laces. All along the edges of the design, prepared as described above, holes are made with the point of the needle at a very short distance between. This card, with the design outlined in holes, is now fastened to two or three layers of strong cotton material which will serve as support for the whole piece of lace. The first section, that of the outline, is now tacked. Use a very strong thread to whip over the edges and through the holes of the design; we advise Coats Mercer-Crochet thread as being suitable. This tacking follows the outline of the design perfectly (Fig. 1). In some Venetian workshops this is worked by machine, with a great saving of time; but at the Burano School work is done entirely by hand.

On completing the tacking, the second stage follows: i.e. the filling-in stitches, nets and the stitches forming the lace itself; this is a complex work which the workers call "guipure", using the French name (Fig. 2). This stage is one of the most important, since on it depends the beauty of the work.

The lace-making stitch is only a Blanket Stitch worked back and forth over a stretched thread. From one part of the design to another, from left to right, or from above to below, a thread is stretched which is then covered with a return row of Blanket Stitches, all alike. On the following row the two movements are repeated. The lace-making stitch is then close and full, whilst the nets, with their spaces, lighten the lace. The bars have already been amply described and illustrated in the chapter on "Renaissance Lace". In Venetian Stitch, the "Venetian" bars are the ones most commonly used, those with picots worked in Buttonhole Stitch. These bars, which join together the different elements of the pattern, are the work of a third section.

A fourth section occupies itself with the finishing of the lace. That is, with giving the lace its particular outline, full of movement, accentuating the light and shade and the reliefs. The outline stitch in Venetian lace is Buttonhole Stitch worked very closely and evenly. It does not only follow the external outline of the design, but goes in to outline leaves and flowers, making them stand out more clearly and giving greater movement to the design. Fig. 4 shows a piece of lace, partly finished, even in its minutest details, and a part which is incomplete, from which can be seen what a great effect the outlines have on the beauty of the lace.

The Burano and Venetian lace-makers have the

Scuola di Burano

Fig. 4. Ladies' cuffs in Venetian lace: on the left the work is unfinished: on the right the finished part is completed with buttonhole stitches richly decorated with picots

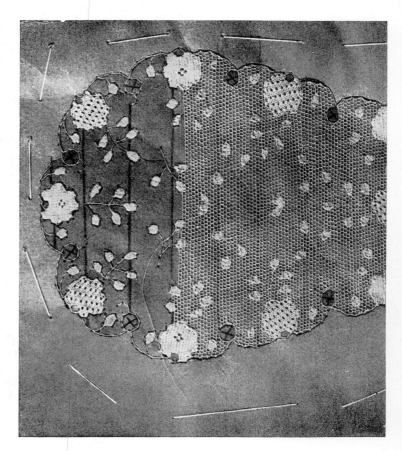

Fig. 5. Lace begun in Burano Stitch: note how the pattern is very much more delicate and lighter than Venetian lace, and the tulle background which joins the various motifs

Fig. 6. Table centre: the internal part of the design stands out on a background in tulle stitch; the external part is worked on a background of Medici Stitch

art of lace-making in their blood. Their surroundings, traditions, their long practice and their ancient patterns have created a graceful spontaneity and creative character in their work which it is impossible to find in any other place where lace is made, apart from Burano and Venice.

Thus in the fourth section of the school the lace is completed; or rather a piece of lace has been completed, because when the work is very large, as for tablecloths, covers, shawls, etc., it is divided into a certain number of parts to be worked separately.

Another section, consisting of the best workers who have reached the highest level of ability, now proceeds to the fastening off and composition of the pieces; this is difficult work, as all the operations already described must be gone over to ensure that no trace of joinings can be seen.

Lastly, the final section takes off the lace from the card. With a pair of scissors, or, better still, with a razor blade, the worker cuts between the lace and the selvedge all the stitches which fixed the first tacking, and with a pair of tweezers takes out all the tacking stitches which have remained

301

attached to the work, then going over all the lace again, joining up bars which may have broken or loose stitches, fastening off threads and working over again the netting which may have broken or a forgotten stitch. This is work requiring great patience and sense of responsibility, because it is the last stage which puts the finishing touches to the work.

After taking the lace off its support, Venetian lace remains rather stiff and solid; it should then be ironed on the wrong side to finish it off completely. The lace is not washed as soon as it is finished; only occasionally, and if absolutely necessary, is it placed in a solution of soapy water and then rinsed in running water, without squeezing.

To work Venetian or Burano lace, the worker rests her work on a kind of pillow, similar to that used when working with bobbins, and this is held on the knees, lengthways. Between the work and the pillow a cylindrical, movable piece of wood, called by the Venetians "murello", is placed and this serves to raise the work to the exact point at which it must be worked. Thus the worker can have both hands free for her work. One holds the needle, and the other places the threads and wraps them round the needle with a quick movement of the wrist.

Work is done from bottom to top. A vertical thread is placed from one point in the tacking at the top and fixed at the bottom, following the design, and going back with a Buttonhole Stitch taking the selvedge stitch up in the first row. On the following row the needle goes into the rib of the Buttonhole Stitch of the preceding line, taking up the stretched thread with each stitch.

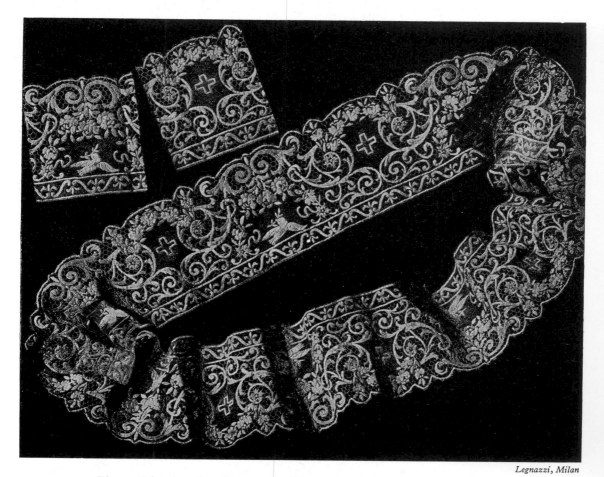

Legnazzi, Milan

Fig. 7. Trimmings for religious vestments, worked in Venetian and Burano lace

302

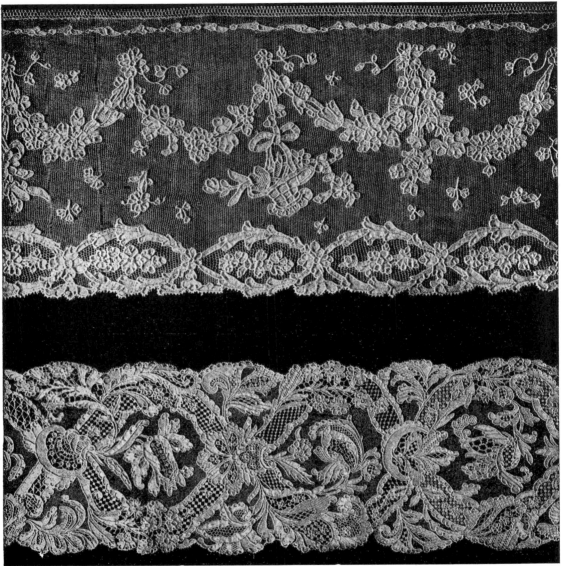

Fig. 8. Patterns of Burano lace: note the beauty of the design and its perfect execution

The Buttonhole Stitching of the outline is also worked "backwards", i.e. from right to left. The bars and outline are always very rich in picots. We have already described the picots used in Venetian laces, pp. 287 and 289, but we now describe how we have seen them worked by workers from Burano.

With the thumb and first finger of the left hand they hold the threaded needle, with the thread doubled. The needle is passed from the last outline stitch or bar, through the top of the thread in the needle, three times; then the three threads are covered with three or four Buttonhole Stitches. Only on arrival at the following picot does the worker unthread the needle and repeat the movement with surprising rapidity.

Venetian Lace in Relief. One of the characteristics of Venetian lace is the high relief which,

303

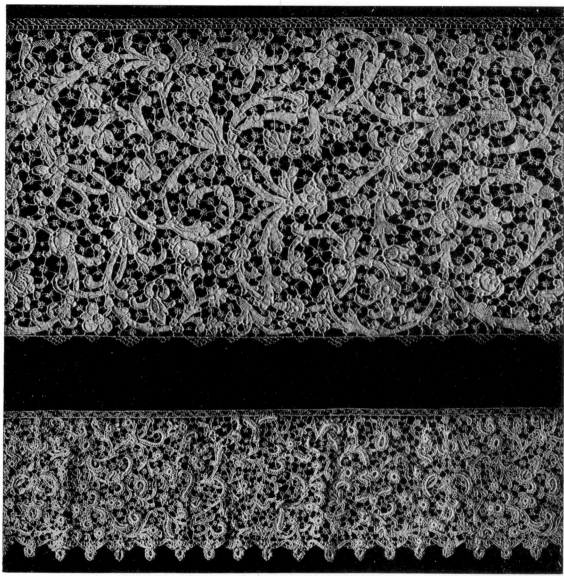

Fig. 9. Patterns of Venetian laces: the special work in the second piece is called "rosaline"

especially in ancient work, gives the richness and luxury typical of this type of lace. The reliefs are only worked in some parts of the design, as, for example, on the outside hems of curves, the petals of flowers, and in leaves, and consists of a large Buttonhole Stitch. This stitch is worked over a thickness of threads which forms a padding and is made by overlapping several soft cotton threads, as, for example, Coats Anchor Stranded Cotton. The

Buttonhole Stitching is begun small and even, as for the rest of the lace, and gradually enlarged, so as to be at its greatest height at the centre, to decrease again on the opposite side.

Sometimes this relief work, which is called "simple" relief, is enriched by other stitches worked in space, placed over and worked on the rib of the first stitch, decorated with an infinite variety of picots.

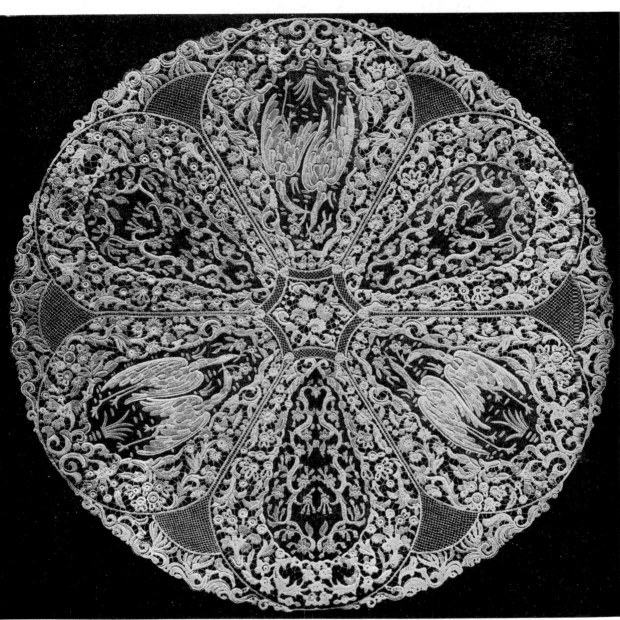

Fig. 10. Attempts have been made to break away from tradition and modernise the designs of Venetian lace. Here is a table centre whose design shows characteristics absolutely different from those of the classical Venetian lace. Given its perfect execution and the elegance of the motifs, it cannot be denied that this piece of work has its own beauty

Fig. 11. This table centre shows an original note which distinguishes it from the usual designs. The entire decorative motif is not worked on a background of bars or tulle, but the curves join and intersect amongst themselves. Only the border and the small centrepiece are rich in bars of the Medici type

306

CHAPTER XXVI

Modàno Lace

This type of work, in netting, also called "filet", gets its name from the Tuscan name "modàno" for the needle with which it is worked. "Filet", a French word, means net, and in fact this lace has the characteristic structure which everyone knows and which is similar to fishing nets. It is therefore work with very ancient origins; it began with primitive man who, with his still inexpert hands, roughly knotted his nets by the seashore. On the beaches of coastal villages it is not an uncommon sight, even today, to see the fishermen mending holes in their nets, and if one stops to watch, it can easily be seen that the movement they use is just that which the embroideress uses in making her filet.

As for all other laces, this one too had a period when it was very fashionable, and forty years ago it was used for decorations of all kinds, both for the house and for clothing. Today, this netting is always in demand for curtains, laces, bags, hairnets and even ladies' stockings.

In Italy, the centres producing modàno are to be found in Venetia, Tuscany, Abruzzi, and above all in Sardinia, where the beautiful nets have a particular and unmistakable character.

Necessary Materials. First of all the "modàno", that is a kind of long, thick needle, generally in metal, with an open eye at each end, is necessary. Under one of these eyes there is a small hole through which the thread is taken and knotted in place, to be then wound round the needle through the two open eyes. These needles are of varying thicknesses, according to the work to be carried out, and of different qualities, in steel, in wood and in bone.

Different threads are necessary according to the fineness of the work to be done. For lace nets, in white or écru, we advise Coats Mercer-Crochet. With Nos. 20, 30, 40, 50, 60, 70 and 80, nets of varying thicknesses can be obtained from the finest to the thickest. For bags and nets with wide spaces, Coats Anchor Coton à Broder, No. 18, is an excellent, well-running thread, which has the advantage of more than 120 colours.

The nets, especially for laces, are then embroidered, as will be seen further on in the chapter. For embroidery on net, work with a thread of the same quality as that used for the net itself. Only for Darning Stitch is it better to use a softer, less twisted thread: in this case the best thread is Coats Anchor Coton à Broder in a thickness suitable to the net to be filled in or Coats Anchor Stranded Cotton. As well as the modàno needle and thread, a rod of wood or metal is also necessary. For nets which are rather thick, the use of an ordinary pencil is advised, and for finer nets, a double-pointed knitting needle is very suitable: the thickness of this rod of wood or metal is what determines the size of the hole in the net.

Richly decorated bed-spread in large squares of filet lace alternating with rectangles embroidered in Slip-stitch and Pisa Stitch, and with squares of pillow lace. The net of this lace is rather wide and worked in double darning stitch

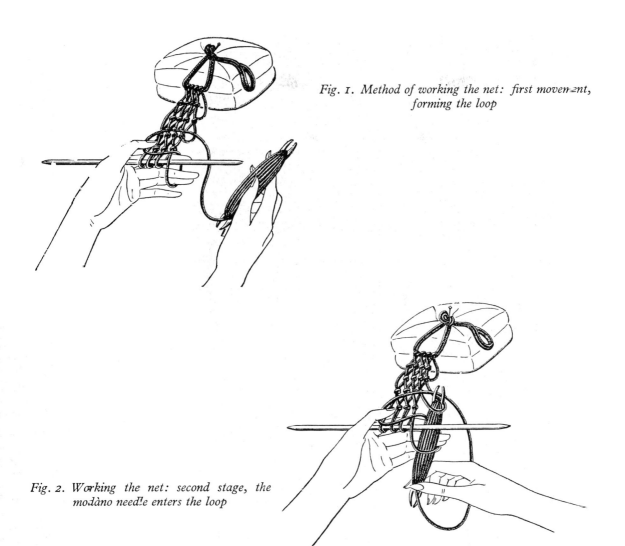

Fig. 1. *Method of working the net: first movement, forming the loop*

Fig. 2. *Working the net: second stage, the modàno needle enters the loop*

A heavy pillow, on which to support the lace, is also necessary, but almost any household object, for example a hook, a key in a drawer, a chairback, etc., will serve the same purpose.

Technique for working Modàno. Embroidery on net can be divided into three distinct types, according to the manner of working. "Cluny Filet", or the classical embroidery on net, in which designs of flowers, leaves, animals, figures, etc., are worked solely in Lace Stitch. "Richelieu Filet", in which the motifs of the design in Lace Stitch and Darning Stitch are outlined by a double thread, thicker than the rest, to make the outline

stand out. In Italy this work is much used in Sardinian filet work.

And lastly, "Italian Filet", in which many different stitches are used.

In the past, embroidery on net was very much more elaborate than it is today, and net was very suitable for all types of work. Further on are given some examples of backgrounds which may be of interest to those specialising in filet work, but the most common stitches in use today are Lace Stitch, Darning Stitch and Ghost Stitch.

To embroider on net, place it over a light frame or, if its size allows, over a piece of card, pulling the stitches well so that the net is well stretched al

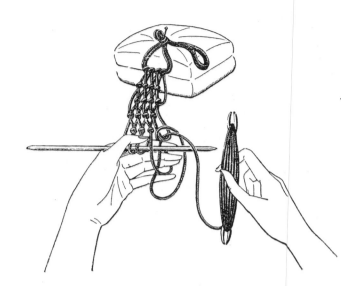

Fig. 3. Working the net: third stage, the little finger does not leave the loop until the knot has been drawn up by pulling on the threads

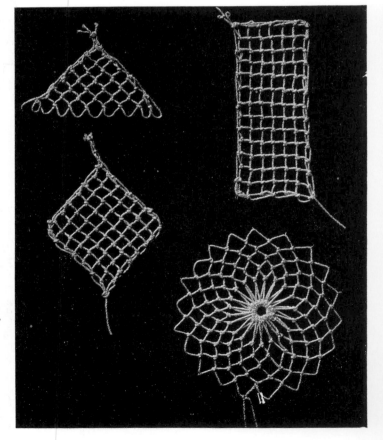

Fig. 4. Beginning a square of netting: the finished square: a rectangle of netting: a circle of netting

over, and the squares forming it are all equal. The needles used for the work should be rather long, with blunt ends.

The patterns for the embroidery must be prepared on squared paper. Each hole in the net corresponds to a square of paper.

Working the Net. Having arranged all the necessary materials, and filled the modàno needle with the most suitable thread, the work can begin. Make a loop in the thread and fix it to the pillow with a safety pin. Fix the end of the thread, wrapped round the needle, to this with a knot. Take the rod of wood in the left hand, pass the thread in front of it and behind the first, middle and third fingers of the left hand, forming a loop which is held firm with the left thumb (Fig. 1). With the right hand pass the needle through the loop below the rod and take it through the smaller loop at the beginning (Fig. 2). At this point, take up the modàno needle again with the right hand, and holding the thread only with the little finger of the left hand, free the other fingers from the loop, pulling the thread with the right hand; hold the thread with the little finger until the loop is almost closed. Only then should the little finger be removed from the loop, at the same time closing the knot which is to be found at the upper side of the rod (Fig. 3). Repeat the movement making as many holes as necessary. Then place in the rod, turn the work and begin another row, resting the rod against the row of holes just worked. The needle passes through each hole of the preceding row, which is worked in the same way, drawing up the knots.

Method of Working a Square of Net. After working the first hole into the basic loop, take out the rod and into this hole work two knots. Take out the rod again, turn the work and work three knots into the two stitches of the preceding row. That is, one into the first stitch and two into the second. Take out the rod, turn the work and continue thus, increasing one stitch on each row, making two stitches in the last stitch on the right. Continue to increase until there is one more stitch than the number necessary for the side of the square. Then, work a row without any increases and on the following row begin to decrease, taking the two last knots on the right into one single stitch. Continue thus until all the stitches have been used up (Fig. 4).

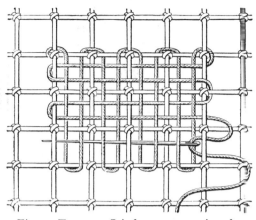

Fig. 5. Tapestry Stitch on net, passing the thread twice

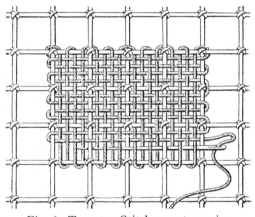

Fig. 6. Tapestry Stitch on net, passing thread four times

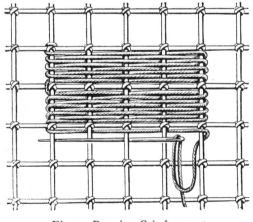

Fig. 7. Darning Stitch on net

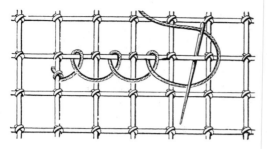

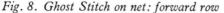

Fig. 8. Ghost Stitch on net: forward row

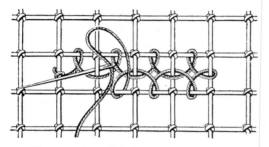

Fig. 9. Ghost Stitch on net: return row

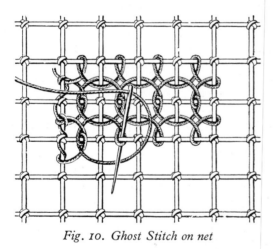

Fig. 10. Ghost Stitch on net

Method of Working a Rectangle or Strip of Net. Proceed as for the square, up to the required width, making one stitch more than the number necessary for the upper side of the rectangle. On the following row decrease, taking two stitches together on the right, turn the work and at the end of the next row, in the last stitch, work two stitches. Turn the work and continue thus, alternating the decreasing and increasing on successive rows. To close the rectangle, proceed as described for the finishing off of the square, that

is, decreasing on every row in the last two stitches until all are taken off (Fig. 4).

Method of Working a Circle in Net. Over a very strong stretched thread (an excellent thread is Coats Mercer-Crochet in a thickness suitable to the work to be done), work twenty or twenty-five stitches. Pull the two ends of the stretched thread, drawing up the central hole as much as possible. Fix the two joined threads to the pillow and work round, taking care that the first stitch is very tight. Bags in netting are worked by this process. To widen the row work a Double Stitch (i.e. into each stitch of the previous row, work two), and then continue to work round for the required length.

If, however, a perfect circle is required, that is, a star in net (for table centres, bed linen, etc.), work in the following manner: for example, if a star with eight rays is required, set on seven stitches over the usual stretched thread (this number will vary according to the size of the star), leaving a length of thread from the setting-on hanging down. This thread will serve to make the passage from one row to the other invisible. After having set on a sufficient number of stitches for the first row, less one (in this case, seven stitches), and after having pulled the ends of the stretched thread as described above, close the first row, using the length of thread left at the beginning. Place the rod through the last stitch worked, i.e. the seventh, and through the first of the row. The joining thread remains below, whilst the thread from the needle stays above the rod. These two threads are knotted together twice (the second time the knot is made in the opposite direction to make it firmer). The next row then begins from this knot and the joining thread is carried in this way through all the rows of the work. Fig. 4 shows, below on the right, a circle of net worked with joining threads.

Joining Thread in Nets and Embroidery on Net. To join threads in the net itself, use a Weaver's Knot (see p. 215).

Try to make the knot half-way along the stitch so that it is covered, on the following row, by the knot of the net.

In embroidery, too, join the threads with Weaver's Knots, whatever the stitch used.

Patterned Nets. The net can be worked with different sizes of rods, giving rise to coarser and finer netting, and using different thicknesses of thread, giving very pleasant contrasting effects.

The joining of three or four stitches into one on the first row, stitches which will be replaced on the following row, forms a prettily-patterned net, as does the working of several knots into one on the first row, leaving them free on the next, forming decorative bows. The self-patterned net can be used for curtains and instead of embroidered nets.

Embroidered Nets. The modàno net can be embroidered after working it. Any design on squared paper can be worked in embroidery on net: each square being equal to one hole in the net. The threads used for embroidery on net should be softer than that with which the net itself is worked. The most advisable are embroidery threads, such as Coats Anchor Coton à Broder, and Coats Anchor Stranded Cotton.

Tapestry Stitch. This is the classical stitch for working embroidery on nets. Fix the needleful of thread to a knot in the net, and then pass the thread backwards and forwards, twice through each hole, for the necessary length. Take care that the threads, whether to left or right, have the same position, so that the stitch is even. The selvedge is formed in this way.

Later, the same stitches are worked in the opposite direction taking up and leaving down a thread of the actual selvedge itself like a Tapestry Stitch.

The Tapestry Stitch can be worked very closely or widely spaced. In the first case the weft and woof threads pass four times through each hole of the net, according to the design and the size of the hole, and in the second case twice through each hole (Fig. 5).

Darning Stitch. This is even simpler than Tapestry Stitch. Fix the thread with a knot, to a knot in the net and make the first movement as in Tapestry Stitch, that is, passing the thread above and below the threads of the net, as many times as necessary to fill the space with rather close stitches (Fig. 7).

Ghost Stitch. This consists of a twist of threads which thickens the net, but gives it a great air of lightness.

It is worked in two stages. Fix the thread halfway along the side of one hole of the net, and work from left to right with a Blanket Stitch as wide as half the following hole. On the second row work from right to left: first work a stitch on the vertical side of the last square, then another on the bottom side, then pass the thread below the left side and above the loop of the preceding row. Figs. 8, 9 and 10 are much clearer than any written explanation could be.

Background on Net.
Fig. 11 shows a background consisting of threads worked in a horizontal direction through the squares of the net, taking one thread of the net below the knot, first at the top and then at the bottom. Work from right to left or from left to right.

Fig. 12 shows a background in Ghost Stitch, worked first from left to right and then going back from right to left, as explained on the preceding page.

Fig. 13. This background is worked in rows of Cross Stitch worked diagonally back and forth, always in the same direction.

Fig. 14. A background consisting of small squares worked in Darning and Ghost Stitches, alternated and interchanged on each line. Work first the squares in Darning Stitch, diagonally, and then those in Ghost Stitch.

Fig. 15. A background consisting of small squares filled-in with Darning Stitch up to the diagonal, alternating the direction of the stitches on every row.

Fig. 16. Background consisting of threads pulled diagonally through the squares in both directions. At the point of intersection work a wheel, using the pulled threads and those of the net.

Fig. 17. A background in rosettes worked on nine squares with the corners in Darning Stitch and with a Ghost Stitch at the centre. Work a wheel among the rosettes in Rib Stitch, covering four squares.

Fig. 18. A background consisting of squares in Tapestry Stitch, occupying four holes of the net, alternated with four holes left empty. Later, in these empty spaces, a Cross Stitch is worked diagonally in both directions, i.e. one going from left to right and one from right to left.

Fig. 19. A motif worked in Darning Stitch outlined with a thread which makes the design stand out.

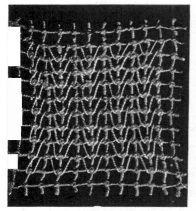

Fig. 11. Background with alternated stretched threads

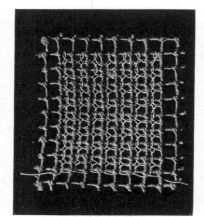

Fig. 12. Background in Ghost Stitch

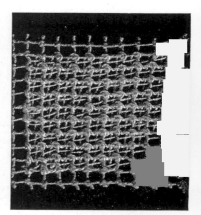

Fig. 13. Background in Cross Stitch worked diagonally

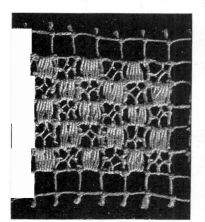

Fig. 14. Background with Darning Stitch and Ghost Stitch

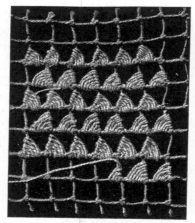

Fig. 15. Background with Darning Stitch in corners of squares

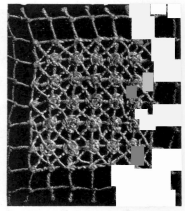

Fig. 16. Background of webs worked diagonally

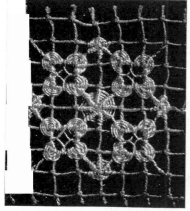

Fig. 17. Background of rosettes in Darning Stitch

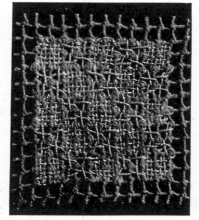

Fig. 18. Background in Tapestry Stitch and crossed threads

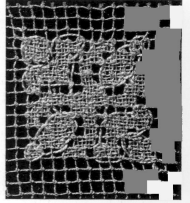

Fig. 19. Motif in Darning Stitch outlined

Example of Sardinian filet. Table centre with stylised cocks and flowers

Example of Sardinian filet work with a typical peacock design: chairback cover

All these backgrounds are worked in Clark's Anchor Coton à Broder, a very soft thread which is very suitable for embroidering on net.

Nice Stitch. The so-called "Nice" Stitch is a modern application of Darning Stitch on modàno net, worked with a special cording in ivory with very large holes.

Stretch the net to be embroidered over a frame, and cut lengths of cord, rather longer than the length desired. Fix the end of the first thread at the upper edge and stretch it vertically on the net until the first motif of the design is met with. Since this motif must be embroidered in Darning Stitch, the cord passes through the holes of the net, forming a weft thread, after which the thread is again stretched as far as the next motif to be worked, when again the cord will form a Darning Stitch through the net; and so on to the other edge of the net. All the necessary cords are thus stretched over the work, close to each other. On completing the placing of the vertical threads, work other cords in horizontal Darning Stitch in all the places where the weft has already been worked. On completing the Darning Stitch in both directions, turn the frame over, and cut away the net which has not been worked, on the back of the work. Thus the net will remain where there is a design in Darning Stitch, but will be removed behind the stretches of perpendicular cording, which will then remain free and loose between one pattern and another. This is rich, elegant work, especially used for curtains and door hangings for modern decoration schemes.

Sardinian Filet. In Sardinia, net work has its own particular characteristics. It is worked by the women in different regions of the island, but the most famous centre for its production is Bosa. Sardinian filet work originated in the fifteenth century, and although there were periods when it was not worked much, alternating with periods of great popularity, it never completely disappeared.

It is worked with a light, natural-coloured linen thread to traditional designs, showing stylised animals (the peacock is very famous), flowers and various figures. All the filled-in motifs are generally worked in Darning Stitch, and then outlined by a thread which passes twice going, and once coming back, and which enriches the design with little flowers, rosettes, whirls, etc.

Sardinian filet is used for working runners, table centres, tablecloths, bed covers, curtains and chairback covers, etc. It is rare work of great beauty, which can take its place with other laces, perhaps more precious, but not so characteristic.

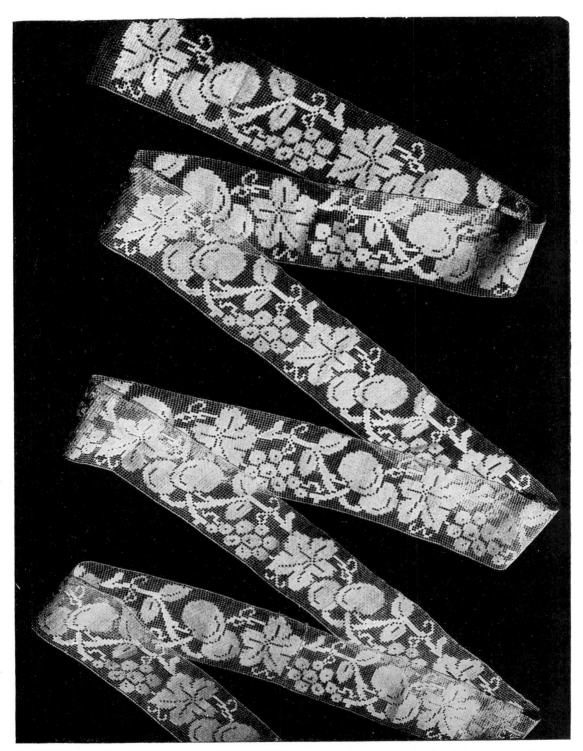

Lace insertion with design of fruit and leaves. The rather fine net is embroidered in Darning Stitch

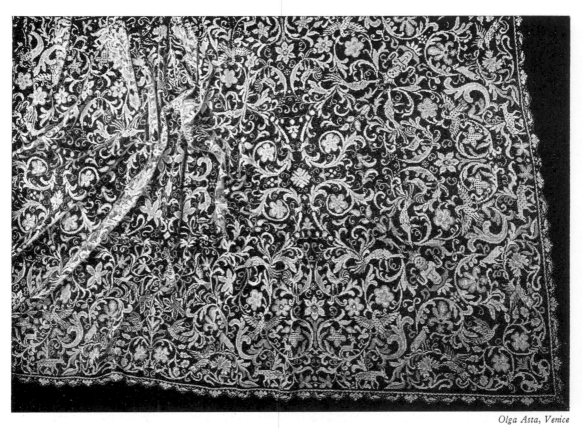

Luxurious table runner embroidered in Tapestry Stitch on fine natural-coloured net
(Below) A detail of the pattern enlarged

CHAPTER XXVII

Bobbin Lace

The gay, placid art of lace-making still lives on in some places because of an unconscious sense of artistry which has been jealously guarded up to the present day.

Venice preserves the majesty of needle-made laces; in some of the villages of the Abruzzi, like Pescocostanzo, lace is made with bobbins, as it is here and there in Tuscany and Liguria, where, however, it does not follow the ancient traditions rigidly. These have, instead, grown up again in the town of Cantù, the classical lace-making district.

How this art grew up here we do not know, since the origins of all bobbin-made laces are obscure. It seems that some nuns of the Benedictine order from Cluny and Alençon imported the secret of how to work this lace, teaching it to their young pupils. But, on studying available documents, another story becomes apparent which insists that Italy was the first country to produce lace made in this way, and not France.

The earliest traces are to be found in a contract of division, made in Milan in 1493, between the sisters Angela and Ippolita Sforza Visconti. This treats of a piece of lace worked "with two bobbins for a sheet". Earlier documents do not exist. In the same contract there is mention of work done with "bones" and we think it highly probable that these "bones" correspond to bobbins. In fact, before being made of wood, the bobbins were in fact made of bone, and so they were called in Cantù and in the Canton of Ticino.

It was only about 1870 that the lace-making industry in Cantù really developed. Able salesmen were substituted for the humble women who carried their laces into the big cities to sell; shops were opened, organised groups formed for working and for the distribution of the work, for procuring material and designs. In the *History of Manufacturing Industry in Lombardy*, the author says that only the inhabitants of Cantù and the district around occupied themselves with lace-making, and that the work had been carried out there by the women and children since 1600. This small army of women worked for a few merchants who supplied them with thread, silk, designs and all the other necessities for their work, at a wage of from 20 centimes to 1 lira per day. In the last decade of the eighteenth century the number of workers rose to nearly 5,000, of which 3,000 were in the District of Cantù and 2,000 in the surrounding districts, earning daily about 20–25 centimes and reaching a maximum of 1 lira and 30 or 40 centimes each. It can well be imagined how cheap the laces were!

But we are not so particularly interested in economic facts, however important they may be, as in historical and artistic ones. A natural question arises: was needle-made lace or bobbin-made lace the first to develop? It appears that they both

A rare example of pillow-made lace. Details of a richly worked, luxurious luncheon cloth

Chair back (or car seat) cover showing the "Rape of Helen at Troy" worked in pillow lace

arose at about the same time. Certainly they are to be found contemporaneously, with characteristics much the same, in countries very far apart, which might lead us to imagine that some mysterious inspiration ensured their simultaneous development.

But while needle-made laces have an aristocratic tradition, bobbin-made ones are essentially a tradition of the people. The first ones constituted the elegant pastime of noblewomen, in their courts of young ladies, so that to find their origin we must go into the old noble families; the second, on the other hand, were reserved entirely to the common people, and formed the basis of a trade which, as we have seen above, was far from lucrative.

At Cantù the industry, as well as being carried on by some firms in the town, also spread to surrounding villages: Carinate, Novedrate, Figino and Mariano.

In the Cantù district there is not a house where lace is not worked in spare moments from the work of the house or the fields, and it is a real "home-industry". The men specialise in iron work for making nails, or they are carpenters or furniture makers: the women make lace.

In the good weather thread and bobbins are to be seen outside in the street, where the younger and less expert workers learn from the agile, expert movements of their more skilled sisters.

The beginner learns when very young, whilst still playing with her dolls and, what is an inexplicable fact, making one believe in some obscure, hereditary law; the Cantù children very quickly learn to work the lace with all the skill and grace of their elders, and with more than that of workers imported from other places, who have to undergo long years of training.

Another curious fact is that the art continues to be preserved in all its characteristics and in the way in which it is worked. It has never been possible to change it, in spite of its commercialisation, and so it has never been affected by the nineteenth-century industrialisation which took almost every other kind of artisan work into the factories. This peculiarity is what has preserved the primitive purity of design of the lace, without those deviations which are so often to be found in popular taste.

It might be said that the best laces, with the finest designs, clarity of detail, etc., are to be found in this town in Brianza, especially so far as imitation of ancient, classical models is concerned. And it is this imitative ability which gives the lace its value, for no collector can say with certainty that the antique "piece" in his collection is not of some much more recent date than the "real seventeenth century" attributed to it.

Necessary Materials.

Bobbins, a kind of wooden rod furnished with a ball at one end, are the first necessities. The thread for the lace-making is wrapped on these bobbins, which are always in pairs.

The Pillow.

This is a round pillow, in the form of a muff, padded with horse-hair, on which the design to be worked is rested. In other European countries this pillow takes different forms: in Normandy it is square; like a cushion in Belgium, and so on. The pillow generally rests on a stand furnished with two curved wooden rests, which hold it still. A pricker serves to prick out holes around the design.

Pins.

These are used to fix the various braids of thread during the course of the work. They must be fine and rather long, in steel or brass, so that they do not rust.

A light green or reddish card is used for copying the design. The design for pillow lace must be carried out perfectly, so that the lace will be perfect. The card should be long enough to go all round the pillow to which it is fixed at the joining point, with pins. The lines of the design should be interrupted at the place where the card joins. If the circumference of the pillow is less than the length of card carrying the design, join on lengths of felt between the card and the pillow, for the length necessary to make the two edges of the design meet.

Punch holes in the outline of the design with the pricker, and fix pins in the holes to hold the thread joinings. In a beginner's designs the holes are marked by serial numbers to aid the worker in following the pattern.

Threads.

The thread used for working pillow-lace must be well twisted in order to stand up to frequent washing. Coats Mercer-Crochet in its various thicknesses is advised. Clark's Anchor Coton à Broder, too, is used on a large scale in the best workrooms.

Pillow lace can also be worked in silk, which produces the famous "Chantilly" lace, and with gold and silver thread, especially for religious garments.

Technique for Working Pillow Lace.

First of all, we must make it clear that it is very difficult to learn this art alone, or with the aid of only a book as guide. As we have already mentioned, in the places where the lace is produced, such as Cantù and Sansepolcro, Pecocostanzo and other places on the Ligurian Riviera, little girls learn the art from their mothers and older sisters, and easily become skilled workers. For anyone not in the trade, however, pillow lace is particularly difficult to make and the new worker should have the help of the teacher. In any case, the basic elements are given here to help the learner with the different stitches, and these will help her to face up to the more difficult work under the guidance of a skilled teacher.

Fixing the Thread to the Bobbins.

The wrapping of the thread to the bobbins can be done by hand, but in the workrooms it is done on a special machine which winds the thread as if on a shuttle. The bobbins should not be too full, in order to avoid dirtying the thread. The thread is fixed to the bobbin, but must run easily at the slightest touch. To this end, make a loop with the thumb and first finger of the left hand. Wrap the thread on to a bobbin and then fill in another in the same way, to make the pair (Fig. 1).

After preparing all the material and tools necessary, as explained above, the work of the actual lace-making can begin. The various methods of turning and crossing the bobbins form the various stitches of the lace. The number of bobbins used for pillow lace varies according to the design. There is work which requires hundreds of bobbins. Naturally, they are not all used at the same time: the ones which are momentarily out of use are rested on the pins to right or left of the pillow. The length of the thread from the bobbin to the lace should not be greater than about seven inches, to avoid knotting.

Large pieces of work are all worked in separate pieces. The different parts are then joined, according to the pattern, and the work is given out in the workroom so that each single worker performs and is specialised in a particular process, as for Venetian lace-making.

When the design card is fixed to the pillow, the Blanket-Stitched part of the lace should always be placed to the right and the part to be attached to the material always to the left of the worker.

Movement of the Bobbins. In pillow work always take four bobbins at a time, i.e. one pair in each hand. In the course of the following explanation, the terminology used by the Cantù school and workers has been adopted, words which are probably different in other districts.

Twisting. This is the name of the movement with which the bobbin on the right passes over that on the left. The movement is carried out with one hand only, and often must be repeated two or more times (Fig. 2).

Crossing. This is the term for the movement in which the inside bobbin of the left-hand pair is passed over the inside bobbin of the right-hand pair. The outer bobbins remain still. This movement is worked with two pairs of bobbins and both hands (Fig. 3).

The Stitch. This is worked in the following manner: hold a pair of bobbins in each hand. Twist the right bobbin over the left, in each hand, and cross the underlying bobbin of the pair in the left hand over the overlying bobbin of the pair in the right hand.

Twisting and crossing the bobbins produces the so-called "half-stitch". When the movement is repeated twice the full stitch is worked, and a "twist" is formed by working the movement several times.

Pillow work almost always goes in a diagonal direction.

Before doing any other work, it is best for the beginner to practise the various stitches and backgrounds. The numbering of the bobbins proceeds from left to right. The first pair, which is also the first described, is fixed to the design on the left, the last pair, on the right, corresponds to the highest number and is the last one described.

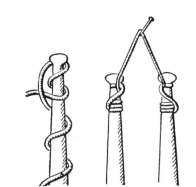

Fig. 1. *Bobbins with thread wrapped and fixed*

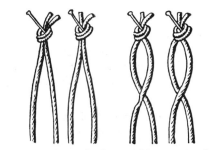

Fig. 2. *Threads ready for working: twisted threads*

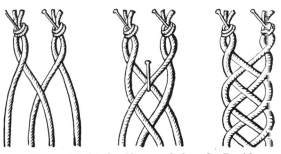

Fig. 3. *Twisted and crossed threads. Braid*

Braids (Fig. 3). The braid is worked with two pairs of bobbins; twist each pair once, then braid the inside threads. Repeat the same movement and a braid is formed.

Full Stitch and Tapestry Stitch. This is one of the first stitches that must be learned. With it, a kind of string is made, from which many laces can be formed, and, generally, the thickest parts of the pattern.

Prepare the model as shown in Fig. 5, and fix two pairs of bobbins wrapped with Coats Mercer-Crochet, No. 40, at points A, B, and C, and then begin the work.

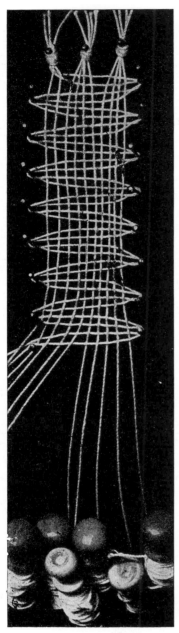

Fig. 4. Tapestry or Full Stitch

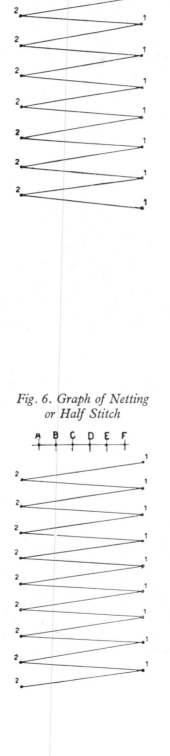

Fig. 5. Graph of Tapestry Stitch

Fig. 6. Graph of Netting or Half Stitch

Fig. 7. Netting Stitch in Half Stitch

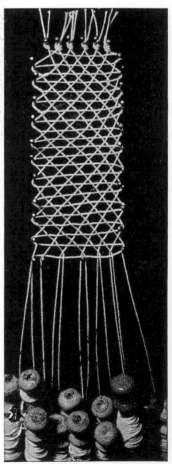

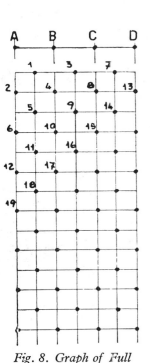

Fig. 8. Graph of Full Stitch in netting and Tulle Stitch

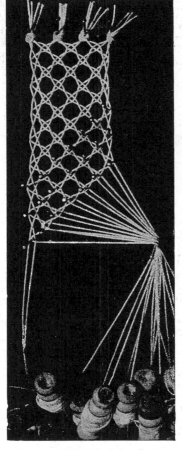

Fig. 9. Full Stitch in netting with a wrapped thread

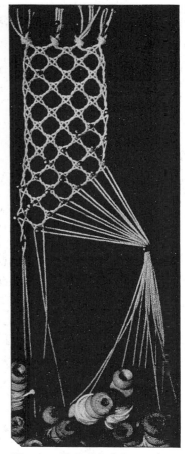

Fig. 10. Full Stitch in netting with two wrappings

Cross the first and the second pair, one stitch (★), cross second and third pairs, one stitch, cross third and fourth pairs, one stitch. Cross fourth and fifth pairs, one stitch. Cross fifth and sixth pairs, one stitch, fix a pin No. 1; twist sixth pair once, cross with fifth not twisted, one stitch. Cross fourth and fifth pairs, one stitch. Cross third and four pairs, one stitch. Cross second and third pair, one stitch. Cross first and second pairs, one stitch; fix a pin in No. 2, twist first pair once, cross with second, not crossed, one stitch. Repeat from (★) (Fig. 4).

Netting Stitch or "Half-stitch". Prepare design as in Fig. 6. Fix a pair of bobbins filled with Coats Mercer-Crochet, No. 40, to points A, B, C, D, E and F.

Then work as follows:

Twist first and second pair once, cross (★). Twist second and third pairs once, cross. Twist third and fourth pairs once, cross. Twist fourth and fifth pairs once, cross. Twist fifth and sixth pairs once, cross, fix a pin at point No. 1. Twist sixth pair twice and fifth pair once, cross. Twist fourth and fifth pairs once, cross. Twist third and fourth pairs once, cross. Twist second and third pairs once, cross; twist first and second pairs once, cross, and fix a pin to No. 2. Twist first pair once, second pair twice, cross and repeat from (★) (Fig. 7).

Full Netting Stitch (Fig. 10). Prepare the design as in Fig. 8. Fix two pairs of bobbins filled with Coats Mercer-Crochet to points A, B, C and D.

Then work thus:

Twist second and third pairs once, cross and fix pin to No. 1, one stitch. Twist first and second pairs once, cross, fix pin to No. 2, one stitch. Twist fourth and fifth pairs once, cross, fix pin to No. 3, one stitch. Twist third and fourth pairs once, cross, fix pin to No. 4, one stitch. Twist second and third pairs once, cross, fix pin to No. 5, one stitch. Twist first and second pairs once, cross, fix pin to No. 6, one stitch. Twist sixth and seventh pairs, cross, fix pin to No. 7, one stitch. Twist fifth and sixth pairs, cross, fix pin to No. 8, one stitch. Twist fourth and fifth pairs once, cross, fix pin to No. 9, one stitch. Twist third and fourth pairs once, cross, fix pin to No. 10, one stitch. Twist second and third pairs once, cross, fix pin to No. 11, one stitch. Twist first and second pairs once, cross, fix pin to No. 12, one stitch (*). Twist seventh and eighth pairs once, cross, fix pin to No. 13, one stitch. Twist sixth and seventh pairs once, cross, fix pin to No. 14, one stitch. Twist fifth and sixth pairs once, cross, fix pin to No. 15, one stitch. Twist fourth and fifth pairs once, cross, fix pin to No. 16, one stitch. Twist third and fourth pairs once, cross, fix pin to No. 17, one stitch. Twist second and third pairs once, cross, fix pin to No. 18, one stitch. Twist first and second pairs once, cross, fix pin to No. 19, one stitch. Repeat from (*) (Fig. 9).

Full Netting Stitch with Two Windings. Prepare design as in Fig. 8 and fix two pairs of bobbins wound with Coats Mercer-Crochet, No. 40, to points A, B, C and D.

Twist second and third pairs twice, cross, fix pin to No. 1, one stitch. Twist first and second pairs twice, cross, fix pin to No. 2, one stitch. Twist fourth and fifth pairs twice, cross, fix pin to No. 3, one stitch. Twist third and fourth pairs twice, cross, fix pin to No. 4, one stitch. Twist second and third pairs twice, cross, fix pin to No. 5, one stitch. Twist first and second pairs twice, cross, fix pin to No. 6, one stitch. Twist sixth and seventh pairs twice, cross, fix pin to No. 7, one stitch. Twist fifth and sixth pairs twice, cross, fix pin to No. 8, one stitch. Twist fourth and fifth pairs twice, cross, fix pin to No. 9, one stitch. Twist third and fourth pairs twice, cross, fix pin to No. 10, one stitch. Twist second and third pairs twice, cross, fix pin to No. 11, one stitch. Twist first and second pairs twice, cross, fix pin to No. 12, one stitch (*). Twist seventh and eighth pairs twice, cross, fix pin to No. 13, one stitch. Twist sixth and seventh pairs twice, cross, fix pin to No. 14, one stitch. Twist fifth and sixth pairs twice, cross, fix pin to No. 15, one stitch. Twist fourth and fifth pairs twice, cross, fix pin to No. 16, one stitch. Twist third and fourth pairs twice, cross, fix pin to No. 17, one stitch. Twist second and third pairs twice, cross, fix pin to No. 18, one stitch. Twist first and second pairs twice, cross, fix pin to No. 19, one stitch. Repeat from (*) (Fig. 10).

Double Netting Stitch. Prepare the pattern as in Fig. 8. Fix two pairs of bobbins wound with Coats Mercer-Crochet, No. 40, at points A, B, C and D. Fix.

Twist second and third pairs twice, cross, one stitch, fix pin to No. 1, two stitches. Twist first and second pairs twice, cross, one stitch, fix pin to No. 2, two stitches. Twist fourth and fifth pairs twice, cross, one stitch, fix pin to No. 3, two stitches. Twist third and fourth pairs twice, cross, one stitch, fix pin to No. 4, two stitches. Twist second and third pairs twice, cross, one stitch, fix pin to No. 5, two stitches. Twist first and second pairs, cross, one stitch, fix pin to No. 6, two stitches. Twist sixth and seventh pairs twice, cross, one stitch, fix pin to No. 7, two stitches. Twist fifth and sixth pairs twice, cross, one stitch, fix pin to No. 9, two stitches. Twist third and fourth pairs twice, cross, one stitch, fix pin to No. 10, two stitches. Twist second and third pairs twice, cross, one stitch, fix pin to No. 11, two stitches. Twist first and second pairs twice, cross, one stitch, fix pin to No. 12, two stitches (*). Twist seventh and eighth pairs twice, cross, one stitch, fix pin to No. 13, two stitches. Twist sixth and seventh pairs twice, cross, one stitch, fix pin to No. 14, two stitches. Twist fifth and sixth pairs twice, cross, one stitch, fix pin to No. 15, two stitches. Twist fourth and fifth pairs, cross, one stitch, fix pin to No. 16, two stitches. Twist third and fourth pairs twice, cross, one stitch, fix pin to No. 17, two stitches. Twist second and third pairs twice, cross, one stitch, fix pin to No. 18, two stitches. Twist first and second pairs twice, cross, one stitch, fix pin to No. 19, two stitches. Repeat from (*) (Fig. 11).

Tulle Stitch. This is so-called because it imitates the material of the same name. Prepare pattern as in Fig. 8, and fix two pairs of bobbins filled with Coats Mercer-Crochet, No. 40, to points A

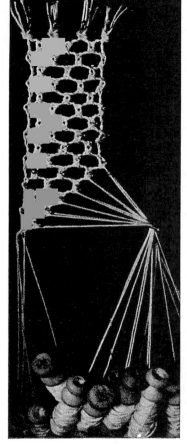

Fig. 11. Full Stitch in netting, double

Fig. 12 (right). Tulle Stitch

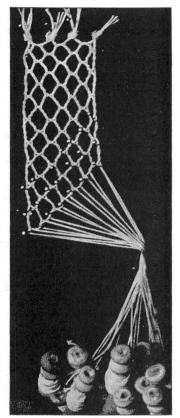

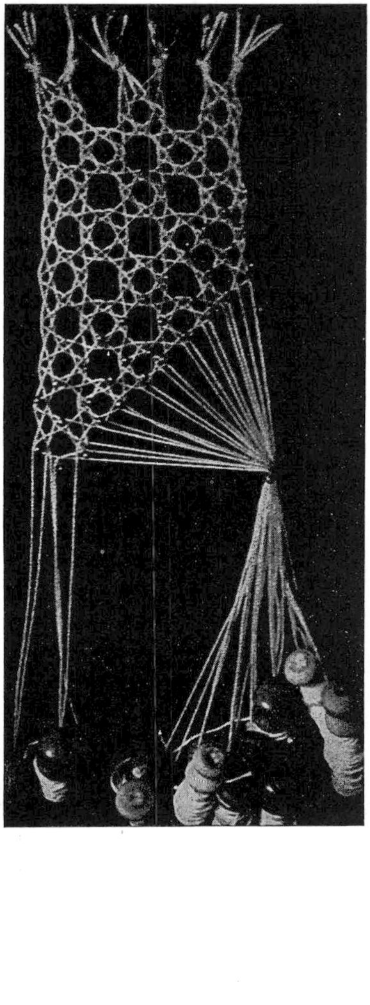

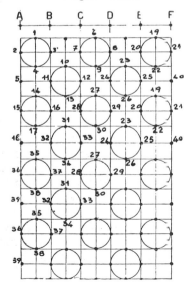

Fig. 14. (below). Graph of "Virgin" Stitch

Fig. 13 (right). "Virgin" Stitch

327

B, C and D. Work diagonally as for the other stitches, proceeding thus: twist the two pairs of bobbins three times and then cross, or make a half-stitch, fix a pin. Repeat in this manner (Fig. 12)

Background in "Virgin" Stitch. Prepare design as in Fig. 14 and fix two pairs of bobbins wound with Coats Mercer-Crochet, No. 40, at points A, B, C, D, E and F.

Twist second and third pairs once, cross, fix pin to No. 1, one stitch. Twist first and second pairs once, cross, fix pin to No. 2, one stitch. Twist third and fourth pairs once, cross, fix pin to No. 3, one stitch. Twist second and third pairs once, cross, fix pin to No. 4, one stitch. Twist first and second pairs once, cross, fix pin to No. 5, one stitch. Twist sixth and seventh pairs once, cross, fix pin to No. 6, one stitch. Twist fifth and sixth pairs once, cross, fix pin to No. 7, one stitch. Twist seventh and eighth pairs once, cross, fix pin to No. 8, one stitch. Twist sixth and seventh pairs once, cross, fix pin to No. 9, one stitch. Twist fifth and sixth pairs, cross. Twist third and fourth pairs, cross. Twist fourth and fifth pairs, cross, fix pin to No. 10, one stitch. Twist third and fourth pairs once, cross, fix pin to No. 11, one stitch. Twist fifth and sixth pairs once, cross, fix pin to No. 12, one stitch. Twist fourth and fifth pairs once, cross, fix pin to No. 13, one stitch. Twist third and fourth pairs once, cross. Twist second and third pairs once, cross, fix pin to No. 14, one stitch. Twist first and second pairs once, cross, fix pin to No. 15, one stitch. Twist third and fourth pairs once, cross, fix pin to No. 16, one stitch. Twist second and third pairs once, cross, fix pin to No. 17, one stitch. Twist first and second pairs once, cross, fix pin to No. 18, one stitch (*). Twist tenth and eleventh pairs once, cross, fix pin to No. 19, one stitch. Twist ninth and tenth pairs once, cross, fix pin to No. 20, one stitch. Twist eleventh and twelfth pairs once, cross, fix pin to No. 21, one stitch. Twist tenth and eleventh pairs once, cross, fix pin to No. 22, one stitch. Twist ninth and tenth pairs once, cross; twist seventh and eighth pairs once, cross. Twist eighth and ninth pairs once, cross, fix pin to No. 23, one stitch. Twist seventh and eighth pairs once, cross, fix pin to No. 24, one stitch. Twist ninth and tenth pairs once, cross, fix pin to No. 25, one stitch. Twist eighth and ninth pairs once, cross, fix pin to No. 26, one stitch. Twist seventh and eighth pairs once. Twist fifth and sixth pairs once, cross. Twist sixth and seventh pairs once, cross, fix pin to No. 27, one stitch. Twist fifth and sixth pairs once, cross, fix pin to No. 28, one stitch. Twist seventh and eighth pairs once, cross, fix pin to No. 29, one stitch. Twist sixth and seventh pairs once, cross, fix pin to No. 30, one stitch. Twist fifth and sixth pairs once, cross. Twist third and fourth pairs once, cross. Twist fourth and fifth pairs once, cross, fix pin to No. 31, one stitch. Twist third and fourth pairs once, cross, fix pin to No. 32, one stitch. Twist fifth and sixth pairs once, cross, fix pin to No. 33, one stitch. Twist fourth and fifth pairs once, cross, fix pin to No. 34, one stitch. Twist third and fourth pairs once. Twist second and third pairs once, cross, fix pin to No. 35, one stitch. Twist first and second pairs once, cross, fix pin to No. 36, one stitch. Twist third and fourth pairs once, cross, fix pin to No. 37, one stitch. Twist second and third pairs once, cross, fix pin to No. 38, one stitch. Twist first and second pairs once, cross, fix pin to No. 39, one stitch. Twist eleventh and twelfth pairs once, cross, fix pin to No. 40, one stitch. Twist ninth and tenth pairs once, cross. Repeat from (*) (Fig. 13).

Braid with Smooth Edge and "Mocchettine". For both types, fix three pairs of bobbins, filled with Coats Mercer-Crochet, No. 40, to the points A and B (Fig. 16), then proceed as follows for the first braid:

Twist second pair twice, cross with third, not twisted, work one stitch, cross third and fourth pairs, one stitch, cross fourth and fifth pairs, one stitch. Twist fifth and sixth pairs twice, cross, one stitch, fix pin to inside of stitch instead of centre, i.e. fix the pin on left of fifth pair (so as to place the pins at the side of the braid, making the difference between the smooth edge and the other "mocchettine"). Leave sixth pair on pin. Twist fifth pair twice, cross with fourth not twisted, one stitch, cross third and fourth pairs, one stitch, cross second and third pairs, one stitch. Twist first and second pairs twice, cross, one stitch, fix pins to inside of stitch, and not in centre, i.e. to right of second pair, leave first pair on a pin and begin again from beginning (Fig. 15).

For the second type proceed as follows:

Twist second pair twice, cross with third, not twisted, one stitch. Cross third and fourth pairs, one stitch. Cross fourth and fifth pairs, one stitch. Twist fifth and sixth pairs twice, cross, one stitch. Fix a pin to No. 1 in centre of four threads,

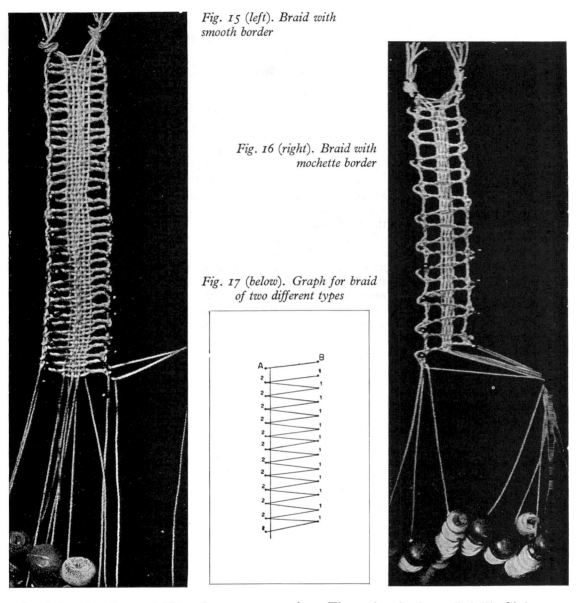

Fig. 15 (left). Braid with smooth border

Fig. 16 (right). Braid with mochette border

Fig. 17 (below). Graph for braid of two different types

twist sixth pair twice, and fifth pair once, cross, one stitch.

Twist fifth pair twice, cross with fourth, not twisted, one stitch. Cross third and fourth pair, one stitch. Cross second and third pairs, one stitch. Twist first and second pairs twice, cross, one stitch, fix pin to No. 2 between the four stitches, twist first pair twice, second pair once, cross, one stitch. Begin again from beginning (Fig. 17).

After having practised the stitches explained so far, the beginner may then begin to work some

lace. The easiest is that called "leaf" lace, as shown in Fig. 18.

First of all prepare 11 pairs of bobbins (that is 22 in all), all filled with Coats Mercer-Crochet, No. 40, and fix the prepared design as in Fig. 19 to the pillow. The scalloped edge, as we have already mentioned, should be on the right of the worker.

Now fix the bobbins on the four holes dividing one scallop from another, in the following order:

Six bobbins (three pairs) in the first hole. Four

bobbins (two pairs) in the second, four (two pairs) in the third and eight (four pairs) in the fourth.

Begin the work from the pricked part, i.e. from the netting on the left and pass from one point to another, twisting each pair of bobbins twice; then make a stitch, fixing it with a pin; go back to twist and work another stitch, then take up another pair of bobbins, always working diagonally, until the netting is complete.

Pass all the bobbins, pair by pair, from right to left, the last pair on the right being twisted twice before making the stitch; fix the pin, go back to twist, make another stitch and work towards the left, twisting only the pair which remains in the left hand

On reaching the hole on the left side, take the

pair that comes from the net, twisting only the pair that goes in again, work a stitch, fix the pin, twist the pair in the left hand twice, and go back, always in the same way up to the half-way point.

On the other half of the leaf, the Tapestry Stitch decreases. Each time the work comes to the hole on the left, leave a pair of bobbins which serve to work the net.

For the Braid Stitch shown in Fig. 20, eleven pairs of bobbins are needed, all wound with Coats Mercer-Crochet, No. 40.

Fix four pairs of bobbins to the design, as shown in Fig. 21, to work the tape which completes the lace, and six pairs for working the braid.

Begin the twisting of the threads to the left making a narrow string in Tapestry Stitch. The bars are worked by braiding and each time two pairs meet, cross them, fixing with a pin. The braids are often decorated with pips.

To make pips in pillow-lace, place a pin under the thread from the bobbin on the right, take the underlying thread of the same bobbin and pass it to the right. Cross it, forming a small loop which is fixed with a pin into the hole which marks the point where it should be worked.

Method of Working Bars. A characteristic design in pillow-lace is the one formed by a winding line with bars at the curves joining two motifs. Place a crochet hook in the point where the bar will be fixed and twisting the threads of the pair of bobbins, take up one of these threads with the crochet hook and, in the loop formed, pass the other bobbin of the pair, twisting the threads again, and going back to the starting point. The bar will thus be double.

Lace with Hearts (Figs. 22 and 23). Twenty pairs of bobbins are necessary.

Begin working on the left, fixing a pin into the first hole with three pairs of bobbins; in the other holes place two pairs to each pin. The net is worked with two pairs of bobbins; twist twice, make a full stitch, fix with the pin, twist again and work another full stitch, put down the pair of bobbins in the left hand and take up the pair in the right hand. Work as already explained and continue thus until the net has been completed.

Pass on to working the scalloped part, using ten pairs of bobbins. Here the work is different; while in the netting the work has holes in it, here it takes the form of a narrow tape.

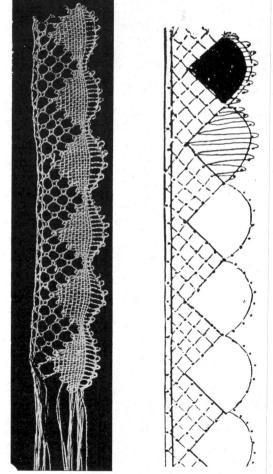

Fig. 18 (left). "Leaf" lace in Netting Stitch and Tapestry Stitch
Fig. 19 (right). Graph of "leaf" lace

330

Pillow prepared for working lace. When the bobbins have to remain momentarily out of use, they are tied into groups with ribbons

Scuola d'Arte Mobile e del Merletto, Cantù

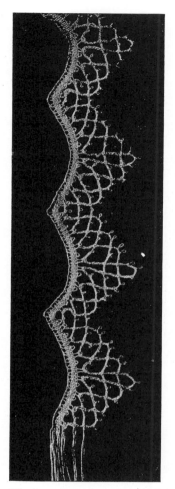

Fig. 20. Lace in twists with
border in Tapestry Stitch

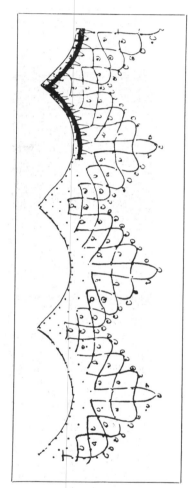

Fig. 21. Graph of twisted lace

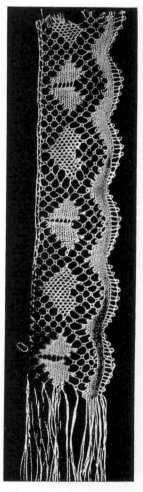

Fig. 22. Lace with hearts
in Tapestry Stitch
and netting

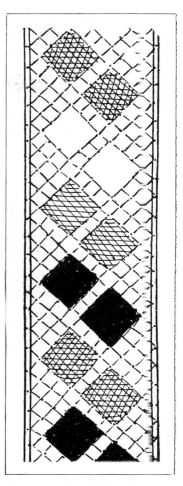

Fig. 25. Graph of lace in squares

Fig. 24. Inset with squares
in Tapestry Stitch
and netting

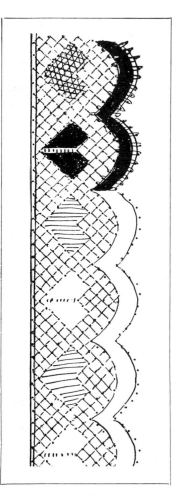

Fig. 23. Graph of lace with hearts

*Enlarged detail of the lace shown in
illustration (Page 331)*

Pass all the bobbins, with full stitches, without twisting, except for the last two on the right, which are twisted before and after having fixed the pin. The small hearts are worked half in half-stitch, beginning with two pairs, one on the right and one on the left, and then passing from right to left, taking all the pairs of bobbins up to the half-way point. For the other half, each time, on turning to left or right, leave out one pair. For the other heart in full-stitch, follow the same procedure, except that at the half-way point twist the bobbins which make the selvedge, twice.

Inset with Squares. Sixteen pairs of bobbins are necessary.

Begin from the left. Begin the square by fixing two pairs of bobbins to each pin, so as to have eight pairs, passing from left to right and leaving out a pair, so that when the square is completed all the bobbins have been eliminated. Pass to the netting, twist twice, make a half stitch, place the pin and repeat two more times.

When the net is completed, begin the second square, taking a pair of bobbins from the right and one pair from the left, and begin with a full stitch when the square is worked in Tapestry Stitch, and

with a half-stitch when the square is perforated. Up to the half-way point, passing from right to left, take a pair of bobbins from each side; in the second half leave out a pair on either side until the square is finished, continuing the netting. Continue thus until the work is complete (Figs. 24 and 25).

Lately the designs for this magnificent type of lace have undergone some modifications by well-known artists, and these have given further life to the beauty and value of an art in which it is difficult to know whether to give the greatest praise to the beauty of design or to the technical skill of the worker, which often reaches perfection.

Illustrated here, for the admiration of the reader, is the tablecloth on page 336, worked by the School for the Art of Furniture and Lace-making in Cantù, in which, in the centre, there is a design with the signs of the zodiac, amongst twining leaves, and which then opens out into a wider circle in which scenes animated by graceful figures alternate with floral designs spread over the background of very fine and extremely delicate net.

The tablecloth by the Galbiati brothers of Cantù, shown on page 320, in which mythological figures dominate over a rich piece of work in very fine Tulle Stitch, is also surrounded by rich ornamental motifs, which are a real work of art.

To the same school is owed the two pieces of work illustrated on pages 321 and 337. One, a Pompeian style table centre, in which the very fine work, accurate in the smallest detail, is to be admired, and the other, a panel, in which the scene of the parting of Helen and Paris from Troy seems to be a living picture rather than a piece of lace.

In Italy, as well as at Cantù, pillow-lace is worked in other localities: in the Abruzzi, where one of the most important centres is Pescocostanzo, the Aquilan lace is worked, with its entirely classical designs. In Liguria, pillow-lace is worked at Portofino, St. Margherita and Rapallo, where it is made in original and modern patterns. In Piedmont it is made at Cogne in the Aosta valley, where the laces are very simple, almost rustic in type. In Venetia, at Pellestrina, a small island in the Venetian Lagoon; in Marche at Porto San Giorgio, at Ascoli Piceno and at Offida, called "the town of the lace-makers"; in Tuscany at Sansepolcro in the province of Arezzo, whose celebrated laces are unmistakable both for the workmanship and the artistic designs which give them some similarity to Venetian laces; and lastly pillow-lace is made in Friuli, Calabria, Sicily and Sardinia.

Example of pillow-made lace worked at the school at Cantù

335

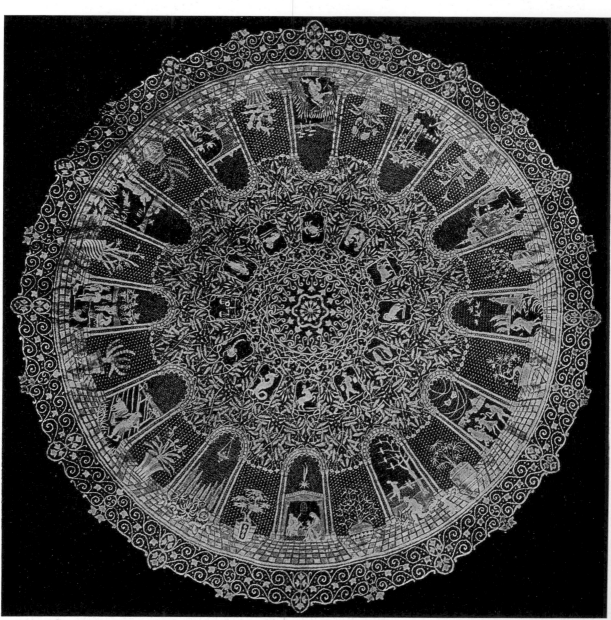

Tea cloth worked in pillow lace. At the centre the signs of the zodiac can be seen, whilst on the outer border scenes of the four seasons stand out on a perforated background. This is a modern and original design by the pupils of the same school: it has been perfectly carried out by the female section

*Place setting in modern style, worked at Pescocostanzo, the largest centre of
pillow-made laces*

Table runner worked on bobbins; the design is Pompeian

337

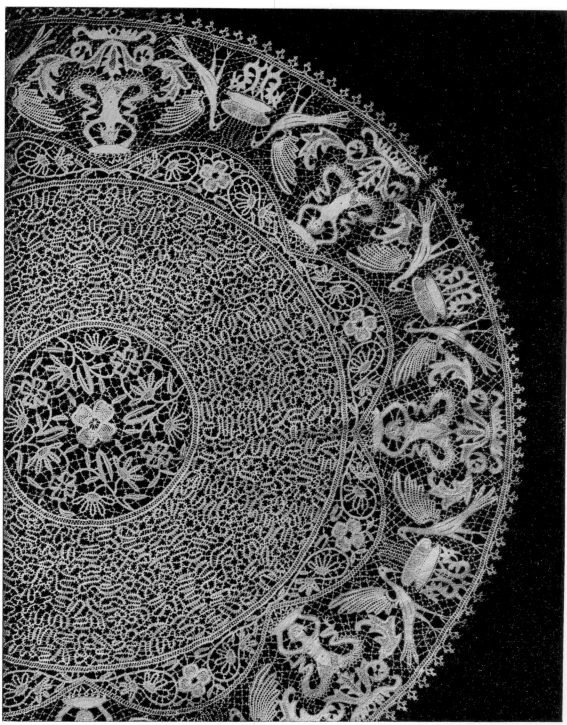

Tamburini Agnese, S. Sepolcro

Table centre worked at Sansepolcro, another well-known centre of the industry. Note the beauty of the design which is original and shows different characteristics from those produced elsewhere

8 Crocheted Laces

CHAPTER XXVIII

Crochet

This type of lace takes its name from the small tool, the crochet hook, with which it is worked. Its origins are obscure, and it is certainly very ancient, but from the details available it has never been possible to give any accurate information as to its history.

Everybody knows the crochet hook: it is a narrow rod, generally made of steel, with a hook at one end which serves to hold the thread, to twist it and to work it in hundreds of different ways.

Pleasant work, which even today has many followers, quick and easy to work, it does not require great attention and it has a variety of uses: laces, insets, edgings, table centres, glass mats, covers, ladies' blouses, collars and cuffs, gloves, hats, berets, etc.

Crochet, if carefully worked with very thin thread, can acquire extraordinary delicacy, and the combination of artistic designs can create expensive and beautiful work. It is, besides, work which is very practical, being resistant to washing, especially because of the type of thread used in making it; and when the thread is Coats Mercer-Crochet results are guaranteed.

Necessary Materials. Given their wide uses, crocheted laces require a vast assortment of threads. Coats Mercer-Crochet in white or écru, a well-twisted, shiny thread, easy running and strong, is sold in 20 gm. balls in Nos. 3, 5, 10, 15, 20, 30, 40, 50, 60, 70 and 80. The threads may be chosen for thickness according to the work to be done, the higher numbers for the finest work, and the lower numbers for heavier work.

The Crochet Hook. Only an expert worker can realise how important is the choice and quality of the hook. It must be suitable to the type of work

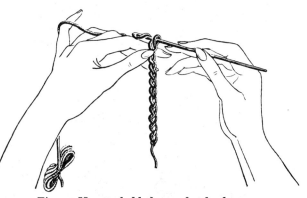

Fig. 1. How to hold the crochet hook

being done and the thread used. It is generally better to use a hook which is finer than the thickness the thread requires. It is also a good idea to have an assortment of hooks in different sizes in the work-basket. These hooks are always numbered, the lower numbers being the thickest and the higher numbers the finest. The best hooks are

339

Table centre in crochet. The procedure is quite clear from the actual-sized detail given below. The work was carried out in Coats Mercer-Crochet, No. 20, in white

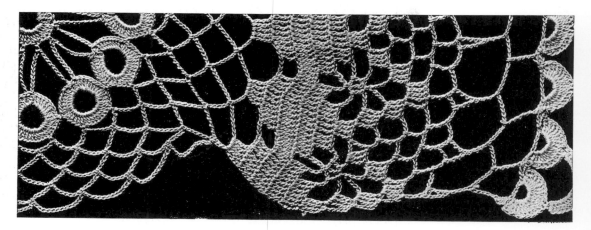

made of steel and should be shiny and slippery, with a well-made hook which will not catch, but slip easily through the thread. For work in wool, a bone or plastic or wooden hook is preferable. As we have already mentioned, the crochet hook consists of a tubular rod with one end shaped into a hook; it is flattened at the centre and this makes a resting place for the thumb when working.

Abbreviations used in the text:

stitch	st.
chain	ch.
double crochet	d.c.
single crochet or slip stitch .	s.s.
half treble	hlf. tr.
treble	tr.
double treble	dbl. tr.
triple treble	tr. tr.
quadruple treble	quad. tr.
block	blk.
repeat	rep.
preceding round	prec. round
preceding row	prec. row
space	sp.
separate	sep.

(*) When, in the course of the work, an asterisk is found, continue to work until the instructions indicate that work should be taken back and repeated from this sign.

Method of working Crochet. The basis of crochet work is Chain Stitch. It might be said that it is the stitch which gives rise to all the different effects, according to the way in which it is used.

Fig. 1 shows the method of working crochet. The hook is held in the right hand, as if it were a pen, whilst the thread is wrapped over the little finger of the left hand and held firm between the thumb and first finger of the same hand. Take up the thread held by the left-hand fingers, with the hook, and pull it through a loop of thread, thus making a stitch. After completing this first stitch, go back to the thread held in the left hand and again take up the thread with the hook in the same way, thus forming a series of stitches all alike—the so-called "Chain Stitch" (Fig. 2 (a)).

Here are some of the stitches derived from this basic stitch.

Double Crochet. In Chain Stitch or any other stitch in a single row already worked, place in the

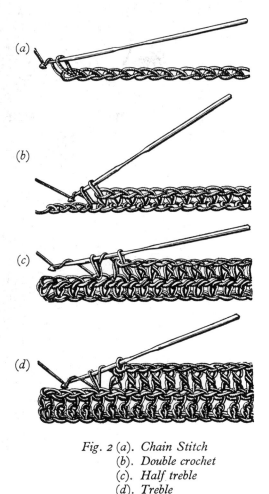

Fig. 2 (a). *Chain Stitch*
(b). *Double crochet*
(c). *Half treble*
(d). *Treble*

hook and take up the thread on to it, going through 2 stitches (Fig. 2 (b)).

Half Treble. Place thread over hook, take up one stitch from chain, or other row of stitches already worked, throw thread over hook again and pull through all 3 threads together (Fig. 2 (c)).

Treble. Place thread over hook, take up one stitch from chain or other stitch already worked on row below, take thread over hook once again, take it first through the first 2 threads, then place thread over hook again and take it through last 2 threads (Fig. 2 (d)).

341

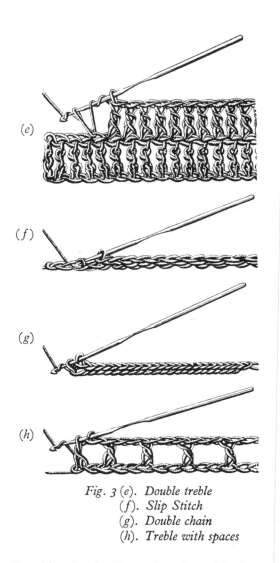

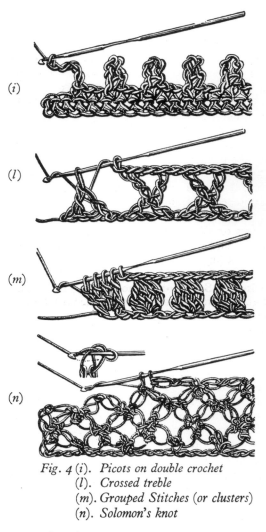

Fig. 3 (e). Double treble
(f). Slip Stitch
(g). Double chain
(h). Treble with spaces

Fig. 4 (i). Picots on double crochet
(l). Crossed treble
(m). Grouped Stitches (or clusters)
(n). Solomon's knot

Double Treble. Proceed as for treble, but take thread twice over hook at beginning and then pull threads through 2 at a time (Fig. 3 (e)).

Triple or Quadruple Treble. Place thread over hook 3 or 4 times, accordingly, pulling through 2 at a time as for other trebles.

Single Crochet or Slip Stitch. When it is necessary to pass from one point to another in a line of Chain Stitch or on an edging, Slip Stitch is used to pass through the stitches already worked. Place the hook in the stitch, take thread over it, and pull through 2 stitches (Fig. 3 (f)).

Fig. 3 (g) shows a **Double Chain Stitch.** The kind of braid which is formed by this stitch can be used to substitute braids and cords in various types of work.

They can be worked in two ways:

1. Never turn the work. Begin with 2 ch.; place hook into first stitch, take thread over hook and work a d.c. Now place the hook under the thread to the left of the stitch worked and work another d.c.

Repeat the procedure.

2. Proceed as above, but instead of working a d.c. taking 2 threads together, work them separately, i.e. first one and then the other. By using this second method the braid is a little thicker.

Fig. 3 (h) shows a series of trebles spaced, with bars of 2 ch.

Fig. 4 (i) shows simple picots consisting of five or six Chain Stitches worked immediately after a d.c. and before the next stitch.

Twisted or Crossed Treble. Fix the thread to a stitch of the one below and work 3 ch. st. (all the same), miss 2 st. on base row, work a tr. into the following st., 5 ch. 1 tr. taking hook into the crossing point of the tr. and ch. (*). Now work a dbl. tr. (taking thread over hook twice), miss 2 base st., work into next free st., leaving last 3 st. on hook. Take thread once more over hook, miss 2 basic st. work into next free st. There will now be 5 threads on hook, to be pulled through in twos. Then work 2 ch. and 1 tr. into crossing-point of tr., 2 ch. and so on, repeating from (*) (Fig. 4 (l)).

Groups or Clusters. Work 4 tr. or dbl. tr. into 1 basic st., and pass thread once only through the 4 st. (Fig. 4 (m)).

Netting, or Solomon's Knot. A very nice, light, decorative stitch is that shown in Fig. 4 (n). Draw a loop on hook out $\frac{1}{4}$ inch, thread over hook and draw through loop on hook. Insert hook between loop and single thread of this ch. and make a d.c. Work another knot in same manner (1 Solomon's Knot made), miss 4 stitches, 1 d.c. into next stitch. Rep. from beginning to end of row. Make $1\frac{1}{2}$ Solomon's Knot to turn, 1 d.c. over double loop at right of first centre knot of prec. row, 1 d.c. over double loop at left of same knot, 1 Solomon's Knot. Rep. to end of row.

To work all the stitches given so far, use Coats Mercer-Crochet in its different thicknesses. This is the perfect thread for this kind of work.

In all types of crochet, the rows are worked backwards and forwards. Work one row, turn the work, working 2 or 3 ch. st. at the turnings so that the stitches are not pulled and then begin the next row.

In some work, however, it is necessary to work on the right side always, as, for example, when working stars or round table centres and in Tunisian Stitch, etc.

To fasten off the thread in crochet, pass it on to the wrong side of the work and work a ch. st., making a very tight knot.

Now we shall give a list of some of the basic stitches in crochet, and for the working of which Coats Mercer-Crochet is advised, as this will make the stitches stand out to the best effect.

Rose Stitch (Fig. 5). This consists of rows of d.c. worked backwards and forwards, passing the hook under the two horizontal threads of the prec. row.

Rib Stitch (Fig. 6). When the hook is taken only into the lower horizontal thread of the stitch a d.c. in rib is formed.

Russian Stitch. This consists of rows of d.c. worked entirely on the right side. This is very practical for working circles. With d.c. worked in rib on the right side only, a close, strong stitch is formed.

Double Stitch (Fig. 7). On length of ch. required, d.c. into first 2 ch. leaving each loop on hook, (3 loops), thread over and draw through all loops (*). For next st., d.c. into same place as last d.c. worked, and into following ch., once again leaving each loop on hook, thread over and draw through 3 loops. Rep. from (*) to end of row, finishing with 1 d.c. into same place as last d.c., 1 ch.; turn. This stitch is suitable for covers, bed-spreads, children's jackets etc., as it is soft and elastic.

Fern Stitch (Fig. 8). Commence by making a chain slightly longer than the desired length.

1st row. 3 tr. into 4th ch. from hook (*), miss 3 ch., 1 d.c. into next ch., 3 ch., 3 tr. into same place as last d.c.; rep. from (*) for desired length, ending with miss 3 ch., 1 d.c. into next ch., 3 ch., turn. Cut off remaining ch.

2nd row. 3 tr. into first d.c., 1 d.c. into first 3 ch. sp. (*), 3 ch., 3 tr. into same sp. as last d.c., 1 d.c. into next 3 ch. sp.; rep. from (*) to end of row, 3 ch., turn.

Rep. 2nd row for length required.

Shell Stitch (Fig. 9). Commence with length of ch. required.

1st row. Work 1 d.c. into 2nd ch. from hook (*), miss 2 ch., 5 tr. into next ch. (shell made) miss 2 ch., 1 d.c. into next ch.; rep. from (*) ending with 5 tr., miss 2 ch., 1 d.c. into next ch., 3 ch., turn.

2nd row. 3 tr. into first d.c. (*) miss 2 tr., 1 d.c. into next tr., miss 2 tr., 5 tr. into next d.c.; rep. from (*) ending with 3 tr. into 3rd of turning ch.

Groups (Fig. 10). Work back over ch. st. with 3 tr. into the 4th. st. counting behind hook (*), miss 3 basic st. and 4 tr. 1 ch. 4 tr. into next st. Rep. from (*) along the whole row. Finish with half blk. On following line work 3 ch. (equal to 1 tr.) 3 tr. into first st., 4 tr., 1 ch. 4 tr. between two blks. of prec. row and so on.

Wave Stitch (Fig. 11). Work a row of d.c. above

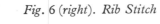

Fig. 5 (left). Rose Stitch

Fig. 6 (right). Rib Stitch

Fig. 7 (left). Double Stitch

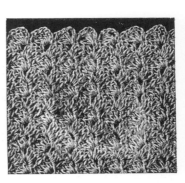

Fig. 8 (right). Fern Stitch

Fig. 9 (left). Shell Stitch

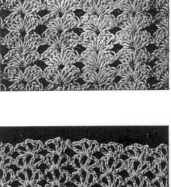

Fig. 10 (right). Blocks of stitches

Fig. 11 (left). Wavy lines of stitches

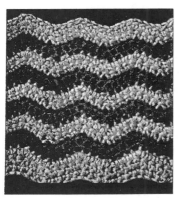

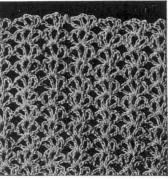

Fig. 12 (right) Another stitch in blocks

344

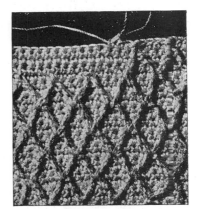

Fig. 13 (left). Crochet with straight lines in relief

Fig. 14 (right). Crochet with diamonds in relief

Fig. 15 (left). Groups of treble in relief

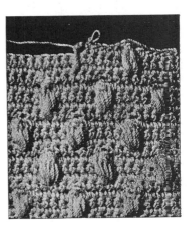

Fig. 16 (right). Another stitch with clusters in relief

a row of ch. st. On following row (★) 4 d.c. over 4 d.c. of prec. row, 2 d.c. into fifth st., 4 into following 4 st. Miss 2 basic st. and rep. from (★). At turning work 1 ch. Rep. same pattern alternating colours every two rows.

Other stitches in Groups (Fig. 12). Into a row of ch. st. and in 5th ch. from hook work 1 tr. 1 ch. 1 tr. 1 ch. 1 tr. (★), miss 3 ch., 1 tr. 1 ch. 1 tr. 1 ch. 1 tr. into next ch.; rep. from (★) to end of row.

2nd row. S.s. into first 3 sts. and into next 1 ch. sp., 4 ch., 1 tr. 1 ch. 1 tr. 1 ch. 1 tr. (★), 1 tr. 1 ch. 1 tr. 1 ch. 1 tr. 1 ch. 1 tr. into centre sp. of next blk.; rep. from (★) to end of row. Rep. 2nd row for length required.

Work three rows into d.c. On 4th row and into 4th st. work a dbl. tr. joining it to thread of 4th st. of first row, then work another 3 d.c., 1 dbl. tr. attaching it to 8th st. of first row, and so on. On

completing the row, turn the work and work a row of d.c., then a 2nd and 3rd. On 4th row, work in the same pattern, alternating the position of the dbl. tr. in relief.

For all types of crochet work, we recommend Coats Mercer-Crochet as being the best.

Treble with Diamonds (Fig. 14). Work 3 rows of d.c. On 4th row work 2 d.c., then working into thread of first st. on first row, work 1 dbl. tr. leaving last 2 threads on hook, place thread over hook twice for dbl. tr. following, pass hook through thread of 4th st. of first row, place thread over hook and work dbl. tr. up to last 3 threads which are taken through together. Miss out st. behind dbl. tr., work 2 d.c. and begin again, working the first following dbl. tr. into same thread as previous dbl. tr., miss 2 sts. of first row, work 2nd dbl. tr. into thread of next st. Work row back in d.c. and then another 2 rows in d.c. and begin from beginning.

Groups of Treble in Almond-shaped Relief (Fig. 15). Work 3 rows in d.c. For next row, work 4 d.c. (*), 1 ch., inserting hook through 4th st. on first row, bring thread through from back of work and work 6 tr. Remove hook from loop of last tr. worked and place hook into ch. st., lift tr. loop and draw up tightly with a ch. st., 1 d.c. into st. below blk. formed, 4 d.c.; rep. from (*) to end of row. Work next row having groups of trs. in between first row of trs.

Another method of working blocks in almond shape is shown in Fig. 16. After 3 rows of d.c. work 4th row with 3 d.c. (*), 5 tr. through 4th st. of first row as before, but leaving last loop of trs. on hook, draw thread through all the loops (cluster made) 1 ch., 5 d.c.; rep. from (*) to end of row.

Furry Stitch (Fig. 17). Place hook into 2 threads of d.c., and place thread round a pencil or stocking needle (according to length of loop to be made), and then work a d.c. very tight. Work d.c. on row back. The stitches form a furry surface on the back of the work, which will be the right side.

The same movement is repeated into each of the following stitches.

Figs. 18, 19 and 20 show some background stitches which are very easy to copy.

Fig. 18. Over a row of ch., insert hook into 8th st. from hook and work 5 tr. into same st., 4 ch. miss 4 basic st. 5 tr. into next st.; rep. to end of row, 7 ch., turn.

2nd row. Into each sp. of blk. work 3 tr. 3 ch. 3 tr. 6 ch. turn.

3rd row. 5 tr. between blk. of 3 tr., 4 ch. Rep. to end of row 7 ch. turn. Rep. 2nd and 3rd rows for desired length.

Fig. 19. Over a row of ch. insert hook into 3rd st. behind hook (thus forming a picot) 2 ch., miss 8 base sts. 1 tr. (*) 5 ch., 1 picot, 2 ch. miss 4 base st. 1 tr.; rep. from (*) to end of row.

2nd row. 8 ch. at turn, 1 picot 2 ch. 1 tr. into first sp. after picot (*) 5 ch., 1 picot 2 ch., 1 tr. into next sp.; rep. from (*) to end of row.

3rd row. 8 ch. at turn, 1 picot 2 ch. 1 tr. into first sp., 5 ch. 1 picot 2 ch. 1 tr. into 2nd sp., 5 ch. 1 picot 2 ch. 1 tr. into 3rd sp. At this point work the almond

Fig. 17 (left). Furry Stitch in crochet

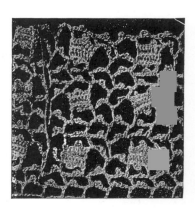

Fig. 19 (right). A second background Stitch

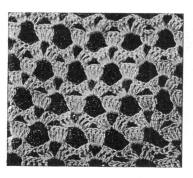

Fig. 18 (left). Background Stitch

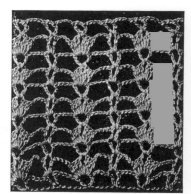

Fig. 20 (right). Third background stitch

346

shape, turn, 7 d.c. into arc just worked, turning picot upside down (this must be below—see illustration). Turn, 7 d.c. in rib. Turn, 7 d.c. in rib. Turn, 3 d.c. 1 picot 4 d.c., then 5 ch. 1 picot 2 ch. 1 tr. into next sp. Continue thus making one almond every 2 sps. Take up work again from first 2 rows.

Fig. 20. Over a piece worked in ch. work a line of blks. of 1 tr. 2 ch. 1 tr. into same st., sep. by 4 ch. On following row work one blk. as explained and then another with 3 tr. 2 ch. 3 tr. sep. by 4 ch. Rep. these two rows.

All these background stitches in our patterns have been worked in Coats Mercer-Crochet.

Picots. Picots are very important both for finishing off laces and in the course of crochet itself. Here we give a variety of picot patterns. The instructions follow the order of the patterns shown in Fig. 21.

Simple Picots. 3 ch., 1 s.s. into first of the 3 ch., 4 ch., 1 s.s. into 3rd st. from hook; rep. to end of row.

Picots for Edgings. Into row of ch., work 4 ch. with 1 s.s. into 4th st. from hook, 1 d.c. into nearby st. at base and so on. To make longer spaces work 2 or 3 d.c. before next picot.

Large Picots. 5 ch., 1 dbl. tr. into 4th st. from hook, 1 d.c. into 5th, and so on.

Round Picots. (*) 5 ch., 3 dbl. tr. into 4th ch. from hook, 1 s.s. into same st., 2 ch.; rep. from (*).

Pointed Picots. 5 ch., miss first st. from hook and work 1 s.s. into 2nd st., 1 d.c. into 3rd st., 1 tr. into 4th st., 1 dbl. tr. into 5th st.; rep. from beginning.

Picots with borders of Double Treble. 7 ch., 1 s.s. into 4th st. from hook, 1 dbl. tr. into first st. of 7 ch. (*), 1 picot of 4 sts., 1 dbl. tr. into half of dbl. tr. just worked; rep. from (*).

Picots in Loops. These picots can serve as a basis for other laces, as well as a decoration. To obtain evenness in the length of the loops, proceed thus:

3 ch. placing a stocking needle under right arm; this should be of a size suitable to the measure of picot required; slip the 3rd st. over it taking it off the hook, place hook into preceding st., i.e. in the 2nd, take up the thread and work 1 dc. then 2 ch. placing the st. on needle and so on.

To work these same picots over a completed row or on finished work, proceed as follows:

1 d.c. into one st. of the row (*) take out hook from this point and place loop of thread over knitting needle: place hook into horizontal thread above, in the stitch on previous row, place thread over hook and pass it over the thread mentioned, then work 1 d.c. into the following st. on that row and rep. from (*).

Here are some other insets for various uses and decorating linen, which can be made in any length since they consist of one motif, which is repeated; for this reason they are also called "eternal".

Fig. 22. Over a row of ch. st. go back to 8th st. from hook with 1 d.c. then work 2 more d.c. near by (one to each st.) (*) 3 ch. miss 3 st. on base, 1 tr. 3 ch. miss 3 st. on base, 3 d.c. Rep. from (*) to finish with 2 d.c.

2nd row. At the turn work 6 ch. (*) 3 d.c. (one into the sp. on a tr., the third into nearby sp.) 3 ch. 1 tr. among 3 d.c. of prec. row 3 ch. Rep. from (*)

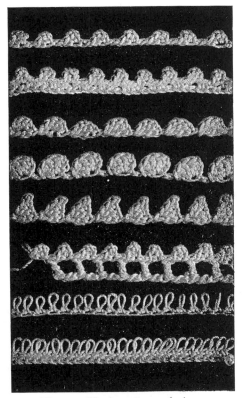

Fig. 21. Various types of picots

and continue in this fashion, alternating the rows.

Fig. 23. Commence with 42 ch.

1st row. Work 1 d.c. (*) 5 ch., miss 3 base sts.,
1 d.c.; rep. from (*) until 10 sps. have been
worked, turn.

2nd row. 7 ch., 1 d.c. into first sp., 5 ch. miss 1 sp.
and into next sp. work 5 dbl. tr. sep. by 1 ch., then
work 5 ch. miss 1 sp., 1 d.c. into next sp., 5 ch. miss
one sp. and into next work 5 dbl. tr. sep. by 1 ch.,
5 ch. miss 1 sp., 1 d.c. into next sp., 5 ch. 2 dbl. tr.
sep. by 1 ch. into last sp. of row, turn.

3rd row. 7 ch., 1 d.c. into d.c. on prec. row (*),
5 ch., 1 d.c. after first dbl. tr. of blk. of prec. row,
5 ch. 1 d.c. between 2nd and 3rd dbl. tr., 5 ch. 1 d.c.
between 4th and 5th dbl. tr., 5 ch. 1 d.c. into d.c. on
prec. row; rep. from (*) then work 5 ch. 1 d.c. into
last sp., turn.

4th row. 7 ch., 1 d.c. into first sp., 5 ch., 1 d.c.
into 2nd sp. and continue thus until 10 sps. have
been worked.

Rep. from 2nd row.

Fig. 24. Commence with 41 ch.

1st row. 1 tr. into 8th ch. from hook (*), miss 2 ch.,
2 ch. 1 tr. into next ch.; rep. from (*) to end of
row (12 sps.).

2nd row. 5 ch., 1 tr. into first tr. (*) 2 ch., 1 tr.
into next tr.; rep. from (*) ending with 2 ch., 1 tr.
into 5th of 7 ch.

3rd row. As 2nd row, ending with 2 ch. 1 tr. into
3rd of 5 ch.

4th row. 6 ch. (*), 1 dbl. tr. into first dbl. tr., 2 dbl.
tr. into sp., 1 dbl. tr. into dbl. tr., 2 dbl. tr. into sp.,
1 dbl. tr. into dbl. tr., miss 1 dbl. tr., 1 trip tr. into
next dbl. tr., 4 ch., 1 trip tr. crossing behind last
trip tr. and into same place as last dbl. tr.; rep.
from (*) ending with 1 dbl. tr. into 3rd of 5 ch.

Fig. 25. This shows a simple method of finishing
off crochet or knitted stockings.

Over a row of d.c. worked from right to left as
usual, turn back with another row of d.c. worked
in the opposite direction, i.e. from left to right,
without turning the work. This is called "Shrimp
Stitch".

All the patterns shown here have been worked
in Coats Mercer-Crochet, the best thread for
crochet work.

On the following pages are given some examples
of medallions worked in crochet, which when
joined together form a type of perforated material
very suitable for bed-spreads, tablecloths, serviettes, table centres, etc.

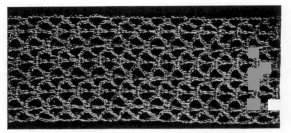

Fig. 22. Inset with repeated motif

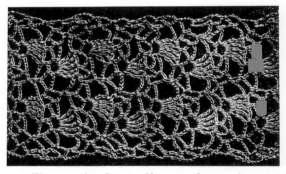

Fig. 23. Another motif repeated on an inset

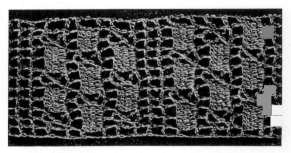

Fig. 24. Third inset with repeated motif

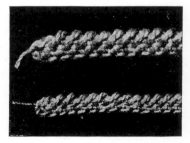

Fig. 25. Shrimp Stitch for edgings

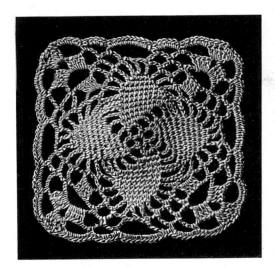

Fig. 26. Star in crochet

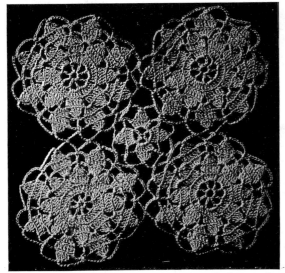

Fig. 27. Stars joined—suitable for a bed-spread

Fig. 26. **Necessary Materials.** Coats Mercer-Crochet, No. 40, and a No. 1.00 hook. Work 6 ch. and close circle with 1 s.s., then, 5 ch. 1 d.c. into circle just worked; rep. 3 times more (4 sps.) join with 1 s.s. into first of 5 ch.

1st row. With 2 s.s. work up to middle of first sp., work 1 d.c. into sp., then 5 ch. 3 d.c. into 2nd sp., 5 ch. 3 d.c. into 3rd sp., 5 ch. 3 d.c. into 4th sp., 5 ch. 2 d.c. into first sp., joining with 1 s.s. into first d.c.

2nd row. 5 ch. 5 d.c. (2 into sp., 3 d.c. into d.c. of prec. row).

3rd row. 5 ch. 7 d.c. (as above).

4th row. 5 ch. 9 d.c. (as above).

5th row. 5 ch. 10 d.c. (as above).

6th row. 5 ch. 11 d.c. (as above).

7th row. 8 ch. 10 d.c. on the 11 of prec. row (miss first st.).

8th row. 5 ch. 1 d.c. into sp. of 8 st. on prec. row, 5 ch. 9 d.c. into 10 of prec. row (miss first st.).

9th row. 5 ch. 1 d.c. into first sp., 5 ch. 1 c.c. into 2nd, 5 ch. 8 d.c. into 9 on prec. row (miss out first st.).

10th row. 5 ch. 1 d.c. into first sp., 5 ch. 4 tr. into 2nd, 5 ch. 1 d.c. into 3rd, 5 ch. 6 d.c. into 8 on prec. row (miss out first and last st.).

11th row. 5 ch. 1 d.c. into first sp., 5 ch. 1 d.c. into 2nd, 10 ch. 1 d.c. into 3rd (after 4 tr.) 5 ch. 1 d.c. into 4th, 5 ch. 4 d.c. into 6 on prec. row (miss out first and last st.).

12th row. 5 ch. 1 d.c. into first sp., 5 ch. 1 d.c. into 2nd, 5 ch. 4 tr. 3 ch. 4 tr. into sp. of 10 st. 5 ch. 1 d.c. into following sp., 5 ch. 1 d.c. into following sp. 2 ch. 1 tr. on 4th d.c. of prec. row. 2 ch. 1 d.c. into first sp.

13th row. 5 ch. 1 d.c. into 2nd sp., 5 ch. 1 d.c. into 3rd (*), 5 ch. 5 tr. between two groups of 4 tr. of prec. row, 5 ch. 1 d.c. into following sp., 5 ch. 1 d.c. into following sp., 8 ch. pass 2 sps., 1 d.c. into next sp., 5 ch., 1 d.c. into next sp.; rep. from (*).

14th row. All in d.c., 6 into small sp., 10 into sp. of 8 st., 5 into corners.

Fig. 27. **Necessary Materials.** Coats Mercer-Crochet, No. 60, and a No. 0.75 hook.

Commence with 6 ch., join with a s.s. to form a ring.

1st row. 6 ch. (*), 1 dbl. tr. into ring, 2 ch.; rep. from (*) 6 times more, join with 1 s.s. to 4th of 6 ch. (8 sps.).

2nd row. S.s. into first sp., 4 ch., 4 dbl. tr. into same sp. (*), 2 ch., 5 dbl. tr. into next sp.; rep. from (*) all round ending with 2 ch., join with 1 s.s. into 4th of 4 ch. (8 dbl. tr. groups).

3rd row. 4 ch., 1 dbl. tr. into same place as s.s., 1 dbl. tr. into each of next 4 dbl. tr., 1 dbl. tr. into next ch. (*), 3 ch., 1 dbl. tr. into next ch., 1 dbl. tr. into each of next 5 dbl. tr., 1 dbl. tr. into next ch.; rep. from (*) all round ending with 3 ch., join with 1 s.s. into 4th of 4 ch.

4th row. 1 s.s. into first dbl. tr., 4 ch., 1 dbl. tr. into each of next 4 dbl. tr. leaving the last loop of each dbl. tr. on hook, thread over and draw through

Fig. 28. Spinning wheel motif

all loops on hook, 1 ch. to fasten (a cluster made) (*), 4 ch., 5 dbl. tr. into next 3 ch. sp., 4 ch., miss first dbl. tr. of next group, 1 dbl. tr. into each of next 5 dbl. tr. working off as for a cluster; rep. from (*) all round ending with 4 ch., 5 dbl. tr. into last 3 ch. sp., 4 ch., join with 1 s.s. into tip of first cluster.

5th row. 8 ch. (*), miss first 3 of 4 ch., 1 dbl. tr. into next ch., 1 dbl. tr. into each of next 5 dbl. tr., 1 dbl. tr. into next ch., 4 ch., 1 dbl. tr. into tip of next cluster, 4 ch.; rep. from (*) all round omitting last dlb. tr. and 4 ch. at end if last rep., join with 1 s.s. into 4th of 8 ch.

6th row. (*) 12 ch., miss first dbl. tr. of next group, 1 dbl. tr. into each of next 5 dbl. tr. working off as for a cluster, 12 ch., 1 d.c. into single dbl. tr. between groups; rep. from (*) all round omitting last d.c. at end of last rep., join with 1 s.s. into s.s. of previous row (16 loops). Fasten off.

On completion of first and second star, join them at the two points on the last row as shown in the illustration.

After four stars are completed, work at centre as follows:

Fill-in Motif

1st row. 8 ch., 1 dbl. tr. into 8th ch. from hook, 4 ch. (1 dbl. tr. into same place, 4 ch.), twice, join with 1 s.s. into 4th of 8 ch. (4 sps.).

2nd row. 4 ch., 6 dbl. tr. into first sp. (*), 5 ch., 7 dbl. tr. into next sp.; rep. from (*) all round, 5 ch., join with 1 s.s. into 4th of 4 ch.

3rd row. 1 s.s. into first dbl. tr., 4 ch., 1 dbl. tr. into each of next 4 dbl. tr. working off as for a cluster, 10 ch., 1 d.c. into next 5 ch. loop, 10 ch. (*), miss first dbl tr. of next group, 1 dbl. tr. into each of next 5 dbl. tr. working off as for a cluster, 10 ch., 1 d.c. into next 5 ch. loop, 10 ch.; rep. from (*) all round, join with 1 s.s. into tip of first cluster. Fasten off.

Fig. 28. Necessary Materials. Coats Mercer-Crochet, No. 60, and a No. 0.75 hook.

Commence at centre with 10 ch., join with s.s. to form a ring.

1st row. 4 ch., 2 dbl. tr. into ring leaving the last loop of each on hook, thread over and draw through all loops on hook (thus a 3 dbl. tr. cluster is made) (*), 6 ch., 3 dbl. tr. into ring leaving the last loop of each on hook, thread over and draw through all loops on hook (another 3 dbl. tr. cluster made); rep. from (*) until 10 clusters in all are made, 6 ch., join with a s.s. to tip of first cluster.

2nd row. 1 s.s. into each of first 3 ch. of next loop, 1 d.c. into same loop (*), 7 ch., into next 6 ch. loop work 3 clusters with 5 ch. between each cluster, 7 ch., 1 d.c. into next loop; rep. from (*) omitting 1 d.c. at end of last rep., 1 s.s. into first d.c.

3rd rows. 1. s. into each of first 4 ch. of next loop, 1 d.c. into same loop (*), 7 ch., 1 d.c. into next loop; rep. from (*) ending with 7 ch., 1 s.s. into first d.c.

4th row. 1 s.s. into each of next 3 ch., 1 d.c. into next ch. (*), 5 ch., 1 d.c. into 4th of next 7 ch.; rep. from (*) ending with 5 ch., 1 s.s. into first d.c.

5th row. 1 s.s. into each of next 3 ch., 3 ch., 1 tr. into same place as last s.s., 2 ch., 2 tr. into same ch. (1 shell made) (*), 2 ch., into 3rd ch. of next loop work 2 tr. 2 ch. and 2 tr. (another shell); rep. from (*) ending with 2 ch., 1 s.s. into 3rd of 3 ch.

6th row. 1 s.s. into next tr., 1 s.s. into 2 ch. sp., 3 ch., 2 tr. into same sp., 3 ch., 3 tr. into same sp. (*), 1 d.c. into next 2 ch. sp. (between shells), into 2 ch. sp. of next shell work 3 tr. 3 ch. and 3 tr.; rep. from (*) ending with 1 d.c. into 2 ch. sp. (between shells), 1 s.s. into 3rd of 3 ch. first made. Fasten off.

Fig. 29. Necessary Materials. Coats Mercer-Crochet, No. 60, and a No. 0.75 crochet hook; a piece of linen 12 in. square. With compasses, mark a circle 12 in. in diameter on to the material. Lay a small hem all round circle and work a round of 352 d.c.

350

2nd row. 8 ch., miss 3 d.c. (*) 1 tr. 5 ch. miss 3 d.c.; rep. from (*) all round (88 sps.).

3rd row. One round in d.c., 5 into each sp.

4th row. (*) 1 d.c. at start of first sp., 12 ch., 1 d.c. after 2nd sp. 8 d.c. over next 10 d.c., turn, 1 ch., 7 d.c. into 8 d.c., turn, 1 ch. 6 d.c. turn, 1 ch.; continue thus dec. 1 st. on each row until 1 d.c. remains. Work down side of triangle formed with 7 s.s., Rep. all round mat from (*).

5th row. Starting from point of a triangle work 12 ch. 4 tr. into arc formed by the 12 ch. of previous row. 12 ch., 1 d.c. into point of triangle following. Rep. all round.

6th row. Starting from point of a triangle work 7 ch., join with s.s. into first of 7 ch. to form a ring. Into a ring work 1 d.c. 1 hlf. tr. 6 tr., 1 hlf. tr., 1 d.c., 1 s.s. into base of disc formed, then 12 d.c. into 12 ch. of prec. row, 12 d.c. into next 12 ch. Rep. all round.

Fig. 30 **Necessary Materials.** Coats Mercer-Crochet, No. 60, and a No. 0.75 crochet hook.

Commence at centre with 12 ch., join with 1 s.s. to form a ring.

1st row. 21 ch., 1 d.c. into 2nd ch. from hook, 1 d.c. into each ch. across (20 d.c.). Work 1 d.c. into ring, 1 ch., turn.

2nd row. Picking up only the back loop of each d.c., miss first d.c., 1 d.c. into each of next 20 c.c., 1 ch., turn.

3rd row. Picking up only the back loop of each d.c., 1 d.c. into each of next 4 d.c. (*), 5 ch., 1 d.c. into each of the next 4 d.c.; rep. from (*) across, ending with 4 d.c. (4 picots made). Work 1 d.c. into ring. This completes first spoke. Do not break off, but continue for the second spoke.

Second Spoke: *1st row.* 20 ch., drop loop from hook, insert hook into 2nd picot from ring and draw dropped loop through, 1 d.c. into each of the next 20 sts. (20 d.c.). Work 1 d.c. into ring, 1 ch., turn. Rep. the 2nd and 3rd rows of first spoke once. Work 4 more spokes same as second spoke (6 in all), but while working the third picot of sixth spoke, attach to first spoke by working 2 ch., 1 s.s. into end of first d.c. of first row of first spoke, 2 ch., and complete the sixth spoke in the usual way.

Fasten off. This completes one motif.

Further ones can be worked separately in the same way and then sewn together later, or, if desired, they can be crocheted together while on the last spoke.

Fig. 31. **Necessary Materials.** Coats Mercer-Crochet, Nos. 20 or 40; a No. 1.25 or No. 1.00 crochet hook.

Commence with 10 ch., close with 1 s.s. into first ch.

Fig. 29. Table centre with crocheted border

351

Fig. 30. Chariot wheel motif

Fig. 31. Medallion suitable for bed-spread

1st row. Work 3 ch., 23 tr. into circle. Join with 1 s.s. into 3rd of 3 ch.

2nd row. 4 ch., miss 1 tr. and work 1 dbl. tr. into next tr., 6 ch. 1 tr. into crossing of tr. and 4 ch.; 3 ch. (*) 1 quad. tr. into next tr. and work leaving last 4 st. on hook, place thread over hook twice, miss one st. and work into next free st. until there are 5 threads on hook, which are now joined in twos. Work 3 ch. and 1 tr. into crossing of the

quad. tr., 3 ch. Rep. from (*) to form 8 crossed groups.

3rd row. Work 6 d.c. into each sp. Work 2 more rounds of d.c. and one round of tr.

7th row. Work a round of crossed sts. as in 2nd row but leaving one st. between each cross (24 blks.). End with 1 s.s. into 3rd of 6 ch.

8th row. S.s. into first sp., 5 ch. 1 tr. into same sp. (*), 2 ch. 1 d.c. into next sp., 2 ch. 1 tr. 2 ch. 1 tr. into next sp., rep. from (*) all round. End with 1 s.s. into 3rd of 5 ch.

9th row. As 8th row but work d.c. into d.c. of previous row.

Fig. 32. This table centre consists of stars worked in crochet joined together by bars worked with a needle. All the stars are worked separately and attached, as shown in the illustration, on to a card or tracing paper, and then proceed to work all the bars decorated with picots. The outer measurements (the shape may be round, square or oval) should be drawn on to the paper and worked over in ch. st. to which the bars will be attached, and on to which the finishing-off lace will be worked.

Fig. 33. **Necessary Materials.** Coats Mercer-Crochet, No. 40 and a No. 1.00 crochet hook.

Motif: Start with 10 ch., join with a s.s. to form a ring.

1st row. 20 d.c. into ring, 1 s.s. into first d.c.

2nd row. 1 d.c. into same place as s.s. (*) 1 d.c. into each of next 3 d.c., 18 ch., 1 d.c. into 10th ch. from hook (3 ch., miss 3 ch., 1 d.c. into next ch.) twice, 1 d.c. into next d.c.; rep. from (*) omitting 1 d.c. at end of last rep., 1 s.s. into first d.c.

3rd row. 1 d.c. into same place as s.s. (*) 1 d.c. into each of next 3 d.c., 6 d.c. into next sp., 6 tr. into next sp., into next sp. work 2 tr., 13 dbl. tr. and 2 tr., 6 tr. into next sp. 6 d.c. into next sp., miss next d.c., 1 d.c. into next d.c.; rep. from (*) omitting 1 d.c. at end of last rep., 1 s.s. into first d.c. Fasten off.

Lace Finishing.

Over the ch. st. joining the bars (see illustration) work 18 d.c. (*) turn, 4 ch., miss 5 d.c., 1 dbl. tr. into next d.c., 4 ch., 1 dbl. tr. into same place as last dbl. tr., 3 times more, 4 ch., miss 5 d.c., 1 d.c. into next d.c., turn, 1 ch., 6 d.c. into 5 ch. sp., 5 d.c. into each 4 ch. sp. and 6 d.c. into last 5 ch. sp. 5 d.c. into ch. on base. Turn 5 ch. 1 d.c. into d.c. of first sp. (*), 5 ch. 1 dbl. tr. into next dbl. tr., 5 ch. 1 d.c. into middle d.c. of next sp.; rep. from (*) with 5 ch. into 5th d.c. on base. Turn, 1 ch., into

Fig. 32. Table centre in crochet and needlework

Fig. 33. Detail of table centre in Fig. 32

Fig. 34. Table centre in Coats Mercer-Crochet, No. 60, in green

each sp. work 7 d.c. and into each dbl. tr. a 3 ch. picot. On coming to base work another 18 d.c. and rep. from (*).

Fig. 34. **Necessary Materials.** Coats Mercer-Crochet, No. 60, 1 ball of 20 grm.; a No. 0.75 crochet hook.

Commence with 8 ch., join with s.s. to form a ring.

1st row. (1 d.c. into ring, 10 ch.) 8 times, 1 s.s. into first d.c.

2nd row. 1 s.s. into each of next 5 ch., 1 d.c. into loop, 6 ch., 1 tr. into same loop (4 ch., into next loop work 1 tr. 3 ch. 1 tr.) 7 times, 4 ch., 1 s.s. into 3rd of 6 ch.

3rd row. 1 s.s. into next sp., 3 ch., into same sp. work 1 tr. 2 ch. 2 tr. (*), 2 ch., 1 d.c. into next sp., 2 ch., into next sp. work 2 tr. 2 ch. 2 tr.; rep. from (*) ending with 2 ch., 1 s.s. into 3rd of 3 ch.

4th row. 1 s.s. into next tr. and into next sp., 3 ch., into same sp. work 2 tr. 2 ch. 3 tr. (*), 3 ch., 1 d.c. into next d.c., 3 ch., into next sp. (between tr. groups) work 3 tr. 2 ch. 3 tr.; rep. from (*) ending with 1 s.s. into 3rd of 3 ch.

5th row. 1 s.s. into each of next 2 tr. and into sp., 4 cn., into same sp. work 1 dbl. tr. 3 ch. 2 dbl. tr. (shell made) (*), 11 ch., into 2 ch. sp. (between tr. groups) work 2 dbl. tr. 3 ch. 2 dbl. tr. (another shell); rep. from (*) ending with 1 s.s. into 4th of 4 ch.

6th row. 1 s.s. into next dbl. tr. and into sp., 4 ch., into same sp. work 2 dbl. tr. 3 ch. 3 dbl. tr. (shell over shell) (*), 3 ch., 9 dbl. tr. into 6th of next 11 ch., 3 ch., into sp. of next shell work 3 dbl. tr. 3 ch. 3 dbl. tr. (shell made over shell); rep. from (*) ending with 1 s.s. into 4th of 4 ch.

7th row. 1 s.s. into each of next 2 dbl. tr. and into sp. (*), shell over shell, 3 ch. (1 dbl. tr. into next dbl. tr., 1 ch.), 8 times, 1 dbl. tr. into next dbl. tr., 3 ch.; rep. from (*) ending with 1 s.s. into 4th of 4 ch.

8th row. 1 s.s. into each of next 2 dbl. tr. and into sp. (*), shell over shell, 3 ch., 1 d.c. into next 1 ch. sp. (3 ch., 1 d.c. into next sp.), 7 times, 3 ch.; rep. from (*) ending with 1 s.s. into 4th of 4 ch.

9th row. 1 s.s. into each of next 2 dbl. tr. and into sp. (*), shell over shell, 5 ch., miss next 3 ch., 1 d.c. into next 3 ch. loop, (5 ch., 1 d.c. into next loop) 6 times, 5 ch.; rep. from (*) ending with 1 s.s. into 4th of 4 ch.

10th row. 1 s.s. into each of next 2 dbl. tr. and into sp., 4 ch., into same sp. work 2 dbl. tr. 2 ch.

1 dbl. tr. 3 ch. 1 dbl. tr. 2 ch. 3 dbl. tr. (*), 5 ch., miss 5 ch., 1 d.c. into next 5 ch. loop (5 ch., 1 d.c. into next loop), 5 times, 5 ch., into sp. of next shell work 3 dbl. tr. 2 ch. 1 dbl. tr. 3 ch. 1 dbl. tr. 2 ch. 3 dbl. tr.; rep. from (*) ending with 1 s.s. into 4th of 4 ch.

11th row. 1 s.s. into each of next 2 dbl. tr. and into sp., 4 ch., into same sp. work 2 dbl. tr. 2 ch. 2 dbl. tr. (*), 2 ch., 5 dbl. tr. into next 3 ch. sp., 2 ch., into next sp. work 2 dbl. tr. 2 ch. 3 dbl. tr., 5 ch., miss next 5 ch., 1 d.c. into next 5 ch. loop, (5 ch., 1 d.c. into next loop) 4 times, 5 ch., miss next 5 ch., into next sp. work 3 dbl. tr. 2 ch. 2 dbl. tr.; rep. from (*) ending with 1 s.s. into 4th of 4 ch.

12th row. 1 s.s. into each of next 2 dbl. tr. and into sp., 4 ch., into same sp. work 2 dbl. tr. 3 ch. 2 dbl. tr. (*), 2 ch., into next sp. work 2 dbl. tr. 2 ch. 1 dbl. tr., 2 ch., miss next dbl. tr., (1 dbl. tr. into next dbl. tr., 1 ch.) 3 times, 1 dbl. tr. into next dbl. tr., 2 ch., into next sp. work 1 dbl. tr. 2 ch. 2 dbl. tr., 2 ch., into next sp. work 2 dbl. tr. 3 ch. 3 dbl. tr., 5 ch., miss next 5 ch., 1 d.c. into next 5 ch. loop, (5 ch., 1 d.c. into next loop) 3 times, 5 ch., miss next 5 ch., into next sp. work 3 dbl. tr. 3 ch. 2 dbl. tr.; rep. from (*) ending with 1 s.s. into 4th of 4 ch.

13th row. 1 s.s. into each of next 2 dbl. tr. and into sp., 4 ch., into same sp. work 2 dbl. tr. 3 ch. 3 dbl. tr. (shell over shell) (*), 3 ch., miss next sp., into next sp. work 3 dbl. tr. 2 ch. 2 dbl. tr., 5 ch., miss next sp., 1 d.c. into next 1 ch. sp. (5 ch., 1 d.c. into next sp.), twice, 5 ch., miss next sp. and dbl. tr., into next sp. work 2 dbl. tr. 2 ch. 3 dbl. tr., 3 ch., miss next sp., into next sp. work 3 dbl. tr. 3 ch. 3 dbl. tr., 5 ch., miss next 5 ch., 1 d.c. into next 5 ch. loop, (5 ch., 1 d.c. into next loop) twice, 5 ch., miss next 5 ch., into next sp. work 3 dbl. tr. 3 ch. 3 dbl. tr.; rep. from (*) ending with 1 s.s. into 4th of 4 ch.

14th row. 1 s.s. into each of next 2 dbl. tr. and into sp., shell over shell (*), 3 ch., 1 d.c. into next sp., 3 ch., shell in next sp., 5 ch., miss next 5 ch., (1 d.c. into next loop, 5 ch.) twice, miss next 5 ch., shell in next sp., 3 ch., 1 d.c. into next sp., 3 ch., shell over shell, 5 ch., miss next 5 ch., (1 d.c. into next loop, 5 ch.) twice, miss next 5 ch., shell over shell; rep. from (*) ending with 1 s.s. into 4th of 4 ch.

15th row. 1 s.s. into each of next 2 dbl. tr. and into sp. (*), shell over shell, 5 ch., 1 d.c. into next d.c., 5 ch., shell over shell, 5 ch., miss next 5 ch.,

1 d.c. into next 5 ch. loop, 5 ch., shell over shell, 5 ch., 1 d.c. into next d.c., 5 ch., shell over shell, 5 ch., miss next 5 ch., 1 d.c. into next loop, 5 ch.; rep. from (*) ending with 1 s.s. into 4th of 4 ch.

16th row. 1 s.s. into each of next 2 dbl. tr. and into sp. (*), shell over shell, 8 ch., 1 d.c. into next d.c., 8 ch., shell over shell, 5 ch.; rep. from (*) ending with 1 s.s. into 4th of 4 ch.

17th row. 1 s.s. into each of next 2 dbl. tr. and into sp., 4 ch., 2 dbl. tr. into same sp. (*), 12 ch., 1 d.c. into next d.c., 12 ch., 3 dbl. tr. into sp. of next shell, 3 ch., into next sp. work 2 dbl. tr. 2 trip tr. 1 quad. tr., 5 ch., 1 d.c. into top of quad. tr., into same sp. work 1 quad. tr. 2 trip. tr. 2 dbl. tr., 3 ch., 3 dbl. tr. into sp. of next shell; rep. from (*) ending with 1 s.s. into 4th of 4 ch. Fasten off.

Fig. 35. **Necessary Materials.** Coats Mercer-Crochet, No. 40; one 20-grm. ball; No. 1.00 crochet hook.

Commence with 8 ch., join with a s.s. to form a ring.

1st row. Into ring work 15 d.c., 1 s.s. into first d.c.

2nd row. 1 d.c. into same place as last s.s. (*), 4 ch., miss 2 d.c., 1 d.c. into next d.c.; rep. from (*) ending with 4 ch., 1 s.s. into first d.c. (5 loops).

3rd row. 1 s.s. into first loop, 4 ch., 6 dbl. tr. into same loop (*), 2 ch., 7 dbl. tr. into next loop; rep. from (*) ending with 2 ch., 1 s.s. into 4th of 4 ch.

4th row. 4 ch., 1 dbl. tr. into same place as last s.s. (*) (1 dbl. tr. into each of next 2 dbl. tr., 2 dbl. tr. into next dbl. tr.), twice, 2 ch., 2 dbl. tr. into next dbl. tr.; rep. from (*) omitting 2 dbl. tr. at end of last rep., 1 s.s. into 4th of 4 ch.

5th row. 4 ch. (*) (1 dbl. tr. into next dbl. tr., 2 dbl. tr. into next dbl. tr.) twice, (2 dbl. tr. into next dbl. tr., 1 dbl. tr. into next dbl. tr.) twice, 1 dbl. tr. into next dbl. tr., 2 ch., 1 dbl. tr. into next dbl. tr.; rep. from (*) omitting 1 dbl. tr. at end of last rep., 1 s.s. into 4th of 4 ch.

6th row. 1 d.c. into same place as last s.s. (*), 1 tr. into next dbl. tr., 2 dbl. tr. into each of next 3 dbl. tr., 1 tr. into next dbl. tr., 1 d.c. into each of next 2 dbl. tr., 1 tr. into next dbl. tr., 2 dbl. tr. into each of next 3 dbl. tr., 1 tr. into next dbl. tr., 1 d.c. into next dbl. tr., 2 d.c. into next sp., 1 d.c. into next dbl. tr.; rep. from (*) omitting 1 d.c. at end of last rep., 1 s.s. into first d.c.

7th row. 1 s.s. into each of next 3 sts., 1 d.c. into each of next 2 dbl. tr. (*), 10 ch., 1 d.c. into each of

Fig. 35. Glass mat

2 centre dbl. tr. of next point; rep. from (*) ending with 10 ch., 1 s.s. into first d.c.

8th row. 3 ch. (*), 1 tr. into next d.c., 1 tr. into each of next 10 ch., 1 tr. into next d.c.; rep. from (*) omitting 1 tr. at end of last rep., 1 s.s. into 3rd of 3 ch.

9th row. 1 d.c. into same place as last s.s. (*), 5 ch., miss 2 tr., 1 d.c. into next tr.; rep. from (*) ending with 5 ch., 1 s.s. into first d.c.

10th row. s.s. to centre of loop, 1 d.c. into loop (*), 5 ch., 1 d.c. into next loop; rep. from (*) ending with 5 ch., 1 s.s. into first d.c.

11th row. s.s. to centre of loop, 1 d.c. into loop (*), 3 ch., 1 d.c. into next loop; rep. from (*) ending with 3 ch., 1 s.s. into first d.c.

12th and 13th rows. s.s. to centre of 3 ch. sp., 1 d.c. into sp. (*), 3 ch., 1 d.c. into next 3 ch. sp.; rep. from (*) ending with 3 ch., 1 s.s. into first d.c., turn.

14th row. 1 s.s. into first 3 ch. sp., 1 d.c. into same sp. (*), 3 ch., 2 tr. into same sp., 1 d.c. into next 3 ch. sp.; rep. from (*) omitting 1 d.c. at end of last rep., 1 s.s. into first d.c. Fasten off.

Slip on to glass.

Various Edgings. The instructions follow the order of the patterns shown in Figs. 36 and 37 from top to bottom.

Pretty examples of centres and mats worked in rather fine thread in Coats Mercer-Crochet, No. 60, in white, écru and colours. These mats stand out well on glass tops or on silverware

Necessary Materials. Coats Mercer-Crochet, No. 60, and a No. 0.75 crochet hook.

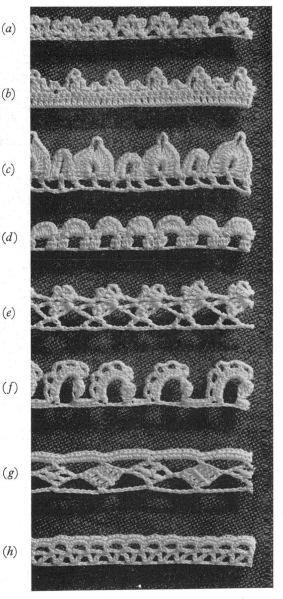

(a)

(a)

Make a chain the length required.

1st row. Into 7th ch. from hook work (1 tr., 2 ch., 1 d.c. into top of last tr.) 3 times, 1 tr. into same ch (*), 2 ch., miss 2 ch., 1 d.c. into next ch., 2 ch., miss 2 ch., into next ch. work (1 tr., 2 ch., 1 d.c. into top of last tr.) 3 times, 1 tr. into same ch.; rep. from (*) to end of row. Fasten off.

(b)

(b)

Make a chain the length required.

1st row. 1 tr. into 4th ch. from hook, 1 tr. into each ch., 3 ch., turn.

2nd row. (*) 3 ch., 1 tr. into each of next 2 tr. leaving the last loop of each on hook, thread over and pull through all loops on hook (cluster made), 3 ch., 1 d.c. into tip of cluster just made, 3 ch., 1 d.c. into each of next 2 tr., 3 ch., 1 d.c. into 3rd ch. from hook, miss 1 tr., 1 d.c. into each of next 2 tr.; rep. from (*) to end of row. Fasten off.

(c)

(c)

1st row. Commence with (*) 13 ch., 1 d.c. into 9th ch. from hook; rep. from (*) for length required, ending with a loop, 1 ch., turn.

2nd row. (*) 11 d.c. into next loop, 1 d.c. over 4 ch. between loops, into next loop work 8 tr. 5 ch. 8 tr., 1 d.c. over next 4 ch.; rep. from (*) to end of row. Do not break off but work across long side as follows 5 ch. (*), 1 tr. into centre of next ring, 3 ch., 1 tr. into next d.c., 3 ch.; rep. from last (*) to end of row. Fasten off.

(d)

(d)

Make a chain the length required.

1st row. 2 tr. into 4th ch. from hook leaving the last loop of each on hook, thread over and pull through all loops on hook (cluster) (*), 1 ch., miss 1 ch., 1 cluster into next ch., 3 ch., miss 3 ch., 1 cluster into next ch.; rep. from (*) ending with 1 cluster, 1 ch., 1 cluster, 1 ch., turn.

2nd row. (*) 1 d.c. into 1 ch. sp., 1 d.c. 1 hlf. tr. 5 tr. 1 hlf. tr. 1 d.c. into next 3 ch. sp.; rep. from (*) to end of row. Fasten off.

(e)

(e)

1st row. 5 ch., 2 tr. into 5th ch. from hook, 3 ch., 1 s.s. into last tr. (picot made), 1 tr. into same ch. as last tr., 2 ch., into same ch. work 2 tr. picot, 2 tr., 5 ch., turn.

2nd row. Into 2 ch. sp. work 1 tr. 3 ch. 1 tr., 4 ch., turn.

3rd row. Into 3 ch. sp. work 2 tr. picot 1 tr. 2 ch.

(f)

(g)

(h)

Fig. 36. Various crochet edgings

2 tr. picot 1 tr., 5 ch., turn. Rep. 2nd and 3rd rows alternately for length required. Do not break off thread but work along side where 5 ch's. appear as follows: (*) into loop formed by turning 5 ch. work 1 tr. 3 ch. 1 tr., 3 ch.; rep. from (*) to end of row. Fasten off.

(f)

Make a chain slightly longer than length required.

357

1st row. (*) 3 tr. into 5th ch. from hook leaving the last loop of each on hook, thread over and pull through all loops on hook, 7 ch., miss 2 ch., 1 s.s. into next ch., turn, into 7 ch. loop work 15 d.c., turn. (3 ch., miss 2 d.c., 1 d.c. into next d.c.) 5 times, 1 d.c. into each of next 5 ch., 5 ch.; rep. from (*) to end of ch. Fasten off.

(g)

Commence with 8 ch.

1st row. 1 tr. into 6th ch. from hook, 1 ch., miss 1 ch., 1 tr. into next ch., 4 ch., turn.

2nd row. 1 tr. into next tr., 1 ch., miss 1 ch. of turning ch., 1 tr. into next ch., 7 ch., do not turn work.

3rd row. 1 tr. into 4th ch. from hook, 1 tr. into each of next 3 ch., 3 ch., turn.

4th row. 1 tr. into each of next 3 tr., 1 tr. into top of turning ch. Rep. these 4 rows for length required. Do not break off thread but work along one long side as follows: 7 ch., 1 d.c. into free tip of same square (*), 7 ch., 1 d.c. into free tip of next square; repeat from (*) across, 1 ch., turn and work 10 d.c. into each 7 ch. loop. Then s.s. to remaining free tip of first square on opposite long side (*), 7 ch., 1 d.c. into free tip of next square; rep. from last (*) across. Fasten off.

(h)

Make a chain slightly longer than length required.

1st row. Into 4th ch. from hook work 1 tr. 2 ch. 1 tr. (*), miss 2 ch., into next ch. work 1 tr. 2 ch. 1 tr.; rep. from (*) to end of ch., 3 ch., turn.

2nd row. (*) Miss 2 ch. and 1 tr., 1 d.c. into next tr., 3 ch.; rep. from (*) to end of row, 1 ch., turn.

3rd row. 5 d.c. into each 3 ch. sp. Fasten off.

(i)

Commence with 11 ch.

1st row. 1 dbl. tr. into first of 11 ch. (*), 7 ch., turn, miss 2 ch. of last loop, 1 dbl. tr. into next ch.; rep. from (*) for length required, 1 ch., do not turn.

2nd row. (*) Into next sp. work 1 hlf. tr. 5 tr. 1 hlf. tr., 1 d.c. into next st., rep. from (*) to end of row.

Rep. 2nd row along other side of first row.

Heading.

Attach thread to 3rd tr. of first scallop on one long side, 10 ch., 1 dbl. tr. into 3rd tr. of next scallop (*), 5 ch., 1 dbl. tr. into 3rd tr. of next scallop; rep. from (*) across. Fasten off.

(l)

Make a chain the length required.

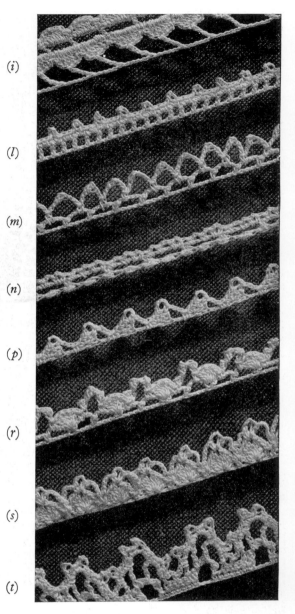

(i)

(l)

(m)

(n)

(p)

(r)

(s)

(t)

Fig. 37. Various edgings worked in Coats Mercer-Crochet

1st row. 1 tr. into 5th ch. from hook (*), 1 ch., miss 1 ch., 1 tr. into next ch.; rep. from (*) to end of row, 1 ch., turn.

2nd row. (*) Into next sp. work 1 d.c., 3 ch., 1 s.s. into 3rd ch. from hook, 1 d.c. into same sp., 2 d.c. into next sp.; rep. from (*) to end of row. Fasten off.

358

Fig. 38. Table centres in crochet. Detailed instructions for their working begin on page 360

(*m*)

Make a chain slightly longer than length required.

1st row. 1 d.c. into 9th ch. from hook (*), 5 ch., miss 3 ch., 1 d.c. into next ch.; rep. from (*) to end of ch., 5 ch., turn.

2nd row. (*) 1 d.c. into 3rd ch. from hook (picot made), 3 ch., 1 d.c. into next loop, 5 ch.; rep. from (*) to end of row. Fasten off.

(*n*)

1st row. 3 ch. (thread over hook, insert hook into 3rd ch. from hook and draw a loop through) twice (*), thread over and draw through all loops on hook (cluster made), 1 ch. Pull loop on hook out until it measures ⅛ in. (thread over, insert hook into 1 ch. and draw a loop through) twice; rep. from (*) for length required, 5 ch., turn.

2nd row. (*) Miss 1 cluster, 1 d.c. on side of next cluster, 5 ch.; rep. from (*) to end of row, 1 ch., turn.

3rd row. Into each 5 ch. loop work (1 d.c., 2 ch.), 3 times and 1 d.c. Fasten off.

(*p*)

1st row. (*) 6 ch., 1 d.c. into 2nd ch. from hook, 1 hlf. tr. into next ch., 1 tr. into next ch.; rep. from (*) for length required. Fasten off.

2nd row. Attach thread in first d.c. made, 1 d.c. into place where thread was attached (*), 1 d.c. into next hlf. tr., 1 d.c. into next tr., 1 d.c. under 2 ch. (between groups), 3 ch., into next d.c. work 1 d.c. 3 ch. 1 d.c.; rep. from (*) to end of row. Fasten off.

(*r*)

Make a chain slightly longer than length required.

1st row. 1 d.c. into 9th ch. from hook (*), 5 ch., miss 3 ch., 1 d.c. into next ch.; rep. from (*) to end of row, 3 ch., turn.

2nd row. (*) 1 d.c. into 3rd ch. from hook (3 ch., 1 d.c. into 3rd ch. from hook) twice, 1 d.c. into next loop, 5 tr. into d.c. between 2 loops, 1 d.c. into next loop, 3 ch.; rep. from (*) ending with 1 d.c. into last loop. Fasten off.

(*s*)

Make a chain the length required.

1st row. Into 4th ch. from hook work 4 tr. 2 ch. 4 tr. (*), miss 2 ch., 1 d.c. into next ch., miss 2 ch., into next ch. work 4 tr. 2 ch. 4 tr.; rep. from (*) to end of row, ending with 1 d.c. into next ch., 5 ch., turn.

2nd row. (*) Into 2 ch. sp. work 1 d.c. 3 ch. 1 d.c., 5 ch., 1 d.c. into next d.c., 5 ch.; rep. from (*) to

end of row. Fasten off.

(*t*)

Make a chain slightly longer than length required.

1st row. 1 d.c. into 2nd ch. from hook (*), (3 ch., 1 d.c. into 3rd ch. from hook) 3 times (3 picots made), miss 2 ch., 1 d.c. into each of next 7 ch.; rep. from (*) ending with 3 picots, miss 2 ch., 1 d.c. into next ch., 5 ch., turn.

2nd row. (*) 1 dbl. tr. between 1st and 2nd picot of next loop, 5 ch., 1 dbl. tr. between 2nd and 3rd picot of same loop, 5 ch., miss 1 d.c., 1 d.c. into each of next 5 d.c., 5 ch.; rep. from (*) ending with 5 ch., 1 s.s. into last d.c., 1 ch., turn.

3rd row. (*) Into next loop work 2 d.c. picot 2 d.c., into next loop work (2 d.c., picot) twice and 2 d.c. into next loop work 2 d.c. picot 2 d.c., 2 ch., miss 2 d.c., 1 d.c. into next d.c., 2 ch.; rep. from (*) to end of row. Fasten off.

Large Table Centre. Necessary Materials.

Coats Mercer-Crochet, No. 20 (20 grm.). 2 balls each White, 623 (Spring Green) and 503 (Coral Pink). This model is worked in these three shades, but any other shades of Mercer-Crochet may be used.

Milwards steel crochet hook No. 1.25.

The above quantity is sufficient for 1 Centrepiece, 1 Place Mat and 1 Glass Mat.

Tension. First 6 rows = 2 in. in diameter.

Measurements. Centrepiece 16 in. in diameter. Place Mat 10½ in. in diameter. Glass Mat 5 in. in diameter.

With Coral Pink, commence with 10 ch., join with a s.s. to form a ring.

1st row. Into ring work 24 d.c., 1 s.s. into first d.c.

2nd row. 1 d.c. into same place as s.s. (*), 5 ch., miss 3 d.c., 1 d.c. into next d.c.; rep. from (*) ending with 5 ch., 1 s.s. into first d.c. (6 loops made).

3rd row. Into each loop work 1 d.c. 1 hlf. tr. 3 tr. 1 hlf. tr. and 1 d.c., 1 s.s. into first d.c. (6 petals made).

4th row. (*) 5 ch., 1 d.c. between next 2 petals; rep. from (*) ending last rep. with 1 s.s. into first ch.

5th row. As 3rd row. Fasten off.

6th row. Attach White into same place as last s.s., 1 s.s. between next d.c. and hlf. tr., 7 ch. (*), 1 trip tr. between next hlf. tr. and tr. (2 ch., 1 trip tr. between this tr. and next tr.) twice, 2 ch., 1 trip tr. between this tr. and next hlf. tr., 2 ch., 1 trip tr.

between this hlf. tr. and next d.c., 2 ch., miss 2 d.c. and 1 hlf. tr., 1 trip tr. between this hlf tr. and next tr., (2 ch., 1 trip tr. between this tr. and next tr.) twice, 2 ch., 1 trip tr. between this tr. and next hlf. tr., 2 ch., 1 trip tr. between this hlf. tr. and next d.c., 2 ch., miss 2 d.c., 1 trip tr. between last d.c. and next hlf. tr., 2 ch.; rep. from (*) ending with 1 trip tr. between last hlf tr. and d.c. of 6th petal, 2 ch., 1 s.s. into 5th of 7 ch. (33 trip tr. counting starting ch. as 1 trip tr.).

7th row. 1 s.s. into next 2 ch. sp., 1 d.c. into same sp. (*), 4 ch., 1 d.c. into next sp; rep. from (*) ending with 4 ch., 1 d.c. into first loop.

8th and 9th rows. (*) 5 ch., 1 d.c. into next loop; rep. from (*) ending with 5 ch., 1 d.c. into first loop.

10th row. As 9th row working 6 ch. loops instead of 5 ch., ending with 3 ch., 1 tr. into first loop.

11th row. (*) (4 ch., 1 tr. into 4th ch. from hook), twice, 1 d.c. into next loop (a 2 group loop made); rep. from (*) omitting a d.c. at end of last repeat, 1 s.s. into tr. of previous row.

12th row. 1 s.s. into each of next 4 ch., 1 d.c. into centre of 2 group loop (*), (4 ch., 1 tr. into 4th ch. from hook) 4 times, 1 d.c. between first and second group just made, 4 ch., 1 tr. into 4th ch. from hook, 1 d.c. into centre of next 2 group loop of previous row (a 5 group loop made) (4 ch., 1 tr. into 4th ch. from hook), twice, 1 d.c. into centre of next 2 group loop of previous row; rep. from (*) 15 times more omitting 1 d.c. at end of last repeat, 1 s.s. into first d.c. Fasten off.

First Leaf

1st row. With Spring Green, commence with 11 ch., 1 d.c. into 2nd ch. from hook, 1 d.c. into each of the following ch., 2 ch., 1 d.c. into same place as last d.c., 1 d.c. into each ch. along opposite side of foundation ch., 1 ch., turn. Hereafter pick up back loop only of each d.c. throughout.

2nd row. 1 d.c. into each d.c. to within 2 ch. sp., into 2 ch. sp. work 1 d.c. 2 ch. and 1 d.c., 1 d.c. into each d.c. along other side to within last d.c., 1 ch., turn (1 d.c. decreased). Rep. 2nd row until there are 14 d.c. on each side of 2 ch. sp., 1 ch., turn. Now join first leaf to *Centre*: With wrong side of *Centre* facing, 1 d.c. into each of next 9 d.c. on leaf, 1 d.c. between 3rd and 4th group of a 5 group loop, 1 d.c. into each remaining d.c. on leaf to within 2 ch. sp., 1 d.c. into 2 ch. sp., 1 ch., 1 d.c. into centre of next 2 group loop on *Centre*, 1 ch., 1 d.c. into 2 ch. sp. on leaf, 1 d.c. into each of next 5 d.c., 1 d.c.

between 2nd and 3rd group of next 5 group loop, 1 d.c. into each of next 9 d.c. on leaf. Fasten off.

Second Leaf

Work as for first leaf until there are 14 d.c. on each side of 2 ch. sp., then join as follows: 1 ch. 1 d.c. into last d.c. worked on previous leaf, turn, 1 d.c. into each of next 9 d.c. on second leaf, 1 d.c. between 3rd and 4th group of same 5 group loop to which previous leaf was joined, 1 d.c. into each of the following d.c. on second leaf to within 2 ch. sp., 1 d.c. into sp., 1 ch., 1 d.c. into centre of next 2 group loop on *Centre*, 1 ch., 1 d.c. into 2 ch. sp. on leaf and complete joining as for first leaf. Fasten off.

Make 14 more leaves in same manner, joining as second leaf was joined to first leaf and joining last leaf to first leaf with 1 d.c. to complete 13th row of doily. Fasten off.

14th row. Miss last st. on last row of any leaf, attach White into next row-end, 7 ch. (*), 1 tr. into 4th ch. from hook, 4 ch., 1 tr. into 4th ch. from hook, miss next 3 row-ends, 1 d.c. into next row-end, (4 ch., 1 tr. into 4th ch. from hook) twice, miss next 4 row-ends, 1 tr. between last row-end missed and next row-end, (4 ch., 1 tr. into 4th ch. from hook) twice, miss next 4 row-ends, 1 d.c. into next row-end, (4 ch., 1 tr. into 4th ch. from hook) twice, miss next 3 row-ends, 1 tr. into next row-end, miss first row-end on next leaf, 1 tr. into next row-end, 4 ch.; rep. from (*) omitting 1 tr. and 4 ch. at end of last rep., 1 s.s. into 3rd of 7 ch.

15th to 17th row. 1 s.s. into each of next 4 ch., 1 d.c. between 2 group loop (*), (4 ch., 1 tr. into 4th ch. from hook) twice, 1 d.c. into centre of next 2 group loop; rep. from (*) omitting 1 d.c. at end of last rep., 1 s.s. into first d.c. Do not fasten off.

Motifs are made individually as follows:

First Petal Motif (make 16).

With Coral Pink, commence with 12 ch., join with a s.s. to form a ring.

1st row. 3 ch., 23 tr. into ring, 1 s.s. into top of 3 ch.

2nd row. 4 ch. (*), 1 tr. into next tr., 1 ch.; rep. from (*) ending with 1 s.s. into 3rd of 4 ch.

3rd row. (*) 1 s.s. into next sp., 9 ch., 1 tr. into 4th ch. from hook, 1 tr. into each of the following 5 ch., 1 d.c. into next sp. on previous row, 2 ch., turn (petal started). Now working along petal work 1 hlf. tr. between first and second tr., 1 hlf. tr. between each of the following tr., 5 hlf. tr. over turning ch. at tip, then work across opposite side to correspond, 1 d.c. into next sp. on previous row,

1 ch., turn, 1 d.c. into each hlf tr. to tip of petal, 3 d.c. into centre hlf. tr. at tip, 1 d.c. into each hlf. tr. across other side ending with 1 d.c. into top of previous 2 turning ch., 1 d.c. into next sp. on previous row (petal completed); rep. from (*) until 8 petals have been made in all ending with 1 s.s. into first d.c. on last row of first petal. Fasten off.

18th row. Pick up White, 1 s.s. into each of next 4 ch., 1 d.c. into centre of 2 group loop (*), 4 ch., 1 tr. into 4th ch. from hook, 1 s.s. into centre d.c. at tip of any petal, 4 ch., 1 tr. into 4th ch. from hook, 1 d.c. into centre of next 2 group loop, (4 ch., 1 tr. into 4th ch. from hook) twice, 1 d.c. into centre of next 2 group loop, 4 ch., 1 tr. into 4th ch. from hook, 1 s.s. into centre d.c. at tip of next petal on same petal motif, 4 ch., 1 tr. into 4th ch. from hook, 1 d.c. into centre of next 2 group loop, (4 ch., 1 tr. into 4th ch. from hook) twice, 1 d.c. into centre of next 2 group loop; rep. from (*) joining 2 petals of each petal motif in each rep. and ending last rep. with 1 s.s. into first d.c. Fasten off.

With Coral Pink, and working on wrong side, oversew tips of petals on each side of petals joined to doily, to corresponding petals on previous motifs as shown in illustration.

Place Mat

Work as centrepiece until 16th row has been completed. Fasten off. Attach Coral Pink into same place as last s.s.

17th row. As previous row. Fasten off.

Glass Mat

Work as centrepiece until 11th row has been completed. Fasten off. Attach Coral Pink into same place as last s.s.

12th row. 1 s.s. into each of next 4 ch., 1 d.c. into centre of 2 group loop (*), (4 ch., 1 tr. into 4th ch. from hook) twice, 1 d.c. into centre of next 2 group loop; rep. from (*) omitting 1 d.c. at end of last rep., 1 s.s. into first d.c. Fasten off.

Damp and pin out to measurements.

Crocheted Gloves (Fig. 39). Necessary Materials.
Coats Mercer-Crochet No. 60 (20 grm.). 2 balls. This model is worked in White, but any shade of Mercer-Crochet may be used. Piece of tubular elastic. Milwards steel crochet hook No. 0.75.

Size of Glove: 7.

Tension: *7 rows—1 in.*
Left Hand

Commence with 120 ch. (do not work ch. tightly), join with a s.s. to form a ring.

1st row. 1 d.c. into same place as s.s., (*) 5 ch., miss 3 ch., 1 d.c. into next ch.; rep. from (*) 28 times more, 5 ch., 1 d.c. into first loop. (30 sps.).

2nd row. (*) 5 ch., 1 d.c. into next loop; rep. from (*) all round. (29 sps.).

Now work in continuous rows (1 row = 1 complete round, ending above where 1st and 2nd rows are joined) increasing at end of 8th, 13th, 16th, 19th and 22nd rows (to increase work 1 d.c. 5 ch. and 1 d.c. into same loop).

23rd row. Work without increasing, ending row on increase loop of previous row.

24th row. Work 9 loops, 5 ch., 1 tr. into next loop, 15 ch., count back 10 loops and work 1 tr. into this loop.

Fig. 39. Gloves in crochet

362

Thumb. *1st row.* (*) 5 ch., 1 d.c. into next loop; repeat from (*) 8 times more, (*) 5 ch., miss 3 of 15 ch., 1 d.c. into next ch.; rep. from last (*) twice more, 5 ch., 1 d.c. into next loop. Work 13 more rows (or length required).

15th row. (*) ch., 1 d.c. into next loop; rep. from (*) to end.

16th row. (*) 2 ch., 1 d.c. into next loop; rep. from (*) to end.

17th row. (*) 1 ch., 1 d.c. into next sp.; rep. from (*) to end.

18th row. 1 d.c. into each 1 ch. sp.

19th row. 1 d.c. into each d.c. Fasten off, Leaving sufficient thread to pull up opening and darn thread away.

Join thread to top of tr. on 24th row at back of thumb.

24th row (continuing). 5 ch., 1 d.c. into same place as last tr., (*) 5 ch., 1 d.c. into next loop; rep. from (*) 29 times more.

Work 8 more rows in these loops, ending last row above where thread was joined.

33rd row. Work 20 loops, 11 ch., count back 9 loops, work 1 d.c. into this loop.

Little finger. *1st row.* (*) 5 ch., 1 d.c. into next loop; rep. from (*) 7 times more, (*) 5 ch., miss 3 of 11 ch., 1 d.c. into next ch.; rep. from last (*) once more, 5 ch., 1 d.c. into next loop. Work 13 more rows (or length required). Finish off as for thumb.

Ring finger. With front of glove facing, join thread into last d.c. on 33rd row and complete row, ending with 1 d.c. into same loop where thread was joined.

Work 4 loops, 7 ch., count back 11 loops and work in same manner as for little finger having 18 rows (or length required), instead of 14, before closing.

Middle finger. Join thread as before and then work as for ring finger.

Fore finger. Join thread in same manner and work round all remaining loops for 16 rows (or length required). Close as for other fingers.

Cuff. Join a piece of elastic to fit wrist. Join thread to foundation ch.

1st row. (working over elastic) 4 d.c. into each 3 ch. sp., join with a s.s. into first d.c.

2nd row. (*) 5 ch., miss 2 d.c., 1 d.c. into next d.c.; rep. from (*) ending with 5 ch., 1 d.c. into first loop.

Continue in loops until 10th row has been completed.

11th row. Into each 5 ch. loop work 3 d.c. 3 ch. and 3 d.c. Fasten off.

Right Hand

Work 23 rows as for left hand, ending with 1 tr. into last loop on 23rd row; 15 ch., count back 10 loops, work 1 tr. into this loop.

Continue as for thumb of left hand.

Join thread to top of tr. on 23rd row at front of thumb, then work 24th row (continuing) until 32nd row is worked.

33rd row. Work 16 loops and continue from little finger having back of glove facing when joining for remaining fingers.

Wheat ear trimming

Commence with 4 ch.

1st row. 4 tr. into 4th ch. from hook, 3 ch., turn.

2nd row. 1 tr. into first tr., 2 tr. into next tr., 2 ch., 1 tr. into next tr., 2 ch., 2 tr. into next tr., 2 tr. into 4th of 4 ch., 3 ch., turn.

3rd row. Miss first tr. leaving the last loop of each on hook work 1 tr. into each of next 3 tr., thread over and draw through all loops on hook (a cluster made), 3 ch., into next tr. work 4 tr. 2 ch. 1 tr. 2 ch. and 4 tr., 3 ch., a 4 tr. cluster over next 3 tr. and turning ch., 4 ch., turn.

4th row. A cluster over next 4 tr., 3 ch., into next tr. work 4 tr. 2 ch. 1 tr. 2 ch. and 4 tr., 3 ch., a cluster over next 4 tr., 1 dbl. tr. into cluster of previous row, 4 ch., turn. Rep. 4th row 9 times more.

14th row. A cluster over next 4 tr., 5 ch., 4 tr. into next tr., 5 ch., a cluster over next 4 tr., 1 dbl. tr. into cluster of previous row, 5 ch., turn.

15th row. 1 d.c. into next 5 ch. loop, 5 ch., a cluster over next 4 tr., 5 ch., 1 d.c. into next 5 ch. loop, 5 ch., 1 d.c. into cluster of previous row. Fasten off.

Sew trimming to gloves as shown in illustration.

Crochet with Netting Background. Here are some patterns of the so-called "netted" crochet, with motifs of flowers, fruit and figures worked in blocks on a background of square holes. The designs for filet and modàno work, as well as those for Cross Stitch in a single colour, all serve very well for this particular type of crochet work. The proportion between the design and the work is one tr. and two missed st. for the spaces and three tr. for the filling in. When worked in very fine cotton thread this crochet takes on the aspect of filet, being, however, easier and quicker to work than filet, and also more resistant to washing.

Fig. 42. Inset with net background

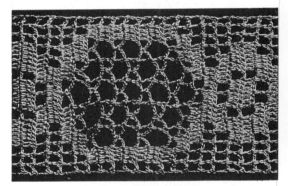

Fig. 40. Table centre with net background,
worked in Coats Mercer-Crochet

Fig. 43. Table centre with net background, worked
in Coats Mercer-Crochet

Fig. 41. Inset with net background

Fig. 44.
Diagram of
design for
table centre
with net
background,
shown in
Fig. 43

364

The net backgrounds must start and finish off with a tr. Thus at the end of a round the work is turned and 3 ch. st. worked, these being equal to a tr.

When a filled-in square is worked between two spaces, work 4 tr. so that the last tr. becomes the first of the following squares; for two squares joined, however, count 7 tr., for 3 squares 10, for 4, 13 and so on, that is, multiply the number of squares by 3 plus one.

The net background, instead of being worked in squares, can also be worked as shown in Fig. 41.

Fig. 45. Attractive place setting, consisting of a central mat in material with crochet work edgings. The illustration is very clear, and the stitches are easy to copy by anyone who has a little experience of this work. So we shall only say that the background material is in pale green and the lacework in crochet is worked in Coats Mercer-Crochet, No. 40, in écru.

Fig. 46 shows a nice use of crochet work. All the decoration on the cloth consist of stars, large and small trellises, worked in crochet and appliquéd to the material with small stitches.

Necessary Materials. Coats Mercer-Crochet, No. 20, in écru, green material in desired size; No. 1.75 crochet hook.

At the centre of the cloth the design is traced before beginning the work. Then work all the parts separately, making the discs to form the stars thus:

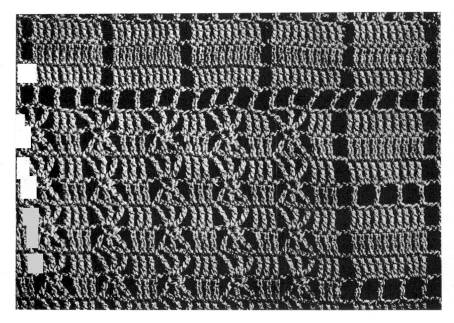

An elegant ladies' blouse worked in crochet. Requires 10–12 balls (20 grm.) of Coats Mercer-Crochet, No. 20. The stitches used are double treble, and chain stitch. The sleeves are worked separately and the back and front in one piece. The design can easily be seen from the picture and is easy to copy from the detail, in actual size, given here. The sleeve is rather wide and gathered at the elbow with round elastic. The collar and sleeves are finished off with a crochet edge

365

Fig. 45. American place settings using easy stitches and Coats Mercer-Crochet, No. 40

4 ch. st. worked into a circle, turn around these 4 st. with d.c. increasing little by little, every now and then until the diameter of the circle is about 1 inch. Make as many of these as are necessary and then work a centre disc which will be bigger. Attach these to the cloth, placing them over the traced design, wrong side up, and fix them down with small hidden stitches and natural-coloured cotton. Prepare separately some yards of chain and attach to the material, following the design and, again, with the wrong side uppermost. Fill in the spaces with oversewing stitches worked rather long, as shown in the picture. The cloth is finished off with a row of ch. st. attached in a wavy line and with oversewing stitches on the curves. This is an amusing, pretty and effective piece of work.

Hairpin Crochet (Fig. 47). By means of a curved metal gadget, similar to a hairpin, a piece of braid can be formed, consisting of a series of knots and wavy lines, from which loops that are then worked with a crochet hook start. Laces, bonnets, scarves, shawls, cot-covers, children's dresses, can all be worked in this hairpin crochet.

For hairpin work, proceed as follows:

With the crochet hook work 1 ch. st., take off from hook and pass the st. (lengthened so as to be half the width of the opening of the hairpin) on to the left side of the hairpin, which is held firm in the left hand (see illustration Fig. 47). Now take the thread in front of and round the right leg of the pin. Place the hook into the loop, lift up the thread, take it through the st. and fix it in place with a d.c., then take the thread, which has remained, behind and over the left leg of the pin. Turn the pin, place the hook, from below above, into the loop on the left leg and work another d.c. Then rep. the movement. The width of the braid will be in proportion to the width of the hairpin: when this is full of st., take them all off and put on 5 or 6 again, to continue work on these.

More than one st. can be worked into each loop. When the first piece is complete, others are worked and then joined together using the crochet hook. To do this, take 2 loops from the first piece, work a ch. st. and take up 2 other loops from the second piece, and so on.

Tunisian Stitch. This is one of the most typical in crochet work. The hook used must be tubular and smooth, like a knitting needle, and can be made of steel, aluminium, celluloid, plastic or wood,

366

Fig. 46. Cloth with Crochet work appliqué. The crochet was done in Coats Mercer-Crochet

according to the thickness of the thread to be used. Instead of holding it like a pen, the hook is, in this case, held from above. There should be a ball at the opposite end from the hook, to avoid st. falling off. Tunisian work is always worked on the right side, never turned, and forms a soft, elastic stitch used specially for scarves, jackets, cot-covers, children's bootees, etc.

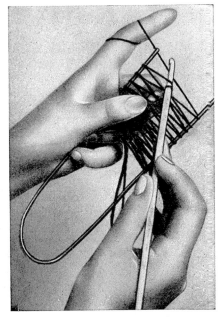

Fig. 47. Hairpin work

Simple Tunisian Stitch. Over a length of ch. st. to the desired length, work back, placing the hook into the second st. behind the hook, take out the st. and so on, successively, into each ch. st., take up the thread but leave the st. on the hook.

At the end of the row there will be as many st. on the hook as there were ch. st. On completing the row, take the thread over the hook, passing it first under a st., then take the thread once again over the hook and pass through 2 st. and so on, in this way, until all the st. have been cast off in twos.

On the following row lift up the vertical thread

Fig. 48. Simple Tunisian Stitch

Fig. 50. Tunisian Stitch with crossed, oblique stitches

Fig. 49. Tunisian Stitch with vertical, crossed stitches

Fig. 51. Tunisian Stitch, with a design of balls

formed, on prec. row, with the hook, picking up a st. from each one and leaving it on the hook. The st. are then cast off the following row, as explained in Fig. 48.

Variations of Tunisian Stitch. First work two rows as explained above for simple Tunisian Stitch. On the third row, first lift up the second vertical thread, then the first, so that the two threads cross. The fourth row back is unchanged. Rep. the two alternating rows for the following rows (Fig. 49).

Oblique, Crossed Tunisian Stitch. Proceed as for preceding stitch up to fourth row. On fifth, lift up the first st., then the third, and lastly the second, then the fifth and then the fourth, and, following, the seventh and then the sixth. The return row is unchanged. Rep. in this way, alternately, and oblique lines are formed on the surface of the Tunisian Stitch (Fig. 50).

Tunisian Stitch with Balls in Relief. Proceed as for Simple Tunisian Stitch. The balls are worked on the return row, thus: on reaching the point where the balls are to be worked, make three or four ch. st. before closing the st., then work five and rep. On the following row, lift up all the st. whose number should equal that on the prec. row, taking the ch. st. on to the right side of the work. On the following rows, alternate the position of the balls: therefore the number of st. must always be counted, so as to obtain accurate work (Fig. 51).

Increasing and Decreasing in Tunisian Stitch. To decrease at the two sides of a piece of work, proceed thus: work a forward row on the right side. At the right, take the first and second vertical threads together making a single st. and continue the row up to the last two st., which are taken together, working back with a single st. To increase take up the horizontal thread at the point indicated, so that a new st. is formed.

Collar and cuff set for child or young lady. From the detail, in actual size, given below, it is easy to follow the design and count the stitches, without being an expert. The set requires 1 ball of Coats Mercer Crochet, No. 20, in white; about a yard and a half of black velvet ribbon to thread through the holes

CHAPTER XXIX

Irish Lace

Light, delicate and airy, Irish lace has a typical appearance which distinguishes it immediately from all other kinds of lace made by crochet. Some examples of the work find a place in art collections, and can very well compete with needle-made laces in their fineness and lightness.

The typical Irish lace, coming from the "Emerald Isle", was once made with specially produced threads, but these can now be substituted very well by Coats Mercer-Crochet in the higher numbers.

For good crochet workers who know all the stitches, Irish lace will not present any great difficulties. Stylised flowers, rosebuds, decorative curves worked in close stitches, standing out in relief, are placed over a wide-spaced and very thin net to make a rich and decorative whole. All the motifs are worked separately and then fixed into place on the net with small hidden stitches, or they may be placed over a design on squared paper, and then joined together by bars worked in crochet.

Necessary Materials. So that the best results are obtained, Irish lace should be worked in Coats Mercer-Crochet, Nos. 20, 40 or 60. The hooks used should be very fine, Nos. 1.25, 1.00 or 0.75. Also a thin cord of twisted thread will be needed, chosen from among the lower numbers of Coats Mercer-Crochet.

Method of working Irish Lace. The stitches used are the normal Chain Stitch, double crochet, treble, picots and double crochet worked on cording. Like all hand work, Irish lace will only be perfect when worked by an experienced worker who can keep the work fresh and clean.

One of the chief elements in working Irish lace is the netting. Here we give three patterns, from among the commonest.

1. Over a length of ch. go back to the 4th st. behind hook, with a s.s., then work (*) 9 ch. miss 5 st. on base, 1 d.c. 4 ch. 1 d.c. into same st. Rep. from (*). On 2nd row work 13 st. at turn then 1 d.c. at centre of arc underneath, 4 ch. a 2nd d.c. very near to first, 9 ch. 1 d.c. into sp. following, and so on. Rep. the 2nd row to required length.

2. Over a length of ch. go back to 3rd st. behind hook (thus working a picot) then 5 ch. miss 4 st. on base, and work 1 d.c. (*) 5 ch. 1 picot (3 st. going back to 3rd with a s.s.) 5 ch. miss 4 st. on base and 1 d.c. Rep. from (*). Into 2nd row work 8 ch. at turn, than 1 d.c. into first sp., then 5 ch. 1 picot 5 ch. 1 d.c. into following sp. and rep.

3. Over a stretch of ch. st. worked to required length (*) go back to 5th st. behind hook with 1 s.s. (picot) then 7 ch. working into 5th st. counting back from hook, with 1 s.s. (another picot) work again into base of first picot with another s.s. 3 ch. miss 4 st. on base, 1 d.c. 8 ch. and rep. from (*). At the turn work 11 ch. into the 2 ch. left between

Fig. 1. American place settings: the place mat is in white linen cloth with a crochet border of the Irish lace type. The various pieces are all finished off with a crochet edge

Fig. 2. From this dtail, in actual size, it is easy to see how t~e lace is worked, uing Coats Merce~ Crochet, No. 60. T~e way to work the rosbuds, joined by trebls and picots, is cleary explained in the cha~ter on "Irish Lace"

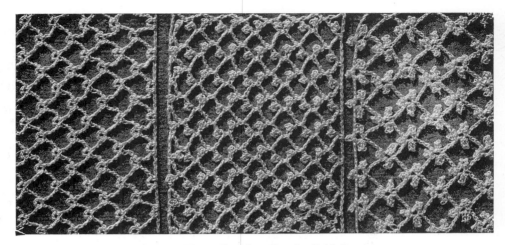

Fig. 3. Examples of netting for Irish lace

Fig. 4. Motifs for Irish lace worked in Coats Mercer-Crochet, explained in the following pages

the 2 picots, with a s.s. then 4 ch. going back with a s.s. into same st. forming a picot (**), 8 ch. going back into 5th st. with a s.s., 7 ch. 1 s.s. in 5th ch. from hook and work into base of first picot again, work as in previous row with a s.s. 3 ch. work into the 2 ch. between next 2 picots, with a s.s. then 4 ch. into same st. forming a picot. Rep. from (**).

Here we explain the method of working the examples of Irish lace given on the preceding page. The explanations follow the order of the pieces in the picture (Fig. 4).

Trefoil. Wrap the thread two or three times round little finger of left hand, fix it with a d.c. and fill circle with 30 d.c. fixed to first d.c. with a s.s.

2nd round. Take a cord under the threads and work 30 other d.c. into first lot worked.

3rd round. 24 ch. st. miss 1 d.c. of base circle and then 9 d.c. three times. Now take the cord together with the 24 ch. and work 33 d.c. into sp., 7 d.c. into the 9 and rep. all round. Cut cord.

4th round. 1 d.c. 3 ch. (16 times) 5 d.c. into the 7 on prec. row.

Last round. 1 d.c. into first sp., 3 ch. 1 d.c. into second and so on. 5 s.s. into the 5 d.c. of prec. row.

Work the stem with 29 ch. st. covered by 29 d.c. using the same cord.

Leaf. Commence with 15 ch.

1st row. 1 d.c. into 2nd ch. from hook, 1 d.c. into each ch. to within last ch., 3 d.c. into last ch. (tip of leaf), 1 d.c. into each ch. along opposite side of foundation, 1 d.c. into same place as last d.c. Hereafter pick up only the back loop of each d.c.; 1 d.c. into each of next 11 d.c., 1 ch, turn.

2nd row. 1 d.c. into each d.c. to within centre d.c. of 3 d.c. group. Into next d.c. work 1 d.c. 1 ch. and 1 d.c., 1 d.c. into each d.c. on other side to within 4 d.c. from centre d.c. at tip of leaf, 1 ch., turn.

3rd row. 1 d.c. into each d.c. to within 1 ch., into 1 ch. sp. work 1 d.c. 1 ch. and 1 d.c., 1 d.c. into each d.c. on other side to within last 3 d.c., 1 ch., turn.

4th row. As 3rd row.

5th row. As 3rd row, making 7 ch. instead of 1 ch.

6th row. 1 d.c. into each d.c. to within 7 ch., into 7 ch. loop work 2 d.c. 5 ch. 3 d.c. 5 ch. 3 d.c. 5 ch. and 2 d.c., 1 d.c. into each d.c. on other side of leaf to within last 3 d.c. Fasten off.

Rosebud. 8 ch. close into circle with a s.s. into

first st. 6 ch. 1 tr. into loop, 3 tr. into loop, so on until 6 sp. are formed. Fasten last st. to third of the 6 ch. worked at beginning.

1st round. Into each sp. work 1 d.c. 1 hlf tr. 3 tr. 1 hlf tr. 1 d.c. (a total of 6 petals).

2nd round. 5 ch. 1 d.c. between first two petals Rep. all round.

3rd round. Into each sp. work 1 d.c. 1 hlf tr. 5 tr. 1 hlf tr. 1 d.c.

4th round. 7 ch. 1 d.c. between petals. Rep. all round.

5th round. Into each sp. work 1 d.c. 1 hlf tr. 7 tr. 1 hlf tr. 1 d.c.

Daisy. Wrap thread round little finger of left hand, fix with a d.c., fill in circle with 24 d.c. Now, on to the usual cording work 16 d.c., turn work and work 16 d.c. into the preceding ones, carrying the cord along. Fix down the small leaf formed with a d.c. to the central circle. Turn work, make 4 d.c. into the first 4 d.c. of the leaf, then continue to work on the cord only for 16 d.c. Turn work and make 16 d.c. into the 2nd leaf. Continue thus until 12 leaves are formed. For the stem work 25 ch. and work back over them with 25 d.c. on the cord.

Flower with Three Leaves. Begin from the stem: 50 ch. working back with 50 d.c. and carrying cord along under threads. Turn. 12 d.c. into first 12 below. Turn. 1 ch. 11 d.c., 4 d.c. into 12th st., 4 d.c. into following st., 11 d.c. into st. below. Turn. 1 ch. 12 d.c., at turn work 2 st. in 1, five times, then 12 d.c. from the other side, 1 d.c. near to the stem and then work on the stem with 38 d.c. 6 d.c. into same st. at turn. 38 d.c. into the 38 below, 1 d.c. near to stem, 4 ch. miss two st. 1 d.c. all round: a total of 12 sp. Into each sp. 1 d.c. 2 tr. 1 d.c. Work three small leaves separately and attach with small stitches. On to the cord work 6 d.c. Turn. 1 ch. 6 d.c. on opposite side. Turn 5 d.c. on to base below. 3 d.c. into sixth st., 3 into the following one, 5 d.c. into opposite side.

Flower with Rosette and Five Leaves.

Necessary Materials. Coats Mercer-Crochet, No. 40; No. 1.00 crochet hook.

20 ch. going back with 20 d.c., taking cord along under threads. Into the twentieth st. work 4 d.c. Turn work and work 20 d.c. on opposite side into the rib of the ch. st. Turn. 1 ch. 20 d.c., taking the ribs of the st. 2 d.c. in 1 st. for 4 st. at turn. 20 d.c.,

Fig. 5. Other motifs in Irish lace worked in Coats Mercer-Crochet

from opposite side. Turn. 4 ch. miss 3 st. 1 d.c. rep. all round. Cut thread. Work the other four leaves in the same way, attaching the last two sp. to the two of the prec. leaf. When the five leaves have all been attached, fill in the sp. with 4 d.c. each. For the rosette which has five leaves, proceed as explained above: also for the stem which has 30 st.

The following explanations are for Fig. 5 in the order of the illustrations.

Large Flower with Seven Petals. Make seven petals in the following way. Begin with a base of 17 ch. Turn on the seventh behind the hook with 1 tr. (*) 2 ch. miss 1 st. 1 tr., into the nearby st. Rep. 4 times from (*). A total of 6 sp. Turn. 1 ch. 3 d.c. in each of the first 5 sp., 10 d.c. into sixth, 3 d.c. from the opposite side to the 5 sp. Turn. 3 ch. into each d.c. 1 tr. Turn. 1 ch. 4 d.c., 1 picot

all round. On completing the seven petals all the same, as shown in the illustration, join them slightly overlapping. There will be a hole of about ½ inch in diameter at the centre. Work the centre separately in this way.

10 ch. Join into a circle. Attach the usual cord and work into the circle taking the cord under the stitches, with 22 d.c. Complete the round thus and then work 10 d.c. on the cord only, turn (*) 1 d.c. into second st. counting from hook. 1 d.c. into each d.c. taking the rib of the st., then 2 d.c. taking 2 d.c. of the central circle (thus completing one pistil). Turn. Miss 2 st. and work 1 d.c. into the st. nearby, then 1 d.c. into each of the two st. following, 7 d.c. on cord only. Turn and rep. from (*) until 11 pistils have been worked. Join the last to the first with a few stitches worked with needle and thread, and appliqué the disc thus formed to

374

Pretty blouse all worked in Irish lace with Coats Mercer-Crochet, No. 40. Two different stitches were used in making it: the properly called "Irish Lace" for the sleeves and front trimming, and a heavier stitch in blocks of treble in different directions for the body of the blouse. The detail reproduced below shows the two stitches in actual size

the centre of the seven petals, fixing with hidden stitches.

Crest. Work 31 ch. going back into the sixth, counting from hook with 1 tr. 2 ch. miss two st. 1 tr. A total of 14 sp. should be worked. Turn. Into each sp. work 4 d.c. Turn. Into each d.c. work a tr. A total of 56 tr. Turn. 2 ch. miss 3 st. 1 tr. into fourth, 3 ch. 1 dbl. tr. into fifth, 1 tr. into sixth and seventh, 1 dbl. tr. into eighth, 1 tr. into ninth, 2 ch. miss 2 st. 1 hlf tr. Rep. all round 5 times. Into each sp. work 3 d.c. 1 picot, 3 d.c. and continue with 3 d.c. into each sp. on the bottom part too.

Flower. Begin from stem, with 50 ch. st. going back into the same st. with 50 d.c. taking a cord along under the st. At the end of the 50 d.c. work 5 d.c. into last st. Turn work and work 50 d.c. on opposite side of the rib of the ch. st. (*) Work 15 ch. Fix last st. to sixth d.c. of stem. Fill in arc formed with 24 d.c. Turn. 24 d.c. into the d.c. just worked. Turn. Go back with again 4 d.c. 1 picot 5 times. Thus the work has been taken back to the centre of the flower. Work a picot of 5 st. which will remain between the two rays of the flower, then rep. from (*) attaching the different rays to the second picot of the prec. one.

Second Flower. Begin from the stem with 50 ch. st. Work back with 50 d.c. taking the cord under the st. Work 5 d.c. into last st. turn work and make 50 d.c. on the opposite side, into the rib of the ch. st. (*) 15 ch. 1 d.c. after 2 st. Turn. 3 ch. (=1 tr.) 23 tr. into sp. formed. Attach at base after 2 d.c. Turn. 23 d.c. into tr. Fix at base with a s.s. then work 15 ch. going on after 2 d.c. Turn. 3 ch. (=1 tr.) 23 tr. into sp. formed, attach on back of first sp. formed. Turn. 24 d.c. and fix again to base. Rep. another 6 times.

Large Trefoil. Commence with 15 ch., hereafter work over a cord (or 4 strands of same thread).

1st row. 1 d.c. into 2nd ch. from hook, 1 d.c. into each ch. to within last ch., 5 d.c. into last ch., 1 d.c. into each ch. along opposite side of foundation, 3 d.c. over cord only. Hereafter pick up only the back loop of each d.c.: 1 d.c. into each d.c. to within 4 d.c. from centre d.c. at tip of leaf, 1 ch., turn.

2nd row. 1 d.c. into each d.c. to within centre of 3 d.c. (over cord), 3 d.c. into centre d.c., 1 d.c. into each d.c. on other side to within 4 d.c. from centre d.c. at tip of leaf, 1 ch., turn.

3rd row. d.c. to within centre of 3 d.c. group, 3 d.c. into centre d.c., d.c. on other side to within last 3 d.c., 1 ch., turn.

4th to 6th row. As 3rd row. Fasten off.

Make 2 more leaves like this.

Sew sides of leaves together to form a triple leaf.

Small Trefoil. 8 ch. Close into circle, 18 d.c. into circle, 3 ch. (=1 tr.) 4 tr. into 5 d.c. Turn. 3 ch. (=1 tr.) 7 tr. into the 5. Turn. 3 ch. (=1 tr.) 9 tr. into the 7. Rep. 3 times, going down to the base of the circle with s.s. After the third leaf, work the stem with 15 ch. Work on cord 15 d.c. Go back in this way to the base of the leaves; work 9 loops round each one with 3 ch. and 1 d.c. and fill them in with 3 d.c. each on the second row.

Large Daisy. Work a disc in d.c. of about $\frac{1}{2}$ inch in diameter. From this disc all the small leaves start, worked in the same way; there will be 21 in all. Work 17 d.c. on the cord, turn the work and go back on to the d.c. with 1 d.c. 1 half tr., 8 tr. 7 d.c. fixing with 1 s.s. to central circle. Turn. 7 d.c. into d.c. then work on cord only 10 d.c. Turn work and go back with 1 d.c. 1 half tr. and 8 tr. 7 d.c. The work is now at the centre again. Continue thus until the disc has been completely filled in with leaves. For the stem, proceed as for the other flowers and attach to back of the daisy.

Another blouse entirely worked in Irish lace. As will be seen from the detail in actual size at the bottom of the page, the blouse consists of numerous squares in Irish lace, joined together. The collar, the sleeves and the waistline are decorated with a fringe of spaces of chain stitches fixed by double crochet; these are clearly seen in the illustration. Use 8 balls of Coats Mercer-Crochet, No. 60

CHAPTER XXX

Orvieto Lace

The airy Orvieto laces, called collectively by their Latin name *Ars Wetana*, are exceptional, characteristic products of Italian handwork.

A group of Umbrian gentlewomen founded, financed and supported a school, situated near the Cathedral of Orvieto, for the production, sale and designing of laces in the Italian tradition.

Birds, figures, leaves, flowers, classical ornaments, worked in close, even stitches, stand out in this lace from a very fine network background, admirably suited to its purpose of clearly showing up the beauty of an artistic design.

Orvieto lace, so fine and delicate, is worked entirely in crochet with a thread specially produced for such work, and requires special skill and an even and light hand, both for the filled in and the netted parts.

Since the technique of working Orvieto lace is related to that of Irish lace, which we have described in the previous pages, we are going to describe it here, although it differs in the very smallness of the work and in the background, which in Orvieto lace is absolutely without the picot which are an essential part of Irish lace.

As for Venetian laces, in which the work is subdivided among the workers, so that each has some particular task, so for Orvieto lace too there are specialists in the decorative parts, in the background and in the finishing off.

Necessary Materials. To work Orvieto lace a special thread is necessary. To work with such very fine thread, very fine crochet hooks must be used. Lastly, the cloth used must be rather strong and resistant.

How to work Orvieto Lace. The patterns for Orvieto lace have been inspired, as has already been seen, by the artistic traditions of Italy. They are, for the greater part, taken from designs on capitols, bas-reliefs, allegoric symbols taken from stone fragments and ornaments in the Orvieto Cathedral. These designs, suitable for table centres, mats, appliqués for tablecloths, serviettes, handkerchiefs, etc., are reproduced in their entirety over a piece of material, and the working of the filled-in parts, after having traced them with a rather thick tacking thread, begins by joining the thread on to the tacking thread and working round the design in double crochet back and forth. After completing the filled-in parts, the outline is worked; this generally consists of rows of double crochet decorated with leaves or picots. At this point the work is handed over to the worker of the so-called "mistake" stitch, that is, the background, which appears as an irregularly-patterned tulle, formed by one or two Chain Stitches, and one double crochet. The unevenness of the stitch, which is apparent even in the most perfect work, is due to the fact that the worker must go through the

Table centre in Orvieto lace

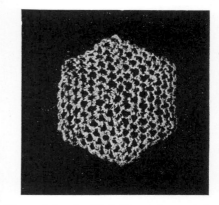

Fig. 1 (left). Table centre in Orvieto lace

Fig. 2 (above). Medallion taken out from background in "misty" stitch. It consists of numerous equal hexagons

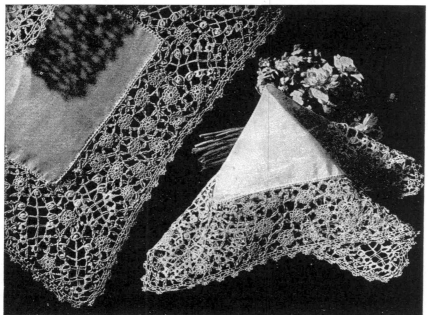

Fig. 3. Handkerchief with border in Orvieto lace composed of rosettes joined by bars in Chain Stitch

background made with small or large spaces, all very irregular, and join all the curves of the design into one harmonious whole.

Another characteristic background of Orvieto lace is the so-called "misty" background. This is formed by numerous perfectly equal hexagons, worked separately and then joined together with a needle or crochet hook. These hexagons shown in Fig. 2 are very simple to work. Six chain stitches are worked and closed into a circle. Into the circle work 3 ch. 1 d.c. six times. On the following row work 3 ch. 1 d.c. into first sp., 3 ch. 1 d.c. into same sp., 3 ch. 1 d.c. into next sp. and so on.

On the third row work 3 ch. 1 d.c. into first sp.,

3 ch. 1 d.c. into same sp., 3 ch. 1 d.c. into same sp., 3 ch 1 d.c. into following sp., 3 ch. 1 d.c. into same sp., and so on for the whole row. On the following rows, rep. the same pattern so that the rays of the small hexagons stand out, divided by simple sp. In the fine table centre shown here in Fig. 1, the rather open background can be seen with bars of double Chain Stitch joined in webs.

The border of the handkerchief shown in Fig. 3 is formed by numerous rosettes worked separately, and then appliquéd on to the material and joined by bars worked in Chain Stitch.

When the table centre, or any other piece of work, has been completed, it is removed from the cloth by cutting away the tacking stitches on the back.

On completing any piece of work, it should be immediately immersed into a water and glue solution, and then ironed rather dry with a rather hot iron, without ever using pins.

Fig. 4. Method of working Orvieto lace: the design is traced on to paper and covered, little by little, with the filled-in parts, which are then joined together by the background

Fig. 5. Table centre "Oakleaves"

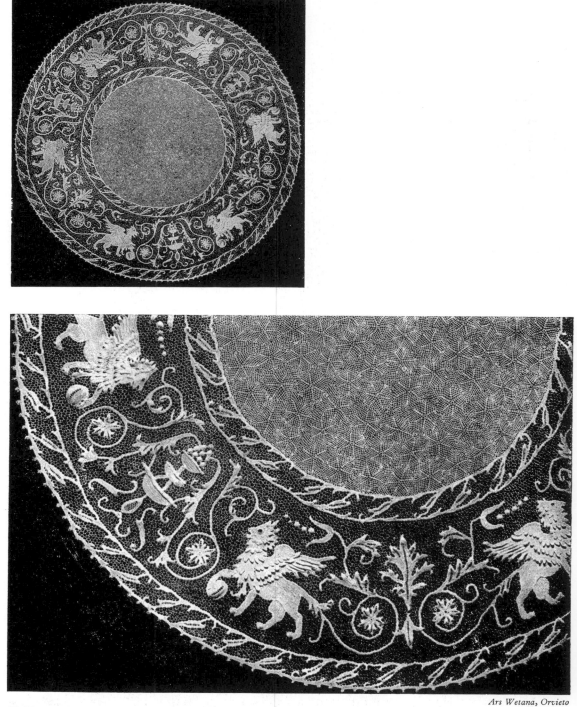

*Table centre in Orvieto lace. This is an enlarged detail of the table centre at the top of the page.
The centre part is worked in "misty" background, and in the border, the filled-in parts stand out on the
background worked in "Mistake" Stitch*

Geremei Partinelli, Orvieto

Table centre with a beautiful, rich design in wide curves. At the top of the page a detail of the work is shown

383

9 *Knitting*

CHAPTER XXXI

Knitting

Knitting has been done by women in all ages. It is simple, easy, housewifely work, which has never been destroyed by time; when threatened by war or plague the craft took refuge in the convents where it continued to flourish and find a use. Fifty years ago, knitting socks was the favourite occupation of our grandmothers, but today every woman does some kind of knitting. Fashion and, above all, sport have given impetus to an infinite variety of knitted garments, which, with the changes in fashion and feminine taste, leads to a continuous supply of beautiful, elegant hand-knitted articles.

Socks, stockings, children's and ladies' jerseys, babies' outfits, shirts, scarves, gloves, hats, all can be worked in wool and thousands of journals and leaflets offer patterns of all kinds, original creations, following the rapid and ever-changing vagaries of fashion.

Knitting can be done by hand or by machine. Although machine-knitting has today gained great importance in modern clothing production, here we shall confine ourselves to giving our readers some hints on hand-worked knitting together with some patterns of stitches which will allow them a wide choice for different types of work.

Necessary Materials. For knitting, the most important essentials are the needles or sock needles, which may be of steel, aluminium, cellu-loid, wood or plastic, and which are sold in the various sizes for the type of work to be done and the wool used.

Apart from wool, the most suitable threads for knitting are Coats Mercer-Crochet, Nos. 10 and 20 (20 gm.), in white, écru and fast colours.

Handknitting. Before beginning a piece of work, it is wise to work a small pattern in order to choose the thickness of thread and needles correctly and to calculate the exact number of stitches required.

Thus, by measuring the pattern with a tape-measure it will be easy to calculate the number of stitches per 25 mm, according to the tension of the

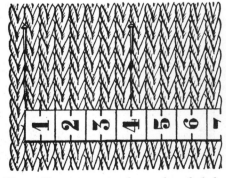

Fig. 1. How to meausre the number of stitches per 25 mm

Corner of a bed-spread worked in separate knitted squares which are then sewn together

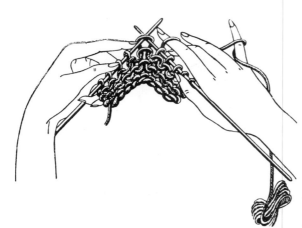

Fig. 2. Position of the hands when knitting with short needles

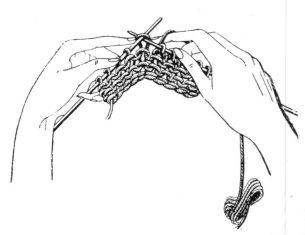

Fig. 3. Position of the hands when knitting with long needles

Fig. 4. Casting on knitting with one needle only

knitted piece. Having obtained this measure, it is then a simple matter to calculate how many stitches will be required for the garment to be worked (Fig. 1).

Try to avoid joining the thread in the course of a piece of work, or at least to get the joins at the end or beginning of a row where they will work in with the edging stitches.

If a join cannot be avoided, no knots should be made. Instead, place the two ends of the thread together, one in either direction, and work them together for four or five stitches, leaving the two ends on the wrong side.

If this joining should be too thick for the work, open out the thread and take only half of it for an inch or two, so that the double thickness of the join will be equal to the thickness of a complete thread. In either case, the ends left on the back are then threaded into a needle and taken through the backs of the stitches.

To make the horizontal lines in different colours, it is not necessary to break off the thread at the end of each colour. Work a double stitch at the end of the row to carry along the thread from one row to another; this can only be done on Stocking Stitch.

Position of the Hands in Knitting. Wrap the thread round the little finger of the right hand, then take it under the third and middle fingers, and over the first finger, which should touch the needle held in the right hand. The left hand, holding the left needle, thrusts the knitting along towards the right-hand needle, whilst the right hand forms the stitch by raising the thread and placing it over the right-hand needle and pulling it through the loop. The position of the hands shown in Fig. 2 is particularly suitable for working with four needles or with short needles. The position given in Fig. 3 is for work with long needles used two at a time.

Abroad, and especially in Switzerland and Germany, the thread is wrapped round the first finger of the left hand, which is held up in order to keep the yarn taut; in Italy, especially in the south, in Apulia, still another system is in use. The women, when working, wrap the yarn round their necks first of all and work the different movements on this. Whatever the method followed, however, the important thing is that the work is well and evenly done.

Casting-on. This is the action of setting on the stitches which serve as a basis for the work.

Simple Casting-on with One Needle. Form a loop with the yarn around left thumb, leaving a length hanging which is sufficient for the number of stitches to be set on. Any join in this thread would ruin the evenness of the work and should be avoided at all costs. With the right hand, place the needle into the loop, then take the yarn over the needle and through the loop, which is then let go, pulling slightly on the left-hand thread. Repeat the movement until the number of stitches desired has been cast on (Fig. 4). If this casting on has been rather loose, then use needles a size larger or two needles together, slipping one out on completion of the row.

If a raised edge is desired, use the yarn double for the casting-on stitches (Fig. 5).

Casting-on with Two Needles. First work a simple casting-on stitch, then take a second needle, place the point of the second needle into the stitch just made, wrap round the thread and pull the stitch through the loop, thus forming a new stitch, which is passed on to the left-hand needle, the right needle remaining free the whole time (Fig. 6).

Casting-on in Slip Stitch. This very simple type of casting-on is used when increases have to be made in the course of the work, for example when making buttonholes. Work a loop of yarn on the left thumb, as for simple casting-on, then place the needle in from below, crossing the thread, and leaving the stitch drop, pull the thread with the left hand, to form a stitch on the right-hand needle (Fig. 7).

Casting on for use with or without elastic. For setting on collars, cuffs, socks, gloves, etc., we advise another type of casting-on, which. apart from being very strong, will not unravel, and allows for threading through an elastic, as is sometimes necessary, for example, for socks.

Cast on a number of stitches which is equal to half the total number required, using two needles, as explained above. Thus, if 100 stitches are required, cast on 50. Then work thus:

1st row. (*) k. 1, cast on 1 by slip stitch method (Fig. 7); rep. from (*) to end.

2nd row. (*) k. 1, yfd, sl. P, yb.; rep. from (*) to end. Rep. 2nd row twice more.

There will now be 100 stitches on the needle.

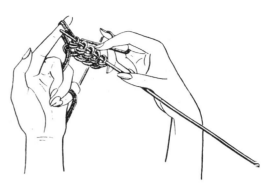

Fig. 5. Casting on with double yarn

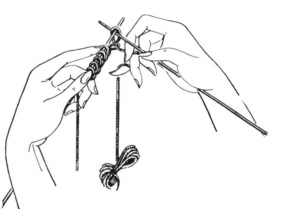

Fig. 6. Casting on with two needles

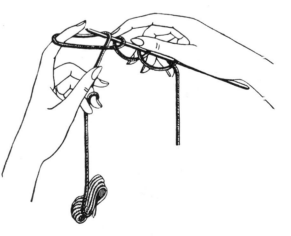

Fig. 7. Casting on slip stitches

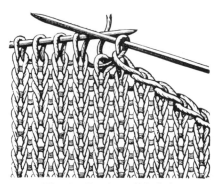

Fig. 8. Casting off knitting

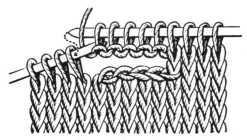

Fig. 9 (a). Horizontal buttonhole

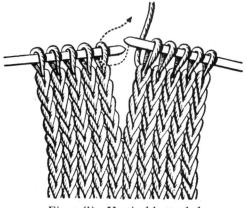

Fig. 9 (b). Vertical buttonhole

3rd row. Work slipped stitch as a plain stitch, slip following stitch as explained above.

4th row. As third.

If elastic has to be run through, repeat the third and fourth rows another two or three times, before beginning on the actual knitting.

On completing this casting-on, cut the thread at the beginning of the casting on and pull it out from the stitches with the help of a sewing needle or stocking needle.

Knitting must have very perfect edges. To obtain these, never work the first stitch of the row. If the second stitch is plain, take the needle into the back of the first stitch and pass it on to the right-hand needle without working it, then working the second stitch plain. If the second stitch is purl, take the needle through the first stitch as for a plain stitch, before slipping it off on to the right-hand needle, working the second stitch as purl.

In Garter Stitch, that is, all worked in plain knitting, work the last stitch on the row into the back, then at the beginning of the next row, slip off the first stitch without working it and work the second stitch in plain knitting. In this way the edge will be very firm, and even.

Casting Off. When the work is completed it must be cast off. To do this, pass a stitch, without working it, from the left-hand needle on to the right-hand one, work the following stitch, and pass the first over the second, and so on, until all the stitches have been taken off (Fig. 8).

Plain knitting is cast off in plain knitting, and purl in purl. This is also the case for a rib, which thus preserves its elasticity.

When casting off has to be done "on the cross", for example, for shoulders, avoid making steps by leaving the stitches forming the taking-off on the needle, and cast off all at the same time.

Increasing and Decreasing in Knitting. To increase when knitting, one of two methods can be used: either by making a stitch by taking the yarn over the needle, or by knitting twice into one stitch. This last method is preferable, because by using the first a hole is formed, spoiling the even look of the work.

Decreasing is worked in Three Ways. When the decreases must slope to the right knit two stitches together. When the decreasing must slope to the left knit two together through back of loops.

A third way of decreasing is to pass one stitch over the other as explained for casting off.

The increases and decreases should always be worked into the second and third stitch on the row, never into the first, in order to keep the edge even.

When decreasing or increasing must be made on both sides of a piece of work (a pullover, sleeves, jacket, etc.), mark the place with a coloured thread so that both sides will be alike. This thread will then be removed on completion of the work.

Making a Stitch. This made stitch is worked by placing the yarn over the needle and continuing to work. On the next row this is worked as a normal stitch.

This made stitch, however, leaves a hole in smooth knitting and serves for working knitting with a pattern of holes as well as for increasing, as explained above.

Buttonholes. For fastenings on jackets and pullovers, first work the side where the buttons go (the left for ladies' garments, the right for men's), so as to be able to calculate exactly the distance between the holes on the opposite side.

Horizontal Buttonhole. On reaching the point where the hole has to be made, cast off two or three stitches (buttonholes must always be worked rather small, as they become much bigger with use). On the following row, cast on these stitches again and continue to work normally. Draw up the stitches at the sides of the buttonhole rather tightly (Fig. 9 (a)).

Vertical Buttonholes. On reaching the point at which the buttonhole must commence, do not complete the row, but turn back and work four rows on one side of the work only. Then cut the yarn and work the other side, near to the edge of the garment, making the same number of rows so that a vertical cut of about $\frac{1}{2}$ inch is made. On completing the space, go back to work the whole of the next row, drawing up the stitches above the space very tightly.

It is sometimes necessary to divide the yarn already wound into balls into two or three threads. This is easy if performed by two people: each one then takes one thread of the yarn to wind and it is as well to stick a pin into the ball to be divided to stop the thread every three or four yards. Thus the operation can be carried out fairly easily without breaking or knotting the thread.

When it is necessary to use again wool which has been used already, wind it into hanks, tie and wash it, drying it with a weight attached so that the yarn dries straight. If it is impossible to wash

Fig. 10 (a). Finishing off a hem with a row of Purl Stitches

Fig. 10 (b). Finishing off a hem with "cat's tooth" edging

Fig. 11. Finishing off with Chain Stitch under the loops of knitting

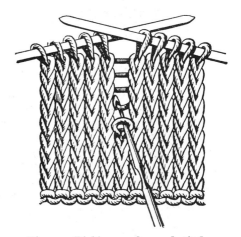

Fig. 12. Picking up dropped stitches

389

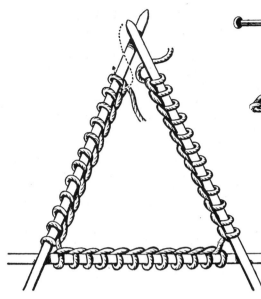

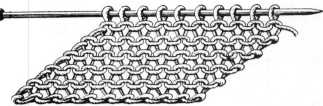

Fig. 14 (a) (above). Knitting worked diagonally

Fig. 13 (left). Casting on on three needles

the yarn, wind it into balls, passing it through a damp cloth and pulling it slightly.

Various Finishings. To make hems on jackets or to finish off sleeves, cuffs, collars, etc., we advise the following method:

1. Work ten rows in Stocking Stitch, then the eleventh in purl on the right side of the work, and then continue with the pattern. The eleventh row marks the exact point for folding in the hem (Fig. 10 (a)).

2. Work ten rows in Stocking Stitch, then work the eleventh taking two stitches together on the right side and make one stitch by throwing wool over. Rep. all along the row. The line of holes thus obtained marks the exact point for turning in the hem, leaving an indented edge called "cat's tooth", which is very pretty (Fig. 10 (b)).

3. A third method of finishing off collars and cuffs is to change the position of the Stocking Stitch, i.e. after working Stocking Stitch on the right side for a certain length, work a row of the opposite kind and continue with Stocking Stitch on the other side of the work, for ten or twelve rows. Cast off the stitches rather tightly, and an effective roll is thus formed.

4. Another type of finishing off for knitting is that worked in crocheting. Double crochet trimmed with picots is, in fact, one of the most simple and common edgings. "Shrimp" Stitch, too, as

explained and illustrated in the chapter on crocheting, is a good edging to use.

5. Fig. 11 shows another method of finishing off knitting. Under the row of casting off, work a row of Chain Stitch using the same yarn as has been used for the knitting itself.

When, in the course of the work, a stitch is dropped, pick it up again with a crochet hook, as shown in Fig. 12.

Knitting is worked on two needles when working separate pieces of a garment. When working round, however, as for socks, gloves, etc., the knitting is worked on four needles. Cast on the stitches on three needles, so that there is an almost equal number of stitches on each needle, and then work with the fourth.

Fig. 13 shows the casting on of knitting on three needles. With the fourth, work the first twelve, then the needle which is thus freed from the stitches is used to work the next needle and so on for the third. The threads should be tightly drawn up between the needles, and it is a good system to work two or three stitches of the following needle on to the one being worked, so that the knitting is more even and without defects.

Working Diagonally. To knit diagonally, as for scarves, work as follows:

Cast on the number of stitches required for the desired width. On the first row make an increase

390

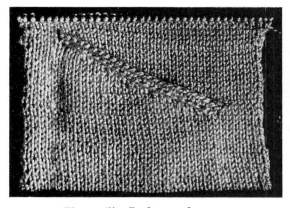

Fig. 14 (b). Pocket on the cross

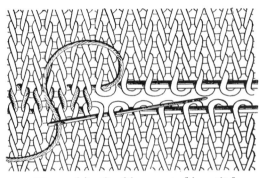

Fig. 15 (a). Grafting on stocking stitch

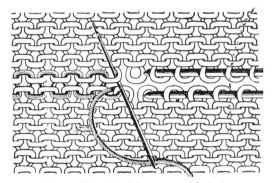

Fig. 15 (b). Grafting on purl knitting

in the second stitch; on the second row knit the second and third stitches together. In this way an increase is worked at one side and a decrease at the other, while the number of stitches on the needle remains unchanged. Pay attention not to confuse the two different operations which, if worked well, give a very effective piece of work on the cross. The best stitch for this type of work is

Garter Stitch, that is, plain knitting on both sides (Fig. 14 (a)).

Finishing Off Knitting. The finishing off of a piece of knitting is very important and should be done very carefully. When the various pieces of a garment have been completed (back, front, sleeves, etc.), they must be pressed before being joined together. First eliminate all unnecessary threads at joining, etc., and then go on to the pressing. Each piece must be pressed on the wrong side; fix the work to the ironing cloth with pins, taking care not to pull the work out of shape: place a slightly damp cloth over the work and press with a rather cool iron.

If there is a raised pattern, press over a very soft cloth with a very cool iron and without damping. Ribbing, which must remain elastic, should not be pressed, or only very lightly. Join the pieces by hand, using the same thread as the knitting, over-sewing the pieces together, or by Back Stitching about 6 mm from the edge of the material. If there are pockets, fix the edges firmly with hidden stitches.

Pockets. If the pockets are not external, in which case they are sewn on with hidden stitches, they open directly into the knitting. Work thus:

At the exact point where the pocket is to be placed, work, on a third needle, a number of stitches to correspond to the opening of the pocket (about 24 stitches); working them back and forth for about 19 mm, then cast off. Then, on to a third needle, cast on the same number of stitches as those cast off and work in Stocking Stitch for about 5 cm or to the required depth of the pocket. Finish with a row on the wrong side. Take up the work again at the point where it was cast off, and work the separate stitches. With a hidden stitch sew the back of the pocket, fixing the short piece of about 19 mm on the front.

Pockets on the Cross. At the exact spot where the pocket has to be placed, discontinue work on that row and cast off 24 stitches in eight goes. In other words, work the stitches preceding the pocket and which will remain unworked until the whole piece is cast off, cast off three stitches, finish the needle and go back. And so on until the 24 stitches have been cast off. Then, on to a third needle cast on 24 stitches, for the inside of the pocket, and work in Stocking Stitch for about

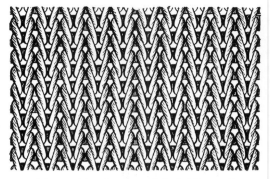

Fig. 16 (a). Stocking Stitch (diagram)

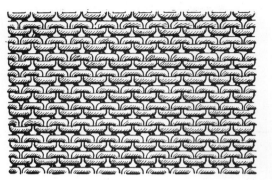

Fig. 16 (b). Purling (diagram)

7 cm. Then begin to work again on the stitches left aside at the beginning of the row and continue to work back and forth for 16 rows. This brings the work to the upper side of the pocket; continue to work all the stitches. The inside of the pocket is sewn to the garment with hidden stitches. Straighten the upper side of the pocket (Fig. 14 (b)) with crocheting.

Grafting. It is sometimes necessary to join two separate pieces of knitting. In this case, take up any unnecessary threads, then place the two pieces on to two needles, placing them so that the sides to be joined touch, and the stitches are opposite each other. Then using the same yarn, begin grafting, i.e. take the sewing needle with the thread into two stitches of the lower side, slipped off the needle, and then into the two stitches of the upper piece, also slipped off from the needle, moving along by one thread, to the left. Pay attention to keep the tension of the sewing thread always the same, so that the joining is perfect and unseen (Fig. 15 (a)).

Fig. 10 shows grafting worked on to purl (Fig. 15 (b)).

Here we give a list of abbreviations used in the following patterns:

k.—knit; p.—purl; st(s).—stitch(es); sl.—slip one stitch from left-hand needle to right-hand needle without working; yfd.—yarn forward by placing yarn over needle before working the following stitch; yb.—yarn back; rep.—repeat; p.s.s.o.—pass slipped stitch over, i.e. pass a stitch from the left-hand needle on to the right-hand needle without working it, work the next stitch and lift the slipped stitch over the worked stitch so that one stitch is formed instead of two; tog.—together; patt.—pattern; tbl.—through back of loop(s); alt.—alternate; yrn.—yarn round needle; sl. 1—slip one stitch knitwise; sl. p.—slip one stitch purlwise; st. st.—stocking stitch; M.—main colour; C.—contrasting colour.

All the following patterns are worked with two needles.

Plain Knitting. This is the simplest of all stitches. Place the right-hand needle into the stitch on the left-hand needle, from below, place yarn over needle from right to left, pull the yarn through the stitch and drop the loop of the stitch off the needle, passing the new loop on to the right-hand needle (Fig. 16 (a)).

Purl. This is generally worked on the wrong side of the work. Place the wool over the right-hand needle, taking the needle through the stitch on the left-hand needle from above; pass the yarn round the right-hand needle and pull the loop through on to the right-hand needle, slipping the loop off the left-hand needle (Fig. 16 (b)).

Some of the Most Usual Stitches

Stocking Stitch. This is worked by making one row knit or plain and one row purl, alternately. If the knit stitches are worked into the back of the stitches, then a very close piece of work will be

392

Fig. 17. Stocking Stitch worked into the backs of the stitches

Fig. 18. Garter Stitch: all plain knitting or all purl

Fig. 19

Fig. 20

Fig. 21

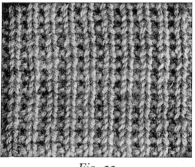

Fig. 22

given, stronger than the usual Stocking Stitch (Fig. 17).

Garter Stitch. This is obtained by working every row in plain knitting or every row in purl. It is very soft and elastic and suitable for children's clothing (Fig. 18).

Moss Stitch. This is worked by making a plain and purl stitch alternately, interchanging them on every row (Fig. 19).

Double Moss Stitch. Work two plain and two purl alternately, interchanging on every second row (Fig. 20).

Ribbing. Work two plain and two purl on the right side, and on the wrong side work the stitches in plain or purl as they come. This is used especially for the cuffs of gloves, socks and the waistbands of pullovers, etc., because of its great elasticity. Rib may be worked with only one knit and one purl stitch (Fig. 21).

Pattern 22
1st row. k. 1, p. 1.
2nd row. p.

Pattern 23. Cast on a multiple of 4, plus 2.
1st row. (*) k. 2, p. 2; rep. from (*) to last 2 sts, k. 2.
2nd row. p. 1, (*) k. 2, p. 2; rep. from (*) to last st., k. 1.

Pattern 24. Cast on an even number of sts.
1st row. k. 1 (*) yfd., sl. p., k. 1; rep. from (*) to last st., k. 1.
2nd row. k. 1 (*) yfd., sl. p., k. 2 tog.; rep. from (*) to last st., k. 1.
The second row forms the pattern and is repeated throughout.

Pattern 25. Cast on a multiple of 4.
1st and 2nd row. (*) k. 2, p. 2; rep. from (*) to end.
3rd row. p. 1, (*) k. 2, p. 2; rep. from (*) to last 3 sts., k. 2, p. 1.
4th row. k. 1, (*) p. 2, k. 2; rep. from (*) to last 3 sts., p. 2, k. 1.
5th and 6th row. (*) p. 2, k. 2; rep. from (*) to end.
7th and 8th row. As fourth and third row.

Pattern 26. Cast on a multiple of 8, plus 1.
1st row. k. 1, (*) p. 7, k. 1; rep. from (*) to end.
2nd row and alt. rows. p.
3rd row. k. 2, (*) p. 5, k. 3; rep. from (*) to last 7 sts., p. 5, k. 2.
5th row. k. 3, (*) p. 3, k. 5; rep from (*) to last 6 sts., p. 3, k. 3.
7th row. k. 4, (*) p. 1, k. 7; rep. from (*) to last 5 sts. p. 1, k. 4.
9th row. p. 4, (*) k. 1, p. 7; rep. from (*) to last 5 sts., k. 1, p. 4.
11th row. p. 3, (*) k. 3, p. 5; rep. from (*) to last 6 sts., k. 3, p. 3.
13th row. p. 2, (*) k. 5, p. 3; rep. from (*) to last 7 sts., k. 5, p. 2.
15th row. p. 1, (*) k. 7, p. 1; rep. from (*) to end.
16th row. As second row.

Pattern 27. Cast on a multiple of 6.
1st row. k.
2nd and alt. rows. p.

3rd and 5th row. (*) k. 2, p. 4; rep. from (*) to end.
7th row. As first.
9th and 11th row. p. 3, (*) k. 2, p. 4; rep. from last 3 sts., k. 2, p. 1.
12th row. p.

Pattern 28. Cast on a multiple of 6.
1st row. p. 1, (*) k. 1, p. 2; rep. from (*) ending last rep. p. 1.
2nd row. k. 1, (*) p. 1, k. 2; rep. from (*) ending last rep. k. 1.
3rd row. p. 1, (*) yfd., k. 1, p. 2, k. 1 sl. yfd. over these 4 sts., p. 2; rep. from (*) ending last rep. p. 1.
4th row. As second row.

Pattern 29. Cast on a multiple of 12, plus 1.
1st row. (*) k. 1, p. 1; rep. from (*) to last st., k. 1.
2nd and alt. rows. k. the p. sts. and p. the k. sts. of previous row.
3rd row. (*) k. 2, (p. 1, k. 1) 5 times; rep from (*) to last st., k. 1.
5th row. (*) k. 3, (p. 1, k. 1) 4 times, k. 1; rep. from (*) to last st., k. 1.
7th row. (*) k. 4, (p. 1, k. 1) 3 times, k. 2; rep. from (*) to last st., k. 1.
9th row. (*) k. 5, (p. 1, k. 1) twice, k. 3; rep. from (*) to last st., k. 1.
11th row. (*) k. 6, p. 1, k. 5; rep. from (*) to last st., k. 1.
13th to 14th row. As first and second row.
15th row. (*) (p. 1, k. 1) 3 times, k. 2, (p. 1, k. 1) twice; rep. from (*) to last st., p. 1.
17th row. (*) (k. 1, p. 1) twice, k. 4, (k. 1, p. 1) twice; rep. from (*) to last st., k. 1.
19th row. (*) (p. 1, k. 1) twice, k. 6, (p. 1, k. 1) once; rep. from (*) to last st., p. 1.
21st row. (*) k. 1, p. 1, k. 9, p. 1; rep. from (*) last st., k. 1.
23rd row. (*) p. 1, k. 11; rep. from (*) to last st., p. 1.
24th row. As second row.

Pattern 30. Cast on a multiple of 12, plus 2.
1st row. (*) p. 2, k. 10; rep. from (*) ending p. 2.
2nd row. (*) k. 2, p. 10; rep. from (*) ending k. 2.
Rep. these 2 rows 4 times more.
11th row. (*) p. 2, sl. next 5 sts. on to cable needle and keep to front of work, k. 5 then k. 5 sts. from cable needle; rep. from (*) to last 2 sts., p. 2.
12th row. As second row.

Pattern 31. Cast on a multiple of 3.
1st row. (*) k. 3, yfd., sl. 3 sts. from left-hand

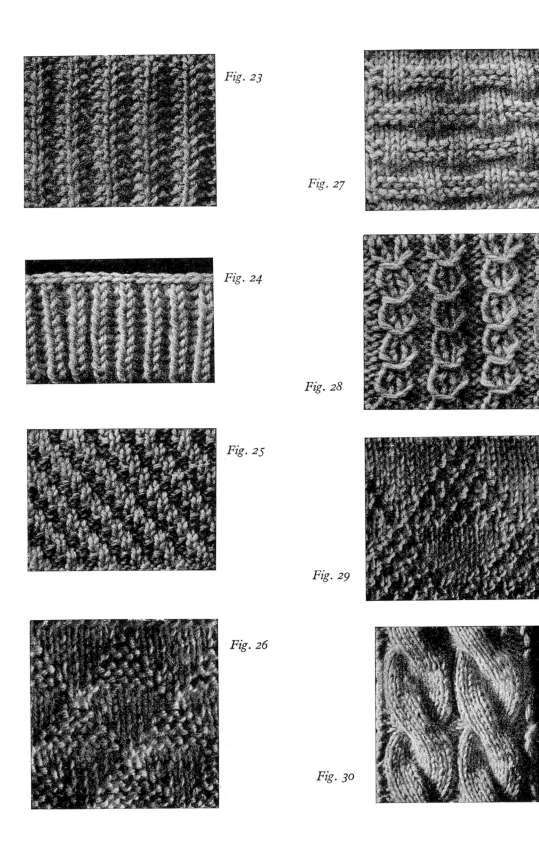

Fig. 23

Fig. 24

Fig. 25

Fig. 26

Fig. 27

Fig. 28

Fig. 29

Fig. 30

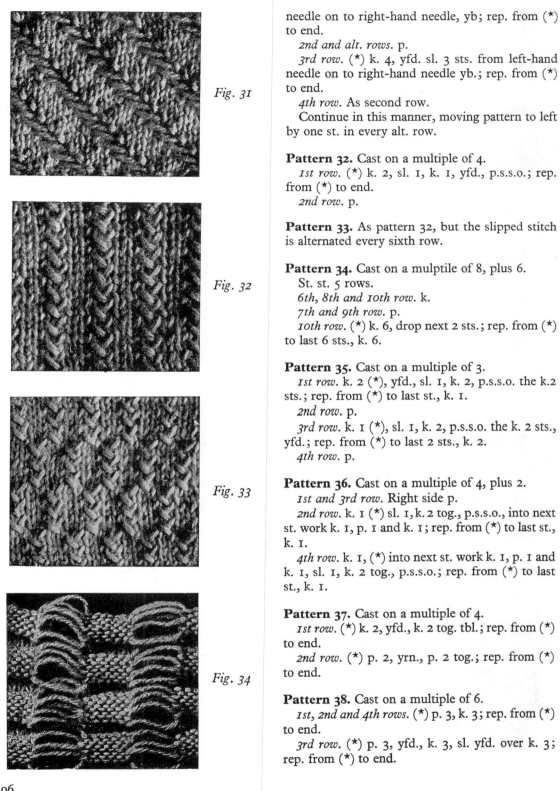

Fig. 31

Fig. 32

Fig. 33

Fig. 34

needle on to right-hand needle, yb; rep. from (*) to end.

2nd and alt. rows. p.

3rd row. (*) k. 4, yfd. sl. 3 sts. from left-hand needle on to right-hand needle yb.; rep. from (*) to end.

4th row. As second row.

Continue in this manner, moving pattern to left by one st. in every alt. row.

Pattern 32. Cast on a multiple of 4.

1st row. (*) k. 2, sl. 1, k. 1, yfd., p.s.s.o.; rep. from (*) to end.

2nd row. p.

Pattern 33. As pattern 32, but the slipped stitch is alternated every sixth row.

Pattern 34. Cast on a mulptile of 8, plus 6.

St. st. 5 rows.

6th, 8th and 10th row. k.

7th and 9th row. p.

10th row. (*) k. 6, drop next 2 sts.; rep. from (*) to last 6 sts., k. 6.

Pattern 35. Cast on a multiple of 3.

1st row. k. 2 (*), yfd., sl. 1, k. 2, p.s.s.o. the k.2 sts.; rep. from (*) to last st., k. 1.

2nd row. p.

3rd row. k. 1 (*), sl. 1, k. 2, p.s.s.o. the k. 2 sts., yfd.; rep. from (*) to last 2 sts., k. 2.

4th row. p.

Pattern 36. Cast on a multiple of 4, plus 2.

1st and 3rd row. Right side p.

2nd row. k. 1 (*) sl. 1, k. 2 tog., p.s.s.o., into next st. work k. 1, p. 1 and k. 1; rep. from (*) to last st., k. 1.

4th row. k. 1, (*) into next st. work k. 1, p. 1 and k. 1, sl. 1, k. 2 tog., p.s.s.o.; rep. from (*) to last st., k. 1.

Pattern 37. Cast on a multiple of 4.

1st row. (*) k. 2, yfd., k. 2 tog. tbl.; rep. from (*) to end.

2nd row. (*) p. 2, yrn., p. 2 tog.; rep. from (*) to end.

Pattern 38. Cast on a multiple of 6.

1st, 2nd and 4th rows. (*) p. 3, k. 3; rep. from (*) to end.

3rd row. (*) p. 3, yfd., k. 3, sl. yfd. over k. 3; rep. from (*) to end.

Fig. 35

Fig. 39

Fig. 36

Fig. 40

Fig. 37

Fig. 41

Fig. 38

Fig. 42

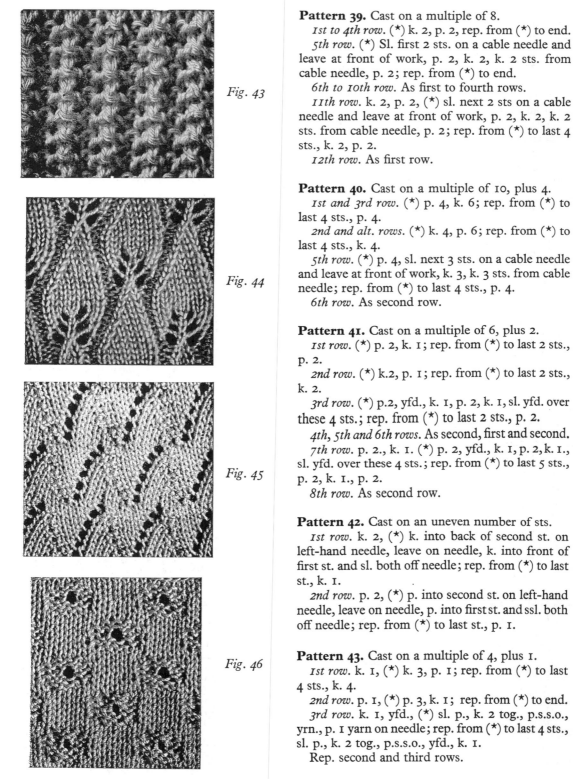

Fig. 43

Fig. 44

Fig. 45

Fig. 46

Pattern 39. Cast on a multiple of 8.

1st to 4th row. (*) k. 2, p. 2, rep. from (*) to end.

5th row. (*) Sl. first 2 sts. on a cable needle and leave at front of work, p. 2, k. 2, k. 2 sts. from cable needle, p. 2; rep. from (*) to end.

6th to 10th row. As first to fourth rows.

11th row. k. 2, p. 2, (*) sl. next 2 sts on a cable needle and leave at front of work, p. 2, k. 2, k. 2 sts. from cable needle, p. 2; rep. from (*) to last 4 sts., k. 2, p. 2.

12th row. As first row.

Pattern 40. Cast on a multiple of 10, plus 4.

1st and 3rd row. (*) p. 4, k. 6; rep. from (*) to last 4 sts., p. 4.

2nd and alt. rows. (*) k. 4, p. 6; rep. from (*) to last 4 sts., k. 4.

5th row. (*) p. 4, sl. next 3 sts. on a cable needle and leave at front of work, k. 3, k. 3 sts. from cable needle; rep. from (*) to last 4 sts., p. 4.

6th row. As second row.

Pattern 41. Cast on a multiple of 6, plus 2.

1st row. (*) p. 2, k. 1; rep. from (*) to last 2 sts., p. 2.

2nd row. (*) k.2, p. 1; rep. from (*) to last 2 sts., k. 2.

3rd row. (*) p.2, yfd., k. 1, p. 2, k. 1, sl. yfd. over these 4 sts.; rep. from (*) to last 2 sts., p. 2.

4th, 5th and 6th rows. As second, first and second.

7th row. p. 2., k. 1. (*) p. 2, yfd., k. 1, p. 2, k. 1., sl. yfd. over these 4 sts.; rep. from (*) to last 5 sts., p. 2, k. 1., p. 2.

8th row. As second row.

Pattern 42. Cast on an uneven number of sts.

1st row. k. 2, (*) k. into back of second st. on left-hand needle, leave on needle, k. into front of first st. and sl. both off needle; rep. from (*) to last st., k. 1.

2nd row. p. 2, (*) p. into second st. on left-hand needle, leave on needle, p. into first st. and ssl. both off needle; rep. from (*) to last st., p. 1.

Pattern 43. Cast on a multiple of 4, plus 1.

1st row. k. 1, (*) k. 3, p. 1; rep. from (*) to last 4 sts., k. 4.

2nd row. p. 1, (*) p. 3, k. 1; rep. from (*) to end.

3rd row. k. 1, yfd., (*) sl. p., k. 2 tog., p.s.s.o., yrn., p. 1 yarn on needle; rep. from (*) to last 4 sts., sl. p., k. 2 tog., p.s.s.o., yfd., k. 1.

Rep. second and third rows.

Pattern 44. Cast on a multiple of 15 sts., plus 2.

1st row. p. 2, (*) k. 7, p. 2, k. 2, k. 2 tog., p. 2; rep. from (*) to end.

2nd row. k. 2, (*) p. 3, k. 2, p. 7, k. 2; rep. from (*) to end.

3rd row. p. 2, (*) k. 7, p. 2, k. 1, k. 2 tog., p. 2; rep. from (*) to end.

4th row. k. 2, (*) p. 2, k. 2, p. 7, k. 2; rep. from (*) to end.

5th row. p. 2, (*) k. 5, k. 2 tog., p. 2, yfd., k. 2. tog., yrn., p. 2; rep. from (*) to end.

6th row. k. 2, (*) p. 3, k. 2, p. 6, k. 2; rep. from (*) to end.

7th row. p. 2, (*) k. 4, k. 2 tog., p. 2, k. 1, yfd., k. 1, yfd., k. 1, p. 2; rep. from (*) to end.

8th row. k. 2, (*) p. 5, k. 2; rep. from (*) to end.

9th row. (*) p. 2, k. 3, k. 2 tog., p. 2, k. 2, yfd., k. 1, yfd., k. 2; rep. from (*) to last 2 sts., p. 2.

10th row. (*) k. 2, p. 7, k. 2, p. 4; rep. from (*) to last 2 sts., k. 2.

11th row. (*) p. 2, k. 2, k. 2 tog., p. 2, k. 7; rep. from (*) to last 2 sts., p. 2.

12th row. (*) k. 2, p. 7, k. 2, p. 3; rep. from (*) to last 2 sts., k. 2.

13th row. (*) p. 2, k. 1, k. 2 tog., p. 2, k. 7; rep. from (*) to last 2 sts., p. 2.

14th row. (*) k. 2, p. 7, k. 2, p. 2; rep. from (*) to last 2 sts., k. 2.

15th row. (*) p. 2, yfd., k. 2 tog., yrn., p. 2, k. 5, k. 2 tog.; rep. from (*) to last 2 sts., p. 2.

16th row. (*) k. 2, p. 6, k. 2, p. 3; rep. from (*) to last 2 sts., k. 2.

17th row. (*) p. 2, k. 1, yfd., k. 1, yfd., k. 1, p. 2, k. 4, k. 2 tog.; rep. from (*) to last 2 sts., k. 2.

18th row. As eighth row.

19th row. (*) p. 2, k. 2, yfd., k. 1, yfd., k. 2, p. 2, k. 3, k. 2 tog.; rep. from (*) to last 2 sts., p. 2.

20th row. (*) k. 2, p. 4, k. 2, k. 7; rep. from (*) to last 2 sts., k. 2.

Pattern 45. Cast on a multiple of 7, plus 5.

1st row. k. 5, (*) yrn., p. 2 tog., k. 5.; rep. from (*) to end.

2nd and alt. rows. p.

3rd row. k. 5, (*) yfd., k. 1, p. 2 tog., k. 4; rep. from (*) to end.

5th row. k. 5, (*) yfd., k. 2, p. 2 tog., k. 3; rep. from (*) to end.

7th row. k. 5, (*) yfd., k. 3, p. 2 tog., k. 2; rep. from (*) to end.

9th row. k. 5, (*) yfd., k. 4, p. 2 tog., k. 1; rep. from (*) to end.

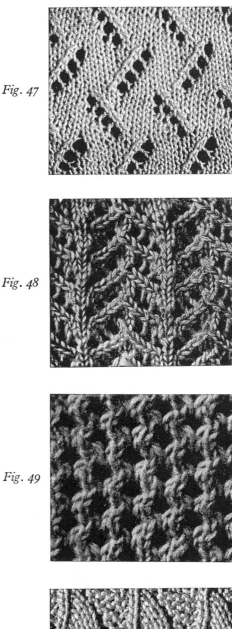

Fig. 47

Fig. 48

Fig. 49

Fig. 50

11th row. k. 5, (*) yfd., k. 5, p. 2 tog.; rep. from (*) to end.

13th row. k. 2, (*) yrn., p. 2 tog., k. 5; rep. from (*) to last 3 sts., yrn., p. 2 tog., k. 1.

15th row. k. 2, (*) yfd., k. 1, p. 2 tog., k. 4; rep. from (*) to last 3 sts., k. 1, yfd., p. 2 tog.

17th row. k. 2, (*) yfd., k. 2, p. 2 tog., k. 3; rep. from (*) to last 3 sts., yfd., k. 1, p. 2 tog.

19th row. k 2, (*) yfd., k. 3, p. 2 tog., k. 2; rep. from (*) to last 3 sts., yfd., k. 1, p. 2 tog.

21st row. k. 2, (*) yfd., k. 4, p. 2 tog., k. 1; rep. from (*) to last 3 sts., yfd., p. 2 tog.

23rd row. k. 2, (*) yfd., k. 5, p. 2 tog.; rep. from (*) to last 3 sts., yfd., k. 1, p. 2 tog.

24th row. As second row.

Pattern 46. Cast on a multiple of 10, plus 7.

1st row. k.

2nd row. p.

3rd row. k. 2, (*) p. 3, k. 7; rep. from (*) ending p. 3, k. 2.

4th row. p. 1, (*) k. 5, p. 5; rep. from (*) ending k. 5, p. 1.

5th row. k .1, (*) p. 2, yrn., p. 2 tog., p. 1, k. 5; rep. from (*) to last 6 sts., p. 2, yrn., p. 2 tog., p. 1., k. 1.

6th to 8th row. As fourth, third and second.

9th row. k. 7, (*) p. 3, k. 7; rep. from (*) to end.

10th row. p. 6, (*) k. 5, p. 5; rep. from (*) to last st., p. 1.

11th row. k. 6, (*) p. 2, yrn., p. 2 tog., p. 1., k. 5; rep. from (*) to last st., k. 1.

12th and 13th row. As tenth and ninth. Rep. from second row.

Pattern 47. Cast on a multiple of 7, plus one.

1st row. (*) k. 5, k. 2 tog., yfd.; rep. from (*) to last st., k. 1.

2nd and alt. rows. p.

3rd row. k. 4, (*) k. 2 tog., yfd., k. 5; rep. from (*) to last 4 sts., k. 2 tog., yfd., k. 2.

5th row. k. 3, (*) k. 2 tog., yfd., k. 5; rep. from (*) to last 5 sts., k. 2 tog., yfd., k. 3.

7th row. k. 2, (*) k. 2 tog., yfd., k. 5; rep. from (*) to last 6 sts., k. 2 tog., yfd., k. 4.

9th row. k. 1., (*) yfd., sl. 1, k. 1, p.s.s.o., k. 5; rep. from (*) to end.

11th row. k. 2, (*) yfd., sl. 1, k. 1, p.s.s.o., k. 5; rep. from (*) to last 6 sts., yfd., sl. 1, k. 1, p.s.s.o., k. 4.

13th row. k. 3, (*) yfd., sl. 1, k. 1, p.s.s.o., k. 5; rep. from (*) to last 5 sts., yfd., sl. 1, k. 1, p.s.s.o., k. 3.

15th row. k. 4, (*) yfd., sl. 1, k. 1, p.s.s.o., k. 5; rep. from (*) to last 4 sts., yfd., sl. 1, k. 1, p.s.s.o., k. 2.

16th row. As second row.

Pattern 48. Cast on a multiple of 8, plus 2.

1st row. (*) k. 3, k. 2 tog., yfd., k. 1, yfd., sl. 1, k. 1, p.s.s.o.; rep. from (*) to last 2 sts., k. 2.

2nd and alt. rows. p.

3rd row. k. 2, (*) k. 2 tog., yfd., k. 3, yfd., sl. 1, k. 1, p.s.s.o., k. 1; rep. from (*) to end.

5th row. k. 1, k. 2 tog., (*) yfd., k. 5, yfd., k. 3 tog.; rep. from (*) ending last rep. k. 2 tog.

6th row. As second row.

Pattern 49 Cast on a multiple of 4.

1st row. (*) Sl. 2 sts. on to a cable needle and keep at front of work. k. 2, then k. 2 from cable needle, sl. 2 sts. on to cable needle and keep to back of work, k. 2, then k. 2 from cable needle; rep. from (*) to end.

2nd and alt. rows. p.

3rd row. (*) Sl. 2 sts. on to cable needle and keep to back of work. k. 2, then k. 2 from cable needle, sl. 2 sts on to cable needle and keep to front of work, k. 2, then k. 2 from cable needle; rep. from (*) to end.

4th row. As second row.

Pattern 50. Cast on a multiple of 7, plus 2.

1st row. Sl. 1, (*) k. 5, k. 2 tog., yfd.; rep. from (*) to last st., k. 1.

2nd row. Sl. 1, (*) k. 1, p. 6; rep. from (*) to last st., k. 1.

3rd row. Sl. 1, (*) k. 4, k. 2 tog., p. 1, yfd.; rep. from (*) to last st., k. 1.

4th row. Sl. 1, (*) k. 2, p. 5; rep. from (*) to last st., k. 1.

5th row. Sl. 1, (*) k. 3, k. 2 tog., p. 2, yfd.; rep. from (*) to last st., k. 1.

6th row. Sl. 1, (*) k. 3, p. 4; rep. from (*) to last st., k. 1.

7th row. Sl. 1, (*) k. 2, k. 2 tog., p. 3, yfd.; rep. from (*) to last st., k. 1.

8th row. Sl. 1, (*) k. 4, p. 3; rep. from (*) to last st., k. 1.

9th row. Sl. 1, (*) k. 1, k. 2 tog., p. 4, yfd.; rep. from (*) to last st., k. 1.

10th row. Sl. 1, (*) k. 5, p. 2; rep. from (*) to last st., k. 1.

11th row. Sl. 1, (*) k. 2 tog., p. 5, yfd.; rep. from (*) to last st., k. 1.

12th row. Sl. 1, (*) p. to last st., k. 1.

13th row. Sl. 1, k. 1, (*) yfd., sl. 1, k. 1, p.s.s.o., k.5; rep. from (*) to end.

14th row. Sl. 1, p. 5, k. 1, (*) p. 6, k. 1; rep. from (*) to last 2 sts., p. 1, k. 1.

15th row. Sl. 1, k. 1, (*) yrn., p. 1, yb., sl. 1, k. 1, p.s.s.o., k. 4; rep. from (*) to end.

16th row. Sl. 1, p. 4, k. 2, (*) p. 5, k. 2; rep. from (*) to last 2 sts., P. 1, k. 1.

17th row. Sl. 1, k. 1, (*) yrn., p. 2, yb., sl. 1, k. 1, p.s.s.o., k. 3; rep. from (*) to end.

18th row. Sl. 1, p. 3, k. 3, (*) p. 4, k. 3; rep. from (*) to last 2 sts., p. 1, k. 1.

19th row. Sl. 1, k. 1, (*) yrn., p. 3, yb., sl. 1, k. 1, p.s.s.o., k. 2; rep. from (*) to end.

20th row. Sl. 1, p. 2, k. 4, (*) p. 3, k. 4; rep. from (*) to last 2 sts., p. 1, k. 1.

21st row. Sl. 1, (*) k. 1, yrn., p. 4, yb., sl. 1, k. 1, p.s.s.o.; rep. from (*) to last st., k. 1.

22nd row. Sl. 1, p. 1, k. 5, (*) p. 2, k. 5; rep. from (*) to last 2 sts., p. 1, k. 1.

23rd row. Sl. 1, k. 1, (*) yrn., p. 5, yb., sl. 1, k. 1, p.s.s.o.; rep. from (*) to end.

24th row. As twelfth row.

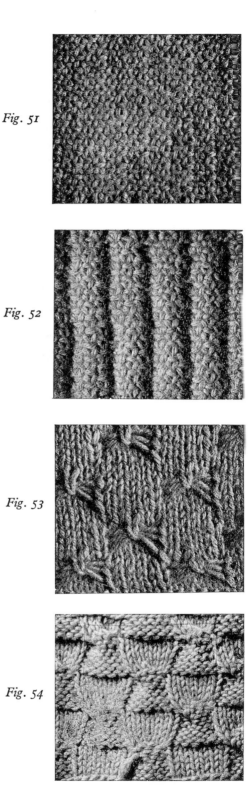

Fig. 51

Fig. 52

Fig. 53

Fig. 54

Pattern 51. Cast on odd numbers of sts.

1st row. (*) k. 1, yfd., sl. p., yb.; rep. from (*) to last st., k. 1.

2nd row. (*) sl. p., p. 1, yb.; rep from (*) to last st., k. 1.

Pattern 52. Cast on a multiple of 4.

1st row. (*) k. 1, yfd., sl. p., yb., k. 1, p. 1; rep. from (*) to end.

2nd row. (*) k. 1, sl. p., p. 1, yb., sl. p.; rep. from (*) to end.

Pattern 53. Cast on a multiple of 10, plus 7.

1st, 3rd and 5th rows. k. 6, (*) yfd., sl. 5, yb., k. 5; rep. from (*) ending k. 6.

2nd and alt. rows. p.

7th row. k. 8, (*) pick up the 3 parallel strands and k. 1 into these, k.1 , sl. the previous st. over this, k. 9; rep. from (*) to end.

9th, 11th and 13th rows. k. 1, (*) yfd., sl. 5, yb., k. 5; rep. from (*) to last 6 sts., yfd., sl. 5, yb., k. 1.

15th row. As seventh row starting with k. 3, and ending k. 3.

16th row. As second row.

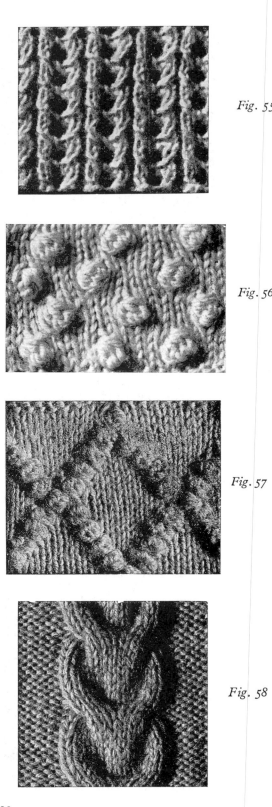

Fig. 55

Fig. 56

Fig. 57

Fig. 58

Pattern 54. Cast on a multiple of 12 sts.

1st to 5th rows. (*) k. 6, p. 6; rep. from (*) to end.

6th row. (*) Sl. 3 sts. on to a cable needle and leave at front of work, p. 3, then p. 3, sts. from cable needle, k. 6; rep. from (*) to end.

7th to 11th row. (*) p. 6, k. 6; rep. from (*) to end.

12th row. (*) k. 6, sl. next 3 sts. on to a cable needle and leave at front of work p. 3, then p. 3 sts. from cable needle; rep. from (*) to end.

Pattern 55. Cast on a multiple of 5, plus 1.

1st row. (*) p. 1, k. 2 tog., yrn., sl. 1, k. 1, p.s.s.o.; rep. from (*) to last st., k. 1.

2nd row. k. 1, (*) p. 2, k. 1, p. 1, k. 1; rep. from (*) to end.

3rd row. p. 1, (*) k. 4, p. 1; rep. from (*) to end.

4th row. k. 1, (*) p. 4, k. 1; rep. from (*) to end.

Patterns 56 and 57. Into the st. where bobble is to be made, k. 1, p. 1, k. 1, p. 1 and k. 1, pass the first 4 sts. over the last st. Pattern 56 shows bobbles made on every 5th st., then interchanged on every 4th row. Pattern 57 shows bobbles made on every 9th st., then on the following k. rows every 7th, 5th, 3rd and first st., forming a diamond pattern.

Pattern 58. Cast on a multiple of 22 sts.

1st row. (*) p. 6, k. 16; rep. from (*) to end.

2nd row. (*) p. 16, k. 6; rep. from (*) to end. Rep. these 2 rows 4 times.

11th row. (*) p. 6, sl. 4 sts. on to a cable needle and keep at back of work, k. 4, then k. 4 from cable needle, sl. next 4 sts. on to a cable needle and keep at front of work, k. 4, then k. 4 from cable needle; rep. from (*) to end.

Pattern 59. Cast on a multiple of 14, plus 2

1st row. k. 5, (*) k. 2 tog., yfd., k. 1, yfd., sl. 1, k. 1, p.s.s.o., k. 9; rep. from (*) ending last rep. k. 6.

2nd and alt. rows. p.

3rd row. k. 4, (*) k. 2 tog., yfd., k. 3, yfd., sl. 1, k. 1, p.s.s.o., k. 7; rep. from (*) ending last rep. k. 5.

5th row. k. 3, (*) k. 2 tog., yfd., k. 2 tog., yfd., k. 1 (yfd., sl. 1, k. 1, p.s.s.o.) twice, k. 5; rep. from (*) ending last rep. k. 4.

7th row. k. 2, (*) k. 2 tog., yfd., k. 2 tog., yfd., k. 3 (yfd., sl. 1, k. 1, p.s.s.o.) twice, k. 3; rep. from (*) to end.

9th row (*) k. 1, k. 2 tog. (yfd., k. 2 tog.) twice, yfd., k. 1 (yfd., sl. 1, k. 1., p.s.s.o.), 3 times; rep. from (*) to last 2 sts., k. 2.

11th row. k. 2 tog., (*) (yfd., k. 2 tog) twice, yfd., k. 3 (yfd., sl. 1, k. 1, p.s.s.o.) twice, yfd., k. 3 tog.; rep. from (*) ending last rep. k. 2 tog., k. 1.

12th row. As second row.

Pattern 60. Cast on a multiple of 3.

1st row. k. 2, (*) yfd., sl. 1, k. 2, p.s.s.o.; rep. from (*) to last st., k. 1.

2nd row. p.

Pattern 61. Cast on a multiple of 8, plus 1.

1st row. (*) k. 2, k. 2 tog., yfd., k. 1, yfd., sl. 1, k. 1, p.s.s.o., k. 1; rep. from (*) to last st., k. 1.

2nd and alt. rows. p.

3rd row. (*) k. 1, k. 2 tog., yfd., k. 3, yfd., sl. 1, k. 1, p.s.s.o.; rep. from (*) to last st., k. 1.

5th row. (*) k. 3, yfd., k. 3 tog., yfd., k. 2; rep. from (*) to last st., k. 1.

7th row. (*) k. 1, yfd., sl. 1, k. 1, p.s.s.o., k. 3, k. 2 tog., yfd.; rep. from (*) to last st., k. 1.

9th row. (*) k. 2, yfd., sl. 1, k. 1, p.s.s.o., k. 1, k. 2 tog., yfd., k. 1; rep. from (*) to last st., k. 1.

11th row. k. 2 tog., (*) yfd., k. 5, yfd., k. 3 tog.; rep. from (*) ending last rep. k. 2 tog.

12th row. As second row.

Pattern 62. Cast on a multiple of 8, plus 3.

1st row. k. 3, (*) yfd., k. 3 tog., yfd., k. 5; rep. from (*) to end.

2nd and alt. rows. p.

3rd row. (*) k. 1, k. 2 tog., yfd., k. 3, yfd., sl. 1, k. 1, p.s.s.o.; rep. from (*) to last 3 sts., k. 3.

5th row. k. 2 tog., (*) yfd., k. 5, yfd., k. 3 tog.; rep. from (*) to last 9 sts., yfd., k. 5, yfd., k. 2 tog., k. 2.

7th row. k. 2, (*) yfd., sl. 1, k. 1, p.s.s.o., k. 1, k. 2 tog., yfd., k. 3.; rep. from (*) to last st., k. 1.

8th row. As second row.

Pattern 63. Cast on a multiple of 8.

1st row. (*) p. 2, k. 1, yfd., k. 1, p. 2, k. 2; rep. from (*) to end.

2nd, 4th and 6th row. (*) p. 2, k. 2, p. 3, k. 2; rep. from (*) to end.

3rd and 5th row. (*) p. 2, k. 3, p. 2, k. 2; rep. from (*) to end.

7th row. (*) p. 2, k. 1, drop next st., k. 1, p. 2, k. 1, yfd., k. 1; rep. from (*) to end.

8th, 10th and 12 row. (*) p. 3, k. 2, p. 2, k. 2; rep. from (*) to end.

Fig. 59

Fig. 60

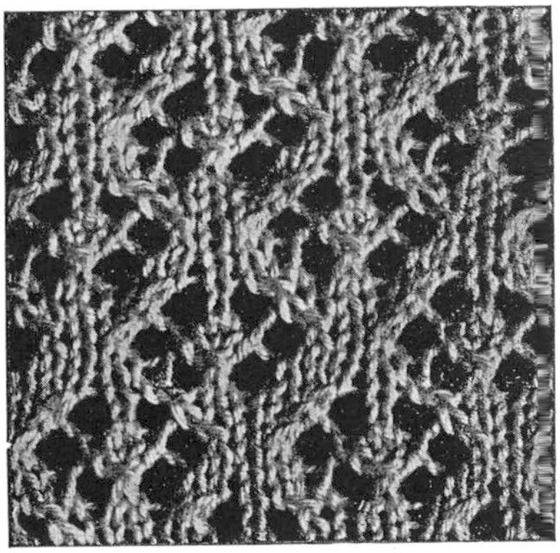

Fig. 61

Fig. 62

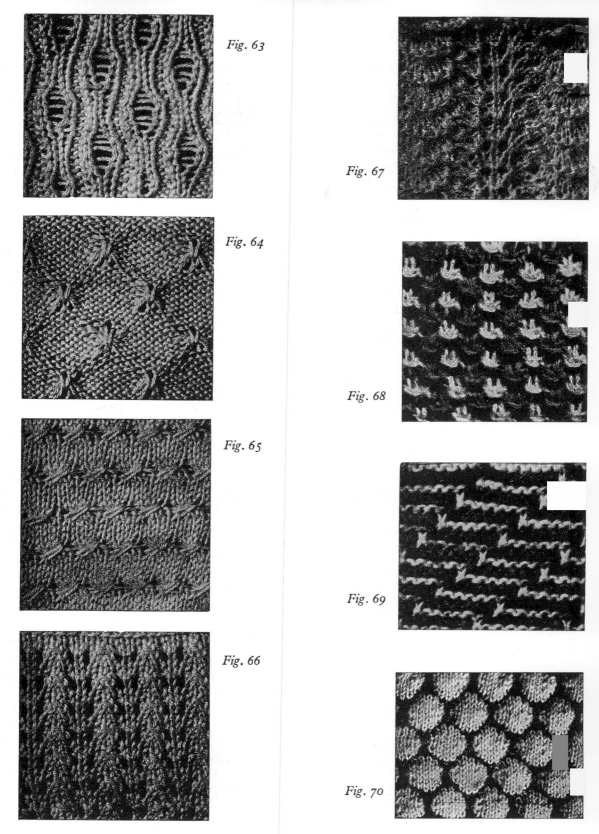

Fig. 63

Fig. 64

Fig. 65

Fig. 66

Fig. 67

Fig. 68

Fig. 69

Fig. 70

9th and 11th row. (*) p. 2, k. 2, p. 2, k. 3; rep. from (*) to end.

13th row. (*) p. 2, k. 1, yfd., k. 1, p. 2, k. 1, drop next st., k. 1; rep. from (*) to end.

14th row. As eighth row.

Rep. from third row.

Pattern 64. Cast on a multiple of 8 plus 3.

St. st. 7 rows.

8th row (*right side*). (*) p. 7, drop the next st. to 5th row below, insert right-hand needle into this st. and under 5 loose strands and k.; rep. from (*) to last 3 sts., k. 3.

St. st. 7 rows.

16th row. p. 3, (*) drop next st. as before, p. 7; rep. from (*) to end.

Pattern 65. Cast on a multiple of 4.

St. st. 4 rows.

5th row. (*) k. into the 4th st. but do not drop off needle, k. first 3 sts., drop 4th st. off needle, rep. from (*) to end.

6th row. p.

St. st. 4 rows.

11th row. k. 2, (*) k. into the 4th st. as before; rep. from (*) to last 2 sts., k. 2.

12th row. As sixth row.

Pattern 66. Cast on a multiple of 4, plus 1.

1st row. k. 1, (*) yfd., k. 3, yfd., k. 1; rep. from (*) to end.

2nd and alt. rows. p.

3rd row. k. 2, (*) sl. 1, k. 2 tog., p.s.s.o., k. 3; rep. from (*) to last 5 sts., sl. 1, k. 2 tog., p.s.s.o., k. 2.

4th row. As second row.

Pattern 67. Cast on a multiple of 18, plus 1.

1st row. p.

2nd row. k.

3rd row. p.

4th row. (k. 1, yfd) twice, k. 1, yrn., (p. 2 tog.) 6 times, (*) (k. 1, yfd.) 5 times, k. 1, yrn., (p. 2 tog.) 6 times; rep. from (*) to last 4 sts. (k. 1, yfd.) 3 times, k. 1.

Pattern 68. Cast on a multiple of 3, plus 2.

1st row. With M., P.

2nd row. (*) k. 3, sl. first st. over 2nd and 3rd st., yfd.; rep. from (*) to last 2 sts., k. 2.

3rd row. With C., P.

4th row. k. 1, (*) yfd., k. 3, sl. first of these 3 sts. over 2nd and 3rd; rep. from (*) to last st., k. 1.

Pattern 69. Cast on a multiple of 8, less 1.

1st row. With M., K.

2nd row. With C., (*) k. 7, sl. p.; rep. from (*) to last 7 sts., k. 7.

3rd row. (*) k. 7, yfd., sl. p., yb.; rep. from (*) to last 7 sts., k. 7.

4th row. With M., k. 6, (*) sl. p., k. 7; rep. from (*) ending last rep., k. 8.

5th Row. k. 8, (*) yfd., sl. p., yb., k. 7; rep. from (*) to last 6 sts., k. 6.

6th row. With C., k. 5, (*) sl. p., k. 7; rep. from (*) to last 2 sts., sl. p. k. 1.

7th row. k. 1, sl. p., (*) yfd., sl. p. yb., k. 7; rep. from (*) to last 5 sts., k. 5.

Continue to slip one st. to the right in every alternate row.

Pattern 70. Cast on a multiple of 6, less 1.

1st row. With C., P.

2nd row. With M., k. 5, (*) yfd., slp. p., k. 5; rep. from (*) to end.

3rd row. p. 5, (*) p. tog the yfd. and sl. p. of previous row, p. 5; rep. from (*) to end.

4th row. k. 5, (*) yfd., insert right-hand needle purlwise under made sts. and through sl. st. of previous row and leave on right-hand needle; k. 5; rep. from (*) to end.

5th row. p. 5, (*) p. tog. sl. st. and made sts. of previous rows, p. 5; rep. from (*) to end.

6th to 9th row. Rep. 4th and 5th rows twice.

10th row. With C., k. 5, (*) k. 1 below next st. on left-hand needle, k. 5; rep. from (*) to end.

11th row. As 1st row.

12th row. With M., k. 2, (*) yfd., sl. p., k. 5; rep. from (*) ending last rep. k. 2.

13th row. p. 2, (*) p. 2 tog. the yfd. and sl. p of previous row, p. 5; rep. from (*) ending last rep. p. 2.

14th row. k. 2, (*) yfd., insert right-hand needle purlwise under made sts. and through sl. st. of previous row and leave on right-hand needle, k. 5; rep. from (*) ending last rep., k. 2.

15th row. p. 2, (*) p. tog. sl. st. and made sts. of previous rows, p. 5; rep. from (*) ending last rep. p. 2.

16th to 19th row. Rep. 14th and 15th rows twice.

20th row. With C., k. 2, (*) k. 1 below next st. on left-hand needle, k. 5; rep. from (*) ending last rep. k. 2. Rep. from first row.

Pattern 71. Cast on a multiple of 34.

1st row. (*) k. 3, k. 2 tog., k. 4, yrn., p. 2, (k. 2,

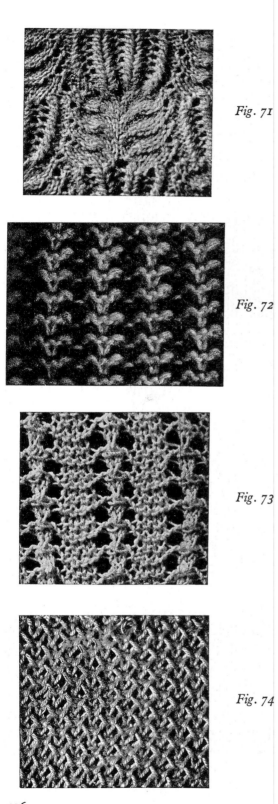

Fig. 71

Fig. 72

Fig. 73

Fig. 74

yfd., sl. 1, k. 1, p.s.s.o.) 3 times, p. 2, yfd., k. 4, sl. 1, k. 1., p.s.s.o., k. 3; rep. from (*) to end.

2nd row. (*) p. 2, p. 2 tog., p. 4, yrn., p. 1., k. 2, (p. 2, yrn., p. 2 tog.) 3 times, k. 2, p. 1, yrn., p. 4, p. 2 tog., p. 2; rep. from (*) end.

3rd row. (*) k. 1., k. 2 tog., k. 4, yfd., k. 2, p. 2, (*) (k. 2, yfd., sl. 1, k. 1, p.s.s.o.) 3 times, p. 2, k. 2, yfd., k. 4, sl. 1, k. 1, p.s.s.o., k. 1; rep. from (*) to end.

4th row. (*) p. 2 tog., p. 4, yrn., p. 3., k. 2, (p. 2, yrn., p. 2 tog.) 3 times, k. 2, p. 3, yrn., p. 4, p. 2 tog.; rep. from (*) to end.

Rep. these 4 rows 3 times more.

17th row. (*) yfd., sl. 1, k. 1, p.s.s.o., k. 2, yfd., sl. 1, k. 1, p.s.s.o., p. 2, yfd., k. 4, sl. 1, k. 1, p.s.s.o., k. 6, k. 2 tog., k. 4, yrn., p. 2, k. 2, yfd., sl. 1, k. 1, p.s.s.o., k. 2; rep. from (*) to end.

18th row. (*) yrn., p. 2 tog., p. 2, yrn., p. 2 tog., k. 2, p. 1, yrn., (p. 4, p. 2 tog.) twice, p. 4, yrn., p. 1, k. 2, p. 2, yrn., p. 2 tog., p. 2; rep. from (*) to end.

19th row. (*) yfd., sl. 1, k. 1, p.s.s.o., k. 2, yfd., sl. 1, k. 1, p.s.s.o., p. 2, k. 2, yfd., k. 4, sl. 1, k. 1, p.s.s.o., k. 2, k. 2 tog., k. 4, yfd., k. 2, p. 2, k. 2, yfd., sl. 1, k. 1, p.s.s.o., k. 2; rep. from (*) to end.

20th row. (*) yrn., p. 2 tog., p. 2, yrn., p. 2 tog., k. 2, p. 3, yrn., p. 4, (p. 2 tog.) twice, p. 4, yrn., p. 3, k. 2, p. 2, yrn., p. 2 tog., p. 2; rep. from (*) to end.

Rep. the last 4 rows 3 times more.

Pattern 72. Cast on a multiple of 4, less 1.

1st row. With M., (*) k. 3, sl. p.; rep. from (*) to last 3 sts., k. 3.

2nd row. (*) k. 3, yfd., sl. p., yb.; rep. from (*) to last 3 sts., k. 3.

3rd row. With C., k. 1, (*) sl. p., k. 3; rep. from (*) ending last rep., k. 1.

4th row. k. 1, (*) yfd., sl. p., yb., k. 3; rep. from (*) ending last rep. k. 1.

Pattern 73. Cast on a multiple of 7, plus 1.

1st row. k. 1, (*) yfd., sl. 1, k. 2 tog., p.s.s.o., yfd., k. 4; rep. from (*) to end.

2nd row. (*) k. 4, p. 3; rep. from (*) to last st., k. 1.

3rd row. k.

4th row. As second row.

Pattern 74. Cast on an odd number of sts.

1st row. k. 1, (*) yfd., sl. p., k. 1; rep. from (*) to end.

2nd row. k. 1, (*) k. made st. leaving loop on left-hand needle, slip next 2 loops purlwise from left-hand needle to right-hand needle, k. 1; rep. from (*) to end.

3rd row. k. 1, (*) k. next 3 loops tog., yfd., sl. p.; rep. from (*) to last 4 sts., k. next 3 loops tog., k. 1.

4th row. k. 2, (*) k. into made st., leaving loop on left-hand needle, slip next 2 loops from left-hand needle to right-hand needle, k. 1, rep. from (*) to last st., k. 1.

5th row. k. 1, (*) yfd., sl. p., k. next 3 loops tog.; rep. from (*) to last 2 loops, yfd. sl. p., k. 1.

Rep. from second row.

Embroidery on Knitting. It is easy to embroider on knitted cloth, and this often enriches what might otherwise be a rather dull piece of knitting. Thus ladies' jumpers, sports articles and children's clothes can often be embroidered according to the fashion of the present day.

Embroidery on woollen garments can be done in two ways: with a needle, or by working in other coloured threads as the knitting progresses. It is easiest to embroider on Stocking Stitch. Knitting Stitch and Cross Stitch are the most suitable stitches for this work. Generally the embroidery is worked in a single light colour on a dark-coloured background and vice versa. However, many-coloured designs can also be very effective.

Knitting Stitch is fully explained and illustrated in the paragraph on "Mending on Knitting", and for further details readers should refer to this. Cross Stitch is worked over knitting, counting the threads carefully. In our illustration, the outlines and dividing lines are worked in Cross Stitch.

More interesting and more difficult at first sight is the method of working the embroidery into the material as work proceeds. This is called Fair Isle work. It is, however, very amusing and fairly quick, requiring only a little care and patience. First prepare the balls of yarns in the various colours required, and begin with a design drawn on squared paper. It is common to begin with one colour, usually the background, and then with the colours forming the pattern, counting the squares on the design, and making one stitch correspond

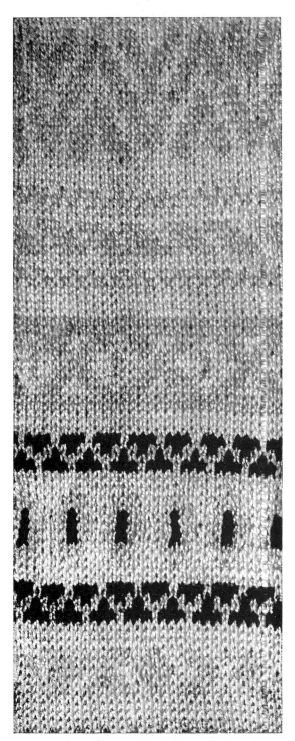

Fig. 75. Embroidery motifs which can be knitted into the knitting in various colours

Fig. 76. *Plain Stocking Stitch in tubular knitting worked on wrong side. The right side is inside*

Fig. 77. *Tubular knitting in Stocking Stitch worked on the right side. The wrong side is on the inside*

Fig. 78. *Tubular knitting in ribbing*

Fig. 79. *Tubular knitting in Moss Stitch*

to one square. After working the requisite number of stitches in one colour, leave the yarn hanging, and continue with another colour, crossing the thread with the first. When there is a big space between one colour and another, the threads should be intertwined every two or three stitches on the back of the work to avoid long lengths of thread.

Tubular Knitting on Two Needles. Tubular knitting worked on two needles is very useful for the working of things like gloves, body-belts, neckscarves, etc.

All the basic knitting stitches (Stocking Stitch, Rib, Moss Stitch, etc.) can be worked round on two needles only. Before beginning to work an important piece, it is wise to practise since, although tubular knitting requires no special skill, it does require particular care.

Always use needles with points at both ends.

Stocking Stitch (worked on wrong side). Cast on an even number of stitches, double that of the size required, i.e. if a length of 25 cm is to be worked, requiring 30 st., cast on sufficient stitches for 20 inches, i.e. 60 st. Then purl half the piece and fold the work so that the two needles are parallel, that half already worked being behind, the part not worked facing the worker. Then take a third needle and slip the stitches alternately from the other two needles on to this one. At the end all the stitches will be on the one needle.

Now take up the yarn where it was left, work the first stitch purl, slip the second, taking it up from behind from the left needle and slip on to right needle without working it, purl the third stitch, slip the fourth and so on to the end of the row. Turn the work and repeat; it will easily be seen how one half of the work is knitted at a time, the other half remaining unworked. In this way, too, the purl stitch will be on the outside of the work and the plain stitch on the inside (Fig. 76), and this is quicker and easier. If so wished, the knit stitch can be worked on the outside (Fig. 77), proceeding thus:

Knit one stitch, lift yarn as for purl, slip, take second stitch into back without working it, take yarn on to back of work and knit a second stitch. Continue thus for the whole needle.

Rib. Cast on a multiple of 4.
p. 1, sl. p., (*) yb., k. 1, yfd., sl. p., p. 1, sl. p.; rep. from (*) to last 2 sts., yb., k. 1, yfd., sl. p.

Moss Stitch.

1st row. As rib.

2nd row. k. 1, yfd., (*) sl. p., p. 1, sl. p., yb., k. 1; rep. from (*) to last 2 sts., yfd., sl. p., p. 1, sl. p.

Casting Off of Tubular Knitting. This operation is the inverse of casting on, i.e.: Take two needles and hold them parallel at a little distance from each other. Pick up a stitch on one needle and the next on the other alternately, so that the work is opened out. When all the stitches have thus been divided on to the two needles, cast them off one at a time with a third needle.

Ribbing for Various Garments. Tubular knitting is also used for the double ribbed edges of pullovers, or stockings and other garments, as this form of rib lasts longer and gives better wear. In this case, once the stitches are cast on, proceed directly to work them with the usual method of one slipped and one worked, but naturally the bottom rib will remain closed. On completing the rib, continue normally.

Tubular knitting is very suitable, as we have already said, for many purposes. One of the most important is for glove making. Working gloves on four needles is rather wearisome; worked on two needles, the gloves show the joining at the fingers. All this is simplified by using tubular knitting.

Increasing in Tubular Knitting. Increases are made preferably into knit stitches. They should always be even in number, equally divided between the back and the front sides. That is, an increase is worked on the first needle (working two stitches into one). On the second needle, when coming to the increase, which is on the back, work a second increase on the front, so as to always have alternate stitches, one back and one front, on the needle.

We give here a way of working gloves in tubular knitting.

Gloves in Tubular Knitting. Figure 80 shows a pair of gloves worked in tubular knitting.

They are worked in Stocking Stitch and ribbing.

Cast on an even number of stitches. This number will vary according to the thickness of the yarn used, the size of the needles and of the hands for which the gloves are made. For thick thread cast on 60 st. Work 30 in alternate knit and purl. Fold work in two, take a third needle and work the other 30 in knit and purl, omitting to work the 30 just worked. Continue thus for about 7 cm Then begin the other part of the knitting.

Now work in tubular knitting for the whole length from the cuff to the finger, about 11 cm. Then begin to work the fingers. Pass a thread through all the stitches so that the stitches do not drop and work in Stocking Stitch in tubular knitting for 15 st. On completing the length of the first finger decrease by a few stitches (always at the end of the needle) on the last two rows, then take out the needle and with a sewing needle take the end of the thread through the open stitches of the finger, draw up and fasten off.

For the middle finger, work 16 st. in the same way, for the third finger 15 st., and 14 st. for the little finger.

This method is certainly the quickest, especially for working the fingers.

For the thumb, cut a stitch at a height of about 6 cm and carefully, with a sewing needle, unravel 10 st. on either side. Slip them on to a needle, alternately from one side and the other, and work them as usual, up to the end, where it is worked as for the first finger.

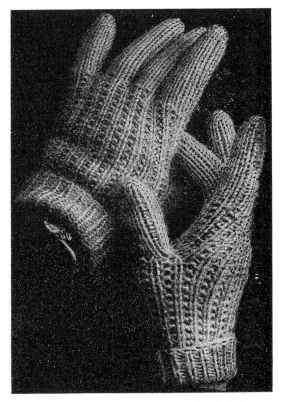

Fig. 80. Gloves worked in tubular knitting

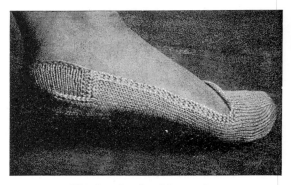

Fig. 81. Insole with toe piece

Stockings or Socks. The use of stockings is not very ancient. The Romans bound their sandals with thongs on bare legs; sometimes these thongs were decorated with metal rings. But at the beginning of the Middle Ages, stockings made of material were already well known and used for a long time, until the appearance, some say in Venice, of the knitted stocking.

Nothing precise is known about the first stocking knitting-machines, or the weaving looms for them: at first stockings were only made in white, then towards the middle of last century, they began to be made in colours and especially in black. In some periods red stockings were favoured, especially for magistrates, prelates, etc.

Finally, after the First World War, the very transparent stocking in real or artificial silk became the uncontested fashion for women, in a wide range of colours, from flesh pink to golden tan and smoke grey. The market became filled with these articles, so that the hand-made stocking lost its popularity and is now no longer worked, except in tiny villages for old men and children. However, sports socks for ski-ing, and children's socks and winter stockings, etc., are still hand-made, so we shall give here some details as to the methods of working them.

A sock consists of a turnover which is generally worked double, for passing an elastic through, the leg, between the heel and the turnover (nowadays socks are worn well below the knee), the heel, and the foot, consisting of the sole and the toecap. The foot of the sock is the first part to wear, the rest very often remaining in good repair. A practical method of overcoming this difficulty is to work an extra footpiece consisting of a heel, sole and toepiece, to be attached to the worn part, by hand.

Working the Sole (Fig. 81). For men's or children's socks the sole should be worked with a strong yarn. If the sole is worked in wool, we advise the use of a cotton thread along with the wool for the heel and toe.

To work the sole, proceed as follows:
Cast on 35 st. and work 8 central ribs (given by a purl st. worked in the centre of a knit row) and 8 side ribs (3 purl st. on a knit row). After working the fifth rib on the right side, leave 9 st. on the left needle. Pass the last stitch worked, over the first of these nine stitches, turn the work, pass the crossed-over stitch on to the right needle without working it, then purl until there are 9 st. on the left needle, purling together the last stitch worked and the first of the nine. Turn the work again, slip the stitches knitted together on to the right needle, without working them and knit the rest of the row up to the point where the last stitch worked is again passed over the first of the 8 st. remaining. Continue thus, back and forth, until all the 9 st. have been worked. Finish on the right side, lift up the 9 rib st. of the first piece, with a free needle and work them crossed. Work thus, the last decrease on the wrong side, lift up the rib stitches and work them crossed. This completes the heel. Continue the sole till there are 25 central and side ribs (this number will vary according to the length of the foot), finishing at the end of a knit row. On to this needle and another two needles cast on a number of stitches equal to those cast on at the beginning (i.e. 35), less 6. Naturally, the side ribs are now omitted, the central ones being continued. These, since the work goes round, will be worked on alternate rows. Work the newly cast-on stitches into the backs of the first row, and then continue to work in Stocking Stitch for about 15 ribs, and then divide the work between the three needles to make the toe.

The Toe. Divide the total number of stitches among the three needles: work with the fourth. Slip a stitch without working it, work the second and p.s.s.o. at the beginning of every row, at first on each alternate round and then on every round. Draw up the yarn tightly between each needle. When 4 st. are left on each needle, cast off by passing a needle threaded with the same yarn through the stitches, pull up and fasten off on back of work.

Men's Socks worked on Four Needles (Fig. 82).

Leg. Cast on 80 st. on three needles. Work in rib for about 16 cm. Then change stitch and work in plain knitting or Stocking Stitch. After another 16 cm, divide the stitches into two lots, leaving two extra on the back and leaving the rest on the other two needles for the moment. Work the other half back and forth on one needle only and begin to form the heel as follows:

Heel. To reinforce this important part of the stocking we advise that the wool should be doubled using another finer strand together with the yarn for the stocking itself, using a cotton thread if the sock is worked in wool.

Begin to work the 42 st. in one row knit and one row purl, until 14 ribs have been worked. On the fifteenth row do not work all the stitches, but leave 12 on the needle. Turn the work, slip the first stitch without working it and purl until there are 12 st. left on the other side too. Turn the work, work the 18 knit st., plus 1 of the 12 left on needle, turn work, work the 19 st. plus 1 of the 12 left on needle on the opposite side.

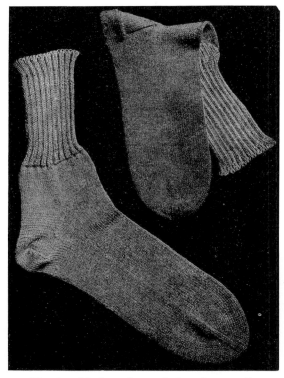

Fig. 82. Men's socks worked on four needles

Continue thus five times, that is until only 7 st. are left on the needle. Now decrease these 7 st on either side in the following manner: on the knit needle, slip last stitch of the central stitches, work the following and p.s.s.o. Turn the work, slip first stitch, work next 27 st. and work the twenty-eighth stitch together with the first of the 7 on the other side. Continue thus until all 14 st. have been taken in: there should be only the 28 heel st. left on the needle. After completing the decreases, take up the 14 on each side of the central rib, working them into the back so as not to leave holes. Begin to work round again with the 38 front st., and, on alternate rows, decrease two of the 28 taken up: i.e. each time the knitting comes round to the base of the heel on the right, slip the last of the 14 st., work the first heel st., and p.s.s.o., and on the left instead, k. two tog., 1 st. from the sock and the first of the 14 picked up. Continue to decrease thus, two stitches every two rows 7 times, making two acute angles at the corners of the heel. On completing the decreases, continue in Stocking Stitch for the desired length (this will be in proportion to the length of the foot), after which work the toe.

Toe. Divide the total number of stitches into four on four needles. Then slip the third and fourth stitches of the first and third needles over each other and knit together the third and fourth from the last stitches, on the second and fourth needles. After each decreasing row, first work two plain rows, and then one. When there are only four stitches left on each needle cast off as above.

Stocking worked in Pieces on Two Needles (Fig. 83). This stocking is worked in various pieces which are then sewn together; it has the advantage of being easily repaired. As we have already mentioned, the heel and the toe are the places which wear first and which need to be often mended, whilst the rest of the sock stays in good repair. With this type of stocking the worn parts can easily be unpicked, cut away and reworked.

Work the leg on four needles as explained for ordinary socks, in rib, and then continue in Stocking Stitch for about 5 cm. At this point divide the stitches in two, plus two from the heel stitches. Supposing there are 78 st., leave 37 apart on one needle and work the 41 remaining st. for the heel on two needles, working back and forth, for about 6 cm. Reinforce this part by adding

Fig. 83. Socks made in separate pieces

another thread in cotton and working thus:

K. 1, slip next st., working into back, k. 1, sl. 1 and so on along the row. On the row back purl all the stitches, the third needle is like the first, but with the slip stitches, interchanged. After working about 6 cm cast off all the stitches.

Take up the work again on the front of the sock, where there are 37 st. Cast on again 20 st. on either side, bringing the total to 77. On the knit needles now decrease one stitch on each side, working, that is, 19 st. k. two tog., 37 k. two tog. (slip 2 st. from left-hand needle to right-hand needle, turn them and replace on left-hand needle and knitting them tog. into back). Then work the next row plain making the same decreases, and so on until all the 20 replaced st. have been taken off. The original 37 st. will thus remain on the needle. Continue to work with two needles only, for about 10 or 12 cm (i.e. for the desired length of the foot) and then begin the toe thus: on the knit rows pass second stitch over third and knit the next to the last and the third from the last stitch together. Cast off when there are 7 or 8 st. left on the needle.

Sole. Now work the under part of the sock, that is, the sole. Cast on 21 st., increase from first row, one stitch into second stitch on needle and one into next to last stitch, until there are 37 st.

Continue to work in Stocking Stitch (one row plain and one row purl), measuring the length with that of the front up to the toe, which is then worked as explained for the other half.

On completion of the various parts, sew together on the wrong side with close oversewing, using the same yarn as used for the work itself.

Child's Sock worked on Two Needles (Fig. 84). Working on four needles is always a little tiresome and cumbersome, so it is certain that this pattern, worked on two needles, will be very welcome to the reader. The sock shown in Fig. 84 is for a young child of a few years of age, and a detailed explanation of it is given here. It can, of course, be made larger by increasing the number of stitches used.

Begin the leg by casting on 52 st. Work in k. 2, p. 2 rib for about 6 cm and then continue in Stocking Stitch (i.e. one row knit and one row purl) for about an inch. At this point begin the half heel, working 14 st. back and forth for twenty rows. Now work 7 st. knit, slip 8 st., from left to right needle, knit next st. and p.s.s.o. Turn work.

Fig. 84. This illustration shows, better than any explanation, how practical is this type of children's sock. Once completed, the sock is joined together, as shown on the left of the picture, with a seam starting from the leg and going right down to the toe. Thus the joining is below the foot

Slip first stitch and work next 7 st. purl. Turn work and repeat as explained until 6 st. have been taken off: after last dec. there will be 8 st. on needle. Now pick up 10 st. with left-hand needle along the length of the 20 st. just worked and knit them into the backs. Now continue to work all the stitches on the needle.

At this point work the other half of the heel on the left thus:

Work the last 14 st. back and forth for twenty rows. Then purl 7 st. and then purl the eighth and ninth tog. Turn work. Slip first stitch and then knit following 7 st. Turn work and continue thus until all 6 st. have been taken off. Pick up the 10 st. along the 20 rows just worked and purl all stitches to end of needle. There will now be 60 st. on the needle: k. 17, slip eighteenth, work the next and p.s.s.o., then k. 22, k. two tog., and then 17. Go back working a plain purl row and continue to decrease 2 st., as already explained, on all knit rows, 6 times. This completes the heel. Now work a piece in Stocking Stitch, according to the length of the foot, and then begin the toe. If the decreases have been correctly worked there will now be 48 st. on the needle. K. 9, sl. 1, k. 1, p.s.s.o., k. 2, k.

two tog., k. 18, sl. 1, k. 1, p.s.s.o., k. 2, k. two tog, k. 9. Purl a row back. Continue thus working one over the other, 4 decreases on each knit row, until there are 16 st. on the needle. Then draw up with a needle threaded with end of the wool. From the toe, work in oversewing along the edge of the sock and fasten off the thread at the edge of the leg

Men's Socks on Two Needles (Fig. 85)

Cast on 116 st., work in rib (k. 1, p. 1) for about 5 cm. Then change stitch and work k. 2, p. 2. After a total length of 30 cm leave 24 st. aside on one side and 24 on the other, working only the 68 central st. for about 22 cm, that is up to the toe, which is worked in Stocking Stitch, decreasing 1 st. per side on the knit rows (then 2 st.), until all the stitches have been taken off.

Now take up and work the stitches left aside, placing all 48 on one needle and working them back and forth. First take off 2 st. on either side on the first two knit rows so that there is a total of 44 st. Then work in Stocking Stitch for twenty-two rows (about 7 cm) and then decrease 1 st.

Fig. 85. Men's socks worked on only two needles. Above: the sock before sewing up; below: the finished sock. See diagram on left and explanation for working on page 415

per side 9 times on the knit rows. Then immediately begin to increase working 1 st. extra on either side 9 times, thus making 44 st. on the needle again (thus forming the heel).

Now continue in Stocking Stitch for about 7 inches, forming the sole and on reaching the toe, proceed as explained above.

On completing the sock, sew first the two parts where the decreases are and then increases forming the heel, and then the two parts of the foot and finally the leg.

Gloves. Ladies', men's and children's gloves can all be knitted. Here we give instructions for various types of gloves.

Glove on Four Needles

Gloves worked on four needles are certainly the most difficult to work, especially the fingers, and the pattern on two needles is advised as being quicker and easier, with nothing to lose as compared with other types. However, many people prefer gloves worked on four needles, so as to avoid the join on the side of the fingers, so here is an explanation which is fairly simple.

Cast on 58 st. on to 3 needles and work in k. 2, p. 2 rib for about 8.8 cm. Then work two rounds in plain knitting. Mark the centre of the glove with a coloured thread and work two increases at the sides of the thread: in other words make a st. on the right of the thread, then k. 2 and then make a stitch again on the other side. Rep. these increases every two or three rows, 9 times, until there are 20 st. between one increase and the other. Place these 20 st. on a safety pin and leave them aside for the time being, continuing to work the glove by casting on 6 st. at base of thumb. Now work for about 2 inches and then divide the stitches for the fingers. Begin with the first finger. The total number of stitches should be 64, and now the separation of the palm and the back of the hand should also be marked with a coloured thread. Place 16 st. on a safety pin for the first finger, 16 on another for the middle finger, 16 for the third finger and 16 for the little finger, taking 8 st. from the back half and 8 from the palm. Now make up the stitches for the first finger, adding 4 new st. for the space between the first and second finger, a total of 20 in all and work for the required length (about thirty rows). At the end of the finger take the stitches together in twos, and then close the end by threading the wool through a needle and passing through the stitches, fastening off on the back. Next work the second and third fingers adding 4 st. for the space between the fingers: a total of 24 st. to be worked for the required length and then fastened off as above. Work the third finger in the same way.

For the little finger, there will be only 20 st. on the needle. Lastly, take up the thumb stitches, that is 20 plus 6 taken up from the glove, and work as for the other fingers for the required length.

Gloves on Two Needles (Fig. 86).

Right hand. Cast on 64 st. and work for about 15 cm in the following pattern.

1st row. p. 2, k. 2.
2nd row. Work the stitches as they come.
3rd row. p. 2, k. 2.
4th row. Knit.

Rep. from first row. Finish after 15 cm and begin the thumb. Work 33 st., work an increase (2 st. into one) then 1 st., and increase into next stitch, then work the remaining 28 st. Rep. these increases 3 times, always on the right side of work and always on the row after a knit row, so as to have 18 st. for the thumb. Now place the 34 st. from one side, and the 28 st. from the other, on to two safety pins. To the 18 thumb stitches add 2 st. on each side so that there are 22 in all. Work for about 10 cm and on last row work 2 st. tog. along the whole row. Then pass a needle threaded with the same yarn as the glove and pass it through the stitches, draw up and fasten off, then with the same needle and thread, sew up the two sides of the thumb to the base. Then pick up the 34 st. left on one side, pick up 6 from the base of the thumb and then 28 from the other pin. There should be 68 st. in all. Continue working for a total depth of about 15 cm, after which begin working the finger. Divide the number of stitches by 2, taking 10 from one side and 10 from the other, in other words, work 24 st., and on the following 20 work the first finger, adding 2 st. on the right and 2 on the left, a total of 24 st. in all. Continue working for 6 cm. For the middle finger, take 8 st. from either side, 4 from the base of the first finger, and, as for first finger, take 2 on either side at the beginning and end of each row. This gives a total of 24 st. to be worked for a length of 8 cm.

Fig. 86. Gloves worked in Clark's Anchor Stranded Cotton in écru, on two needles

Use the same method of working the third finger, with 24 st., and 6 cm in length. The little finger will be worked with 20 st. to a length of 5.7 cm.

On completion sew up the fingers and sides of the gloves on the right side, using the same yarn.

Work the left-hand glove in the same way, but reversing the instructions i.e.:

Begin the pattern row with k. 2, p. 2, and on coming to the thumb, work 28 st before the first increase and 34 after the second.

Knitted Gloves, worked Lengthways (Fig. 87)

Cast on 56 st. Work in Garter Stitch for six ribs, that is twelve rows, then cast off 19 st. (half little

Fig. 87. Gloves worked lengthways

finger). Continue on the same row and, working back, cast on 23 st. again for the third finger. Work another six ribs (twelve rows) and then cast off 23 st. Continue working and on the row back cast on 25 st. for the middle finger and work in the same way for the first finger, for which 23 st. should be cast on again. On completing the first finger, cast off all the stitches thus completing the upper half.

The bottom half is worked in the same way as far as the middle finger: on completing this, carry on by working 14 st., from the palm of the hand, threading the other stitches left on to a thread or safety pin apart. Now cast on, as well as the 14 st., 19 st. from the part towards the cuff; these will form the thumb. Work them back and add 23 st. on the opposite side for the first finger. Continue in Garter Stitch for another six ribs (twelve rows). Then cast off all the stitches. Now pick up again the stitches on the pin or thread, and work them, beginning from the inside. First work 8 and then turn back, then another 8 and turn back, and lastly work all the stitches on the needle. Then only cast on another 19 for the other half of the thumb. Work six ribs (twelve rows) and then cast

off all the stitches. Sew the glove on the wrong side, turn inside out and work the cuff ribbing (on four needles or in tubular knitting) picking up about 64 st. and working in k. 1, p. 1 rib for about 1¾ inches. Other sizes for larger hands: 68 st., little finger, 26; third finger, 30; middle finger, 32; first finger, 30; thumb, 26.

Bedroom Slippers (Fig. 88). These are worked in two pieces, the sole and the upper separately; on completing the two parts and after sewing them together, the short leg piece is worked. Our pattern shows bedroom slippers (Fig. 88) worked in blue and pink yarn.

Sole. Cast on 17 st. in blue thread (that is the background colour) and work in plain knitting for four rows (two ribs). Now begin the pattern in Furry Stitch (Fig. 89), as follows:

With blue yarn work k. 3, then wrap the pink yarn around first finger of the left hand four or five times, pass the right-hand needle below the fourth stitch and below the threads wrapped round the first finger, bringing the group of pink threads back through the blue stitch without working it, but instead knitting the following blue stitch and drawing up the stitch tightly. Rep. into the sixth and seventh stitches, and continue thus all along the needle. Knit last 3 st. Break off pink thread.

The return row is knitted in blue, through all the stitches, both pink and blue. Knit another three rows, and work the following one as the fifth already explained. From the diagram in Fig. 90 it will be easy to see how the threads of the pink thread are increased and decreased according to the shape the work must have. The pink stitches must be counted, and increased or decreased on the plain knit rows. Thus, for example, the first row of the sole is formed by 5 st., the second by 7. Since each stitch requires, in effect, 2 st., 4 st. must be added on the knit rows and the same for the decreases, i.e. for every stitch less in pink, decrease 2 st. on the knit row. Both the increases and decreases should be worked in the centre of the rows.

Upper. Cast on 19 st. and work as explained for the sole, increasing according to the diagram, until there are 21 pink st. Then divide the stitches. There should be a total of 47. Knit the first 3, then 7 pink st. and then place the next 13 st. on a

Fig. 89 (below). Pattern of Furry Stitch (wrong side)

Fig. 88 (above). Bedroom slippers in Furry Stitch

safety pin apart, then work 7 pink st. and 3 knit. Work the two parts separately for thirteen rows of pink stitches.

On completion of both sole and upper, sew together on wrong side with oversewing. Then, on the right side, pick up all the side stitches (40 on each side) and the thirteen central stitches, placing them on three needles. Now work a k. 2 p. 2 rib, except for the 16 central st., which are always worked in plain knitting for about 19 cm. Work a row of holes to thread the ribbon through, and then work another inch in the same way; plain knitting for another 30 mm and then cast off.

This last piece is rolled over, as shown in the illustration of the finished slipper.

Thread a ribbon or cord through the holes and the slipper is finished. Work the other exactly the same.

The Second Type (Fig. 91). Cast on 100 st. and work sixteen rows (eight ribs) in plain knitting. On the seventeenth row work: k. 47, k. two tog., k. 2, sl. 1, k. 1, p.s.s.o., k. 47. Purl eighteenth row.

Rep. seventeenth and eighteenth rows until there are 54 st. on the needle. Work the holes for the ribbon (k. two tog., yfd), and then another four rows knit, then cast off all the stitches. Thread a ribbon or cord through the holes.

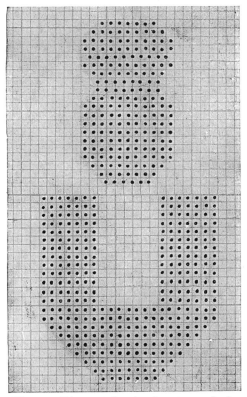

Fig. 90. Diagram showing how to work the bedroom slipper

Fig. 91. Another type of bedroom slipper, easy to make

Pattern. Ten rows (i.e. five ribs) in Garter Stitch (plain knitting) and eight rows in Stocking Stitch (one row knit, one row purl). The 4 central st. will always be in Stocking Stitch. Use Clark's Anchor Stranded Cotton (50-gm. ball) in cardinal 599, grey 418, or cobalt blue 592 and coral pink 503.

Darning on Knitting. It is unnecessary to dwell long upon the mending of modern stockings which, as everyone knows, can be mended in the usual way for holes in material, when there is a hole in the toe; and where there are ladders, these are best repaired by expert menders using special electrical machines which pick up the loops very easily and quickly and at a low cost.

However, a hole or tear in thick knitting can be repaired perfectly by using a needle and yarn.

These darns are used in two instances, as in the case of material: either to reinforce the material in weak spots, or to mend a hole in the material.

Reinforcing Knitting. When the knitting is slightly worn it is a good idea to reinforce it before it breaks away completely. This reinforcement can be done in one of two ways.

In the first case, as shown in Fig. 92, work over the old threads, taking up half a stitch in a vertical direction, that is with a stitch going from top to bottom and vice versa, alternately.

In the second case, work a Knitting Stitch, that is an imitation, using needle and thread, of the actual stitch made by the knitting needles themselves. Work in a horizontal direction: take up two threads of one stitch from below, then the two threads of the following stitch from above and so on. On the following row, turn the work and bring

out the needle between the two threads of the last stitch worked, going down to pick up the two threads of the stitch lying underneath, and then going back into the same place to take up the threads of the nearby stitch to the left and so on (Fig. 93).

Darning on Knitting. When the material is broken or torn so as to leave a hole, tack the torn part on to a stiffened card and, as in darning on material, straighten off the edges of the tear. Cut away the worn part and unpick worn threads, folding the uneven edges on to the wrong side and fixing them down with hidden stitches, so as to form perfectly straight edges at the sides, leaving the loops of knitting at the top and bottom (Fig. 94). Then begin the actual mending in one of two directions, both vertical and horizontal.

Mending on Vertical Threads. Pass vertical threads from a stitch above to the corresponding stitch below. The thread should pass twice through every stitch (Fig. 95).

Then, after attaching the thread to a good stitch, pass the threaded needle with the same wool or yarn into the first stitch above, taking a horizontal stitch over the two threads and then going below the two taut vertical threads, then back into the stitch above to take up another two threads. Continue thus along the whole row and at the end turn the work so as to work always from right to left and repeat the movement (Fig. 96).

Darning on Horizontal Threads. This second method does not give such perfect results as the first: but it is, perhaps, easier to carry out. After straightening the edges of the hole, as described above, place horizontal threads, as many as there are lines of knitting to substitute, working into the good stitches at either side (Fig. 97). Then work vertically on these threads making a kind of Stem Stitch first in one direction and then in the other; each stitch of knitting requires two rows of Stem Stitch (Fig. 98).

Mending on Purl Knitting. To mend on purling proceed as in Fig. 95. Make vertical threads, as explained for mending on Stocking Stitch, then pass the needle below a thread, from below to above, and then from above below, picking up the next vertical thread (Fig. 99).

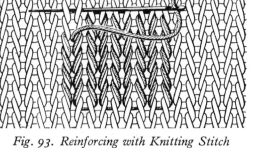

Fig. 92. Reinforcing worn knitted material

Fig. 93. Reinforcing with Knitting Stitch

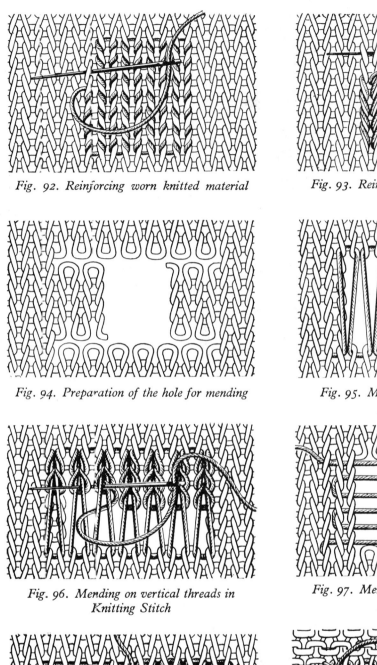

Fig. 94. Preparation of the hole for mending

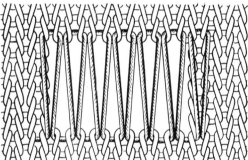

*Fig. 95. Mending on vertical threads:
placing threads*

*Fig. 96. Mending on vertical threads in
Knitting Stitch*

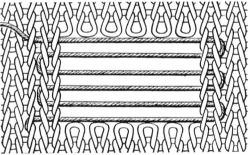

*Fig. 97. Mending on horizontal threads:
placing threads*

Fig. 98. Mending on horizontal threads

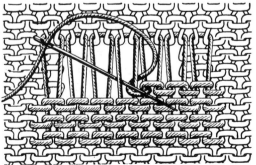

*Fig. 99. Mending on vertical threads on
purl knitting*

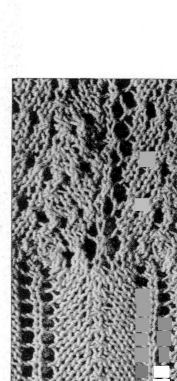

Lady's pullover

Pattern Stitches. The pullover is begun with a border in k. 1, p. 1 rib and then the pattern stitch, which is worked as follows:

Cast on a multiple of 10.

1st row. k. 2 tog., k. 3, (*) yfd., k. 1, yfd., k. 3, sl. 1, k. 2 tog., p.s.s.o., k. 3; rep. from (*) to last 5 sts., yfd., k. 1, yfd., k. 2, k. 2 tog.

2nd row. p.

The shoulders and sleeves are worked in a perforated stitch as follows, and require a multiple of 12 plus 1.

1st row. k. 1, (*) yfd., k. 2 tog.; rep. from (*) to end.

2nd and alt. rows. p.

3rd and 5th rows. (*) k. 1, yfd., k. 4, sl. 1, k. 2 tog., p.s.s.o., k. 4, yfd.; rep. from (*) to last st., k. 1.

6th row. As second row.

A row of double crochet finishes off the sleeves and collar.

Facing page
Long-sleeved jumper

Pattern Stitches

1st row (right side): * p.2, k.2, p.2 yon, sl. 1, k.1, psso, k.2; rep from * to last 6 sts, p.2, k.2, p.2.

2nd and alt rows: * k.2, p.2, k.2, p.4; rep from * to last 6 sts, k.2, p.2, k.2.

3rd row: * p.2, k.2, p.2, k.1, yfd., sl. 1, k.1, psso, k.1; rep from * to last 6 sts, p.2, k.2, p.2.

5th row: * p.2, tw.2, p.2, k.2, yfd., sl. 1, k.1, psso; rep from * to last 6 sts, p.1, tw.2, p.2.

6th row: as 2nd row.

These 6 rows for the patt. Continue in pattern until work measures 33 cm ending with a 6th pattern row.

Long-sleeved jumper

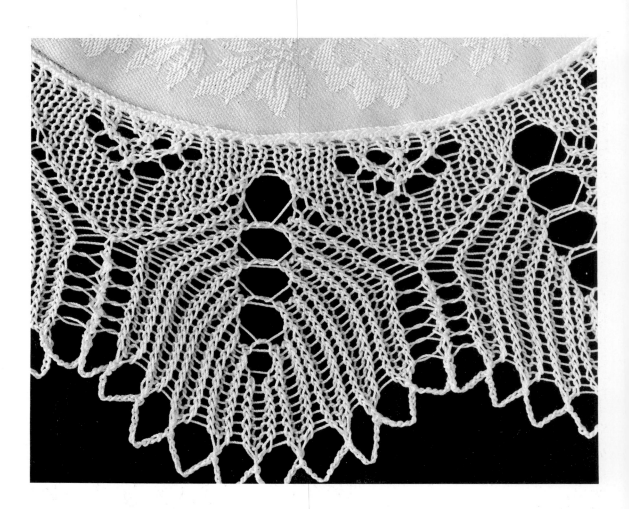

Doily with knitted lace edging

Materials

Coats Anchor Mercer-Crochet Cotton No. 20 (10 g)
2 balls selected colour.
It is advisable to purchase at one time the number of
balls sufficient for your requirements.
Set of four 2.75 mm (no. 12) Milward knitting need-
les with points at both ends (if your knitting is loose
use a size finer needle, if tight use a size larger
needle).
Milward steel crochet hook 1.25 (no. 3).
Piece of fabric 25 cm in diameter.
Coats Drima (polyester) thread.
Coats bias binding (optional).

Tension

8 sts and 11 rows to 2.5 cm square over stocking
stitch.

Measurement

Depth of edging – 9.5 cm
Finished size – 42 cm in diameter.

Abbreviations

k – knit; p – purl; st(s) – stitch(es); sl – slip; tog –
together; psso – pass slipped stitch over; yfd – yarn
forward; yrn – yarn round needle; m2 (make 2) –
into next stitch work k.1 p.1 and k.1; tbl – through
back of loop; alt – alternate; dc – double crochet; ch
– chain; ss – slip stitch.

Doily with knitted lace edging

Cast on 204 sts, 60 on each of 3 needles. K3 rounds.

4th round: ★ sl. 1, k.2 tog, psso., yfd., k.2 tog., yfd., k.10, yfd., sl. 1, k.1, psso., yfd.; rep. from ★ to end.

5th round: k.

6th round: ★ k.1, k.2 tog., yfd., k.4, k.2 tog., yrn. twice, sl. 1, k.1, psso., k.4, yfd., sl. 1, k.1, psso.; rep. from ★ to end.

7th and alt rounds: k, working k.1 and p.1 into each 'yrn. twice' of previous round.

8th round: Before commencing round k. first 2 sts from left hand needle on to right hand needle, mark beginning of round with a coloured thread. ★ yfd., k.4, k.2 tog., (M2) twice, sl. 1, k.1, psso., k.4, yfd., sl. 1, k.2 tog., psso.; rep. from ★ to end. 228 sts.

10th round: ★ k.4, k.2 tog., k.1 tbl., p.1, k.1 tbl., yrn. twice, k.1 tbl., p.1, k.1 tbl., sl. 1, k.1, psso., k.3, k.2 tog., yfd.; rep. from ★ to end.

11th and alt rounds: As 7th round working k. tbl. into tbl. sts. of previous round and p. into p. sts. of previous round.

12th round: ★ k.3, k.2. tog., k.1 tbl., p.1, k.1 tbl., (M2) twice, k.1 tbl., p.1, k.1 tbl., sl. 1, k.1, psso., k.4; rep. from ★ to end. 252 sts.

14th round: ★ k.2, k.2 tog., (k.1 tbl., p.1, k.1 tbl.) twice, yrn. twice, (k.1 tbl., p.1, k.1 tbl.) twice, sl. 1, k.1, psso., k.3; rep. from ★ to end.

16th round: ★ k.1, k.2 tog., (k.1 tbl., p.1, k.1 tbl.) twice, (M2) twice, (k.1 tbl., p.1, k.1 tbl.) twice, sl. 1, k.1, psso., k.2; rep. from ★ to end. 276 sts.

18th round: ★ k.2 tog., (k.1 tbl., p.1, k.1 tbl.) 3 times, yrn. twice, (k.1 tbl., p.1, k.1 tbl.) 3 times, sl. 1, k.1, psso., k.1; rep. from ★ to end.

20th round: Before commencing round k. first st. of left hand needle on to right hand needle, ★ (k.1 tbl., p.1, k.1, tbl.) 3 times, (M2) twice, (k.1 tbl., p.1, k.1 tbl.) 3 times, sl. 1, k.2 tog., psso.; rep. from ★ to end. 300 sts.

22nd round: ★ (k.1 tbl., p.1, k.1 tbl.) 4 times, yfd., (k.1 tbl., p.1, k.1 tbl) 4 times, yfd., k.1 tbl., yfd.; rep. from ★ to end. 336 sts.

24th round: ★ (k.1 tbl., p.1, k.1 tbl.) 4 times, M2, (k.1 tbl., p.1, k.1 tbl.) 4 times, yfd., sl. 1, k.2 tog., psso., yfd.; rep. from ★ to end. 360 sts.

26th, 28th and 30th rounds: ★ (k.1 tbl., p.1, k.1 tbl.) 9 times, yfd., sl. 1, k.2 tog., psso., yfd.; rep. from ★ to end.

32nd round: Work sts. as set. 360 sts.

Outer edging

Using crochet hook work ★ 1 dc. into 3 sts. and slip off needle, 10 ch.; rep. from ★ ending with 1 ss. into first dc. Fasten off.

Inner edging

With right side facing attach thread to cast on edge and work a row of dc. evenly round cast on edge ending with 1 ss. into first dc.

Fasten off.

Damp and pin out to measurement.

To make up

Turn back a small hem on fabric or face with bias binding. Place edging to fabric and sew neatly in position.

*Table centre worked in knitting using Coats Mercer-Crochet, No. 20, in écru.
The edging is in crochet*

The patterns for this type of work have been especially studied so that each design is explained by means of conventional signs placed on a network of lines corresponding to the different stitches. The diagram generally shows a complete pattern of the design, which is then repeated as many times as necessary.

Very fine stocking needles are required to work this stitch as well as a special well-twisted yarn which should be very strong. An excellent one is Coats Mercer-Crochet in No. 60.

These laces are preferably worked in white or natural, rather than in colours, because they are imitations of valuable laces. For oval or round pieces begin to work in the centre, casting on stitches, on to a circle of yarn with a crochet hook. These stitches are then passed on to a knitting needle, working round, on four needles.

For working backwards and forwards, simply cast on to a stocking needle.

The finishings off of this work are generally worked in crocheting. Group together three or four stitches with the crocheting, letting them off the needle and then passing on to another group by means of ten or twelve Chain Stitches.

Stocking Stitch lace only takes on form after being starched and ironed. These are very important for the success of the work. We should like to draw our readers' attention to the chapter on "Washing and Pressing" where the process of ironing lace is fully explained.

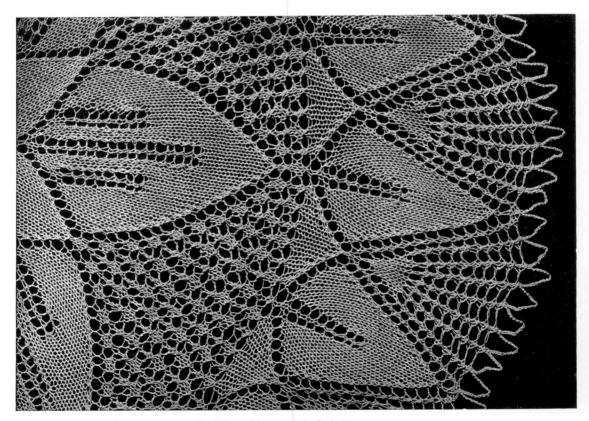

Detail of the table centre in knitting on page 425

426

10 *Various Types of Embroidery*

CHAPTER XXXII

Italian Embroidery

It could be said that in every corner of Italy there is a different kind of embroidery. Thus we have the Drawn-thread Work of Sicily and Sardinia, the laces of Venice and Cantù, the tablecloths of Assisi, the ancient stitches deriving from antique lace; Orvieto, Siena, Parma are only some of the centres, but there are many others throughout Italy.

In this book some of the more important regional stitches of Italy have already been mentioned. For example, Sicilian and Sardinian Drawn-thread Work, Assisi embroidery, Venetian stitch, the laces of Orvieto, Puncetto work, Sardinian filet, etc. All these are found in the chapters on particular types of embroidery or lace.

In this chapter other regional types of embroidery are illustrated, together with clear and simple explanations of the technique of each and of the various stitches. A brief mention of the historical background is also given.

Bandera Embroidery. Amongst the regional work of Italy, Bandera embroidery is the one which most certainly originated in Piedmont.

It seems that the seventeenth-century fashion, derived from France, of covering furniture such as armchairs, divans and stools to protect them from dust and dirt became very widespread among rich Piedmontese families. These covers, which were at first quite simple, were later enriched with Bandera embroidery in the style of the period, the designs being inspired by the brocades, damasks and velvets of the time. Thus Bandera embroidery followed the Baroque style of the seventeenth century, often with geometrical lines enclosing fruit and floral motifs. Later, in the eighteenth century, new motifs were introduced including figures, birds and draperies. The technique, however, remained the same.

As happens to every form of minor art which follows the fashion of the time, Bandera embroidery went out of fashion and was only revived again at the end of the last century by the efforts of two Piedmontese ladies, Countess Sofia di Bricherasio and Mrs. Lampugnani. In 1907, the Countess Bricherasio founded and managed a workroom which took the name of "The Piedmont Bandera School", and the work is still inspired by the Italian designs of the seventeenth and eighteenth centuries.

Bandera embroidery is very rich in design. Flowers, fruit, leaves, posies, garlands, birds and butterflies are all worked in a great range of colour on natural-coloured rough twill, with a rather strongly twisted thread. The original work was carried out in wool, but a twisted cotton thread may be used successfully.

The embroidery stitches in which Bandera embroidery is worked include Satin Stitch and Stem Stitch, but the decorative lines which often

Screen in natural linen in Bandera embroidery. The design is a repeating pattern taken from an old motif. It is worked in shades of old gold, blue, cardinal red, sea-green and violet

Motif in Bandera embroidery

429

Decorative panel in Bandera embroidery. This was worked in the Countess Sofia di Bricherasio's Piedmontese school

Corner of a napkin in Palestrina embroidery

occur are worked in close rows of Chain Stitch in graded colours to give a delicate shading.

Palestrina Embroidery. This work takes its name from a village in Lazio, Palestrina. It is worked in a particularly interesting stitch of the same name and examples of this embroidery, made by the girls of the "Ciociaria", the Palestrina School, are exported today.

Palestrina Stitch is worked on rather thick, natural or coloured fabric, in a single light colour, such as white or natural on a dark background, or in dark red, rust, blue on white or pale-coloured fabrics.

Palestrina embroidery is worked in a knotted stitch called "Palestrina Stitch", Rush Stitch, Knots and Stem Stitch.

Palestrina Stitch is worked horizontally from left to right. Draw the needle out of the fabric and make a stitch from above to below taking up five or six threads. Go back into the stitch, without taking up the fabric, and keeping the thread to the right with the thread under the thumb of the left hand, go back again into the first stitch. Repeat this stitch. When the design has curved lines, the stitches are made slightly obliquely. On the wrong side of the fabric Palestrina Stitch shows a series of vertical stitches which, if the stitch is well made,

Palestrina Stitch or Double Knot Stitch

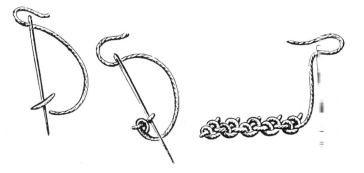

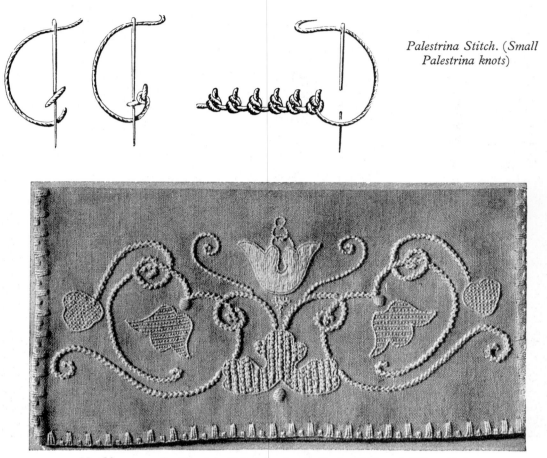

Napkin case embroidered in Palestrina knots, Rush Stitch and filling stitches

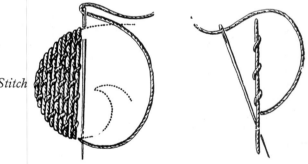

Rush Stitch

appear at regular intervals and are all of the same length.

Another knotted stitch used in Palestrina embroidery is also illustrated. The diagram is very clear. Begin as for the previously explained stitch and work two Blanket Stitches in the opposite direction, i.e. from right to left without taking up the fabric and repeat the movement. These knots are smaller than the others. Coats Anchor Coton à Broder may be used for these knotted stitches.

Rush Stitch is another important feature of Palestrina embroidery and is used to fill large

Detail of Perugino embroidery worked on a table mat

spaces. The stitch is quickly worked almost always on the straight thread of the fabric. Lay a thread between the two lines of the design as shown in the illustration, from bottom to top, and go back over it, sewing it down with small, slightly oblique stitches. Begin again, taking care to alternate the small stitches. Rush Stitch thus makes an area of heavy, close embroidery. It is very similar to Bokhara Couching.

Generally, in Palestrina embroidery, Rush Stitch is outlined with Stem Stitch in the same colour as the rest of the embroidery.

In some pieces of work, the background is worked in Rush Stitch, whilst in others the motifs themselves are worked. The different directions of the stitch, which can be worked either horizontally or vertically, and in some cases obliquely, give interesting variations of light and shade to work carried out in a single colour.

In Palestrina embroidery other stitches are also used, such as Stem Stitch and French Knots. These are explained and illustrated in the chapter "Various Embroidery Stitches". The edges of Palestrina embroidery are finished by turning in a hem and decorating with Blanket Stitch. Palestrina embroidery is easy to work and very effective for cushions, curtains, bed-spreads and other objects which require a bold treatment.

Perugino Embroidery. This embroidery is worked by placing Satin Stitches one beside the other, over four or five threads in width, following a given design. The stitches should be counted and placed closely side by side without overlapping. The designs are inspired by stylised animals, flowers, figures or geometrical motifs, first worked out on squared paper, with a given number of stitches, four, five or six, according to the thickness of the fabric represented by one square. The background cloth should be rather

433

Linen table mats and napkins decorated with Perugino embroidery

strong, with a regular weave, so that it is possible to count the threads easily. The embroidery is generally worked in a single colour, blue, rust or light brown, or bright red. Coats Anchor Stranded Cotton may be used, the number of strands being selected according to the thickness of the fabric. Table mats, beach bags and cushion covers are suitable for decoration with this stitch. The table mats and napkins shown here have been carried out in two tones of natural thread on ivory fabric.

Perugino Stitch is worked in Sardinia, as well as in other districts of Italy. In Sardinia it is worked in many colours, for mats and tablecloth borders.

Sienese Embroidery. The first examples of Sienese embroidery were exhibited at the Siena Samples Fair in 1921, when the Sienese section of the National Council of Italian Women, presided over by Mrs. Maria Martini Mari, created a Committee of Ars Senensis, which developed into an organisation for the encouragement of women's work and the economic improvement of the workers. The original Sienese embroidery was inspired by stone fragments with designs of primitive flowers and animals, from antique monuments in the church of St. Antonio, from Roman bas-reliefs, from ancient palaces and medieval buildings in which Siena is rich, or from paintings by Sienese artists.

The fabric, colours, and stitch are all characteristic of Sienese work. The background fabric is a coarse, thick cloth in a natural colour, often woven especially for the work. The colours for the embroidery are generally blue and black. Sienese embroidery is very quick to work because it is always carried out on rather thick fabric.

434

Sienese Stitch

Several well-known stitches are used in Sienese embroidery, together with a new one called Sienese Stitch. It is this stitch which makes the ornamental part of the designs stand out, whilst the flowers and figures and animals are worked in Rush Stitch. Rush Stitch has been fully explained in the paragraph on Palestrina Stitch.

Sienese Stitch is easily worked from the diagram. Work between two parallel lines. Bring out the needle on the bottom line of the design, throw the thread up with a vertical stitch and take the needle into the upper line and out again on the lower line. Go back to the centre of the vertical stitch and make a Blanket Stitch, without picking up the fabric underneath. Go back through the upper line to come out again on the lower one a little further to the right. Sienese Stitch is generally completed by a line of Stem Stitch in black worked along each edge. On the curves, the stitches must be worked closer together on the inner edge and wider apart on the outer edge. The most suitable thread is Coats Anchor Coton à Broder in rust, blue or black.

Byzantine Work. This type of embroidery, usually worked in rust colour or blue, originated and developed in Ravenna where Byzantine art in the churches and palaces offers an inexhaustible source of inspiration.

The designs are, in fact, taken from the architecture of Ravenna and from the famous mosaics which decorate the Cathedral.

The background is worked in Rush Stitch, and the design outlined in Stem Stitch in the same colour, or very often in black. Finer lines are worked within the shapes in Stem Stitch. Use Coats Anchor Stranded Cotton for this embroidery.

Napkin case with a motif in Sienese embroidery worked in rust and black

Byzantine embroidery. On white linen, the background of the design is worked in Rush Stitch in blue

Monna Vanna Embroidery. The stitch originated in a legend. A young maiden called Monna Vanna was tired of waiting anxiously for her lover to return from the Crusades and so she began to work a crochet. Growing tired of this monotonous work, she picked it up one day and threw it away. The chain fell into whirls and patterns and suggested how this embroidery might be carried out. Long chains of crochet are sewn invisibly on to thick fabric in geometrical designs. These chains are always worked in white or natural and applied to fabric of the same colour. The work is then enriched with flowers embroidered in colour, scattered here and there or placed regularly inside the shapes created by the chain design. Monna Vanna embroidery is easy to work and suitable for simple everyday objects such as work bags, table runners, garden cushions and cloths.

The illustration shows a tea cosy worked on ivory coloured cloth. The chain, worked in Coats Anchor Coton à Broder in white, is applied to the fabric as already explained. The small flowers completing the design are worked in Coats Anchor Stranded Cotton.

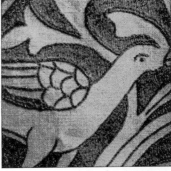

A detail of the Byzantine embroidery

Sorbello Embroidery. Sorbello embroidery is worked on thick linen or crash and is so called after the small Neapolitan village where it is worked. The stitch is similar to Palestrina Stitch and it is used to decorate small mats, table runners, bags and cushion covers. It is worked in white on natural or coloured cloth, or in brown on white or natural cloth, using a thick thread.

The diagram is quite clear. Work a horizontal stitch and an oblique stitch towards the left, and then, without going through the fabric, work two Blanket Stitches. After the second stitch go back

436

Bandera embroidery adapted for a chairback cover

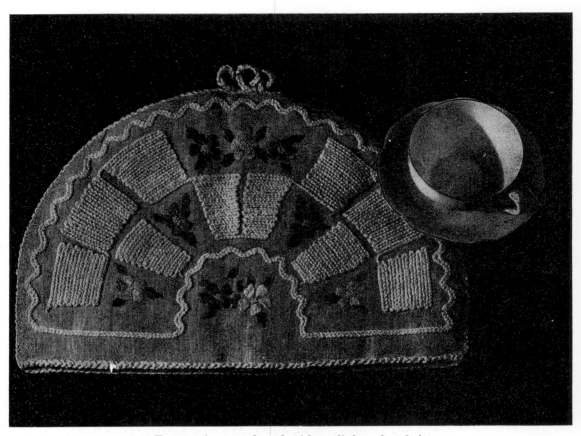

Tea cosy in natural crash with applied crochet chains

into the fabric with a vertical stitch on the wrong side and make a horizontal stitch. Repeat the movement from the first horizontal stitch.

This is simple, easy work, which is very decorative. The table runner shown on page 439 is worked in Coats Anchor Coton à Broder in brown on natural-coloured cloth and the design is worked in Sorbello Stitch.

Catherine de Medici Stitch or Madame Stitch. This originated in Umbria, where it was in fashion at the Florentine Court in the first half of the sixteenth century. Catherine de Medici, a patron of the needlework in which she herself excelled, encouraged her ladies to work this stitch, and so it came to be called by her name. In France the stitch was later called "Madame" Stitch after the name which the people gave to this severe Queen when she became the wife of Henry II.

The embroidery is easy to work, and it has a particular beauty of its own. The background is a loosely woven dark grey fabric. The thread used today for working the stitch is Coats Anchor Coton à Broder in white or écru.

The stitch is worked over counted threads, so that it is not necessary to transfer a design to the fabric. The designs used have not changed very much with time and no attempt has been made to modernise them. They still preserve their ancient characteristics; stylised birds and animals and trees, arabesques and lines set amongst geometrical decorations.

The working consists of a Double Running Stitch generally over two threads of the fabric, as in Holbein Stitch. On the row back, however, the needle should be placed into the fabric once to the right and once to the left of the stitch on the forward row, so that the stitch looks twisted. If this is worked well, the back of the work should be like the front.

438

Today, Madame Stitch is still worked in Umbria, in Perugia, and Deruta, and in Tuscany in the traditional style.

The edges are generally finished off with double crochet worked with picots at regular intervals, over a very small hem.

Casalguidi Embroidery. Casalguidi, a small place near Pistoia, gives its name to this type of embroidery. The embroidery presents an appearance of strong contrasts as the background is worked either in a Pulled Fabric Filling or in Drawn-thread Work and the rest of the embroidery is Corded in a rather special way.

Casalguidi work is rather heavy, but rich and suitable for bags, cushion covers, curtains and even carpets. It is worked on rather strong coloured fabric (Florentine linen) and the embroidery is usually in pure white, contrasting vividly with the coloured background. On white cloth the design is worked, instead, in natural. Coats Anchor Coton à Broder is suitable for carrying out this work.

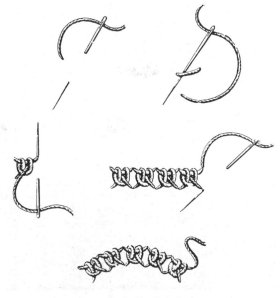

Sorbello Stitch

A runner in natural-coloured cloth, embroidered in Sorbello Stitch

439

For the openwork background, the threads are drawn out and secured with simple Hemstitching. Rodi Stitch may also be used for the background without drawing any threads out from the fabric. (See chapter on "Filling Stitches".) The whole of the background must be worked, the actual Casalguidi embroidery being superimposed afterwards.

As can be seen from the illustrations, the essential element of the embroidery is a thick cord, arranged in geometrical shapes, which surrounds other embroidered sections.

The shapes to be worked are traced on to the perforated background with Running Stitches. The illustration shows the tracing of the design with Running Stitch, and the application of the padding for the cord. Take a group of threads (Clark's Anchor Stranded Cotton) and fix down at regular intervals. Then cover by oversewing, keeping the stitches even, but not too close together. On completing the oversewing, work rows of close Stem Stitch, taking two of the oversewing stitches at a time until the whole cord has been covered.

These cords are often joined together or attached to the background by loops made in Cording. That is, three or four threads are passed round the cord and covered with Cording Stitch.

One of the most common Casalguidi motifs is the rosette in Venetian Stitch. To make a petal,

begin from the base of the small triangle by working Blanket Stitch with nine or ten stitches over a laid thread. Work back and forth, decreasing by one stitch every row until only one stitch is left. This is the point of the triangle which is then fixed to the fabric, taking care that the petal stands out well. The six small petals are joined at their points by small Curl Stitches.

The same illustration shows other decorative stitches in Casalguidi embroidery, such as small trees in Cording and Blanket Stitch, groups of Bullion Knots and leaves in Venetian Stitch.

The edges of Casalguidi embroidery may be finished off with a simple Hemstitched hem. Tassels, loops and balls, worked in crochet, are sometimes used to decorate the corners of bags and mats.

Antique Stitch or Tuscan Stitch. To find examples of this stitch it is necessary to go back to the fourteenth and the beginning of the fifteenth centuries, when it was much used for the brightly coloured household linen.

Antique Stitch, which has undergone many changes in the course of time, is still a valuable embroidery stitch. Worked on a natural-coloured cloth in white, or natural, and sometimes in very pale tones of colour, it is one of a group of stitches best used for geometrical designs. Since the stitch

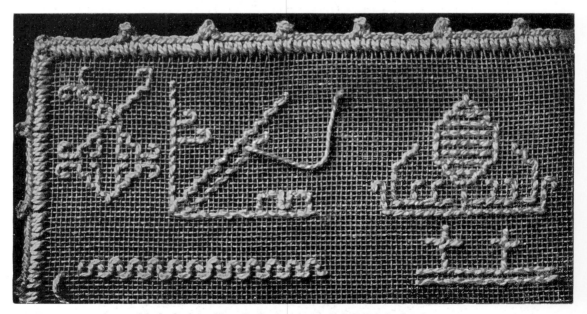

Method of working Catherine de Medici Stitch is clearly seen

Table runner in Catherine de Medici Stitch

Motifs worked in Catherine de Medici Stitch

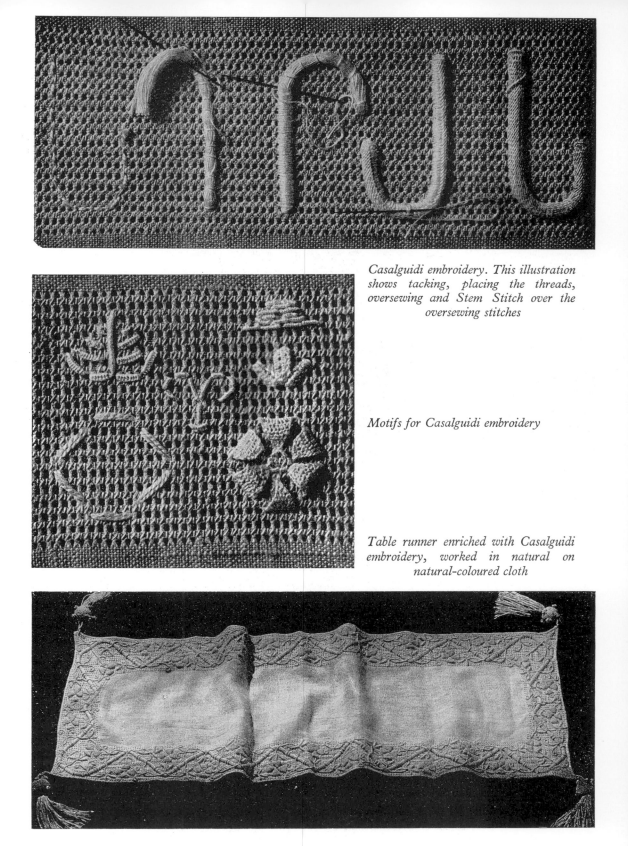

Casalguidi embroidery. This illustration shows tacking, placing the threads, oversewing and Stem Stitch over the oversewing stitches

Motifs for Casalguidi embroidery

Table runner enriched with Casalguidi embroidery, worked in natural on natural-coloured cloth

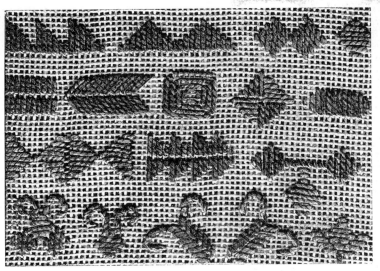

Satin Stitch worked on fabric with a very open weave to show the working method clearly

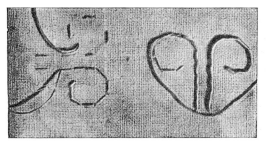

Method of working Curl Stitch

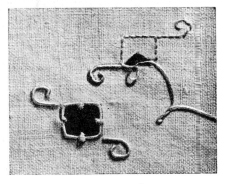

Squares outlined in Cording with picots

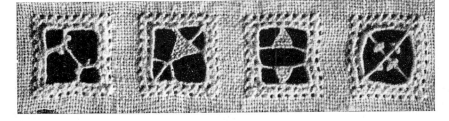

Squares in Aemilia Ars outlined with Four-sided Stitch

Squares in Aemilia Ars worked in Anchor Coton à Broder

143

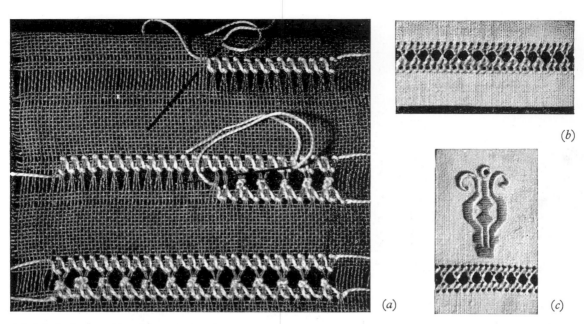

(a) *Method of working Fleur de Lys Stitch;* (b) *Fleur de Lys Stitch worked on fine material;* (c) *Motif in Satin Stitch, Curl Stitch and Fleur de Lys Stitch*

Napkin case in Antique Stitch embroidered on yellow linen

444

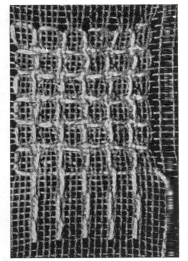

Deruta embroidery: preparatory
Running Stitches

Vertical and horizontal
Running Stitches

A piece of the finished work.
Note the twists at the corners

developed in Tuscany it is also called "Tuscan Stitch".

The stitch should be worked on a cloth which is evenly woven, but not too fine, since it is worked by the counted threads and the geometrical designs must be worked out on squared paper.

The best thread for this stitch is Coats Anchor Coton à Broder or Coats Anchor Stranded Cotton.

Antique Stitch is a flat Satin Stitch, without padding, always worked on the straight thread of the cloth. The stitches should never overlap, but lie side by side.

Curl Stitch consists of a cord in relief. To work this stitch make a row of Running Stitches, taking up five or six threads of material and leaving the same number. Then make a second row to cover the spaces, as in Holbein Stitch. Work over the Running Stitches by oversewing so that any unevenness is avoided, and lastly work Cording Stitch, without taking up the threads of fabric, so that the effect is that of a cord in relief.

Four-sided Stitch is worked both on the straight thread and diagonally. It is used for subdividing a pattern into squares or diamonds, to finish off hems, to outline perforated squares. The explanation of the stitch, both diagonal and horizontal, is to be found in the chapter headed "Hemstitch". Sometimes the stitch is used diagonally and reversed, that is, worked on the wrong side of the fabric.

Here we give some suggestions for open squares. To work squares (these may be, instead, triangles or rectangles), first mark the shape with Running Stitch as explained for Curl Stitch, then cut the fabric with very sharp scissors, beginning from the centre and cutting towards the corners. Turn back the pieces of fabric and work in Cording. Four of the squares shown in the illustration are then surrounded by simple Square Stitch, worked before cutting away the fabric.

Fleur de Lys Stitch. This is a form of Hemstitching which is often used for finishing off the edges in Antique Work or Assisi Work. Make a foundation by drawing out a thread from the fabric, leaving three or four and drawing out six or eight, leaving in three or four again, and lastly drawing out one.

Work on the right side of the work from right to left.

1st row. Take three drawn threads from above with a horizontal stitch and then take the needle down to three threads below, making an oblique stitch on the back. Take the same three threads of the central row of drawn threads with a horizontal stitch and go up again with an oblique stitch on the right side of the work. Taking the three following threads, bring the needle out three threads to the left of the first stitch. Take up these

Corner of a rich luncheon cloth in Antique Stitch, worked in natural on white cloth. The border, enclosed between two rows of Fleur de Lys Stitch, is composed of motifs in Satin Stitch and Curl Stitch alternating with open squares. The corner is worked in the same way

Tea cloth in Deruta Stitch with squares filled in Aemilia Ars

(Below) A detail of the cloth

447

Detail of a rich luncheon cloth in Canusina embroidery. The cloth is divided into many squares, which are repeated around the edge of the cloth, leaving the centre of the cloth unworked. The background material is ivory-coloured linen and the embroidery is worked in brown, natural, dark blue and sea-green

448

three threads with a horizontal stitch and repeat.

2nd row. Work the same stitch on the lower row of drawn threads and, at the same time, the knot binding the two groups. Proceed thus: always working from right to left, take up with the needle three threads from the bottom row of drawn threads, then three from the central line, bringing the needle out three threads further to the left. Take up these three threads with a horizontal stitch and go down with an oblique stitch on the back of the work to take up again the three free threads on the lower line, making a horizontal stitch and going up again with an oblique stitch on the right side to take up the three threads of the second group. Before working the horizontal stitch at this point, draw up the two groups with a knot which should be seen on the right side of the work, then going down to make the horizontal stitch of the second group, bringing the needle out three threads more to the left of the lower row of drawn threads. Then begin again from the beginning. The knot is the same as made in other types of Drawn-thread Work (see chapter on "Hemstitch").

Deruta Embroidery. The small town in Umbria called Deruta has given its name to two types of embroidery: one in bright colours which imitates the ceramics of Deruta, Gualdo Tadino, Gubbio, and Orvieto, on material. The vivid, almost iridescent colours of the pottery are worked in Satin Stitch in graduated shades of colours in which deep blue and green predominate. Outlining in Stem Stitch in black is often used to define the pattern. The background fabric may vary from heavy linen to delicate, almost transparent, lawn. The best thread to use for this embroidery is Coats Anchor Stranded Cotton because the wide range of colours makes it possible to match up the colours in pottery designs.

The other type of "Deruta" embroidery is quite different as it is worked by the counted thread of the fabric. It is neutral in colour, generally being worked in white or natural on a very dark fabric which makes it suitable for rooms in which the furnishing is rather severe. The background fabric is loosely woven and not unlike canvas, but much softer in texture. The designs are almost always geometrical, with sometimes imaginary or stylised animals.

The most suitable threads for the embroidery are Clark's Anchor Coton à Broder and Clark's Anchor Stranded Cotton.

Begin with a vertical Running Stitch, taking up four threads of the fabric and leaving the same number and go back to fill in the spaces. Repeat the Running Stitch at a distance of four threads (see illustrations). Then make a row of Running Stitches in the opposite direction, that is horizontally, twisting the threads at the crossings at the corners. Draw up the stitches tightly.

Canusina Embroidery. This work takes its name from the town of Canossa and it is of fairly recent origin. It was developed at the Colonia Marro School, a craft organisation directed by Dr. Mary Bertolani and Professor Giuseppi Baroni. The work of this school included other crafts as well as embroidery—pottery, tooled leather work and wrought iron. There is a similarity of design in all of these as it is chiefly inspired by the study of motifs which may be found in the sculptured decorations of the local castles and churches. All the work produced at the school bears the emblem of the Countess Matilde di Canossa, who in 1077 witnessed the legendary scene between Pope Gregory VII and the Emperor Henry IV. This emblem consists of the letter "M" within which are intertwined the emblem of the city of Reggio Calabria and that of the Canossa family.

Many stitches are used in this type of embroidery, but the most important is Stem Stitch. This stitch is worked in close rows to fill in large areas and the colours are often used to give a shaded effect. Small pieces of embroidery are worked in the hand and larger pieces in a frame.

The Stem Stitch should be rather long (each stitch being about 6 mm) and follow the outline of the design, the worker holding the needle pointed towards herself and keeping the thread to the right. After working the first line of stitches, the embroidery is turned round and the next row is worked so that the stitches alternate with those in the first line. The work proceeds backwards and forwards. This method of working Stem Stitch creates a very closely stitched surface.

The thread to be used in Canusina embroidery depends upon the type of background fabric. Coats Anchor Stranded Cotton, using a number of strands to give the desired weight, is very suitable for working this embroidery.

The illustration shows part of a luncheon cloth worked in Canusina embroidery. As can easily be seen in the illustration, all the linear part is worked in Stem Stitch. The flower shapes in the outer border are also outlined in Stem Stitch, and the inner parts filled with a counted thread stitch. In the centre, the same filling with a Stem Stitch outline is used for the decoration, and the birds are worked in Stem Stitch in different colours and graduated shades. The fabric from which the cloth is made is natural-coloured linen, and the thread is Coats Anchor Stranded Cotton.

Parma Embroidery. The embroidery was developed by a group of workers under the direction of Professor Bianca Bonfigli Bignotti, helped by Professor Irma Lanza Balestrieri, in the little town of Parma in the province of Lombardy.

The designs worked in Parma embroidery are often taken from the decorative details of the Cathedral and Baptistery of Parma, using such scenes as the "Hunt" from the doorway of the cathedral and the bizarre animals from the group around the Baptistery, motifs taken from the cathedrals of Fidenza and the Church of Pomposa, and designs taken from fragments of doorways and from the borders of copes and stoles.

The embroidery is worked on strong, heavy, natural linen cloth with a natural-coloured cotton thread, using various thicknesses in the same piece of work. Sometimes work is carried out in coloured thread, generally brown, on a light back-

ground. Coats Anchor Coton à Broder may be used for this embroidery.

Many familiar embroidery stitches are used in this work. There is, however, a stitch which is absolutely characteristic of the embroidery and found in every piece of Parma embroidery.

The other stitches, which include French Knots, Chain Stitch, Seeding Stitch, Cross Stitch and Stem Stitch, are all to be found illustrated in other chapters.

Typical Parma Embroidery Stitch. A heavy line which stands out in relief on the background fabric, and is found in most examples of this embroidery, is worked as follows:

Work three rows of Chain Stitch very close together in the same direction taking care to see that all the stitches lie side by side. Whilst it is easy to work the stitches in this way on a straight line, care must be taken on the curves, making the stitches shorter on the inside of the curve and longer on the outer side.

After completing these three rows work Blanket Stitch over the Chain Stitches without going through the fabric underneath. This is shown clearly in the illustration.

The edges of Parma embroideries are decorated with large Blanket Stitches and Four-sided Stitch.

Parma embroidery is very suitable for heavy furnishings such as curtains, cushions and bed-covers.

Part of a cushion cover in Parma embroidery. The background is brown with the embroidery in ivory

Method of working Parma embroidery: the illustration shows various stitches which may be combined for Parma work

Bricco Embroidery. The Countess Tarsilla Petiti di Roreto, at the beginning of this century, was inspired by a precious vestment in the parish church of a small village in Piedmont, and developed from this a type of embroidery which provided work for the girls of the village. She founded a school called "Bricco Embroideries", where she taught a modern adaptation of this particular embroidery. The actual vestment is made from fine linen embroidered with linen threads and with silver.

Modern Bricco embroidery is worked upon rather strong cloth with coloured cotton thread. The designs, which are rich in heraldic emblems, stylised flowers and various birds, are worked in a great variety of stitches, such as Satin Stitch, Stem Stitch, Chain Stitch, and Knots. Buttonhole Stitch rather widely spaced is, however, the most important stitch in this work.

A single colour of thread is generally used for each piece of work. The best thread for the work is Coats Anchor Coton à Broder.

Arezzo Embroidery. Towards the end of last century some ancient pieces of fabric with an uneven weave, embroidered in Cross Stitch in rust and blue, were found in the course of excavations being made in Arezzo.

The quality of the fabric, the design and the colours suggested that these interesting pieces must have been worked about 1400. Following this discovery a group of women tried to revive interest in this type of embroidery. Modified forms of the old designs were made using traditional motifs such as stylised birds and imaginary animals enclosed in geometrical shapes. Special fabric was hand woven in the nearby town of Città di Castello. Their initiative, however, had little success, and the traditional embroidery was eventually carried on by Florentine embroideresses.

At first sight, the embroidery of Arezzo may be confused with that of Assisi, since it is also worked in Cross Stitch in similar colour schemes. But while in Assisi work the background is embroidered, in Arezzo embroidery the motifs are worked and the background is left plain. The greatest difference between the two, however, is that all the Cross Stitches in Assisi work must be made in the same direction, and in Arezzo embroidery the stitches may be made otherwise.

The background fabric for Arezzo embroidery is rather thick and dark, with an irregular weave, which was a characteristic of the ancient fabric. Coats Anchor Coton à Broder in rust or blue may be used for this embroidery.

There are two basic stitches. The filled-in parts of the design are worked in a stitch which is not the usual Cross Stitch, but is similar to Slav Cross Stitch (see chapter headed "Cross Stitch"). The

Cushion cover in Bricco embroidery worked on natural-coloured cloth

452

Ricamo Lampugnani

"The Silver Pheasant." Design worked in silver grey on a black background

linear parts of the design which, in Assisi work, are carried out in Holbein Stitch, consist in Arezzo embroidery of simple stitches worked over four threads of fabric in a forward direction.

Narrow hems are worked in Four-sided Stitch, at a distance of four threads from the design.

The Work of Teresita Lampugnani. Teresita Lampugnani has in recent years developed an original type of embroidery worked entirely in Running Stitch. Mrs. Lampugnani works on many different kinds of fabric and uses Running Stitch as a medium for interpreting her vigorously drawn designs. Geometrical patterns, butterflies, birds and flowers are worked in brilliant colours with great variation in tone.

The "Silver Pheasant" shown here is one of Signora Lampugnani's most important pieces.

Split Stitch Embroidery Designed by Francesco dal Pozzo. This interesting embroidery was originated by the Italian painter, Francesco dal Pozzo, as a means for carrying out some of his compositions in fabric and thread.

The design is traced on to very light fabric in a frame. Split Stitch is worked following the straight thread of the fabric in vertical or horizontal lines. All the stitches must be worked in the same direction and the interest of the work lies in the use of colour and in the vigorous and personal interpretation of the designs. The thread is usually embroidery wool, but Coats Anchor Stranded Cotton could be used for very fine and delicate pieces.

Florentine or Italian Quilting. The two famous Sicilian hangings telling the story of Tristan and Isolda, one of which is in the National Museum at Florence and the other in the Victoria and Albert Museum, London, are the most antique and precious examples of this type of quilting. They were made in 1300 and there are very few other existing examples of this work.

Modern Florentine or Italian Quilting has come back into fashion in the last few years in a simplified form for dressing gowns, cushions, bed covers and for babies' pram and cot covers. Suitable fabrics to use are pure silk and rayon crêpes and shantung silk for quilted garments. Heavier silks and cotton poplin are often used for furnishings. Fine muslin is required for the underside of the work. For the sewing, which is carried out in Running Stitch, use Coats Anchor Stranded Cotton on fine fabrics and Coats Drima (polyester) for heavier work. Thick, soft wool is necessary for the padding.

When planning a design for Florentine or Italian Quilting bear in mind the fact that double rows of stitching are required as these will form channels through which the padding wool is passed. The illustrations in this chapter show clearly the type of design which is required.

Working Method. Trace the design on to the muslin backing and tack securely to the silk. This

Detail of the wall panel by Francesco Dal Pozzo. Note the perfect execution of the stitches, which all lie in the same direction, and the clarity of the outlines even in the minutest details of the design

Wall panel, "The Signs of the Zodiac", a composition by the painter Francesco Dal Pozzo

tacking must be very carefully done so that the two fabrics lie smoothly together. Make the first line of tacking horizontally across the centre of the work and let the second, vertical one, cross at right angles. Other supplementary rows must then be made. When this preparation is complete, work around the design in Running Stitch, using a fine thread in the same colour as the background fabric or in a contrasting colour, or black if desired. Each stitch must pass through both layers of fabric.

Padding. When the Running Stitch is finished the padding is threaded in between the lines of the design. Take a thick wool needle without a point, thread it with the thick wool and pass it between the double lines of each part of the design. To do this, work from the back and push the needle through the soft muslin backing. Look at the right side of the work often to see that the padding is even and do not pull too tightly as this will cause puckering. When threading round a curve bring out the needle at intervals, leave a small loop of wool and return the needle into the same hole to continue the padding. Regulate the padding by easing it carefully with the fingers as the work proceeds.

The finished quilting may be lined with the

Florentine or Italian quilting. Right side of finished work

same, or a similar, silk as that used for the background.

When the background silk is very fine, a pleasant effect can be given by using coloured wool for the padding.

There is another type of quilting which is very practical and warm for bed-quilts and cot covers. Work as follows:

On the silk material spread a layer of soft cotton wool, and on top of this a sheet of tissue paper on which the design has been traced. This should have a very simple all over pattern, such as diamonds, squares or circles. Tack the three layers together carefully. Work Running Stitch along the outlines of the design, taking up all three layers. As the work proceeds, the soft tissue paper may be torn away. The quilting is then lined to match the upper fabric.

Sometimes embroidered motifs are used to enrich quilting. When this is so the embroidery should be worked and well pressed before beginning the quilting. A finished quilt is never pressed.

Three examples of modern quilting are illustrated in this chapter. These have been worked in the Emilia Bellini School in Florence. The three quilts are double sided and worked in two colours.

Albertina Sanpietro Beccari

*Corner of a quilted bedcover in red with
a rich traditional design*

456

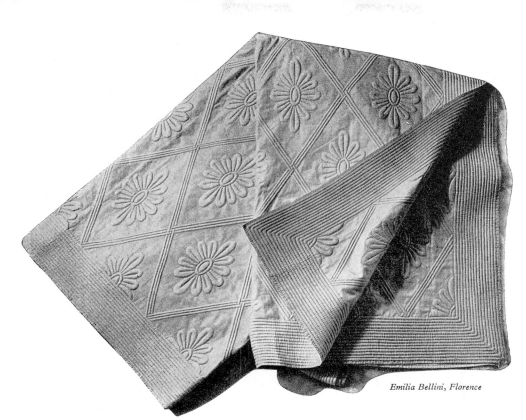

Double-sided bed-spread. Green on one side and straw colour on the other

Emilia Bellini, Florence

Bed-spread. Rose-coloured on one side and blue on the other. The design is geometrical, each square enclosing a flower

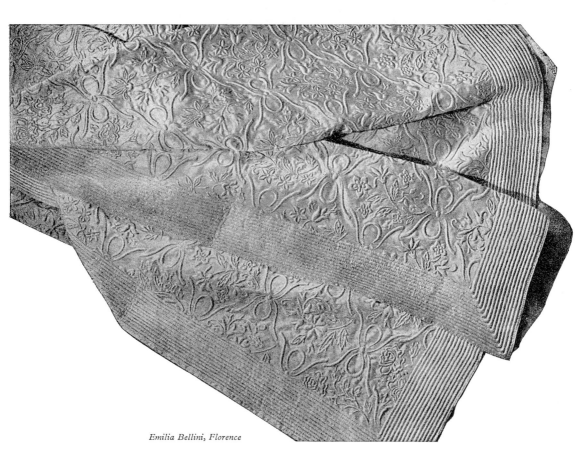

Rich, double-sided bed-spread. White on one side and lilac-coloured on the other

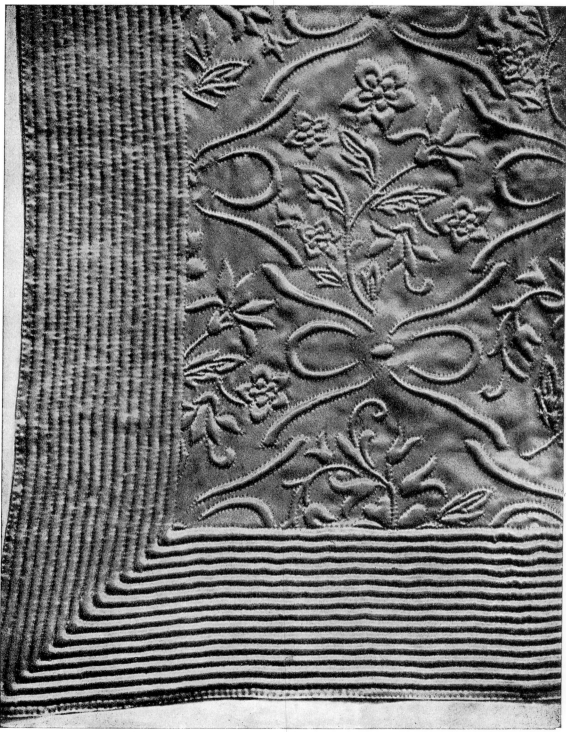

Detail of bedcover with a rich design of flowers and true-lovers' knots

CHAPTER XXXIII

Embroidery in Gold

Embroidery in gold and metal threads is one of the most ancient of the needlecrafts. It is also one of the most difficult, requiring great precision and technical skill in the handling of the threads.

In England during the thirteenth and early fourteenth centuries embroidery of fabulous beauty was carried out and some of this work is preserved in our museums. This early embroidery, which was given the name of "Opus Anglicanum", was enriched with gold and precious jewels. Today work in gold is still used for ecclesiastical furnishings and vestments as well as for ceremonial embroideries, emblems and badges. In this chapter brief notes are given on materials and some methods of working.

Materials. For work in precious threads the background fabric must be of the very best quality whether it is satin, brocade or velvet. The choice will depend upon the effect required and in one embroidery it may be desirable to use several different fabrics to give contrasts of colour and texture.

A great variety of threads is available including gold and silver. Aluminium thread is sometimes used as this does not tarnish and there are now certain synthetic materials which have the appearance of gold, silver, copper or other metals.

Gold embroidery must always be worked in a frame and the fabric should be mounted on a fine unbleached linen. Other necessities for gold embroidery are:

One or more bobbins, similar to those used for lace making on which the metal threads are wound, as these may tarnish if they remain in contact with the hand of the worker.

A stiletto for making holes through which the thread will be passed.

A box in which to keep threads and small equipment. The box should be lined with felt and have divisions so that the threads and objects do not slide about and become entangled.

Some Methods for Working with Gold. Trace the design on to the surface fabric by means of the pricking and pouncing method described in the last chapter of this book. Frame up the lining and fabric very carefully, taking great care to match the straight threads.

Gold and other metal threads may be couched in position. That is, laid upon the surface of the fabric and held in place with a small stitch taken at right angles to the metal thread. Use a fine, strong silk thread for this purpose. The beginning and end of the thread are later taken through to the back of the work and finished off by sewing down with the silk thread (Fig. 1).

Gold work is sometimes padded by means of cardboard or felt shapes. These may be secured in place with stitches and with a little paste (Fig. 2).

Eighteenth-century chasuble in red velvet embroidered in silver. Minerbio in the diocese of Bologna

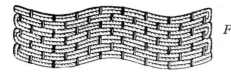

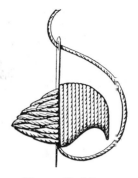

Fig. 1. Couched gold threads
placed side by side

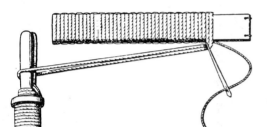

Fig. 2. Cardboard shapes applied to the background fabric
by means of stitches through
holes made in the cardboard

Fig. 5. Padding a
leaf shape

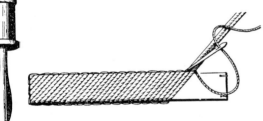

Fig. 3. Bobbin wound with a double gold thread.
Vertical and diagonal gold threads laid over
cardboard shapes and stitched in position

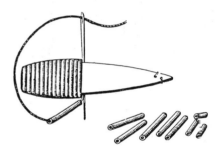

Fig. 6. Cardboard shape in process of
being covered with lengths of gold "purl"

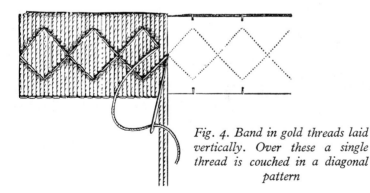

Fig. 4. Band in gold threads laid
vertically. Over these a single
thread is couched in a diagonal
pattern

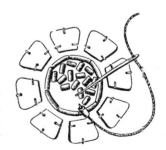

Fig. 7. Application of "purl"
sections to the centre of a flower.
Cardboard shapes stitched in
place to pad the flower petals

463

Altar frontal embroidered in silk and gold (Parish of Cusina, St. Giminiano, Florence)

Enlarged detail of the altar frontal

If card is used, colour it with yellow paint so that it does not show through between the stitches. For more rounded shapes the padding for gold embroidery is worked as for Satin Stitch. For this a soft thread is necessary and Coats Anchor Stranded Cotton, using four, five or six strands at a time, is suitable. Pad with rows of overlapping stitches until the required thickness is obtained. When these stitches are complete cover with Satin Stitch worked in the opposite direction to that in which the gold thread will be laid (Fig. 5).

The metal thread on a bobbin is gradually unwound and held in place with small stitches on each side of the padding or the cardboard shape. The illustrations show double threads laid in vertical and oblique directions (Fig. 3).

When using "purl" cut the pieces to the required sizes as shown in the drawing. Sew in position by passing a thread through the centre of each section. Use a fine silk thread matching the gold in colour (Fig. 6).

Fig. 7 shows a flower shape prepared for covering in gold. The centre is filled with small pieces of "purl" sewn on like beads. The worker must take care when working in gold to keep the edges of the shapes as even as possible. A fine metal cord or a gold thread may be used to outline the worked areas of the design. Fig. 4 shows a band of gold work in which a gold thread is couched down in a simple design over laid gold threads.

Embroidery on Silk or Velvet. On these rich fabrics always use a silk thread. Frame up a firm lining such as fine, unbleached linen. Stretch the fabric over this and secure with close stitching.

A great many different stitches may be worked on silk but the most popular one is Satin Stitch. Trace the design on the fabric by the pricking and pouncing method and keep the original design near at hand, complete with the colour scheme, so that it may be consulted as the work proceeds.

Sometimes it is necessary to work reversible embroidery, as for example on a shawl, fan or curtain. When this is so great care should be taken to finish off neatly and avoid passing threads across the back from one part of the design to another.

On brocades which have strands of gold and silver in them it is a good idea not to embroider directly on the fabric since the silk embroidery thread is easily frayed when it comes in contact with the metal strands. Instead, work the embroidery separately on a smooth silk background and apply this to the brocade.

This is also a suitable method for dealing with worn embroideries such as vestments and ecclesiastical furnishings. The embroidery may be cut away from the old, worn background and applied to new fabric. This may be done almost invisibly or with an embroidered decoration in keeping with the style of the original embroidery.

Detail of the ivory-coloured chasuble

CHAPTER XXXIV

Appliqué Work

Appliqué, or applied work, is the name given to embroidery in which the design is made by applying one fabric to another. It may be that the background and the applied shapes are of the same fabric, but different in colour as seen in the linen tablecloth illustrated, or the background and the applied pieces may be quite different as, for example, in an altar frontal where velvet and satin are applied to a heavy corded silk.

Although popular today, appliqué is not a new method and traces of the work can be found as far back as the Middle Ages.

For carrying out appliqué work in precious fabrics such as heavy silk, velvet and brocade, proceed as follows:

Trace the design on to the background and mount this in a frame over a foundation fabric. Prepare the pieces to be applied. First mount the fabric on to thin paper by sticking it with a little paste. Then press between two boards and leave until dry. Trace the required shapes on to this fabric and cut out with very sharp scissors (the paste and the paper will prevent fraying). Apply the pieces to the background fabric, pasting them lightly to keep in position. Lastly, sew each piece down with small stitches taken over the edges and finishing with Cording or some other embroidery stitch. This method is very suitable for embroideries such as altar frontals, banners and wall panels.

Appliqué work can be successfully used for decorating household furnishings and the method of working is less complicated. The sections to be applied should not be lined with paper or pasted, but tacked directly on to the background fabric, taking care to match the straight threads of background and applied shapes.

For lingerie a shiny fabric is often applied to a matt surfaced fabric, e.g. satin to crêpe. Again take great care to see that the straight threads are well matched or there will be puckering when the garment is laundered.

Hemmed Appliqué. If the fabric is fine and the embroidery is to be laundered frequently, the applied shapes may be hemmed down. Cut out each shape, allowing $\frac{1}{4}$-inch turnings all round. Fold in the turnings to the wrong side and tack with small Running Stitches. Care must be taken to keep the edge of the shape smooth and accurate and to do this successfully the turnings may have to be snipped at frequent intervals. Place the shapes in position, matching the straight threads of background and application and tack. Hem with small stitches. The work, as indeed all appliqué work, may be further enriched with embroidery stitches.

Coats Anchor Stranded Cotton and Coats Drima (polyester) may be used for this work upon linen and cotton fabrics.

Istituto Professionale Femminile, Forlì

Luncheon cloth in fine green linen enriched with appliqué embroidery in pink for the flowers, green for the leaves, reddish-brown for the birds and gold for the bows

Detail of the tablecloth. The applied shapes are secured with Paris Stitch worked in Coats Anchor Stranded Cotton in the exact shades of the linen

Bedhead with an applied motif

The application of fabric to tulle is often used for the decoration of lingerie. Trace the design on to the fabric and tack it to the tulle with small stitches. Work Cording closely round the design and on completing this, cut away the surplus fabric along the edge of the Cording, so that the design rests on a delicate tulle background.

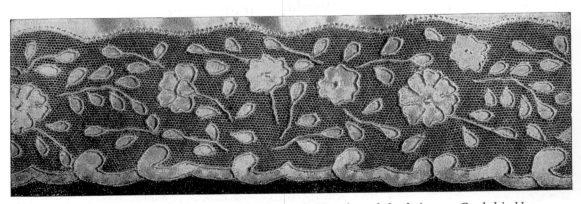

Appliqué work in blue silk on a tulle background. The edges of the design are Corded in blue

Screen in ash grey satin worked in coloured appliqué from a design by Alina Alliaga di Ricaldone

CHAPTER XXXV

Embroidery with Beads and Sequins

At the end of the last century, bead embroidery was excessively popular, and beads were used everywhere: on bags and purses, necklaces and belts, as well as for making flowers, decorations for dresses and hats and fringes of all kinds. Pictures, frames, cushion covers and lamp shades were all covered with beadwork.

Venice, or more exactly Murano, did great business by putting on the market enormous quantities of many coloured glass beads and these were very widely used. Later, the craze died out. Today, however, beadwork has come back into fashion, especially for the decoration of evening and cocktail dresses and for evening bags. Beads and sequins are used to give added sparkle to embroidered pictures and boxes.

Materials. As well as pearls, beads and sequins, a good, strong thread is necessary as the holes through the beads may quickly wear this away. Coats Anchor Coton à Broder may be safely used for threading. If necessary the thread may be used doubled. When the hole in the bead is so small that the finest needle must be used, thread the needle with a very fine, but strong thread and re-pass it through the eye to form a loop. Pass the thread which will hold the bead into this loop and pull gently. The bead will then go easily on to the thread.

Beads may be made of glass, steel, porcelain, etc., and may be round, oval, long, smooth or carved, transparent or opaque, in single colours or iridescent. For separate flowers, or garlands of flowers, a very thin metal wire may be used to give various shapes and to hold them firmly in position.

Beads may be attached to a background in various ways:

(a) One by one. Bring the needle out through the fabric. Thread a bead and replace the needle into the hole it came out of or a little further along.

(b) Thread the beads on to a length of thread, fixing the end of the thread to the beginning of the design. Push a bead along and make a small stitch over the thread immediately after the bead. Push the next bead along and repeat the process along the line of the design.

(c) Tambour Stitch. Beads may also be attached by means of Tambour Stitch. Trace the design on to the wrong side of the fabric and place in a frame with the wrong side uppermost. The beads are secured with a chain-like stitch for which a special hook, similar to a crochet hook, is necessary. The beads are threaded on a long thread and this is held under the frame against the right side of the work. Push the hook through the fabric and bring up the thread from below to form a chain. With the left hand push a bead along for every stitch. Continue in this way.

(d) For bags and purses there is another easy method. Thread the beads on a ball of thread.

Bands of sequin and flower shapes. Tulle or other very transparent fabric is used for the background. The border at the bottom of the illustration consists of long beads forming a very close pattern on a tulle background

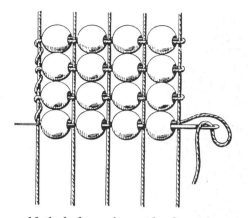

Method of carrying out bead weaving

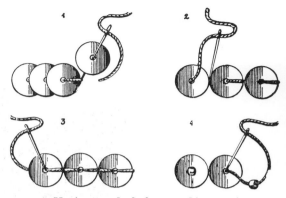

Various methods for attaching sequins

Then beginning from the centre of the bag, form a circle in double crochet. Continue to work round and before working the d.c., push a bead along close to the hook and make another d.c. The back of the work will be the right side, and will look like material made entirely in beads. With this method, too, various designs can be worked, by counting the beads, and alternating crochet stitches with more solid beadwork.

Loom Beadwork. Fix five or more threads over a small loom frame at a short distance from each other, that is, about the width of a bead. Then thread four beads (one less than the number of threads) and pass them behind the stretched threads. With the left hand push the beads along into the spaces between the five stretched threads (one per space) whilst, with the right hand, pass a needle through the four beads in front of the threads. Then go back to thread another four beads and proceed in the same way. Thus a very close beaded material is formed. The illustration shows this process. Use Coats Anchor Coton à Broder for the foundation threads, as these must be strong and match the beads in colour.

On knitting, it is sufficient to separate the stitch on to which the bead is to be fixed, by working a stitch in a different pattern from the background (e.g. a purl on a Stocking Stitch background or vice versa).

Fringes, too, may be made with beads. By counting a fixed number of beads, and alternating the colours, pretty fringes for various purposes can

be made. A looped fringe is very practical and simple to make. Thread the beads on to a strong thread and fold over, fixing the thread to the starting point.

Various Methods of Attaching Sequins. Sequins are small circles of a shiny material, very light and sparkling, with a hole through the centre. They may be black, white, mother-of-pearl, opal, silver, gold, and many iridescent colours. The illustration shows various ways in which sequins may be sewn on to fabric, either overlapping, which is the most common method, or attached one by one, with a small stitch, or a double, decorative stitch, and lastly by means of a round bead, so that the thread is invisible on the right side of the work.

To work the bead chain for which the design is given, take a length of thread double the length required for the chain. At each end thread a fine needle over which the beads can pass easily. Begin by threading ten beads, which form the first loop, half-way along the thread. On one side thread a great many beads, and on the other only three, then leave three, pass the left-hand needle between two beads, from above to below, pull the thread through and the second loop is formed. Now pass the right-hand thread to the left: thread another three beads on the right, count three beads on the left and place the needle in between two other beads from below to above forming a third loop; continue thus for the required length. This is easily followed by looking at the illustration.

474

Motif in sequins and glass beads for an evening or cocktail dress

A motif for an evening dress worked in sequins

Lovers' knot in sequins on a tulle background

*Bag in ivory-coloured beads with a
design in blue beads*

*The small bag on the centre left is crocheted,
using the method explained in the text*

*Small bag in natural-coloured fabric.
The decoration is worked in beads in
old gold*

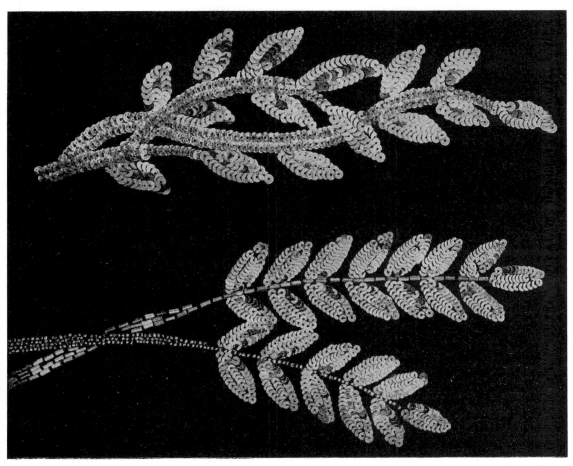

Decoration for evening caps and dresses or for wearing in the hair. The sequins are attached to tulle by the overlapping method, for which an illustration is given

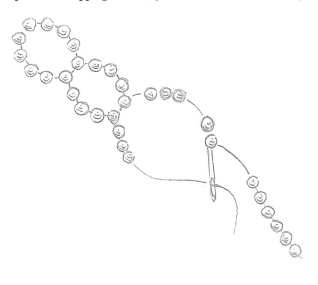

Some embroidered borders for finishing household linen worked in Clark's Anchor Stranded Cotton in white. Blanket Stitch, Eyelet embroidery and Satin Stitch are used for these designs

478

CHAPTER XXXVI

Finishings and Decorations for Embroidery

The finishing of hems has been explained in the chapter on "Sewing" as well as in the chapter entitled "Hemstitch". In this chapter some other decorative finishings are described and illustrated. The finish used depends largely upon the fabric and the type of embroidery. This is especially true in regional work and has been already emphasised in the chapter dealing with Italian embroidery. For example in Assisi and Antique embroidery the Fleur-de-lys Stitch is used. Four-sided Stitch makes an important edge in Deruta work and in Catherine de Medici embroidery the hem is decorated with crochet.

Very narrow hems, simple Cording or Stem Stitch, Blanket Stitch or scallops or a finely worked crochet edging, are much used today. Fringe makes an interesting decorative finish for curtains, bedcovers and tablecloths. It has the double advantage of being quick to work and takes nothing away from the actual measurements of the fabric.

Making a Fringe. Draw out a thread at a distance of about an inch from the edge at each side of the work, and work Hemstitch into the space, taking up four or five threads of the fabric. On completing the Hemstitch, draw out all the threads between the Hemstitch and the edges. Using a crochet hook, decorate this fringe with additional lengths of thread to match the embroidery. These may be

made in Coats Anchor Stranded Cotton, taken six strands at a time. Cut in even lengths by wrapping round a piece of card as shown in the illustration (Fig. 1).

Crocheted Balls and Acorns. Work small circles in crochet, working round one stitch, and increasing little by little, one stitch every four or five. When the circle is about 13 mm in diameter,

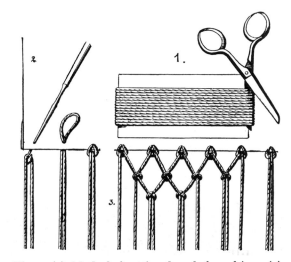

Fig. 1. (*1*) *Method of cutting threads for a fringe.* (*2*) *Attaching the loop of double thread with a crochet hook.* (*3*) *Fringe knotted together every two threads*

479

continue to work in d.c. without increasing. The little pocket so formed is then filled with cotton wool packed tightly. Finish off by decreasing one stitch every three or four, until there are none left (Fig. 2). These balls and acorns can also be decorated with embroidery stitches.

Tassels. These can be made from cotton thread, or in wool or silk. Wrap the thread round a strip of card, of a width equal to the required length of the tassel. Cut the threads at one end and tie them very tightly together at the other. Trim the ends and fray out a little with the needle (Fig. 3).

To work a looped tassel, slip the threads off the card instead of cutting them and tie together as already explained. Fig. 4 shows a decoration of tassels fixed directly on to the hem. To make these tassels, fasten the thread on to the back of the work and place the needle in about 6 mm from the edge of the work. Place the first finger of the left hand on the edge and wrap the thread round it, passing behind the finger and going back into

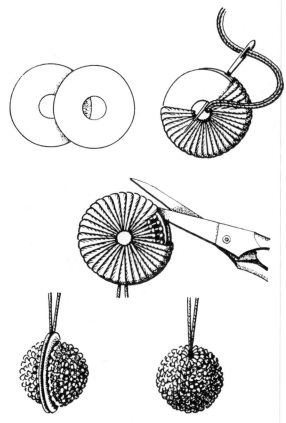

Method of making pompons

the first stitch. Repeat this movement about ten times, then, before withdrawing the finger, fasten the group together with three Blanket Stitches. Work the next tassel in the same way.

Bobbles. These are often used for trimming embroidery in Umbria, Sardinia and Sicily. Make in cotton, woollen or silk thread to go with the object being decorated.

Take 4, 6, or 8 strands of thread, according to the desired size. Knot the strands together with a simple knot and about 19 mm from that make another knot. Make a series of these at equal distances. Then cut the strands after every two knots, so as to form small tufts of threads knotted at both ends. Take a thick needle threaded with double thread of the same type as the knots, to serve as a support for the bobble. Take each tuft half-way along, and then thread them one after the other, like beads, to make a kind of ball. When this is large enough fasten the supporting thread near to the last tuft with a knot. One, two or more of these may be placed at the corners of carpets and are very decorative (Figs. 5 and 6).

They are often attached to the work by coloured china beads.

Spirals. Fig. 7 shows a tassel with three pendants, which is very decorative and simple to make. Using Coats Anchor Coton à Broder, make a length of chain about 22 cm long. Then, counting back from the crochet hook, work into the fourth stitch with three trebles. Work another three trebles into each following Chain Stitch. After filling in all the Chain Stitches, a kind of curl or spiral will be formed, as shown in the illustration.

Making a Twisted Cord. This is the easiest Cord. Take an equal number of threads (2, 4 or 6 as the case may be). Knot together at each end and fix to a point in the room, e.g. a nail, a hook, handle, or doorknob. Pull them out to their full length. Hold tightly at the other end and twist them between the thumb and first finger of the right hand. When the threads have been sufficiently twisted, fold in half and hold the two ends firmly together, letting the rest go free. The cord will then twist itself.

Hand-made Cord. Here is a practical, speedy method of working a strong cord. Join two threads.

Fig. 2. Balls and acorns in crochet

Fig. 4. Closed tassels worked directly on
to the hem

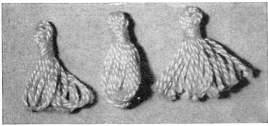

Fig. 3. Cut and looped tassels

Figs. 5 and 6. Bobbles made
of knotted threads

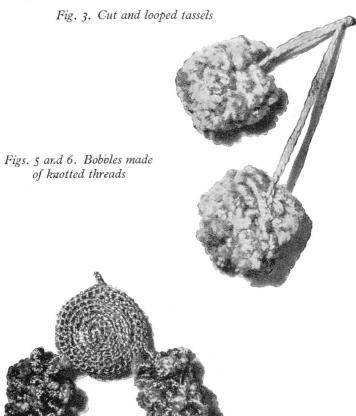

Fig. 7. Bobbles made with
treble crochet

Clark's Anchor Soft Embroidery thread is excellent for this cord. Make a loop with the left hand, holding it high with the first finger. Place the first finger of the right hand into this loop, and pull through the second thread. Meanwhile, with the left hand pull the thread and pass the work into the right hand. Then proceed in the same way, that is, bringing the thread from the other side, out through the loop held in the right hand, at the same time pulling the thread and passing the work into the left hand and so on. This work may also be done in two colours. The work is clearly shown in Fig. 8.

Crocheted Cord. Begin with four Chain Stitches, close these into a circle and, taking the edge of the stitch, work a s.s. into each stitch continuing to turn the work around all the time.

Pompons. Cut out two circles of cardboard as big as the ball is desired, and make a hole in the centre. These two circles are then covered with cotton thread or wool going from the centre round to the edges of the circle; this wrapping should be very closely placed. Continue until the hole in the centre is almost completely closed. Cut the threads around the edge, open out and separate the two circles and tie the threads together at the centre with an additional thread which will form the string for the pompom, pulling it up very tightly. Tear away the two card circles. Trim the pompon and fray the threads out a little.

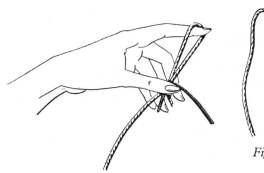

Fig. 8 (a). Method for making a hand-made cord. First movement: fix the thread with a knot and make a loop. Hold firm with the thumb and middle finger of the left hand

Fig. 8a

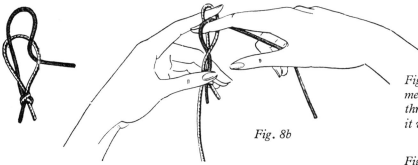

Fig. 8b

Fig. 8 (b). Second movement: pulling the thread through the loop and holding it with the first finger of the right hand

Fig 8 (c). Third movement: pull the left-hand thread

Fig. 8 (d). Finished cord

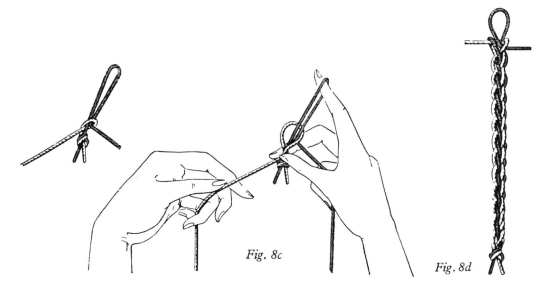

Fig. 8c

Fig. 8d

11 *Miscellaneous*

Design in Embroidery

Sources of design are many and various. A design may grow naturally from the right use of a particular fabric as, for example, in counted thread work or embroidery upon tulle or net where the fabric weave or mesh immediately suggests the use of certain stitches and patterns.

The purpose for which the finished object will be used may suggest other ideas—an embroidered cushion must withstand hard wear and the design should look well when it is placed at any angle in a chair.

An embroidered picture, on the other hand, will be hung in one position only and as it is likely to be framed under glass the wearing qualities of the fabric and threads need not be considered.

Natural forms are another source of inspiration for the designer and it is useful to keep a sketch book at hand in order to make notes of leaves, flowers, pebbles, feathers and other interesting information such as textures, colours and patterns.

Exhibitions, current magazines, especially dealing with interior design, and shop windows should be studied for contemporary trends in fabric, furniture, pottery and dress design. Museums provide opportunities for looking at old and precious traditional pieces and motifs from these may often be adapted to suit modern needs and materials. If the embroidery of today is to be a vital and living craft it is necessary for the designer to be fully aware of the changes taking place in other crafts as

well as keeping in mind the traditions in which the craft is rooted.

The following practical suggestions are useful for the designer:

1. If the design is geometrical or symmetrical, a quarter of it may be drawn on tracing paper and then the sheet can be folded into half, vertically and horizontally, and the design completed by tracing.

2. To repeat a design on the other half of the paper. Draw the motif with a very soft pencil. Fold the right sides of the paper together and rub with the finger nails. It will then be reproduced on the other side, and can be completed by drawing over it with a sharp pencil.

3. To make a design from one already worked. Place a piece of thin white paper over the work and fix it in place with pins and weights. Then rub a piece of cobbler's wax over the paper. The design will thus be reproduced on the white paper. Any irregularities may then be corrected by comparison with the original.

Enlarging and Decreasing the Size of a Design. Sometimes it is necessary to make a design smaller or larger. To do this draw a series of squares in pencil over the design. If this is not convenient, draw the squares on thin tracing paper and fix this over the design. Then take a sheet of paper and draw on it squares which are

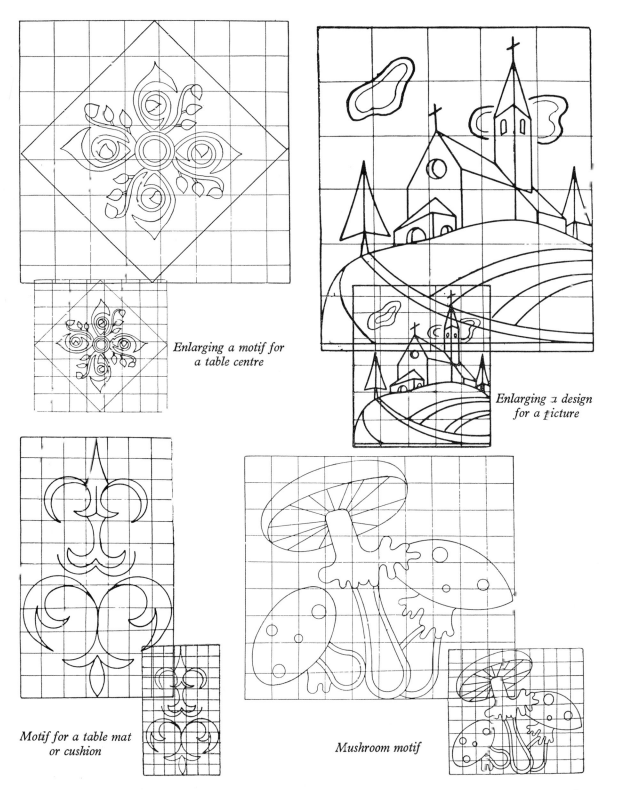

*Enlarging a motif for
a table centre*

*Enlarging a design
for a picture*

*Motif for a table mat
or cushion*

Mushroom motif

485

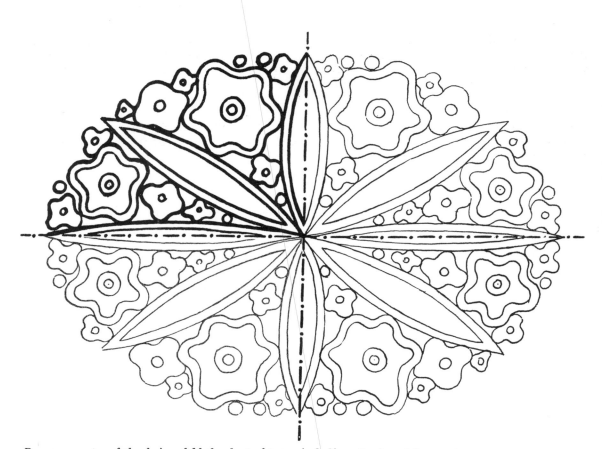

Draw a quarter of the design, fold the sheet of paper in half on the dotted line, and rub over the design with the fingernail on the wrong side so that the design is transferred to the other half. Repeat for the other sections

larger or smaller by a quarter, a third, or a half of the original design, according to the final size required. Sketch in the design, following it carefully square for square. Thus the design will become either larger or smaller (see page 485).

Transferring a Design on to Fabric. Before transferring a design the fabric must be prepared with care.

Find the centre of the piece and fold the fabric horizontally and vertically. Press the folds lightly with a warm iron, so that they are clearly visible. If the fabric cannot be pressed, e.g. felt or velvet, tack the lines in with a contrasting colour. This preparation is very important for the placing of the design.

For designs in the corners, fold the fabric diagonally.

Waxed Transferring Paper. The easiest method for putting on a design is by tracing over waxed transferring paper. Place the design on the fabric fixing it with pins or tacks along the edges so that the straight threads of the fabric coincide with the straight lines of the design. Then slip a sheet of waxed paper (yellow, red or blue for light colours, white for dark ones) between the design and the fabric, and draw over the design with a sharp pencil. If the colouring anywhere is too heavy or the lines too thick, press soft bread on the place, before beginning to work, in order to remove the surplus colour.

Pricking and Pouncing. This method is the traditional one.

Trace the design on to thin tracing paper. Prick

holes all round the lines of the design. To do this place the design over a soft felt pad and prick with a fine needle. Make the holes very close together. Leaving a margin of about 5 to 7 cm all around the design to avoid the pouncing powder falling on to the fabric, place the perforated design over the fabric and hold in position with weights (paperweights or an iron will do). Then pass a felt pad dipped in the pouncing powder over the design. Carefully remove the weights and the tracing and paint over the pricked lines with water-colour paint and a very fine brush. The same perforated design can then be used again to reproduce the same design.

Pouncing powder may be made by mixing powdered cuttlefish and french chalk for dark fabrics and powdered cuttlefish and charcoal for light fabrics.

CHAPTER XXXVIII

Practical Rules for the Washing and Pressing of Embroidery and Laces

Washing White Embroidery. White embroidery worked on good quality fabric with Coats Anchor Embroidery Cottons may be safely laundered. Any coloured embroidery should be washed with caution—especially if there are stains which must be removed.

Removal of Stains. Before washing remove any stains. This can be done more easily with white work as harsh treatment may result in the removal of the dye from coloured embroidery.

1. *Ink stains.* Soak the stain in a cup of warm milk, leaving it for some time and then place in lemon juice in which a little kitchen salt has been dissolved. Rinse frequently.

2. *Tea or Coffee stains.* Remove immediately by washing in soapy, tepid water. They will disappear entirely after laundering.

3. *Wine and fruit stains.* These are more difficult to remove. First cover the stain with table salt, then rub with a piece of damp soap. Leave for a few hours. Rinse. This will lighten the stain.

Afterwards wash with bleaching powder as explained later in the text.

4. *Copying ink pencil marks.* These may be removed with ordinary spirit. Spread the stained part over a white cloth. Dab with a pad of cottonwool soaked in spirit and repeat until the mark has disappeared, changing the cottonwool frequently.

5. *Rust marks.* These can be removed with the powder of wool sorrel, which is actually a mixture of oxalic acid, which may be bought from a chemist. Damp the mark with hot water, cover with a pinch of this powder and leave for some minutes. Rinse well in running water. Take care to keep this powder away from foodstuffs and out of reach of children. It is very poisonous.

6. *Grease marks.* If the mark has not spread very much and is still fresh, cover it with dry talcum powder and leave this on the mark for some hours. The mark will disappear. These marks can also be removed with cleaning fluid. To do this, place blotting paper underneath the marked place and rub briskly with a clean rag or a pad of cottonwool changed frequently.

7. *Tobacco or nicotine stains.* Remove with lemon juice.

8. *Wax marks.* Place a sheet of blotting paper over the place and rub with a clean silver teaspoon.

9. Sometimes, when sewing, the finger is packed leaving a drop of blood upon the fabric. Do not leave the mark to dry, but with a pad of cottonwool, damped with saliva, press the spot again and again until it disappears.

Simple Washing. After removing marks and stains, wash with hot soapy water, to which a few drops of ammonia have been added. If the embroidery has been worked in Anchor Embroidery Cottons, there need to be no fear that the colours will run.

489

Washing and Bleaching. Prepare a solution of tepid water and bleaching powder or solution, in the proportion of half a tumbler of bleach to 15 parts of water. Soak the embroidery in this, leaving it for about ten minutes, then rinse well in running water. Take care not to use too strong a bleach.

Washing with Soap Flakes. Dissolve soap-flakes in tepid water. When the soap has dissolved, place the embroidery in the solution and boil for half an hour. Rinse in running water.

Today there is an infinite variety of soap powders and detergents on the market, which save time and energy in washing delicate garments, and these can also be used for washing embroidery.

Washing Embroidery worked in Silk. Good soap flakes only should be used for this type of work, together with tepid water. Silk embroidery should never be placed into a bleaching solution or soda. At the most, a few drops of ammonia may be added. Squeeze gently and on no account twist or wring the fabric.

Washing and Pressing Embroidery and Lace. Never twist or pull, but squeeze gently again and again. To revive the colours, if they have become a little faded, place the embroidery, after washing, in clean water containing half a tumbler of white vinegar.

Never pile a coloured embroidery on top of other articles, or fold it over itself. Avoid hanging it outside, drying it for preference rolled between two clean, dry cloths. Press whilst the work is still rather damp.

Pressing. It is very important to watch the temperature of the iron: if too hot there is a risk of burning or singeing the work, whereas if it is too cool it will crease or dirty the fabric. Most electric irons can be switched to a suitable temperature for the fabric which is going to be pressed.

Damp the work thoroughly before pressing and press on a fairly soft pad, over which a clean cloth has been spread. Press on the wrong side of the work and smooth the right side only at the end when the iron is cool, to avoid giving the embroidery a shiny appearance. Follow the straight thread of the fabric when pressing, using the left hand to arrange and adjust the damp fabric before the hot iron dries it completely. Avoid pulling the fabric out of shape, and try to keep the movement rhythmic and even. If some of the colours appear to change, this is brought about by the action of the heat and they will go back to their original tones on cooling in contact with the air.

If the embroidery is very much padded, press over a very soft blanket, using the tip of the iron where necessary.

Some embroidery, especially table linen trimmed with lace, is better washed with the addition of a little starch. If the embroidery or lace is very wet and the iron very hot, the work will become rather stiff, without further help. For fine work take a piece of new organdie, wet it and spread it over the wrong side of the embroidery. Press over it until it is completely dry. The special finishing starch in the organdie will pass into the embroidery imparting a certain stiffness.

The best method for stiffening embroidery is by starching with common starch.

Simple Starch. Dissolve grains of starch in cold water so that it becomes milky. Dip the wet or dry embroidery into this and squeeze well. Wrap in a clean cloth for an hour, and then press with a very hot iron.

Boiled Starch. When a much greater degree of stiffening is required, use boiled starch. Dissolve grains of starch in cold water, and mix well with a wooden spoon so that it is free from lumps. Heat half of this amount, and bring to the boil for a few minutes. Leave to cool. Pour it into the rest of the cold starch and add more cold water until a rather thick solution is obtained. Place the embroidery into this, squeeze, wrap in a clean cloth, leaving it for about an hour, and then press.

Fish Glue. Another practical method for stiffening lace well is to use fish glue. Dissolve a few grains of fish glue in tepid water, until a fairly thin and colourless solution is obtained. Bring this to the boil and leave to cool. When the solution has cooled a little, put the lace into it, squeezing slightly. Pin it out as explained later.

Rice Water. By placing the fabric in this solution, it will take on a slight stiffness without, however, becoming too rigid. Cook a little rice in water and strain through muslin. Use the water tepid for white fabrics and cold for coloured. Place the work into the solution, and squeeze it gently. Wrap in a clean white cloth and press after about an hour.

For the inexperienced worker, it is a wise plan to test a piece for consistency and for the heat of the iron.

Tragacanth. This is excellent for starching lace and canvas embroidery. Leave a little tragacanth to soak in cold water for three or four hours, so that it swells up well, and then mix with a wooden spoon. Stir it up into the water to form a fairly thick, colourless solution. Leave the embroidery stretched in the waiting frame, and spread the solution over the back with the hands so that it is completely damped. Go over it two or three times. Then leave to dry away from direct heat.

Laces. To wash fine lace well, wrap it round a bottle, fixing in place with white tacking stitches. Half fill the bottle to give it weight and cork it, and then immerse in a bowl containing cold water, in which good quality soap flakes have been dissolved. Add a pinch of soda, and boil for about an hour. When the water becomes dirty repeat the operation until it remains clean. Rinse, leaving the bottle under the running tap for some time, so that any soap residue is removed. Squeeze out the lace carefully and dry. Black lace is washed in vinegar and water or beer and water.

Before pressing laces, stiffen them so that they come up like new. For very fine, delicate work use the organdie pressing method as explained for embroidery, whilst for heavier types, simple starching, and for thick laces (curtains, mats, etc.) use boiled starch. Always press lace whilst it is very damp. First straighten out carefully with the hands, pulling out all the points and straightening

leaves and flowers, then press until completely dry. Take care not to catch the tip of the iron in the openings of the pattern, as may happen when the worker is not paying attention or is in a hurry. This may cause breaking and tearing which cannot be successfully repaired.

To give a natural colour to white lace, dip it when dry into a solution of weak tea or coffee.

Some laces, for example knitted lace, should be pulled out rather than ironed, and then pinned into shape. For this method, use plain, stainless metal pins. Spread the starched lace over a clean, dry board whilst it is very wet. Fix at the bottom with pins placed at regular intervals, then pull carefully and pin down all the points and scallops.

For lace table centres, first of all fix the pins

round the centre and then, pulling well with the hands, spread out the lace, little by little, and fix it down with pins in concentric circles, following the design. It is a good idea to make a circle on the board with compasses so that this may be used as a guide. The lace should then be left to dry completely before removing from the board.

Index
to
Subjects and Stitches

Index to Subjects and Stitches